D1700272

Klaus-Peter Köpping

# Shattering Frames

Transgressions
and Transformations in Anthropological
Discourse and Practice

Dietrich Reimer Verlag Berlin

Gedruckt mit Unterstützung
der Universität Heidelberg

Die Deutsche Bibliothek – CIP-Einheitsaufnahme

Ein Titeldatensatz für diese Publikation
ist bei Der Deutschen Bibliothek erhältlich

© 2002 by Dietrich Reimer Verlag GmbH
Zimmerstraße 26–27
D-10969 Berlin

Satzherstellung von Nina Poneleit, Heidelberg

Umschlaggestaltung von Nicola Willam, Berlin,
unter Verwendung der Abbildung
*The Sleeping Fool* von Cecil Collins, 1943
(© Tate London 2001)

ISBN 3-496-02497-6

# Contents

# Preface and Acknowledgements

The following essays have been specially selected and edited from previous publications in English or German. However, in spite of the revisions the gist of the argument of each piece has been left untouched though some footnotes indicate the changed trajectory anthropology and the interest of the author have taken over the last two decades; some of the underlying research stretches back in its initial phases to just over three decades. The original places of publication are as follows:

Melancholy appeared first in the *Neue Zürcher Zeitung* on Jan. 11, 1997; the piece on Bastian dates from the volume *Fieldwork and Footnotes*, edited for Routledge by H. Vermeulen and Arturo A. Roldan in 1995 after the conference of the European Association of Social Anthropologists in Prague; the original idea about Malinowski was published in the *Journal of Humanities and Social Sciences* of Nagoya City University in 1999, after an oral presentation upon the invitation by Masahiko Tsuchiya and Yoshimi Bessho; the piece on Husserl goes back to a conference volume, *Proceedings of Phenomenology Conference*, edited by Maurita Harney from the Research School at ANU, Canberra 1976; the essay on the Ungarinyin dates from the 1987 edition of the *Encyclopedia of Religion*, edited by the late Mircea Eliade, an idea born during a pleasant lunch at the staff club of Chicago University with the late Joseph Kitagawa, and of course influenced by the teaching of the late Helmut Petri whom I had the pleasure to accompany to that research area of his in the 1970s; the essay on the Festive was originally commissioned by Christoph Wulf for his *Handbuch Historische Anthropologie*, "Vom Menschen", 1997, while the description of a range of Japanese Matsuri dates from the volume *Im Rausch des Rituals*, edited by the author and Ursula Rao in 2000. The Trickster reverts back to one of the earliest theoretical interests of the author and appeared in the journal *History of Religions*, vol. 24 in 1985, while a different version appeared in the journal *Kölner Zeitschrift für Soziologie und Sozialpsychologie* (Sonderband 26 of 1984, "Ethnologie als Sozialwissenschaft" under the editorship of Werner Ernst Müller, Paul Drechsel and the author), under the general editorship of the late Rene Koenig, my erstwhile mentor and long-time friend. The Satire was conceived for the journal *CHAI* ("Criticism, Heresay and Interpretation") founded at the University of Melbourne by the author while occupying the Baldwin Spencer Chair of Anthropology (the essay appeared in vol. 2 in 1989 under the editorship of John Hutnyk). The article on Leiris was conceived for a special issue on ritual for the journal *The World of Music*, No. 40, in 1998 on the invitation by Martin Zenck whose acuity and versatility in bridging disciplinary boundaries I enjoyed during many debates during the annual meetings in Berlin since 1997 of the research group involved in the program on theatricality under the chair of Erika Fischer-Lichte and supported by the German Science Foundation (DFG). Christoph Wulf commissioned the piece on Bataille for the journal *Paragrana* with the special issue-title of "Jenseits", No. 7 in 1998. I am deeply indebted for his interest and constant support for questions beyond the narrow confines of a specific discipline. The end piece on Hermes as anthropologist appeared after an international conference, organised by Karl-Heinz Kohl, in the journal *Paideuma* 45 in 1994, and its tenor is not least due to the stimulating formal as well as informal discussions with the many members of the symposium, with special thanks to the invigorating debates with Vincent Crapanzano who appreciated the close affinity of the metaphorical concepts, while Barbara and Dennis Tedlock encouraged the foray into literary transformations of anthropological reflexivity which found earlier expression in the essay on Satire.

I am indebted to a great number of colleagues attending the various conferences. As great is my indebtedness to the many graduate students who shared their enthusiasm and curiosity with me in California, in Brisbane and Melbourne as well as in Heidelberg. I should also like to express my special thanks to the translators Elaine Griffith and Karen Leube as well as to Nina Poneleit for seeing the manuscript through its final editing stages for the publisher.

# List of Figures

# FRAMES

*Figure 1*: Penal one of six of *Les Transformes* by Jean-Michel Atlan and
Christian Dotrement, © VG Bild-Kunst, Bonn 2001

# Transgression/Transformation :
# Intersubjectivity/Intertextuality

Designating the practice and discourse of anthropology as one of framing or naming the conceptual categories different actors give the social world is hardly new, but that the term and its inherent ambiguity encompasses both transformations and transgressions forms the core of my argument in this introduction and, incipiently or more explicitly, in what follows. Framing as naming *can* change perception – hence Greenblatt's stress on the Conquistadors' naming as a taking possession of the lands and their inhabitants in more than a mental or ideational sense. As Austin's speech theory has it, "naming" performs the illocutionary act in word or gesture or, more simply, *saying* both *does* and *effects*. It evokes, even exposes, the new reality and excludes any return to the status quo even if the interlocutors, as the Indians *vis-à-vis* the Conquistadors, did not understand the utterance which disempowered them. Set up, "framed" indeed, by the powerful framer (Greenblatt 1994; for a critical re-appraisal of the performative approach in political and legal contests, see Butler 1997).

Yet that is far from the whole story, for while the frame bordering a picture is passive, *living* frames, being also framers, can be active, can shatter the picture and thereby re-make themselves. But what does this concept of framing and, even more, the continual lurking potential for the shattering of frames, have to say about the processes of doing and writing anthropology, about agency and responsibility, interaction between frame and content, agent and patient? Who indeed, is active and who passive, who frames, who shatters, who and what is being framed and shattered? Or do both, researcher and researched, play out a game of words and gestures which may well transform as it transgresses? And who has the last laugh in the power-stakes?

Transformation aptly describes the enormous and positive changes in domain, scope and production of ethnography over the last century, and is equally applicable to the impact of the fieldwork process on the researcher, an experience which can give the writing authority and authenticity. Transgression, however, usually describes forerunners' mistakes or those of other disciplines which bowdlerise participant observation, ethnography's most hallowed mark of distinction or disciplinary boundary maintenance. Rarely do ethnographers connect transgression and transformation in their own work, in spite of a spate of self-recriminations in the wake of post-colonial theorising.

*Shattering frames* wants to reflect upon this by making explicit the processes of change and transformation that are brought about through communicative encounters of many different type. A number of essays is presented on the cultural practices and narratives such as shamanic possession rituals, trick-ster tales, festive performances or the notion of creative "Dreaming". Anthro-pologists, and the respective societies, gloss them all as transgressions which must be done but which go beyond the boundaries of the normal of what is culturally permitted or humanly possible. I am also including essays on some protagonists who in the process of establishing the discipline of anthropology as lived practice and as discursive field tested and extended, even trans-formed, the boundaries of what is possible or desirable to such an extent that their activities are still hotly contested.

While the choice is arbitrary, the key issues and figures assembled here can be taken as paradigms for the success as well as failure to bring into focus the many issues of epistemological and existential conundrums besetting the constitution of a science of different people's mental and cultural ordering of the natural and the social. Both, the natural and the social, are prone to ever new seperate yet linked contingencies of biological as well as historical acci-dents, of evolution and events. All social structures respond to these contin-gencies and try to gain control over them through culturally variable rule-sys-tems to eliminate inconsistencies and anomalies and ensure predictability of action. Yet as Mary Douglas neatly pointed out, untidy contingencies are part of live and lived experience (Douglas 1966).

Categorical ordering tries to control dangers to the system by protecting the social boundaries, but it is precisley at the very margins of the social sys-tem, or the interstices of the categorical, where dangers arise. The narratives of tricksters and shamans and the social performances of festivals or the Abo-riginal Dreaming are ritually controlled spaces and times allowing and even requiring a free rein to the chaotic and anomalous which otherwise threatens the categorical (and social) boundaries, indeed the very hierarchy of ordering itself. Such controlled transgressions are but one of many strategies which social systems employ to cope with that which threatens the boundaries, some of which, re-definitions of categories or physical control, are mentioned by Douglas (Douglas 1984[1966]: 39). As Lévi-Strauss similarly intimated, social systems cope with anomalies by either ingestion (the anthropophagic) or expulsion (the anthropo-emetic), strangers being either assimilated, or expelled, or ghettoised.

Sahlins (1985) may be right in seeing the performative as the *sine qua non* for the shattering of structures, the structures – imaginary or not – neverthe-less being the mutual constituents in this dialectic process. Yet, there may be cultures which are *prescriptive*, so structurally determined that they do not allow the contingent to have the power to vary the frames. But what does framing and shattering say about the craft and role of anthropologists, tena-ciously teetering on the edge of others' life-world, a world which, for good or ill, establishes their authority in this other, the academic, world? The very discipline was delineated as a bridge, a tightrope between an abstract Universal Mankind and the resulting concrete specifics of each cultural creation.

Living on such a tightrope, being aware of the chasm between, is dangerous, volatile and vulnerable – liminal in every sense of that word – intensely active yet necessarily passive, obediently learning yet inevitably, necessarily, transgressing in the living, temporary frames giving transforming permanence for a day, shattering them the next through further knowledge-giving transgression.

And what *is* this "knowledge", from where, for what? Anthropologists moved from "representation of" through "participation in" and even "surrender to" the various milieu in which they worked, yet the contradictions besetting the enterprise led theoreticians such as Zygmunt Bauman to wonder if anthropology could ever be considered a normal scientific formation which, following Foucault, would find its legitimation from within its own discourse (see Bauman 1992: 70f.). As anthropologists are involved in and part of the taken for granted life-world which they make the object of their attention, the legitimation for their interpretations can only come from their own experiences. Michael Jackson puts in his plea for what he calls, following William James, a "radical empiricism":

> "A radically empirical method includes the experience of the observer and defines the experimental field as one of interactions and intersubjectivity" (Jackson 1989: 4).

No form of hair-splitting about the objectivity attainable through distancing, from the self through immersion into foreign life-worlds, can hide the obstinate fact of knowledge acquisition through practice with its inherent contingencies incumbant on its necessarily performative aspects.

Hastrup notes that "practice always puts structure at risk" (1995: 140). The ongoing "transfiguring" and "evocative" conversations of Rorty (1980) risk the shattering of disciplinary and personal boundaries while reflexivity ideally exposes, transgresses and transforms the theoretical presuppositions. Yet the process is neither so clear-cut or so inevitable. Acerbic debates about writing apart, one thing is clear: knowledge acquisition in the field is inseparable from knowledge production in the study, for the doing cannot be divorced from the theoretical perception about the doing. As Handelman among others shows, the asking of questions, the comprehension of the world being observed and lived, cannot possibly be free of the knowledge of questions asked by other anthropologists in crudely defined "similar" circumstances, or even with the same interlocutors, let alone the egoistic eye focussed on publication, on conferences, on grants, on promotion, and even disciplinary boundary defence (see Handelman 1993). In short, the implicit and explicit discourses of our personally and socially performed frame, or what is nowadays called "intertextuality", inevitably clog our minds in the field and back home, where we often intentionally remodel the life-world of others in our collusion with the culture of writing.

The problem is not peculiar to anthropology, and should not lead us – no more or less than others – to agonise self-indulgently over the epistemic, methodological or theoretical status of our discipline. Rather might we creatively if metaphorically renovate it by embracing rather than excusing that liminality which depends on, indeed is created by, transformation through transgression. Certainly the interactional framework of knowledge acquired in and from intimate *doing-field* encounter with individual actors for an anonymous *reading-field* is complex, as it looks back and relives the performed participation, performed from multiple texts and for multiple past and present audiences, for yet another unknown and unknowing future audience. Such audiences may traduce the author through their re-interpretations as much as the author abducts the imagination of the reader through his rhetoric. Let us however rather assume that there is, as Barthes wants us to realise the pleasure of texts and that we *all* sometimes enjoy having our agency removed through the unknown, the reader through adventures told, the writer through seducing his audience with reports about adventures encountered in the flesh.

It is indeed one thing to realise reflexively that anomalies are an inherent feature of classificatory systems, that the beginning of a line or boundary is maybe mathematically indefinable, that fuzziness is a built-in perturbance where the inside and the outside become blurred. It is quite another to see how different social systems respond to it, whether in the performative mode of the ludic – as Sahlins implies for the Hawaiian encounter with the West, adaptively incorporating foreign elements and adjusting structure to contingency through such aleatoric practices as the traditional games of sexuality – or, at the opposite end of ideal-typical structural attitudes, through prescriptive structures where all happenings are "valued for their similarity to the system as constituted" (Sahlins 1985: XII; see Koepping 1997a).

Ostracism and genocide may be the more well-worn tracks of redefinition and physical elimination of dangerous anomalies, and it may indeed be the typical way of such imperial and colonial systems as those which were produced and reproduced by European powers. But many cultural systems, such as the Aztec sacrificial cultural idiom – which Todorov (1984) opposes to the European genocidal one – use anomalies to provide a liminal and often sacred time and space in the central fabric of the system for renewal from within. Anomaly as categorical fuzziness which permeates every drawing of boundaries is thus not evaded, re-defined or expunged. Rather is its special ambivalence made use of. Still perceived as dangerous and threatening, it is taken as a source of that invigorating power which can re-constitute the social and the cultural and thus effect a transformation of reality, of nature and society, of individual status and power-relations, of perception and imagination.

Using the analogy of organic living systems such as cell structures, boundary maintenance seems as important for the *auto-poietic* replication as is the replicating core, as no system can be seen as continuous and replicable if it does not establish itself as distinct from the "environment" or other systems – on which it must feed to grow – for otherwise it would just become a shapeless and undifferentiated "soup" (Maturana and Varela 1987: 53). Since social systems are conceived of as living systems as well – the "natural" of the social – their renewal does depend on both boundary maintenance as well as the porosity of these boundaries, re-acting to an environment and making use of it. Similarly, any conceptual system can be seen as having interstices between categories which are not only logically necessary but existentially required to accommodate as well as to enable new experiences to transform the system itself. The contingent being a part of all living systems, it cannot be completely excluded nor be controlled *a priori*.

If we take this roundabout route from system-theory, structural and symbolic anthropology, the question of the relation between transgression and transformation in regard to the change through replication or reproduction of a system remains a challenge. Transgressions and anomalies can be coped with and included into the system of expected and even required behaviour, felicitously and aptly labelled by Gluckman (1954) as "rituals of rebellion" in its political orientation, as "licentiousness in ritual" when used for social and existential crises and renewal. Turner saw transgression as part of all ritual processes, necessarily occurring in a "liminal" space and period (Turner 1969). The question arises whether the inclusion of those transgressions into the system leads to a simple reproduction or to a veritable transformation. Is "before and after" the playing out of the social drama qualitatively really that different, as is often assumed from these planned ritual and festive performances for which the historian Le Goff (1980) has coined the phrase "cataclysmic"? The intervention of nature through floods, earth-quakes, volcanic eruptions or diseases is inevitably perceived as cataclysmic because it is an unanticipated "event".

How can anomalies which are expected and therefore anticipated as well as learned, rehearsed and staged ("performed") be seen as cataclysmic events transforming instead of only re-producing the known? Turner saw the problem early when, similarly to Mary Douglas' notion of "the system at war with itself" (Douglas 1966), he suggested that the ritual redress of social dramas cannot truly get out of the conundrum of conflicts if these are based in structural imbalances themselves, for each healing of a breach stays within the boundaries of a cyclical repetition (see Turner 1957).

A *first* point is that the emphasis on the maintenance of continuity through *iterative* action should not distract us from the possibility that even under circumstances of repetition and cyclical re-alignment a real transformation, understood as a truly substantive and qualitative change, does occur[1].

However, this change may not be perceived as a progression from a state A to a different and completely new state B, as is often suggested in the literature on ritual processes with initiatory reversals from the social to the natural and back in the time-space of the liminal. This condition that is at the end may be conceived of – and is obviously so perceived by the participants, as Terence Turner rightly pointed out – as a kind of fusion or merger of two states of being (Terence Turner 1977). One is "son" or "child" and newly ritually admitted "adult" at the same time, any confusion which initially occurs eventually becoming a regular and habitual acceptance of both states of being.

This is not to imply that the merger of attributes as states of being and the reactions to this confusing condition will always be free of conflict, intergenerational strife being almost a universal feature regardless of the social structural arrangements. But the past is *not* erased, nor are the memories, emotions or relational attitudes. Indeed, the marker for living systems is the coming to grips or coping with these incremental accretions to individuals and collectivities, the finding of the balance between conflicting layers of experience.

A *second* important point is the effect of the performative activity itself, a feature often overlooked by symbolic structuralists: the transformative potential of enactment, however much staged from the start, is that which overwhelms the performer. As was noticed early by researchers like Lienhardt (1961), even the most "ritualised" performance has the power to evoke and channel emotions and attitudes into new directions. While much may depend on the skills and competence of performers and on the imaginary "ideal" of what a good performance is supposed to be, it is often the participation in performative activities itself, whether in ritual, theatre or art-production, which transforms the agency of the performer as well as the observer into the realm of an emergent reality. Such is the danger – chance and risk – of the contagion of the performative, as noted by Schieffelin for ritual studies, by Grotowski for theatrical modes, and by Gell for art productions (Schieffelin 1993; Grotowski 1969; Gell 1998).

There is probably no better example for the realisation of indigenous performers about the efficacy of staged ritual performances than that reported by Strehlow about those Aborigines who tell their initiates that the belief in the presence of the divine in the form of the sound of the bull-roarer is nothing but man-made pretence, while adding cautionary that the ritual has neverthe-

---

[1]  I do concur here rather with Derrida 1988 on the problem of iterability than with Bourdieu 1990 on the automatism of the replication of authority; see the critique by Butler 1999 on the authority of non-authorised speaking and performing.

less to be performed and be kept secret (from children and women) for otherwise the world would come to an end (Radin 1937: 85ff.).[2] This may be one of
the strongest statements about the power of the performative for constituting
reality, and contrary to the taken-for-granted idea of theatricality as "make-
believe" which permeates modern European understanding.

Naming as one form of the performative is here taken to be efficacious in
transforming reality according to a prototypical performance of ancestors
whose activities are mimetically iterated while the action itself re-constitutes
the performing individuals in their social relations, re-evaluates them, re-
affirms them, contests them or transforms them from one status to another,
giving them a new perception about their own power of agency in relation to
geographical environment and social group, thus being truly creative and poie-
tic. While maintaining the fiction in their mimetic performance, they thereby
cover up the truth of a necessary deception, known discursively, and they keep
the deception secret in order to hide the fictional character not from the divinities (they are thus not blasphemous) but of the performative mimetic identification as an existing reality, rather opting for the power of agency to make
performatively present that which is believed to be fact – the descent of the
group from mimetically enacted ancestor divinities – through hiding the performative mechanism from public recognition.

Again, as early students of reactions to masked performances like Preuss
noted, it is impossible clearly to separate "pretence" from the reality of fear or
dread of the holy, to use Rudolf Otto's words, even when those masks which
are the living ancestors or spirits or deities are known to be worn by living
relatives and friends (Preuss 1912). As Handelman put it succinctly: the characters displayed become for the perceiver what they portray, not what they are
in their ordinary lives (Handelman 1979: 186) or, as I would rather like to
argue, both these roles may merge for the audience as much as for the performer, ambiguity being present all the time.

This double or ambiguous nature of transformative processes and their
perception has a long tradition as a prominent *topos* in the European mythological, literary and philosophical tradition. Many aspects of wilful as well as
involuntary deception and identity-confusion, a common feature of the comic,
have their roots in such transgressions of boundaries or the fudging of frames
and are ultimately traceable to mythic themes. Thus the birth of heroes such as
Heracles – as much an "anomaly" as demi-gods like Prometheus – is due to
the *metamorphic* habits of divinities, in this case of Zeus appearing in the
guise of Alcmene's husband Amphitryon, Hermes playing Sosias as herald,
thus colluding in the deceptive framing.

[2] Radin is probably the first anthropologist to use the terminology of "ritual drama" which became
the main-stock of performance studies only about thirty years later. The case-study is taken from C.
Strehlow's work of 1913, *Das soziale Leben der Aranda- und Loritja-Stämme*, Frankfurt, pp.25-6
(see further in the chapter on the Dreaming in this volume).

But the paradox of the transformation remained one for the performers as well as for the audiences in much the same way as the multi-layered gender-transformations of Shakespeare's *Midsummer Nights Dream* still disconcert viewers today. Zeus as divinity does not disappear when he takes on the shape of a human; the face of tragedy looms underneath the comic surface as soon as the viewer switches gaze and emotional attention to the deceived woman or the cuckolded husband. Horror strikes when in modern scientific versions of metamorphosis a Dr. Jeckyll cannot escape from Hyde, his evil other self, or the were-wolf cannot escape his transformed "nature", for the skin has stuck to the wearer and the performance carried away the performer so that he becomes what he portrays. The ritual of sacrifice with which the performer of a *Wayang Kulit* shadow play (the *dalang*) submits to the supernatural forces of the divinities portrayed is therefore an understandable gesture to avert the danger of complete and irreversible transformation, the loss of identity of substance (see Firth 1967). Both, performers as well as the puppets are more than what they seem to be: both are divine as well, thus truly transformed, yet only when performatively enacted and embodied, a dual state from which they have to be made to return again.

By emphasising in this introduction and in the title the relation of the anthropological enterprise, in particular of fieldwork, to the notions of transgression and transformation ensuing from performative action, I do not intend to add to the mystification of knowledge acquisition which Dan Sperber has called to our self-reflective attention. As Sperber pointed out, anthropologists are prone to overstress the relativity and incompatibility of world-views and lived practices in the abstract while in their actual activities, reporting about the Other and their own successful rapport, they actually disprove the non-comprehensibility of other worlds (Sperber 1985; see also Bowman 1997).

What I instead attempt with the collection is to point to the importance which should be accorded transgression and transformation in their performative and practical rather than their rhetorical sense. Geertz' grasp of transgression is merely the bridging of geographical and metaphorical distance from "Being There" to "Being Here", to convince readers of the shift of the ever-distant anthropologist from one to the other realm (Geertz 1988). Not for Geertz the re-awakened grief for a brother "back home" which Danforth experienced at a funeral in the field. Geertz prefers the existential rupture of the crossing of a "shadow line" in which, as in the famous/notorious cock-fight, he figures as the Conradian imperialist hero, an Almayer or Kurtz, transformed into the world's court anthropologist (Geertz 1973). Kolakowski's court-jester would be more useful, opting for the role of the fool who puts common sense as well as authority into question and discovers the reasonable in the absurd, a philosophy which is irreconcilable with that of a priestly absolutism (see Kolakowski 1976: 256-286).

I concur with Asad's suggestion that a dramatic performance may be a more appropriate medium than the current "translating" a culture through ethnography (Asad 1993: 193). Yet, I would add that both, translation as well as re-staging, are distortions when looked at negatively from the vantage point of an ideological interpretation of "authenticity", but are positive if perceived as transformative adaptations. Both ethnography and performance are forms of de-familiarisation of the known through encountering the alienation of the Other. However, Asad's reflections on present-day ethnography that a dramatic performative discourse is a utopian hope, given the power of the metaphor of culture as a text, especially when – *pace* Geertz – the text is only read "over the shoulder of natives". It seems that the "imperial gaze", to use Louise Pratt's felicitous phrase (1992), has not yet left anthropology, as some of us do not yet engage easily with the eyes of others or confront them – and ourselves – straightforwardly in a true form of dialogue which is radically different, as Ginsburg pointed out so cogently when chiding social scientists for their blue-eyed naivety, from the friendly chat-show. Such a dumbing down of dialogue would be, as I pointed out previously, a thorough misreading of the notion of "surrender" introduced as a methodological attitude by Kurt Wolff on the basis of a phenomenological foundation of fieldwork (Wolff 1976 and 1994; see Koepping 1994b; for a thorough phenomenological "reading" of and engagement with the idea of the stranger see also Waldenfels 1990).

Anthropology can potentially shatter frames of thinking and of practices in the Here as well as in the There, through the transgressions of de-textualisation as well as re-textualisation, an interweaving of intertextuality in the head and intersubjectivity in field practices which leads to a transformation of one through the other in a never-ending process of the performative switch from action to reflection and back. The practices of anthropologists can change their own life-worlds of the academic and the every day. Lisette Josephides stated it clearly: "time and return are crucial factors" in fieldwork, adding the personal remark:

> "I constantly carry my Kewa friends around with me, back to the field, to conferences, to classes" (1997: 25).

Here the transformation has obviously occurred on a personal level and the absent other whose non-authority over ethnographic writing has for so long been agonised over is always present, but in a different form, one achieved through the transgression of the researcher's identity which in turn would not have been possible had it not been mutual. Surrender here comes to the fore as a form of transgression which, while it can be sought intentionally, does not always result in transformation. It cannot be willed, but it may happen. The experience of Josephides and other researchers (and writers about the imagined, like Bataille, I should add, the "field" being found in various contexts) would not be possible without the inter-personal notion of compassion and curiosity, the *sine qua non* of surrender.

The context of compassion which one can neither will nor learn from a method book is very apt here – and was very close to Kurt Wolff's mind and heart when he developed the notion of surrender as methodological requirement. "Surrender to", or as Goffman (1974) put it in the context of the discussion of "frame", "attending to", is one of those deeply ingrained notions of the European understanding of the search for knowledge (and beauty) in the form of the drive of the Eros, that curiosity which is fed by the sensuous desires of the body to obtain the idea of the beautiful as a possession which can never be achieved, thus keeping the yearning and seduction of the desire alive (see Wilhelm Schmid 2000 in extension of Foucault).

It was after all this curiosity which brought an explorer like de Lery (in his travel reports of 1585) to shed his negative attitude toward indigenous rituals in south America as despicable devil worship to one of astonishment and rapture when letting himself as participant observer be carried away by the rhythm and dance to such an extent that he felt a "fluttering of the heart". If, so argues Greenblatt convincingly, we maintain this ability to be astonished (by the miraculous, the unexpected, when the normal categorical thought is paralysed) we at least obtain an ideological "suppleness", leading to a very different strategy of representation (see Greenblatt 1991=1994: 41).

Anthropology should not be too anxious about carrying its own intertextuality back into the field, as long as curiosity is still alive. Rather than perceiving this attitude as a contaminating burden which makes the experience of otherness inauthentic, we might embrace it as the prime transgression which shows who we truly are, and that we are taking seriously in practice the demand of Gouldner for that radical sociology which gets away from the shibboleth of methodological dualism separating knowledge as information from knowledge as self-awareness (Gouldner 1971: 490). Taking anthropological practice as performative, as Kerstin Hastrup proposed, may indeed be more sincere than pretending to come with a value-free attitude to otherness. Yet, the researcher who reflects on his reflections like the actor on the stage has the same positive potential for transformation. The power of the performance, as in ritual, can carry the performer away, add layers to his or her identity and even become acceptable to the audience of the Other.

Here we come back to the notion of the ethnographer as a trickster. Elenore Bowen became aware of a drawback in her own trickster status, for the trickster, "seems to be what he is not and who professes faith in what he does not believe" (1964: 290). With this she meant the realisation that neither the prototypical notion of the detached fieldworker nor the one who becomes one heart and soul with his interlocutors are concretely bearable or morally defensible. Bowen concludes:

> "But even the greatest trickster cannot transform himself ..., his personal habits always betray him, as they betray all of us for what we are" (op.cit.: 290).

That may be all too true, but then one of the great tricksters, Wadjungkaga of the Winnebago tales, does become reflexively aware of his own stupidity yet is nevertheless the great transformer who can constitute the world as it is. Admitting that we are performing "fieldwork" we would as anthropologists have to admit that we are of two minds, in two worlds at the same time, and that the real pretence would be that we can forget or undo one of the two or multiple worlds of our imagination or our practices. That easily leads to self-delusion which often goes under the term of tolerance, yet it is a pathetic tolerance which keeps silent over what one cannot condone. This, as Zygmunt Bauman pointed out, is the opposite of dialogic empowerment of others, of "attending to" or "surrender to", the opposite of that desire for knowledge which even for Socrates is tightly connected and inseparable from the sensual delights of the body (Schmid 2000). The seduction by this desire is the linking transgression between mind and body, and the transformation of ideas cannot occur without the surrender to practice which is inscribed in our bodies and only expressible or re-traceable through the sensual encounter with the environment and thus through performative praxis.

Meta-discussions on the objectives and methods of anthropological work are littered with shattered frames, even just from Malinowski's, never mind from Bastian's times. Yet the incipient drive toward the transformation started in practices they tried as a fusion of a personal quest and a scientific aim. Bastian did this in his restless multiple circum-navigations of the world searching for the laws of cosmic harmony, fully aware of and expressing his belief in the micro-cosmological balance between mental and sexual drives long before Freud: Malinowski in his image of fieldwork as redemptive process of forging together the bones, the flesh and the spirit of other life-ways (their structure, their practices and their thoughts about these practices). Both transfigured anthropological knowledge. Both also transgressed the then normative, Bastian through his writings which were later considered unreadable, but through which he lets readers partake in the very process of intertextuality as it went through his head in an almost Bergsonian flow of an enduring presence, Malinowski in admitting to his failures in private musings which in times of political correctness are still considered controversial.

They both found their successors in figures like Leiris and Bataille. Leiris made unending efforts to approach the rupture between life and writing through ever finer and more meticulous observations of his mental activities, while knowing only too well that he could not escape his own *disposition* either by writing or by travelling, who while yearning for a fusion with his research subjects knew he could not abandon his reflexive inclinations. Meeting with much scorn from his American colleagues for his attention to his body states, he undertook the impossible task of catching the *imaginary*, while at the same time developing a fine sense for the political pragmatics as well as the poetics of the split consciousness of hybrid cultures (see the development of *Negretude* in African as well as Caribbean literature, as for instance represented by Leiris' close friend Aimé Césaire).

Bataille in turn, possibly the most radical thinker of the surrealist movement, vented his iconoclasm through recourse to reconstructed and imagined prehistoric and primitive communities, touching on some of the most guarded taboos of our own societies, as he transgressed in his novels and his scholarly work by lionising the necessity of excessive expenditure of energies as the perfect connection between the biological and the cultural. It is here that the history of anthropological thought seems to have come full circle: Bastian too thought in metaphors of excess, when he compared primitive societies and their mental make-up to the growth of luxuriant rain-forests, modern societies to the English lawn, the opposite actually to the hot-cold distinction introduced by Lévi-Strauss (see Koepping 1983; Köpping and Buchheit 2001). This connects us back to the origins about the modern perception about the contrast of primitive and civilised in Montaigne's image of the difference of taste between the preferable wild fruits which we have adulterated through pruning to our debased taste.

Let me close these musings about transgression with an epigrammatic statement by Martial who considered the buyer of a fool himself foolish to ask for re-imbursement from the slave auctioneer when he discovered that the moron was a very wise and clever man. It is inherent in the paradox of wisdom and foolishness that the fool (also the self-reflexive trickster) is hired to tell the truth to the powerful, who can pretend not to take his gibes, insults and insights seriously because he is insane. This pretence no fool or court-jester should unveil. Or should he? If he does, he admits to the pretence of performing. Yet, here the paradox curls back on itself, for the performance may overtake the performer unexpectedly, practice making perfect.

*Chance* and *risk* of the anthropological endeavour can be interpreted from the expressions used for the title of this introduction: they concern the close connection between fieldwork and writing, whereby the *intertextual* cannot easily be separated from the *intersubjective*, both being embraced by the ambiguous term of "ethnography". Similar questions are raised more metaphorically by the book cover of the *Sleeping Fool* of 1943 by Cecil Collins: As the fool is often shown with his *anima*, is this the dream of the anthropologist about the Other? Other questions about *the imaginary of intertextuality* are raised by the two panels of six which Jean Michel Atlan and Christian Dotremont, members of the art-group which called itself *COBRA* (Copenhagen-Brussels-Amsterdam), labelled *Les Transformes*. The panels seem most apt to illustrate the power of textuality in performative transformations, where the viewer's imagination operates as transforming agent. The letters are made to perform clownish movements, the signs dance, the squiggles become meaningful signifiers in a ballet of the imagination, though even here understanding requires a pre-knowledge and pre-formed judgement about what writing is.

Is this the way in which our works, ideas and those of our fore-runners play with our own imagination and with our perception of the Other? Are we, or are the Others, puppets of our *imaginary repertoire*? Do we make them dance, or does the repertoire make us perform movements of thought which transform reality, including our performances, in our perception and imagination? The question remains: who or what constitutes us, the Other and our work about the Other, and where does the rhetorical have its boundaries in the ongoing interplay between intersubjectivity and intertextuality? Is the *imaginary* of the "primitive" a feature which constitutes our reality as much as it does that of the Other, once the concept has been born, even if the real primitive either never existed or vanished, as Baudrillard (1968) has it, at the moment he became an object of interest? Is then each act of doing ethnography as much as the writing an act of resuscitating the imaginary and the vanishing? Or does the performance and co-performing constitute the vanishing? *What* do we then encounter or surrender to?

*Figure 2*: Penal five of six of *Les Transformes* by Jean-Michel Atlan and
Christian Dotrement, © VG Bild-Kunst, Bonn 2001

# Melancholy: Ambiguities in Method and Morality

*Since its beginnings ethnology has fluctuated between activism and melancholy in its moral attitude towards disappearing indigenous peoples. This indecision has its origins in the fluctuation between two contradictory theoretical and methodical preconditions: theoretically between the search for the universal in humanity on the basis of the unique character of every culture, methodologically between proximity and distance, participation and observation. These preconditions seem suited to an ambiguous morality founded on the context of a dialogical and situative research praxis, but also eliminating the separation between researchers and private individuals.*

## Professional Provocations

Anthropology and the public perception of this discipline, otherwise stigmatised as exotic, has in the last forty years been shaken up by the publications of two of the most well-known names in the discipline. The shock waves of the double provocation can be felt inside and outside professional circles to this day. The first shock wave was sparked by Lévi-Strauss. In 1955 his work *Tristes Tropiques* was a mixture of autobiography and scientific description of the doomed cultures of the Amazon – recalling the rhetoric of Rousseau's *Confessions*. Here Lévi-Strauss accused professional ethnologists of schizophrenic morality. He claimed they were the greatest critics of existing political and social conditions at home, but as soon as they were out in the field in a foreign society they bowed down before practices of the most conservative sort.

The second shock was caused by the doyen of modern anthropology, Bronislaw Malinowski, who also rendered the dubious concept of "participatory observation" acceptable. In his *A Diary in the Strict Sense of the Term* (published posthumously 1967) he was revealed to be an individual with normal prejudices who, in contrast to the mythical picture of "ethnologists as heroes", expressed his private feelings about "dirty niggers". Both these works showed that traditional ethnographies about other ways of life were purified versions of these realities covering the personal prejudices of the researchers in "neutral analysis".

The profession responded with two strategies to these doubts about the lack of moral direction implied by Lévi-Strauss and about the validity of describing reality that surfaced through Malinowski's diary.

The *first* strategy was a forward movement by taking on the challenge of commitment, getting away from the ambivalence of relativising all values, instead supporting universal ones like equality, freedom from oppression and other human rights.

The *second* strategy, that followed the first one, if the prominence of publications is a criterion, was more an inward-looking navel-gazing of intradisciplinary arguments about the depiction of other cultures and the role of representing different perceptions of reality. This turn constituted an important milestone in the rethinking of the connection between structures of prejudice and processes of recognition and communication. It ended up, however, in a fruitless rhetorical discussion of stylistic nuances.

Neither of the two strategies led to a clear-cut moral line which all practitioners would feel committed to. We can even go so far as to say that the hermeneutic turn-about so broadly discussed recently led to virtually the same refraining from asking moral questions as was incorporated in the melancholy of Lévi-Strauss. In an interview with Susan Sontag he had admitted to being a "moral cripple" at home[1]. He felt compelled to adopt this stance for reasons of logic: if we recognise the peculiarity and justification of all cultures we must apply the same value standards to our own culture too. So we can condemn neither the other societies nor our own. *Ergo*: we cannot afford to make any judgements, even if we may regret that the advance of our own, technological culture condemns the others to extinction. It seems that melancholy and moral ambivalence have pervaded social anthropology since its foundation, despite all moral outrage and all nostalgia about the disappearance of "authentic cultural creations", and despite all reformist efforts.

The deeper reason for this ambivalence lies, however, less in the inability to make moral judgements than in the ambiguous historical legacy of social anthropology as that discipline which, as the youngest among the established social sciences, attempts to combine the objectives of both the French Enlightenment and the German Late Enlightenment and Romantic Period. This ambivalent historical legacy is closely connected with the hybrid construction of the method of "participatory observation" introduced in 1922 by Malinowski. It was supposed to bring about a cultural description "with the eyes of the natives"[2].

## The Strategy of Activism

At the climax of the US student revolt of the 60s the anthropologists there also called for a radical change in orientation of their discipline. Traditionally it

---

[1] "The Anthropologist as Hero". In: N. Hayes and T. Hayes (eds.) 1970: *Claude Lévi-Strauss – The Anthropologist as Hero.*

[2] Foreword to the *Argonauts of the Western Pacific* 1979 (originally 1922).

had been concerned with the exploring of "primitive" or "illiterate", generally small "indigenous" peoples, who seemed doomed to die out under the influence of western technology, Christian ideology and capitalist exploitation. Instead of purely antiseptic research, frequently without any emotional involvement and reduced to pedantic collection of data, prominent American anthropologists wanted to dedicate themselves to liberating the peoples they were studying from poverty, injustice and oppression. In a nice mixture of Marxist-inspired liberation ideology and the belief in their own competence they noted that the social sciences were ethically obliged to help humanity. Since this humanity is divided today into groups of conflicting interests based on class, ethnicity or nation, and one cannot serve all interests at the same time, the responsibility of anthropologists was in supporting the "oppressed" since, as one of the representatives of this radical wing of applied anthropology put it, "there lies our specific competence" (Gjessing in *Current Anthropology*, 1968). This demand was tantamount to a commitment to contribute to a social, economic and political emancipation of the research subjects. This direction of applied science is in many respects similar to the Frankfurt School of Horkheimer and Adorno, which claimed that the social sciences could not remain only a discipline reflecting reality, raising the *status quo* to a goal; instead, they had the responsibility to be critical and emancipatory.

Yet this emancipatory thrust of US Anthropology soon ran into resistance, not just in an ever more complex reality, which no longer followed binary thought patterns. The anthropology colleagues in the developing world also felt challenged to protest by this patronising form of "intellectual aid". They called the whole "anthropology" project into question. For example, the Ethiopian Asmarom Legesse accused the whole of Western social science of identifying with a technocratic cultural concept. The native American lawyer and historian Vine Deloria (in *Custer Died for Your Sins* and *We Talk, You Listen* of 1971) scourged the whole of anthropology as an accomplice in the policies of oppression and extermination of indigenous peoples, doubting whether anthropologists were of any use at all. "We can tell our own stories" about sums up this criticism. Latin American anthropologists, by contrast, felt patronised by their North American counterparts and argued, strongly linked with liberation theology in terms of ideological orientation, for an indigenous anthropology. This, they claimed was more effective and justified in working to improve living conditions since it could *fully* identify with the population of its country. Many "Third World" anthropologists thereby terminated the consensus about the mirror paradigm that you could only learn about yourself *via* the other. One can naturally also argue that they were not very different from proponents of "European anthropology", that repatriation of comparative cultural studies which empirically concerns itself with the researcher's own backyard. However, the movement is not far from the ideology that says that the "native" understands his/her own culture best. That would practically abolish anthropology if it did not have something "different" about it, that hybrid method of participatory observation which comes about through voluntary alienation from one's own culture.

Such criticism hit the American anthropological scene hard. At the time Marxist-influenced anthropologists like Berreman, Kathleen Gough, Eric Wolf and Stanley Diamond were establishing themselves in association with Chomsky as critics of the American system. Furthermore, people were just discovering that a large number of their colleagues were working on secret "counter-revolutionary" projects, in particular in South America and South East Asia, as shown by the files on the notorious project "Camelot" (Horowitz 1967). The concept of the good of humanity was proving pretty ambiguous since Applied Anthropology never really answered the question as to who the oppressed were; colleague A helped tribe X and colleague B helped the neighbouring people. Who had morality on their side? Civil wars waged between tribal groups as assault parties for different ideologies made it hard for anthropologists to postulate clear guidelines for morality in the sense of assistance for the oppressed parts of humanity beyond a specific case. The attacks by colleagues from the South prompted a minority of primarily American colleagues to part from academe and take a new direction in Applied Anthropology under the heading of "partisan anthropology". This turned its back on the ambivalent fluctuation of traditional anthropology between commitment and scientific distance, opting for a single party line, that of researched community.

## The Strategy of Rhetoric

The conflictual and not always very successful attempts to create a morally acceptable Applied Anthropology has led since the 80s to that turning-inwards that was a result of a withdrawal to the meta-level of self-reflection in research. While it produced texts the harvest was meagre: instead of the "local realities" more was heard about the state of mind of the researchers or the significance of rhetorical tricks. What began with an interpretative turn-about in anthropology, when Geertz spoke of that dense description that was supposed to draw the author into text production (*The Interpretation of Cultures*, 1973) deteriorated into a literature of confession in the style of "the natives and me", to that kind of introspective navel-gazing where the Other, by whom these personal insights were stimulated, faded into an indistinct shadow. This development was finally too much even for a Geertz who poored scorn on such abortive attempts to overcome oneself that threatened to gel into self-pity. Instead, he argued for imitating the rhetorical skill of the founders of modern ethnology (Malinowski, Firth, Lévi-Strauss or Ruth Benedict) in order to convince the reader at home that they had been in a strange country (*Works and Lives*, 1988).

This rhetorical turn taken by anthropology may be understood as a response to the disappointment of the preceding euphoria about the possibility of changing the world. However, it remains the best excuse for an armchair anthropology for literary circles since Frazer's notorious reply to William James inquiry as to whether he had ever seen the "savages" himself. "For Heaven's sake!"

## Anthropology between the Universal and the Particular

The classical theoretical orientation derived anthropology from the ideas of the French Enlightenment about the classification of all human and natural phenomena and the Late Enlightenment rebellion of Herder against this schematic approach. Anthropology never abandoned the search for universals, but at the same time – in the spirit of Herder – it considered its main task to be that of according each culture its autonomy and thereby its own value. In addition, the 19th century saw the search begin for the use of knowledge which, it was hoped in Enlightenment hybris, would lead to a perfect ordering of society. Anthropology too began as a "reform science", even if its early representatives did not succumb to the megalomania of an Auguste Comte, who believed that sociology could replace religion and the social engineer politics. Edward Burnett Tylor, at the end of his two-volume compendium *Primitive Culture* (1871 II: 456f.), put forward the fitting claim, still used primarily as legitimation for anthropological work, that a survey on the different cultures of the world would benefit those who want to foster the health of society and to eradicate the sickness of modern culture (anthropology as the science of cultural hygiene indeed!).

## Saving the Imagined Primal Culture or Entropy?

This statement shows the trend more or less predominant to this day in this branch of intercultural social sciences: that with their collected wisdom scholars wanted to change things in their own societies, not in the others, at least not at first. Behind this utilitarian approach, which was shared by all evolutionists, including Marxists, was a generous portion of melancholy, not to say guilt feeling, about the decline of "primitive cultures" brought about by the Europeans. They concealed this bad conscience behind the notion that these "primitives" were the surviving example of the original forms of our own and all civilisations, and thereby could be seen as mirrors of our own progress – or decline. Nevertheless Tylor's statement contains two trends of comparative cultural studies, which to this day have never quite matched: *first*, the idea of preserving the lives of those cultures, and *second* the usefulness of knowledge about them for one's own life. The drive to preserve what was regarded as the heritage of all humankind now threatened by European expansion led, on the one hand, to a reservation mentality (to keep threatened species in a kind of zoo) which would grant declining small groups if not a habitat for survival at least an undisturbed space to die out (this was the diction of Australian reservation policy around 1940, yet effective in the minds of Aboriginal Affairs Departments in some Australian States until the mid-70s)[3].

However, this led, on the one hand, to that possessive pedantic collection mania for collecting empirical data which, according to Nietzsche, is a sign of antiquarian history without reverence, which was little concerned for responsibility towards the subjects, let alone for their rights. In other words, the appraisal of positivist science that was gaining ground in the 19th century, and that wanted to measure everything and depict it as exactly as possible as a reflection of reality, found its justification in a nostalgic evolutionism. A fine example of this attitude is the exclamation of the founder of modern German ethnology, Adolf Bastian (1826-1905):

> "It is burning all around us ... and nobody moves a hand ... Treasures of documentation of the sacred temples of mankind's history irrevocably lost – lost forever"[4],

and he continues:

> "We watch it all as if it does not concern us, instead of crying out in horror ... We should at least request their salvage if we cannot quench the fire, because what is destroyed here in raging haste are mankind's spiritual goods which belong to us all, us and our descendants, and it is our duty at least to preserve them, even if we cannot ... use them ourselves".[5]

A hundred years later the structuralist Lévi-Strauss turned this emotion into

---

[3]  See K.-P. Koepping, How to remain human in an asylum? Some fieldnotes from Cherbourg Aboriginal Settlement in Queensland. In: *Occasional Papers in Anthropology*, (Peter Lauer and Klaus-Peter Koepping, eds.), 6: 28-47. Brisbane 1976. University of Queensland Press, Anthropology Museum.

[4]  My translation, from Adolf Bastian, *Der Völkergedanke im Aufbau einer Wissenschaft vom Menschen und seine Begründung auf ethnologische Sammlungen*. Berlin 1881: 180.

[5]  Op.cit.: 170. See K.-P. Koepping, *Adolf Bastian and the Psychic Unity of Mankind*. Brisbane: University of Queensland Press, Scholars' Library, 1983.

melancholy about the law of entropy: "... there will never be another New World", and in a similar vein, "I am a modern traveller, running after the vestiges of a vanished reality"[6]. In comparison to the hectic Romantic Bastian, Lévi-Strauss seems the paragon of melancholy: "Nor, even if Man himself is condemned, are his vain efforts directed towards the arresting of a universal process of decline"[7].

## A Method of Self-Knowledge and the Problem of Difference

All anthropologists still share the paradigm of research described very early by the German emigrant Helmuth Plessner in his Groningen inaugural lecture of 1936 as "seeing with other eyes": we can only become aware of what is ours *via* the detour of experienced strangeness. He continued: "One must have become foreign to the zone of familiarity in order to be able to see it again" (*Zwischen Philosophie und Gesellschaft*, 1979). A prerequisite for any understanding according to Plessner is, however, the shock and pain of the estranged gaze and it is this critical view of one's own, which both for Malinowski and for Boas, the German emigrant and founder of American cultural anthropology, should be the result of experience the strange. However, the over-estimation of difference is one of the great dangers that anthropology can succumb to. The deceased British anthropologist Sir Edmund Leach warned his colleagues back in 1967 that the absolutising and hierarchising of differences can lead to fratricide since it is a "regrettable illusion" that one can only be free in cultural seperateness (Reith Lectures in *The Listener* of 1968). This remark contains a clear moral view of the political participation in the world, which professes its solidarity through the discovery of the human-all-too-human, but also the inhuman in one's own actions and those of the strange culture. This attitude is fully shared by Edward Said in his *Culture and Imperialism* (London, 1993), which sees the hierarchisation of one's own and the strange as fuel for the "bloody massacres" of fratricidal wars and returns to the Renaissance ideal of the emigrant as a cosmopolitan.[8]

---

[6]  Lévi-Strauss, *Tristes Tropiques*, Paris 1955: 44-45 and 454.

[7]  In *Tristes Tropiques*, where he opts for labeling anthropology by the more appropriate term "entropology"; from the English edition, New York 1971: 397.

[8]  What Said may have had in mind would be statements quoted by Jacob Burckhardt from Ghiberi and Codrus Uceus to the effect "Wherever a learned man fixes his seat there is home"; see Burckhardt, *The Civilisation of the Renaissance in Italy*, New York, 1958: 147ff. (original Engl. Translation 1929). See Koepping, From the Dilemma of the Ethnographer to the Idea of Humanitas. In: *Occasional Papers in Anthropology*, Queensland Anthropology Museum (Peter Lauer and Klaus-Peter Koepping, eds.), Brisbane 1975, 4: 124ff.

### A Moral Story

Elenore Bowen (pseudonym for the researcher Laura Bohannan) describes in her book *Return to Laughter* (1954) an anecdote illustrating the precarious but also the indispensability of participating in the lives of others when the limits of principles and prejudices are to be reflected upon morally and not only as mental games. While she can sill laugh about the way her informant parodies a missionary rebuking a "native" for wanting to sit down in his presence in order to listen to the wonderful story of the origin of all human beings from Adam and Eve – descent being of vital traditional interest and the native a specialist thereof – she cannot raise a smile at a pantomime about a blind man stumbling over a snake. This made her aware that one cannot love everything that one understands, for the longer and more intensively one has shared in the life of another society the more clearly one becomes aware that one cannot be part of it without violating one's own personal integrity.

### A New Morality through Devotion to the Context?

The result seems at the moral level to be a withdrawal to the randomness of individual and situational decisions of the respective field situation. This includes the insight that, as Roger Bastide put it back in 1973 in his *Applied Anthropology*, the plurality of groups also entails a plurality of objectives and values. Ethnology therefore has to adapt to the increasing complexity of reality, if it is to include application, and – in keeping with the fragmentation of value systems – regroup itself again and again in research praxis.

The preconditions of a research that is still legitimate and morally acceptable in a pluralist world are suggested by two emigrants who both distil their demands from their ethnographic and emigrant experiences. Unfortunately their work is hardly known as yet in the German-speaking world. One demand stems from Kurt Wolff, born in Darmstadt, retired professor from Brandeis University and the last surviving student of Karl Mannheim. He terms "surrender" and "catch" the appropriate stance for research. This calls for the attitude of "cognitive love" from the researcher which begins with the suspension of all preconceptions and prejudices through surrender to a task, a person or a thing. Surrender is only the way, not the goal, however, says Wolff in an analogy. "We do not abandon ourselves to love in order to lose ourselves but in order to find ourselves" (*Surrender and Catch, 1976*). Through its stress on listening and being drawn in this demand means a reversal of predominant research ethic which until recently started from that Foucault-like observation that Nietzsche had already damned as indecent. This view is extraordinarily apt if you think that the Australian Aborigines strictly refuse to market their religious ceremonies. "Why do you want to take away the last thing that belongs to us", they ask. Here modern anthropology could still derive its research morality from Herodotus, who recorded nothing in his writings about the secret Apis rituals of Egyptian women: that would have been an infringement of the highly respected Greek virtue of keeping holy secrets. As Horace once said, he would not trust anyone who let out such secrets as the Eleusinian mysteries.

This methodical morality of Kurt Wolff is supplemented by the theoretical ethics of the social philosophy of another émigré, the polish sociologist Zygmunt Bauman. Bauman calls for tolerance and solidarity, characterised by taking the other seriously as a partner in research and dialogue and not just noting difference but granting the legitimacy of their interests. That is a different tolerance from the one which accepts the other in the awareness of one's own superiority. This would only be a disguised form of that patronising, complacent arrogance shown by the ruling classes towards colonised peoples and their own inferiors (*Intimations of Postmodernity, 1972*). This tolerance, to be negotiated in dialogue, and the demand for surrender reduce the distance normally stemming from a researcher's academic obligation, without leading to a loss of identity. Ideally it obliterates the separation of the researcher and the private person, as Kirsten Hastrup recently advocated (*A Passage to Anthropology* 1995), and it relies on the shared common ground of the methodological morality of mutual recognition as a person between researcher and dialogue partner as Crapanzano put it (*Tuhami* 1983).

*Figure 3*: Claude Lévi-Strauss

# TRANSFIGURING KNOWLEDGE

*Figure 4*: Adolf Bastian

# Bastian: Digesting Reality

*Questions in the History of Anthropology*

Many writers on the history of the discipline like to set the start of truly modern anthropology with either Boas or Malinowski (see for example Evans-Pritchard 1951; Hymes 1969; Bauman 1973; Kuper 1983; Stocking 1987). This view is justified if by modern we mean only the emphasis on empirical fieldwork in depth within a single socio-cultural group. Evans-Pritchard formulated it cogently:

> "The viewpoint in social anthropology today may be summed up by saying that we now think we can learn more about the nature of human society by really detailed intensive and observational studies, conducted in a series of a few selected societies with the aim of solving limited problems, than by attempting generalizations on a wider scale from literature" (Evans-Pritchard 1951: 91-2).

The shadow of Durkheim as the theoretical godfather certainly loomed as large for Evans-Pritchard as is implied in Bauman's critical assessment of the Durkheimian "vaccine injected into the blood of the modern study of culture in its infancy ... by its midwives, Malinowski and Boas" (Bauman 1973: 45). Modern anthropology also depends upon the tenets of empirical validation conventionally labelled participant observation. Less clear is the resolution of the Boasian "eternal tension" between "seeking to subsume a variety of them [phenomena] under a general law" and "seeking to penetrate the secrets of the individual phenomenon" (Stocking 1987: xvi).

Our problem is merging two seemingly incompatible epistemological paradigms: the subjective and objective, the unique and the comparative, the inner view and the outside analysis, the particular and the general. Did these tensions really arise between the 1890s and the mid-1920s? Can all criticism of as well as homage to this yoking together of opposite epistemologies be laid at the feet of the two historical icons, Boas and Malinowski?

As I shall show, this kind of study, combining the universal human trait of the creation of culture with the malleability and variability of human nature as shown through the expression of different and specifically unique cultural manifestations, was already present in the mid-nineteenth century. It is doubtless a result of the convergence of diametrically opposed currents of thought: the Enlightenment urge for generalized statements about generic human nature, and the Romantic attempt to salvage the importance of cultural creations as unique expressions of specific collectivities. These two currents, of the universalism of rational criteria for comparison and of the particularism of unique creativity (the Romantic notion of genius in its collective forms), re-emerged in different discourses throughout the 19th as well as the 20th century – about nature and nurture, about natural and cultural evolution as well as about structuralist and interpretationist approaches.

I shall trace this fusion of the twin impulses of the Enlightenment and Romanticism in the work of Adolf Bastian (1826-1905), Bastian's work is a focal point because his first written statements appear at the same time as the nature-nurture controversy. This debate had already occupied the 18th century savants (Voltaire) and resurfaced in this period through the scientific publications of Darwin. Bastian can be considered a pivotal link for the emergence of modern anthropology as his work, though only marginally mentioned in recent histories of the discipline, exerted a considerable influence on the works of later "founders" of the anthropological enterprise. Tylor, as well as Boas, was aware of considerable portions of Bastian's works, particularly the notion of *the psychic unity of mankind* (see Tylor 1865: 378; Tylor 1871; Boas 1911: 43 and 154ff.). The variety of anthropological influences on such modern founders as Boas has to a large extent been demonstrated (Kluckhohn and Pufer 1959; Stocking 1974; Koepping 1983: 124ff.). Yet why the epistemological conundrum as inherited from Enlightenment and Romanticism appears in all its acuteness by the middle of the 19th century is less well understood.

After showing the relevance of anthropology's double aims in its modern foundations through the figures of Malinowski and Boas, the ensuing discussion will centre on the expressions which the Enlightenment and the Romantic impulse found in Bastian's writings.

*Malinowski, Boas and Modern Anthropological Sensibilities*

Both Boas and Malinowski's statements reveal the inherited tensions. While Malinowski maintained at one time that "to grasp the native's point of view, his relation to life, to realize his vision of his world ... we have to study man, and we must study what concerns him most intimately, that is, the hold which life has on him" (1922: 25), he later insisted on the following requirement for anthropological comparative work: "The principles of social organization ... have to be constructed by the observer out of a multitude of manifestations of varying significance and relevance" (1935, 1: 317).

One may, as Leach has done, charge Malinowski with epistemological naivety (Leach 1964: 134). Yet even those authors who facetiously challenge the paradigm of the "inside view" as a form of "ventriloquism" (see Geertz 1988) admit to the twin vision of anthropology, the necessity of merging the micro- with the macro-view. "We are the miniaturists of the social sciences, painting on lilliputian canvases with what we take to be delicate strokes. We hope to find in the little what eludes us in the large, to stumble upon general truths while sorting through special cases" (Geertz 1975: 4).

The epistemological conundrum is clearly stated in these remarks: are we really able to accept both the rationality of scientific construction and the relativity of world-views? Do we really stress differences – at least on an intellectual level – while looking for the universal? The more theoretical aspect of this very same question is voiced by Boas as a goal of anthropological work: "Which are the social tendencies that are general human characteristics? ... Thus a critical examination of what is generally valid for all humanity and what is specifically valid for different cultural types comes to be a matter of great concern to students of society" (Boas 1940 in 1968: 261).

Anthropologists may have contributed to an emerging awareness of the precariousness of the empirical method, along with contemporary sociological and philosophical epistemologists during the first third of this century. However, it does appear that combining inside and outside views was a hope posited without much reflection. Anthropology had to wait for this pointed reminder in Lévi-Strauss's despairing personal notes, where he puts the problem in the existential rather than the epistemological terms:

"Either the anthropologist clings to the norms of his own group, in which case the others can only inspire in him an ephemeral curiosity in which there is always an element of disapproval; or he makes himself over completely to the objects of his studies, in which case he can never be perfectly objective, because in giving himself to all societies he cannot but refuse himself ... to one among them" (Lévi-Strauss 1971: 381).

Lévi-Strauss's 1955 statement epitomizes what in more recent times has been called the "predicament of culture" (Clifford 1988), which I take to be really the predicament of the anthropologist.

### *The Mid-nineteenth Century Fusion of Two Currents in Anthropological Orientation*

The "anthropologization" of the world took place through the systems devised by the savants of the eighteenth century (Evans-Pritchard 1951; Foucault 1966; Harris 1968; Diamond 1974; Lepenies 1976 and 1988). The Romantic Johann Gottfried Herder's firm rejection of the mindless and mechanical external classifications of French Enlightenment thought, and his plea to judge each time and culture by its own canon of values, brought about the new emphasis in anthropology on specific cultural configurations as collective expressions of a "folk". The more general question about the nature of culture *sui generis* remained. The tension continued surrounding connections between nature and culture on the one hand, and between the diverse synchronic and diachronic manifestations of culture on the other. There is a considerable gap between Herder's work and Bastian's first publications in 1860. Intervening important writers throughout the humanities spread the message of the Romantic revolt after 1800, from folklore and mythology studies (Jacob Grimm; Lazarus) to linguistics and folk psychology (Steinthal), from legal studies to historiography, from literary criticism (Friedrich and August Wilhelm Schlegel) to philosophy (Schelling and the Neo-Kantians), to mention but a few of the important intellectual currents of the first half of the nineteenth century in the humanities (Koepping 1983: 77-94). But the key methodological impulse encapsulated in the above-mentioned existential quandary of Lévi-Strauss, namely the impossibility of committing oneself to a singular culture without denying all other cultures, appears clearly in the following outburst of Herder:

> "Admittedly, we could derive from it all the common places about the right and the good, maxims of philanthropy and wisdom, views of all times and peoples for all times and peoples. For all times and peoples? That means, alas, precisely not for the very people whom the particular code of law was meant to fit like clothing" (Herder in Barnard 1969: 201).

Herder had earlier seen the epistemological problem of combining the two modes of generalization based on classificatory principles and of giving one's due to the creative genius of each unique cultural or historical production:

> "Nobody in the world feels the weakness of general characterization more than me. One depicts a whole people, era, region – what has one depicted? ... Who has not noticed what an inexpressible matter is the uniqueness of a person: who is able to speak with discernment about difference" (Herder's *Journal* of 1769, in Herder 1976: 36, my translation);

and further:

> "Each estate, each form of life, has its own customs" (1976: 27).

It only needed the fieldworker, the first-hand collector of data on the diversity of customs, to combine Herder's critique of the Enlightenment with the Romantic revolt which gave uniqueness its place. Adolf Bastian was the scholar who proposed a programme of anthropology similar to that endorsed by Boas and Malinowski in this century.

The most direct connection can be established between Herder's idea of the importance of the social formation of an ethnic group (*Volk*) and its animating impulse in the folk-soul (*Volksseele*) with what Bastian was to call the "soul of society" (*Gesellschaftsseele*). This socio-psychological concept of the collective mind finds its objective expressions in material culture as well as in art, religion or legal custom. Once elaborated it becomes, as I shall show in more detail, the basis for those "folk-ideas" (*Völkergedanken*), which are but the diversely patterned forms of collective representations (*Gesellschafts-gedanken*), expressed in their culturally unique formations. Bastian takes his cue from Herder whom he quotes approvingly:

"Though complete in itself, the individual is endowed in such a way that it can reach the highest form of actualization when it fits itself into a totality, as a fulfillment of its destiny, because the individual is a means and an end both for itself and also for higher purposes" (cited in Bastian 1900: 119).

He had much earlier found the adage "It thinks in us" (Bastian 1868: 1)[1]. The main problems of the dichotomous approach of anthropology – the scientific and the humanistic, the positivist and the hermeneutic – were discussed by Bastian. We may nowadays criticize the hasty, almost breathless, execution of the programme as well as his inept writing which either undermines his good intentions or makes it almost impossible to judge how far he succeeded in fulfilling his theoretical goals. As he wrote his first three-volume compendium in 1860, he would normally be incorporated among the many cultural evolution prophets of the nineteenth century (the controversy has been raised by Bidney 1968 and critically discussed by Koepping 1983). However, Bastian had a practical and healthy scepticism towards simplistic evolutionary progression theories. His five journeys around the world, his erudition as well as his scientific and medical training, all contributed to this scepticism.

He was trained as a medical practitioner, and taught the fields of evolutionary biology, comparative anatomy and physiology by his lifelong friend, the pathologist Rudolf Virchow. Bastian employed his grasp of 19th century scientific knowledge towards analysing cultural data and the vast diversity of the "collective representations" of groups, what he called anthropology's main aim (his *Gesellschaftsgedanken*). This abstraction was balanced by his

---

[1] This notion is a standing topos which seems to appear first in the writings of Christoph Lichtenberg and to be repeated or taken up without reference to sources still by Lévi-Strauss.

demand for first-hand field investigations into the manifold manifestations of the collective representations in the form of collective "ethnic idea frames"or his *Völkergedanken*.

*Bastian and the Enlightenment Vision:*
*the Link through Alexander von Humboldt*

Reading Bastian's turgid prose, one becomes aware of the two strains of our anthropological ancestry: the Enlightenment of mainly French persuasion (on the precepts of English 17th century philosophy as well as on the base-line of Descartes) and the Romantic movement as a conscious German counter-movement (led by Johann Gottfried Herder, who quite openly relied on English predecessors, such as Shaftesbury or many of the Scottish representatives of the Enlightenment). To appreciate the marriage of these two disparate streams in Bastian's scientific anthropology it is necessary to summarize and to delve into these two positions.

The French Enlightenment provided the scientific, even scientistic, orientation towards human phenomena which pervaded positivism (and its off-shoots evolutionism and Marxism) from the 19th century onwards. Both human affairs and nature were believed to be governed by the same kind of laws. These rules of necessity could be discerned by applying the power of reason. Cartesian rationalism and English empiricism became the two ruling paradigms for the study of society. Finding the natural laws of society (and of religion, education etc.) would enable people, who were seen as infinitely perfectable, to attain a better state of existence through steady progress. Reason replaced authority and tradition as the principle governing human conduct. Montesquieu exemplified this when he stated: "Man, being a physical being, is, like other bodies, governed by invariable laws. ... It is of course essential that the intellectual world, the world of the mind, should be as well regulated as the physical world" (Montesquieu quoted in Hazard 1965: 375).

What may seem a splendid vision when put into Kant's terms where Enlightenment is paraphrased by the adage of Horace, *sapere aude*, "dare to think" – becomes, in the writings of the French savants, a threatening vision of "man as machine", a totalitarian nightmare of education and control. Interestingly, this joyless vision of human affairs, with its presumed lawlike conformity to universal progress through rationality, had but a short life[2].

The Enlightenment tended to assume liberty and equality were ruled by the laws of reason, on the one hand, and by the rules of etiquette, property relations and hierarchies of natural organization on the other hand. This vision

---

[2] With the exception of it becoming the main stay of socio/political engeneering, as pointed out extensively in the writing of Foucault.

became the paradigmatic presupposition for the foundation of the social sciences (see Koepping 1983)[3]. Through Comte and Durkheim, the conservative stream of the Enlightenment engendered the following propositions:

Society can be studied through the application of the scientific method, and its lawful empirical results can and should be used to improve the state of society; society rests on organization and hierarchy for survival (these conservative visions were shared by Turgot, Holbach, d'Alembert, Voltaire and Condorcet).

However, there was a more radical stream among the savants, represented by Saint-Simon, Rousseau, Diderot and Helvetius, many of whom believed in the possibility of true equality through education. Their ideas were to influence Marx as well as English liberal reformers such as John Stuart Mill. All of them, radicals as well as conservatives, in the period between the Enlightenment and the mid-nineteenth century, believed in laws underlying human conduct, in progress, in universals and in the empirical accessibility of human reality.

The Enlightenment played out in a modern discourse the very same contradictions which have beset the notion of natural law since antiquity. The conservative stream was represented both by Plato, in regard to hierarchical organization and totalitarian control of social life, and by the Stoics, who believed in the universal laws of necessity (though in circular form) in nature, society and the mind. Liberal streams, such as the Sophists, interpreted natural law as an indication that customs which are socially created could be overthrown.

Bastian received this influence of the Enlightenment vision directly through one of his teachers, Alexander von Humboldt (1769-1859; Bastian spoke at his funeral; Bastian 1869). His vision of the natural and human world which Bastian was to adopt and cite is worth quoting:

"We hope to find laws which regulate the difference of temperature and climate ... before we can hope to explain the involved causes of vegetable distribution; and it is thus that the observer ... is led from one class of phenomena to another, by means of the mutual dependence and connection existing between them" (Alexander von Humboldt 1844: viii).

It would be but a small step from this to connect the kingdoms of nature and humanity, and to apply insight from one to the other. Alexander's brother, Wilhelm, summed up these expectations and became at the same time a prophet for the job Bastian was trying to accomplish. Wilhelm von Humboldt wrote: "If anybody is able to do it, I would say it is my brother, for he might

---

[3] I am pararphrasing to a large degree the summary given by Zygmunt Bauman 1992.

connect the study of physical nature with that of moral nature, and thus bring the universe as we know it into true harmony, or if this surpasses the abilities of one man, prepare the study of physical nature in such a way that the second step will become easier" (Wilhelm von Humboldt 1836 in 1967: 159).

The ultimate vision is one of harmony in nature and society, by equalizing differentials. Bastian shared this belief with Alexander von Humboldt. Bastian echoes Humboldt's idea of the universal harmony as the heritage of the best of the Enlightenment optimism (really a scientific eschatology) in the following words:

> "Being part of the totality that constitutes the world, man can only per-
> ceive those connections through which the world relates to him ...
> Being juxtaposed in space, all things react to each other inasmuch as
> their totality makes up the whole of the universe they must, as parts, be
> interdependent ... the microcosm is in reality only a mental distillation
> of the macrocosmic realm in an individuality which is but a part of it.
> Properly speaking, the mind and the body are one, and together make
> man. This unity of mind and matter, created anew each moment, is the
> essence of the nature of man" (Bastian 1860, vol. I: 1).

### Bastian's Adoption of Herderian Concepts

The Romanticist reaction against this Enlightenment vision can be summed up in a short quote by Herder, giving the gist of the argument:

> "that another Montesquieu would come and really offer us the spirit of
> the laws and governments of our globe, instead of a mere classification
> of governments into three or four empty categories. ... A classification
> of states, based on political principles, is also of little avail. ... Least of
> all are we in need of a scissors and paste approach, where examples are
> assembled at random from all nations, times and climates, until we can
> no longer see the wood for the trees; the genius of our earth as one
> entity is lost" (Herder 1774, in Barnard 1969: 325).

And even more pronounced:

> "This is a time when the art of legislation is considered the sole method
> of civilizing nations. Yet this method has been employed, in the strang-
> est fashion to produce mostly general philosophies of the human race,
> rational axioms of human behaviour and what have you! Doubtless the

undertaking was more dazzling than useful" (Herder, in Barnard 1969: 201; Bastian in Koepping 1983: 179, originally 1860, takes up this proposition).

From this Bastian derives his emphasis on the specificity of each cultural creation as expressed in his *Völkergedanken*. The link is made explicitly. Lévi-Strauss, in his 1962 Geneva address for the 250th anniversary of Rousseau, traced the foundations of comparative ethnology to the saying of Rousseau that it was deplorable not to find a savant of the order of Montesquieu or Buffon to study people and their customs instead of stones and plants (cited in Lévi-Strauss 1973, chapter 2). This same demand is uncannily pre-empted by a quote which Bastian takes from Herder (who undoubtedly knew his Rousseau well): "As Herder said with great amazement, it is about time that, having studied the kingdom of minerals, plants and animals, we make an attempt to understand man". Bastian then continues with a definition of ethnology: "Ethnology really is directed towards the study of the "ethnos", the collective representations of social groups or what I have called social thoughts (*Gesellschaftsgedanken*)". A few lines previously, Bastian referred to his notion of the folk-idea: "The folk-idea itself (*Völkergedanke*), if used merely as a mental crutch, is useless unless it is supported by detailed micro-studies" (Bastian in Koepping 1983: 174 and 175, originally Bastian 1893-4: 20, 53, 58 ff.). Thus the notion of variability of cultures and the specificity of each unique ethnic creation go hand in hand with the demand for close observation. Those who think that research into the subjectively meaningful forms of ideas, the "native's point of view", was first introduced by Malinowski should read Bastian's thoughts on the study of folk-ideas:

"The main aim for ethnology has become the securing and collecting of these folk ideas. ... In contrast to the classical sciences of minerals, plants and animals, the science of man has to take cognisance of the subjective angle, the object being man himself in the subjectively created world of ideas" (Bastian in Koepping 1983: 171; originally Bastian 1893-4: 20-1).

This quote shows that Bastian tried to stress the subjective view of social action, and to capture that through a collection and analysis of the idea-systems. For Bastian ideas encompass items of material culture as well, since, for him, the world of human-made things gives us access to thought processes. Whereas Herder remained a historian, interpreting different cultures on the diachronic axis through recourse to written sources on his alien Other, the

Middle Ages, did Bastian act out the same programme by travelling through-out the mid-nineteenth century world on the synchronic axis with living oral cultures.

Herder maintained there are certain universal requirements for the devel-opment of civilized social life. He included the value of *Humanität*, by which he meant the reliance on reason and common sense (*Vernunft und Billigkeit*). Here, perhaps, lies the true source of all modern anthropological dilemmas. There is an insoluble contradiction between relativism, the equal importance and value of all ethnic groups and their expressions in language, art, or social organization, and the axiological demand for a binding universal morality (which for Herder included fraternity, without which liberty or equality would be useless; see Berlin 1980; Spitz 1955). For Herder the common people did not need high-flown philosophical theories, but common sense (Herder, *Werke, vol. V*, 1982: 18; *Briefe zur Beförderung der Humanität*, orig. 1793). This reliance on the common-sense philosophies of populations attracted Bas-tian. This may well have influenced his aim to collect evidence for pervasive folk-ideas which persist in bounded ethnic groups within specific territories.

*Elementary and Folk-Ideas as Tools of Analysis*

Having traced the roots of Bastian's cohesive anthropological programme, with its double roots in Enlightenment and Romanticism, it is necessary to clarify finally the distinction between elementary ideas and folk-ideas and their connection in Bastian's system of and programme for the analysis of cul-tures. "Elementary ideas", *Elementargedanken*, for which Bastian uses also the Stoic term *logoi spermatikoi*, "pregnant thoughts" or thought-seeds, are never directly observable, but are only indirectly deducible from the plethora of folk-ideas. Elementary ideas are abstract generalizations which cannot be located in real social life. They are hidden in the cloaks of ethnic diversity. Yet, because Bastian starts from the proposition that all humans have an equal intellectual potential (widely quoted as his idea of the psychic unity of man-kind), a developmental sequence or a mental process of some kind must lead from elementary to folk-ideas.

The basic prerequisite for Bastian is the biologically given mental endow-ment, equal in all individuals and collectivities, to solve problems. Given that people everywhere tend to hit on the same solutions with monotonous regular-ity, how can elementary ideas change and vary? Until proven, Bastian did not believe in diffusion, though he never denied it. Ratzel mistakenly implies a denial in a heated and polemic controversy in the 1880s: modern literature on the history of anthropological theories continues this mistake (see Bastian 1873; 1885; Ratzel 1887; Bastian 1894; see Koepping 1983: 65ff.).

The forces for changing elementary ideas are of a twofold nature. *First,* there is an inbuilt potential in an idea which can be expanded to its utmost. Bastian uses the analogy from the natural sciences, in this case from physics, about potential and kinetic energy. Elementary ideas are energy-loaded mental seeds which follow an entelechetic law, developing in diverse directions up to an initially given expenditure of energy. *Second,* there are external geographical and historical forces at work: the environment works on ideas and shapes them according to the demands of human survival, while history and/or migration of population groups changes idea-systems constantly.

The notion of folk-ideas may nowadays not require much further elaboration, as the concept has become common in the anthropology of ethnicity, identity, the diversity of time perception, on notions of space, of person or any other category. Folk-ideas largely coincide with the modern concept of culture prevalent in American cultural anthropology and the nineteenth century *Kulturwissenschaften*. Both are defined as a learned pattern of behaviour and thought, shared by an ethnically bounded community and transmitted by enculturative practices. Bastian expresses it in one of his more elaborate definitions thus:

> "The object of our study is the ethnically coloured world of ideas, that world of the creations of the Folk Ideas (*Völkergedanken*) which are expressions of the collective social representations (*Gesellschaftsgedanken*), and we are to study them in their variability deriving from their historical-geographic conditions" (Bastian 1893-4, vol. IV: 311).

The concept of folk-ideas can easily be identified as the notion of the cultural repository of an ethnic group and be traced to the Herderian concept of *Volksseele*. The elementary idea has remained a largely puzzling concept in both origin and connection to the folk-ideas. To understand Bastian on this point, we need to quote some of the numerous analogies from the natural sciences he uses to explain the concept. He states:

> "The physical unity of the species man has been anthropologically established, and as a consequence we now look for the psychic unity of mankind. The psychic unity of social thought underlies the basic elements of the body social. The world over we will find a monotonous sub-stratum of identical elementary ideas" (Bastian in Koepping 1983: 176; originally 1877: 183ff.).

Scientific metaphors concerning elementary ideas abound in Bastian's work: they are compared with a nucleus, with a cell, with the simple plant forms of cryptogams (which, as he puts it, are not to be neglected or looked down upon, as all complex plants develop from the simple ferns and mosses), and so on. To put it simply, we can say that elementary ideas possess an innate propensity to change, grow and react to environmental stimuli and historical changes. As these elementary ideas are reductive analytical categories, it may not surprise us to have so few mentioned in Bastian's whole ceuvre of over a hundred books. Yet there are striking examples, such as the notion of propulsion instruments by artificial extension of the body, which finds its folk-idea realization in such diverse forms as the bow, spear and spear-thrower. That the bow did not develop among Australian Aborigines does not indicate for Bastian the inferior mental equipment of these ethnic groups. Rather it is the result of environmental factors. Australia has no trees which are flexible enough to develop the bow. So the spear-thrower and the boomerang represent alternative folk-ideas.

This leads to a further question: where do we find elementary ideas most pristinely, if at all? Here his answer is clear: to find the simplest, least complex elaborations of elementary ideas we must turn to people who apparently had the least historical contact due to geographical isolation. As Bastian puts it:

> "Like the physical habitus, so does the psychic habitus carry the imprint of the climatical agents, and thus we find the elementary ideas embedded in their specific milieu. Only when the elementary ideas of the savage tribe come into contact with outside stimuli do they develop their inherent potential through a growth process in historical forms of cultural development" (Bastian in Koepping 1983: 167; originally Bastian 1871: 172).

The study of so-called simple, primitive or *Naturvölker* is a way to recapture elementary ideas in their pristine state. The terms evolution and development should not be taken for notions from classical evolutionism, as Bastian categorically states: "No factual evidence exists for the postulate of an uninterrupted and constant progression in the evolution of culture, a regularly ascending line from lower to higher stages" (Bastian in Koepping 1983: 167; originally Bastian 1871), or again: "the idea of a process of evolution to higher forms in which mankind progresses to ultimate perfection can be no more than a hypothesis". (Bastian in Koepping 1983: 166; originally Bastian 1871). While the *Naturvölker* show a closer affinity to original elementary ideas, this does not imply for Bastian a lower state of mental development:

> "Europeans were for so long deluding themselves in the conviction that they represent the ideal of all mankind, and in so doing despised all other ages and nations which dared to derive different ideals from their

unique variations of social life ... maybe the question about the nature of man is to be decided by the majority; in that case Europeans would be the eccentric ones when compared with average man" (Bastian 1860, 1: 230).

Here we find a clear indication of the Herderian influence in twofold form: the reliance on the average man, reminding us of the disdain of elaborate philosophies as also expressed by Herder, and the relativistic gaze on other cultures. This is strongly expressed in the following quote, which clearly contains the spirit of Montaigne: "in our own European civilization ... we would most certainly find a form of mental barbarism that not only equals that of the African or American Indian, but surpasses in stupidity any savage society" (Bastian in Koepping 1983: 169; originally Bastian 1871).

I think the uncanny mixture of the adulation of science mixed with a genuine appreciation of cultural diversity is proved by these quotes from different periods of Bastian's writings. One might ask in the end how this untiring traveller, who spent more than thirty years of his life overseas, repeating the Asian as well as the American crossings of his teacher Humboldt and much more, put his programme into action: how did he collect his data? He never makes this clear, though we do know that he always tried to learn local languages, as he did quickly when retained in Burma for more than two years as personal physician to the king. Instead of a method book, we find him appreciatively quoting an adage from another Romantic follower of Herder, Jacob Grimm, whose method of collecting folktales Bastian rendered applicable to anthropological collecting of data: "rare flowers have to be picked with chaste hands" (Grimm 1844, *"Vorrede zur Deutschen Mythologie"*, in 1981: xi, quoted by Bastian 1885: 39).

Bastian expressed the combination of this sensitivity and sensibility of a Romantic with the Enlightenment programmes for a future culture in the following lines: "The power of the mind of man must break the chains imposed upon it by mythical fantasies and selfforged delusions" (Bastian 1860 vol. 1: 126).

*Conclusion*

Bastian may have failed to fulfil his aims. His view of the applicability of scientific principles to human affairs may have been overly naive and optimistic, while his restless collecting activities, instead of steady and limited fieldwork, might strike us as amateurish. Yet his passionate enthusiasm to put the ideas of Alexander von Humboldt and Herder into practice, and his equally passionate aim to unite thereby Enlightenment and Romanticism (paralleled by some natural scientists such as Fechner), give him a secure place among founders of the discipline as a field of academic teaching.

The epistemologies he pursued may forever remain logically contradictory. Yet, without the universal message of the Enlightenment with its belief in reason, and without the mitigating caution against overgeneralizations and facile categorization as proposed by Herder, a genuine science of culture is scarcely imaginable. We may put the aims of anthropology and the description of our results into a different language today. We may use a different discourse to appear neither corny nor naive, neither inhumanly objectifying nor navel-gazing, by stating, as Michael Jackson did in his *Paths toward a Clearing*, that our ethnographies are co-productions between researcher and research subjects, or that they are creations from within a dialogue (Jackson 1989).

Yet we have to believe in the universality of the human potential behind the relativity of diversity, which in turn we can only grasp through the specificity of a particular formation. Without this double aim, we sink into the cynicism of inauthenticity, of which Stanley Diamond warned in his critique of civilization (1974) and to which we are prone if we consider anthropology and ethnography as mere rhetorical ruses to convince others about our authority (a warning also voiced by Geertz 1988: 142). If credibility becomes a market strategy instead of a willingness to be open to an encounter which carries the risk of losing ourselves, then anthropology has lost its heritage as well as its legitimacy.

*Figure 5*: Bronislaw Malinowski

# Malinowski and the Myth of Method

*Preamble*

Bronislaw Malinowski (1884-1942) is one of the great innovators of social anthropology of the 20th century. There can be no doubt – judging from the debate over the relationship between the production of knowledge during research and the transmission of this knowledge through the writing of ethnographies – that the continuing impact of Malinowski's approach lies in what one could label an emphasis on the pragmatic angle of human action in the diversity of cultural settings. Malinowski was an empiricist and pragmatist, for whom it was rather more important to see what people *do* than to inquire what they *say* they are doing.

He played such a large part in establishing the methodological foundations for the anthropological field that the practical research procedures of social anthropology (or cultural anthropology in the US, ethnology in Europe) are inscribed with Malinowski's name, making the research methodology almost synonymous with the term of his coinage, *participant observation.*

With this required procedure Malinowski bequeathed to us the ambiguity implicit in the oxymoron, the contradiction in the terminology. On the one hand, the procedure stresses the participation of the researcher in the field, so that through his subjective immersion in the daily life-course of the actors their point of view is transmitted to the reader of the ethnography. This then could ideally lead to an empowerment of the social actors themselves, as their views are taken as serious data for understanding and interpreting their own way of life. On the other hand, the epistemological status of the knowledge thus acquired is not made more transparent, as the recorder of the views is still the researcher as subject who through his lens of perception and cognition filters the indigenous view-point.

Furthermore, Malinowski himself insisted that this recording of the indigenous points of view was only one leg of the research procedure, the other being observation, from a distance as it were, with the implied schedule of the researcher's own agenda in mind, be it theoretically or personally framed. Thus, anthropologists are also prone to use a form of disempowering strategy, not only because it is finally their authorship which establishes the ethnography, but also, as Malinowski indicated, because anthropologists can through their distanced view put forward what he labelled "the charter of native institutions" by processing their data to deduce from concrete individual observations the structures and patterns by which the indigenous life seems to be governed, "unbeknown to the actors".

However, we would probably do him injustice by requiring that he produce an answer to this conundrum which till today the scientific discussion has not solved in any satisfactory manner. In this sense Malinowski was a true successor of the anthropological orientation which, through Herder's influence, entered the academic curriculum in the nineteenth century as a mixture of Enlightenment attitudes (scientific ordering) and Romantic yearning (to "understand" the unique). Malinowski as much as Herder before him tried to take cognisance of the particularity of each cultural arrangement but also to look for the universal features of and in all cultures throughout history. While dispensing with what he considered the fruitless search for origins and historical derivations of the extant cultures of the globe, he developed the *functional paradigm*, a theory of culture which combined the human biological and physiological foundations with that what was at the same time in American anthropology called the "superorganic" nature of culture as man-made instrumentarium which has to satisfy the "needs" of the biological organism.

For Malinowski, a culture or society was only viable if it developed an apparatus to fulfil these "basic needs". He recognised that social life can only continue when the organisational or institutional base-line which arose from the very fact of the man-made order of social living were also dealt with. Those needs derived from the fact of social life having to be governed by rules, can be summarised in the following way:

> a) an economic system of production, consumption and exchange; b) an educational system for the recruitment of new members and their "enculturation" into the tradition of a specific society; c) the marriage- and kinship-system for regulating the rights or reproduction, inheritance and property management; d) a system for dealing with internal and external relations and threats, with boundary-maintenance through warfare or diplomacy, which we normally call a political organisation; e) finally, there is the functional imperative for the social system to maintain itself as bounded entity through recourse to commonly held values, religious or otherwise.

While this is a sketchy summary of the functional prerequisites of social life, seen from the basis of needs deriving from the biological organism as well as from the "social organism", it catches Malinowski's wide aim of defining "culture" as an instrument to fulfil these basic and derived needs. The problem arises here of course at the very same moment when one tries to allocate a particular "function" or "purpose" to or for any particular "custom" or "habit": these terms are not clearly separated by Malinowski, so that one gets at times the impression that some kind of "purpose", in an almost teleological form, lies behind "culture" as a disembodied or free-floating collective agency of the "conscience collective". Thus one could argue that a particular custom such as headhunting or infanticide may have a "function" for either survival of groups in difficult environments or for boundary-maintenance.

The danger is on the one hand that one confuses the significance of any activity with its obvious purpose when looked at from the angel of survival or adaptational advantage (though Malinowski disavowed evolutionary explanations)[1]. On the other hand, all groups may have developed different strategies for coping with the same "danger" or "threat": if we concentrate on the objectively given threat of – let us say – overpopulation for survival, then we could from logic as well as through surveying extant methods of different cultures for "dealing" with this problem (in a kind of social policy) come up with a great variety of possibilities of "culture's" response to the problem:

> infanticide, killing of the aged, migration, expansion, raiding, killing of girls (gender-selective infanticide), or the borrowing of technological improvements for increasing production output per person, contraception, abortion or even a drive toward celibacy for all first-born through devotion to monastic orders and religion.

The main question, however, would be why any particular society chooses one or the other method. Malinowski's functionalistic view runs here into the problems of explanatory power. While his scheme served the purpose of "explaining" the most "weird" customs of diverse cultures for a European world-view which on the whole in the early half of the century considered many cultures without writing systems as "primitive" in the sense of "irrational", it leaves the specific custom open to diverse interpretations, not least of which is the possibly "symbolic" interpretation of the actors themselves. Malinowski's functionalism also ran into difficulties through his other basic assumption that "cultures" are integrated wholes. He saw the economic, the educational, the social and the value systems (if one were able to separate human activities into such clearly demarcated abstractions of domains) not only as *bounded* entities, but also as *interdependent* activities and institutions.

In some cases, his point is still worth consideration. With the introduction of modern mechanised agricultural methods, we find that some South American shifting cultivators abandoned their polygynous households. As the new techniques did not require so much manpower for the feeding of the same sized family, the several women attached to the male of an extended household were no longer required, leading to an influx of single females into cities and further to exploitational practices there. On the other hand, it may be impossible to introduce new technologies such as the plow into cultures which

---

[1]  See Malinowski's "Recantation" of his evolutionist views of 1916 in his Special Forword to the 3rd edition of *The Sexual Life of Savages in Northwestern Melanesia*, London 1932: XXIIff.

consider the deep penetration of the soil as a "violation of the womb of mother Earth" and therefore as impious. The general point of a functional and holistic approach may still be salutary for many development agencies in their drive for modernising so-called "traditional" societies insofar as a thorough familiarity with the ideas and principles of the "subjects" of such "improvements" may avoid a paternalising attitude.

Most societies have changed over time through the incorporation of multiple elements from other cultural repertoires, by force or through choice, and the co-existence of diverse techniques and ideas, of rules and values, rarely makes an interdependent and/or integrative whole. Most cultures, if we dare define them as bounded entities attached to definable social groups (and recent ethnographies have shown this to be one of the great myths of the history of anthropological theorising) rather resemble a patch-work quilt of odds and ends the integration of which into a functional whole is more than doubtful, despite this worn-out model of bounded and integrated social and cultural systems being an ideologically beloved tool for modern nation-building as well as for separatist dreams and demands for "cultural" and often also for political autonomy (as titles about the *Invention of Tradition* point out).

Malinowski's theoretical universalism is outmoded today, in times when the boundedness of meaning and motivation for action may have irretrievably been displaced by the plethora of co-existing life-styles and life-projects in the modern social environment, even if such outmoded "anthropological" models have become the main-stay of authenticating collective identities. Yet his focus on the acquisition and production of knowledge about the diversity of cultural repertoires, in short, his pragmatic empiricist approach, has remained a guiding beacon. How translatable are concepts of other languages, and how comprehensible are activities of other people? How can we reconcile the "insider's" views and opinions with the mostly scientific "outsider's" explanatory models? It is the putting together of the Hermeneutics, Semiotics and Pragmatics which Malinowski envisioned which still activates "anthropological" research and analysis beyond the narrow confines of disciplinary boundaries.

The following considerations about the importance and impact of the "prejudices" and "presuppositions" of the scholar as much as the human actor Malinowski on his reflections about the lives of the Melanesians as well as on his self-reflections which shine through his diaries and letters are an attempt to show the "imponderabilia" – one of Malinowski's favoured words for the "unexpected" in social life as well as the "ungraspable" quality of it – of the anthropological enterprise caught between the scientific demand for objective knowledge and the humanist search for self-discovery. It seems to me that Malinowski's personal notes about the "field" and the "informants" as much as his ruminations about his own attitudes foreshadow much of the conundrum of the discussion about Self and Otherness in recent literature. If the Self is only discernible through the encounter with Otherness, even if an imagined Otherness, a fabricated one, a utopian one, then we are all caught in the anthropological enterprise in our daily lives everywhere. Few, however, make the practice of life into a professional enterprise.

*Ancestors*

When asked to choose an "ancestor" of the discipline of anthropology whom I would like to introduce to the general public as well as to students, I was torn between Bronislaw Malinowski (1884-1942) and the equally intriguing figure of Paul Radin (1883-1959). Both share traits which make them important, two or three generations after their deaths, to a new cohort of readers. They met during Malinowski's first visit to the United States in 1926 in New York: Malinowski's letter of March 9, 1926 states laconically: "I have not met very many people, that is except the important anthropologists: Boas, Wissler; Radin and Goddard ..." (Wayne 1995, II: 62).

Both were strong critics and promulgators of "canon" of minimal require-ments for anthropological field methods, though Radin's almost forgotten classic *The Method and Theory of Ethnology* of 1933 contains only one criti-cal reference to Malinowski, chiding him for his theoretical preconceptions which Malinowski considered as inevitable tools with which to approach the field[2]. Both criticised their forebears and colleagues. Radin's critique of what he considered Margaret Mead's shoddy field work, her overblown, unreliable and inaccurate publications aroused little controversy (in contrast to the storm in the American tea-cup after Freeman's 1983 tour de force) and reads very much like the criticism levelled by Malinowski against his predecessors or contemporaries such as Rivers. Radin wrote: "It is the amazing assumption that any outsider can obtain the type of information she specifies except after an intensive study of a lifetime. Indeed, I seriously doubt whether an outsider can ever obtain it" (Radin 1933: 178-79).

In the same vein, Malinowski had earlier written against the revered Riv-ers' belief in the unreflective submission of savages to custom due to "group-sentiments", "group-instincts" or "mental inertia": "we must enter a protest". As to Rivers' notions on primitive communism and against the Durkheimian trend of "clan-solidarity", with its generalising and abstracting from individual incidents to whole categories of people, Malinowski placed his revolutionary field methods: "Nothing could be more mistaken than such generalisations. There is a strict distinction and definition in the rights of every one and this makes ownership anything but communistic" (1926: 19). Malinowski then

---

[2] See Radin 1933: 255.

proceeds to the general methodological imperative exemplified by reference to canoe ownership in the Trobriands: "The only correct proceeding is to describe the legal state of affairs in terms of concrete fact" (ibid.).

Here the resemblance to Radin is overwhelming: "But the recognition of specific men and women should bring with it the realisation that there are all types of individual and that it is not, for instance, a Crow Indian who has made such and such a statement, ... but a particular Crow Indian" (Radin 1933: 177).

### Private Person versus Research Interest

Questions seem to circle around precisely the issues raised both by Malinowski and Radin in exemplary manner, although from here on I shall have to put Radin aside in order to sort out the case for Malinowski. These issues which are still creating a lot of anxiety could be summarised under the broad categories of the negotiation between the *private persona* of the researcher and informants in the field, and the negotiation between the *public persona* who writes an ethnography and the audience in the indigenous society as well as in that of the researcher.

The private musings of researchers and their published results, though occurring in the same time-space during the field encounter, are still published separately. Even during their production this is the case, for most researchers keep a private diary as well as ethnographic fieldnote books. Ethnographies are still generally published in the mode of generalisations about structure and processes, performances and games, exemplary case histories or extended events, while personal negotiations in the field appear in separate volumes of collected essays, in short introductory chapters on method and stay in the field, or even in disguise as fiction.

### The Diary

This pervasive practice comes down to us from Malinowski who wrote several ethnographies about the institutions of the Trobriand Islanders while his private thoughts about himself and his relations to the informants went into his *"Diary"*. Its posthumous publication in 1967 became notorious, causing embarrassment and anger among professionals. Much has been written about Malinowski and the assumed discrepancy between his public pronouncements and his private attitude, so that Nigel Rapport (1990) could exclaim tongue in cheek in his recent re-evaluation of the relationship between Malinowski, Conrad (previously hinted at by Stocking in 1968) and Sassoon "Surely everything has already been said about Malinowski's diary!" However, the recent publication of the two volumes of the correspondence between Malinowski and Elsie Masson, his first wife, by their daughter Helena (Wayne 1995), seems to me a good starting point to re-assess the interface between public and private in the field situation through recourse to the official "canon" promulgated by Malinowski in relation to his self-perception about his negotiation of the actual "field".

I do not want to go so far as Rapport who suggested that the diary discussion has hitherto overemphasised the dichotomy of private versus public (Rapport 1990: 6). The reaction to the diary, as presumed destroyer of the myth of anthropological fieldwork, suggests that it hit a sensitive spot in most practitioners, and few felt safe to talk about skeletons in closets. That is one layer of myth which needs uncovering, or at least confronting, if we do not want to lose face in public or faith with our own students. A second reason for dealing with it is that Malinowski's own practice created a dichotomy which is also deeply inscribed in our own literary tradition, the genre of ethnography being a "scientific" treatise, the diaries belonging to another genre, veering between fantasy and partial recollection. When designed for publication, life is always constructed as a trajectory.

Nowadays we are aware, if we believe Geertz, that ethnographies lie midway between an "author-evacuated" scientific treatise and an "author-saturated" novel. We may excuse the genre separation on the ground that at every point of a trajectory a person is different, and at all points of time the persona is a multiple conglomerate of different "role-bundles": different *genres* thus activate different *facets of self*. Why must a person be from one rounded and whole cast, all of whose facets fit together like a puzzle in such a way that no discrepancies between the different "faces" obtrude, each piece being consistent with each other"? Such a demand may be another European myth that the moral personality must be a consistent, self/contained and self-created unit. Even if we were to accept the *fragmented self*, there may be sound reasons for keeping the different facets apart, as we do when we fulfil different roles in life, but there are nevertheless compelling reasons for considering at least two facets of Malinowski together, given the deeply personal nature of fieldwork. The discussion of public ethnographic writing and the writing of the "canon" must therefore be seen as an ensemble which includes the private musings, especially for persons whose identity is largely shaped or changed and even possibly *transformed* through the encounter with the cultural Other. Luckily, in contrast to public persons like Jane Austen or Richard Burton whose private letters were burned by well-meaning or fearful relatives so that the "public myth" is all we have to go by, in Malinowski's case we can compare the two and learn about ourselves and our professional short-comings when we plumb the public and private inconsistencies, and even find a little uniformity, if not comfort.

### The Irony of the Myth-Maker

The epithet "Maker of Myth" was given to Malinowski by the Trobrianders. As he reports in a letter to his future wife Elsie Masson (15th April 1918) he is now referred to by the Trobrianders not by the earlier designation of "Man from Omarakana", but as *tolilibogwo* which he translates as "the man of old talk", or, "to put it nicely", he adds, "Master of Myth".

In a typically deprecating jocular aside he adds that the designation is not one of reverence, but rather of scorn: "that chap, who is dotty ..." (Wayne 1995, I: 128).

The very ambiguity implied in this Trobriand ascription of Master of Myth seems a fitting summation for Malinowski as anthropologist, and it is the very ambivalence expressed in his own gloss of the indigenous term which nicely encompasses his own attitude, one which has given rise to much controversy if not downright misunderstanding. As one of his first disciples, Raymond Firth, already noted in 1957, it was Malinowski's dry and often self-deprecating humour which threw people off balance, such as when he wrote, in the Special Forward to *The Sexual Life of Savages* that "the magnificent title of the Functional School of Anthropology has been bestowed by myself, in a way on myself, and to a large extent out of my own sense of irresponsibility", or when he wrote on a dinner invitation "Professor B. Malinowski (functionalist in Partibus Infidelium) ... hyper-, epi-, meta-functionalist-in-law ..." (Firth 1957: 11). Firth adds that it was this sense of humour which was "one of the most difficult things to swallow in Malinowski for those who were not prepared to surrender themselves to him" (ibid.: 10).

Myth-maker indeed, but a tricky one! He does collect the myths of the Trobrianders; does it mean, and did the Trobrianders mean, that his writings about them are a myth? He also created the canon of anthropological field work; is this also a myth, because his diary invalidates the canon? Does his self-irony make a myth out of his own pronouncements? Or does he want to say: I see what you make of me, a myth, and I hereby disown it by showing that I do not quite believe it myself?

Much hinges on the interpretation of such issues, on the understanding of irony, and in particular distancing self-irony, and much of what Malinowski said about "his boys" and "me and my nigs" may have to be re-interpreted in the light of self-mockery which if convincingly proved makes a mockery of all attacks against his presumed racism and imperialism as well as personal grandstanding. On the other hand, if we only concentrate on items of self-mockery, the "true person", the "inner self" of Malinowski would recede even further. Given that his private musings are not all in the mode of self-mockery, we have a chance to see his self-perception quite clearly, and in his later writings on issues of applied anthropology and the defence of freedom, he certainly does not mock his support for specific values:

> "There are many who condemn value judgements in the vested interests of academic futility, laziness, and irrelevancy. The best remedy here is to recognise that the soundest test of an adequate theory is always to be found in practical applications" (1944: 19).

The combination of this sense of humour which poked fun at his own profession, when combined with that ruthless honesty and candour with which he scrutinised his own field approach, are the very traits which make Malinowski in my opinion one of the most informative "ancestors" for anthropology. What attracts me is precisely this ambivalence and ambiguity toward the whole enterprise. Yet, even this self-mocking, combined with his public as well as private candour, has been criticised recently.

It may be true, as Ioan Lewis has suggested, that Malinowski would have approved of the publication of his infamous *"Diary"* in 1967, since the published ethnographic public works as well as the private reflections show that he certainly possessed an almost ruthless intellectual honesty. Yet, Michael Young makes the scathing suggestion that his "extreme candour" may have been "another of his publicity tricks" (in relation to Malinowski's "confessions of ignorance and failure" in Appendix II of *Coral Gardens and their Magic*, see Young 1979: 11). Others see it rather as proof of his self-critical will to confront his own deficiencies. After reading the letters to Elsie Masson this judgement must surely be amended. Both, diary and letters, show a researcher who is candid to the point of constantly perceiving himself as falling short of his own standards of decency and morality and of methodological rigour.

### Tolerance through Distancing

Despite his otherwise vituperative and ironic derision of the Malinowskian endeavour and of Malinowski as person, Geertz accurately discerns this trait of his "ancestor", noting after the publication of the diary that Malinowski's mood during fieldwork moved from sexual fantasy to guilt and expiation in ethnographic drudgery (Geertz 1967). If the publication of the private ruminations of a researcher still needs any excuse, it lies in the possibility for others to gain insight into what Stocking has perceptively called the grounding of the canon of fieldwork in the personal ambiguity and ambivalence of a single researcher. Through this publication, says Stocking, we understand something of how "hard-won" was the stance of tolerance and sympathy, if not of identification, with research subjects "at a particular moment in the history of Western European culture by men who carried with them many residual manifestations of the belief in Western European superiority and much of the repressive psychic structure of their culture" (Stocking 1968: 193).

In this way, Malinowski is indeed a "Maker of Myth", any narcissism being rather unimportant. Yet, Geertz interprets many of the revelations of the "Diary" as proof for Malinowski being a "crabbed, self-preoccupied, hypochondriacal narcissist" (maybe it takes a narcissist to discover one, if we recall the "arrival sequence" at the Balinese cock-fight). Despising the "charter of fieldwork" given in the introduction to *Argonauts of the Western Pacific*, Geertz thinks Malinowski's diary demolishes the "unsophisticated conception of rapport" which would "enfold the anthropologist and informant into a single moral, emotional, and intellectual universe" by apparently proving that Malinowski made up for his inadequate empathy through sheer industry (Geertz 1967). This biased view cannot be substantiated, indeed a careful, "thick" reading of Malinowski's various public and private writings proves quite the contrary. Malinowski was a very caring and concerned individual who showed humanity and love for his wife and children as well as concern for the progress of his students and the advance of anthropology as a discipline; his was indeed a spirit of generosity. On a personal self-reflective level, he was a most demanding assessor of his own performance. To judge his personality from his own entanglements of the heart which occurred before his marriage to her, as his diary and his letters to Elsie show, and thus to make him out to be a moral "bounder", as does Mulvaney (1985) in his otherwise exemplary historiographical discussion, is unreasonable. Certainly the sudden rift with Sir Baldwin Spencer in Melbourne was due to Malinowski's attachment to Elsie for whom Spencer, as Mulvaney notes, felt avuncular concern. Yet moralising from this point is as mistaken as judging Malinowski's attitude to research subjects from his frustrated outbursts of loneliness and plain sexual deprivation in the field.

### Derision and Empathy

Stocking has made thoughtful suggestions about the use of the term "nigger" for native populations. He addressed this most painful issue for all anthropologists when he suggests that Australian slang may have influenced Malinowski's linguistic usage, as it only appears after 1915 in the diary, not in his earlier non-Australian influenced one on Mailu (1968: 189). Stocking may be on the right track here, as the angry but also self-mocking remark by Malinowski about his recollection of feeling sea-sick on board a ship in a letter to Elsie shows: "I was not seasick ... if your own body is buggared up this Goddamned, old bloody carcasse (sic) becomes a kind ... – centre of the Universe" (Letter of Sunday, 23rd of December 1917 about the events of the 15th, in Wayne 1995, II:81); this sentence is actually only comprehensible for Australians! Certainly Malinowski used the term "nigger" about his informants, and while this sounds slanderous or patronising or both, Australianisms can be both endearment and curse, as I found often in field discussions with white as well as Aborigines in the Australian outback where the term "bugger" is used in this ambiguous manner.

But the problem goes deeper: which fieldworker has not at times used all kinds of unpleasant epithets for informants, for officials (one may only think of the scorn poured by Nigel Barley on bureaucratic snags in West Africa), for the political situation, even for persons most near and dearly loved, in the face of personal frustration? A family row does not indicate a break-down of the relationship or the disappearance of a deep positive undercurrent of love. Temporary expressions of fury do not negate a lasting bond. What other way is there to express these feelings, no dialogic partner (spouse, children, friends, co-workers) being present, but to a diary? At least one avoids rupturing the very relationship one wants to maintain. It is less the "prevalence of deceit" which Bailey adduces to much anthropological work as well as to all social relations, but the rather normal negotiations of social intercourse. In Malinowski's case the outbursts may be as extreme as was the moral "superego" which he erected for himself, in the web of which he was enmeshed through his time, upbringing and professional aspirations.

I think the outbursts show the contrary to what Geertz implies: Malinowski's deep involvement with the Trobriand culture and many of its representatives. The following note of his letter of December 23rd, 1917 to Elsie clearly shows this:

"I did feel a thrill to see all these niggers again, whom I used to see day after day and who then were quite familiar to me and not altogether devoid of attractiveness or repulsiveness. Then, they all suddenly ceased to exist and became a sort of myth in my working out of the material. And here they were again. It was this breaking of the unreal, this coming to life of a self-made myth, that gave me the keenest pleasure in my return to work and to Kiriwina" (Wayne 1995, I: 81).

This sentence alone could stand as explanation of the essay's subtitle. But let me be more discursive. Only if one is really involved does one feel great emotional upheaval at being scorned by those to whom one wants to get close (instead of gazing over their shoulders, as Geertz has us do). We may have to be more generous to Malinowski, and for that matter to ourselves as researchers in similar situations, by admitting to personal failings while not letting them colour our public writing about others. It is interesting to note that Mulvaney who is so shocked about the outbursts of Malinowski against Baldwin Spencer, judiciously gives Spencer the benefit of the moral high ground for not having disowned Malinowski as anthropologist even after the personal rift over his emotional attachment to Elsie. Similarly, we should heed Leach who, in spite of his incisive critique of the epistemology of Malinowski's theoretical position, comes to the conclusion that Malinowski was "in bondage" to his predecessors and thus resented them. This tension is in my opinion clearly visible in Malinowski's ambivalent attitude to Rivers whose notions he savagely attacks in *Crime and Custom in Savage Society* but whose methodological canon he repeatedly praises in his diary as well as in his letters. He wants to be better than Rivers! Leach ends his critique with the following very telling self-reflective note: "Some of us perhaps feel the same about Bronislaw Malinowski" (Leach 1957: 137).

## *Writing and Encounter*

Why I would therefore recommend Malinowski's ethnographies as well as his diary and letters for students at all levels of their career in anthropology is precisely that he once and for all dismantled the "myth" of the saintly fieldworker. Notwithstanding his poor showing in terms of the now so fashionable "political correctness", which goes so overboard in deferring to the possible vulnerabilities of any and every category of people that it leads to deceit and hypocrisy, I prefer the candour of a Malinowski who freely admits to reading trashy novels in the field (though Austen, Swinburne, Conrad and other "highbrow" authors also appear). Both the vituperative outbursts and the reading of novels show us how participation is possible without becoming schizoid by this re-establishing of distance within the nearness of the research process: this is the pre-condition for writing ethnography. The aim of anthropological work is after all to communicate, and this is the only positive contribution of the "writing culture" fad emerging over the last 15 years from American anthropological meta-theory. Yet, this focus does not mean that the ideal-typical framework which Malinowski established in his formal writing on fieldwork is to be abandoned. Quite the opposite. I think that the rough "canon" he establishes in *Argonauts of the Western Pacific* is the best antidote to the overblown advocates of the "writing culture" mania: before writing comes the face-to-face encounter. Contrary to Geertz, we should probably rather ask, as did Anthony Cohen recently, why we are so reluctant to include the researcher's self in any epistemological equation about the research process, since we have never had any qualms in considering the other the appropriate tool with which to get to know ourselves better (Cohen 1992).

As true Malinowskians we should indeed include the self of the researcher even more into the writing of anthropology. This does not mean that the attempt at "grasping the native's point of view", or to use another phrase of Malinowski, "to realise his vision of *his* world" (both 1922: 7), is "ventriloquism", as Geertz later (1988) derisively labelled speaking with the voice of others[3]. As he blithely continued, writing ethnography "dramatised for Malinowski his hopes of self-transcendence; for many of his most faithful descendants, it dramatises their fears of self-deception" (Geertz 1988: 22-23).

I cannot find any attempt at self-transcendence in the classical canon or in Malinowski's diary or his letter. The diary does indeed contain a lot of self-reflection and candid self-criticism, even self-loathing, all part of the process and hope for self-improvement. As he put it once to Elsie, after giving up the nice veranda life with European settlers and French cooking of Mme. Raff, in order intentionally to immerse himself again in the field: "I was wavering whether to go or not, but as I want to shake off my cunctorial habits ... I decided to leave Billi's comfortable ... veranda and the amoenities (*sic*) of Raffael's nice company". He characteristically carries on to ask Elsie: "Do you understand this necessity to be in a place ...? There is something attractive in this craving, which expresses the desire to translate an extremely abstract idea, that of a geographical spot, into concrete experience. It is almost like touching a theoretical conception or abstraction" (letter from Vakuta on April 16, 1918; in Wayne 1995, I: 129).

*Identification and Identity*

Here we have the palpable desire for immersion or participation which, however, as one of Malinowski's disciples, Hortense Powdermaker, observed acutely, has nothing to do with "identification" or "going native": "Although I had enjoyed those brief moments of feeling at one with the women dancers at the initiation rites and although I was fairly involved in this ... society, I never fooled myself that I had 'gone native'. I participated rather freely, but remained an anthropologist" (Powdermaker 1966: 115). The distance does remain, and, if ethnography as written "corpus" is ever to be effected, has to

---

[3] The true ventriloquist, either without being aware of it or trying to dupe his audience through his erudition, is of course Geertz himself, as it is quite apparent that the term ventriloquism is borrowed from Alvin Gouldner's 1971 work, where the latter however is referring to a mistaken methodological dualism which seperates the personal from the professional pronouncements, which actually is the opposite of what Geertz implies.

remain or be re-established. Yet, that, alas, is the same with desire and that seduction through the Other to which Malinowski's references to eroticism and sexual urges testify: at the point of fulfilment it disappears, so that one yearns again for desire.

A more recent fieldworker, Michael Jackson, has neatly summed up the seduction of "life" in fieldwork against the distancing and super-ego requirements of having to write about others: "On one hand I found myself striving for a wealth of data which I could convert into a book ... Running counter to this will to amass knowledge was a profound desire to give up and let go, to allow my consciousness to be flooded by the African ambience" (Jackson 1989: 163). It goes without saying that the constant shift from participation to distance is a vital ingredient for that famous hermeneutic exercise – some may call it foolishness – of trying to translate and compare with "reference to the familiar" into a "comprehensible scheme", as Malinowski glossed the process of translation and comparison in his Foreword to the First Edition of *The Sexual Life of Savages* (1932: XIV).

As to the issue of how "authoritarian" or "authoritative" Malinowski as author really was, much has been made about his magisterial style and his references to the Trobriand materials as his "magnum opus", often anticipated in his diary in 1918. Maybe we can also read this in a different light: must the designation of *corpus inscriptionum Kiriwiniensum* mean that Malinowski was carried away by some kind of megalomania? I would like to argue that with that time-honoured ascription pregnant with the notion of a classical Greco-Roman as well as Germanic tradition of scholarship (be it through Grimm or Wilamowitz) he actually positioned the oral materials of a pre-literate culture on a par with the sources of the European tradition (like other *corpus inscriptionum* collated by antiquarians, encyclopedists, and in particular classicists).

*A Hidden Symbolism*

To reiterate, why do I still and again encourage the reading of Malinowski? One reason is the concise framework he gives for ideal fieldwork which, as Frazer said in his introduction to *Argonauts of the Western Pacific*, enabled the seeing of man "in the round and not in the flat" (the Copernican revolution metaphor would certainly have delighted Malinowski and be grist to the mills of busy deconstructionists today; see Frazer in Malinowski 1961: IX). How did Malinowski construct this "roundness"? He uses, and to my knowledge this has not been noticed so far, the image of a full human in the Greco-Christian idiom, one consisting of *skeleton, flesh and blood and spirit*. Field research has to establish the skeleton of the "structure" which, he admits, does not hold much interest for him being dry and abstract. "Besides the data of daily life and ordinary behaviour, which are, so to speak, its flesh and blood", and here comes the punch-line: "there is still to be recorded the spirit – the native's views and opinions and utterances" (1922: 22).

Taken together with the diary and the letters, we get the ideal *Charter*, though even there despondency and self-criticism are integral parts of what he calls in the Argonauts the "methodological candour" of a researcher in search of self, stumbling, searching, full of dissonances and passions. It is Malinowski's very unease, the fight against complacency, the plumbing of the abyss of what Stocking called appropriately the "heart of darkness" not in some abstract literary Conradian fashion, but of his own heart which I find moving and instructive. It is also a great consolation for the real vagaries of fieldwork, and it can perhaps only come to the fore in the interstices between private and public writing. This makes the Malinowskian ensemble of private and public so outstanding, and so different from the high tone of commiserating with the "entropy of the world" in Lévi-Straussian intellectual hauteur, or the very moving autobiography fashioned by Margaret Mead with its almost pre-ordained field process, every new fieldwork leading to a new anthropological co-mate, new theoretical vistas, and finally world-fame.

### The "Catch" of Surrender to the "Other": Possession/Passion

Errors, mistakes, preconceptions and prejudices: all these shortcomings in Malinowski have been amply deciphered by cohorts of epigones: what else is missing? Is there anything we can still learn? I would opt for including more of the personal interface in the field into the ethnographic report. While this may seem contradictory, I would suggest that Malinowski told us too much about himself and not enough about the individual fates of his informants, neither in his ethnographies nor in his private writings. Self-possession may have been his greatest enemy leading to his failure to see the importance of the passions of others, or at least not to consider them worthy enough to record. Did Malinowski ever "surrender" to the field in line with the felicitous phrase of Kurt Wolff for the research process which ideally swings from surrender to the "catch" of a theory, a concept? (see Wolff 1976; compare Koepping 1994b). We do get some idea of his interface: "I was madly happy to be alone again with N.G. boys" (*Diary*, p. 92), or: ... I felt joie de vivre tropicale, and something like being drunk on strong wine" (*Diary*, p. 80), and, after what he calls lecherous thoughts: "To submerge myself in the deeper, metaphysical stream of life, where you are not swept by undercurrents or tossed about by the waves. There these things don't exist; there I am myself, I possess myself, and I am free". This is a very telling comment on his hope to be free from, but also the fear of being possessed by, *uncontrollable*, surrender. The illumination of the field and the darkness of his heart are in constant strife. His escape? The Diary, to which he also surrenders. Here the "catch" (in German Wolff used the term *Begriff*) is not only the insight into the self, but the empowering strength to carry on: "Laziness: I'd like to break the monotony, to 'take a day off'. This is one of my worst tendencies! But I shall do the opposite: finish some routine tasks, 'the ethnographic diary', rewrite my census notes and yesterday's impressions" (*Diary*, p. 160).

This sounds very much like the advice of Voltaire's Candide: let us tend our garden! Maybe, we, the readers, should also tend our gardens and at times surrender to Malinowski's works. Maybe that is where the "universality", but not the uniformity, of a "science of mankind" could be found, in our recognition of ourselves in the passion of the self-reflections of this Other, this Malinowski who read trashy novels despite his admonitions (Diary, p. 161). If we read Malinowski's writings as a closely connected ensemble of diary and ethnography, we may realise that he revolutionised the method in our discipline insofar as he tried to live a research existence which the reflexive sociology of Gouldner would later advocate, abandoning the traditional methodological dualism which separates knowledge as information from knowledge as self-awareness (Gouldner 1971: 497). It is up to us epigones to make the myth as real as possible.

# Phenomenological Reductions

*The following paper is exploratory in nature, since it attempts to relate two seemingly unconnected fields in the humanities – anthropology and phenomenology – by supplying the practical method of the former with an epistemological foundation taken from the latter. The approach is by necessity eclectic and at times possibly inconsistent. It should be understood as a hermeneutic attempt, as interpretation in process. The main tenor of the paper is for Husserl the radical searcher, it is against Husserl the creator of certitude. The aim: to stimulate doubt, not to preserve complacency; to praise scepticism, a sign of perfectibility, not to elevate consistency, a sign of mental evasion.*

## Method and Selection of Problems

In this essay I shall *firstly* point to some aspects in the phenomenology of Husserl which have a direct bearing on the main method used in the field of socio-cultural anthropology which is considered an indispensable tool of the trade: participant observation. It is my contention that the requirement of fieldwork for modern anthropologists implicitly contains a mental as well as an existential attitude which is proposed by Husserl in his postulate of phenomenological reduction. The curious fact remains that anthropologists have in practice used the method of participant observation since the beginning of this century but have given little thought to its epistemological foundations or its implication for their theories on culture.

I shall *secondly* outline in analytical fashion the steps which are involved in this main anthropological method and discuss to what extent the method could be seen as a paradigmatic application of parts of Husserl's phenomenology.

*Thirdly*, I shall point to the limitations of the applicability of a purely phenomenological approach and to the possible extensions and variations which have to be taken into consideration in order for this focal method to be viable.

*Fourthly*, I shall discuss whether any of the variations of the so-called phenomenological stream in philosophy as for instance hermeneutics can provide an epistemological framework; this will only be possible after establishing the cognitive procedures and existential positions which I consider as vital for a kind of *ideal type* of participatory fieldwork. These ideally posited procedures are contingent upon the *a priori* postulates of the anthropological enterprise, its implicit aims and orientations, and also upon the actual processes of fieldwork. These processual forms of fieldwork are analytically abstracted from a great number of individual and specific cases of description and reporting by many researchers with diverse theoretical orientations.

### *In Defence of an Eclectic and Critical Approach to Husserl*

It is difficult, if not impossible, to assess the life-work and Husserl's systematic philosophy in these short remarks. Yet in order to understand in what way his seminal approach is of importance to the anthropologist, we have to be eclectic and take those morsels from the whole oeuvre which seem relevant for our own goals.

Though Husserl was rather disdainful of people who had not the patience to understand his whole system, he would have been the first to endorse and eclectic approach for he said, in an added note to his *Cartesian Meditations*:

> "If someone were to object that on the contrary, science, philosophy, takes its rise in the co-operative labour of the scientific community of philosophers and, at each level, acquires its perfection only therein, Descartes' answer might well be: I, the solitary individual philosopher, owe much to others; but what they accept as true ... is for me at first only something they claim. If I am to accept it, I must justify it by a perfect insight on my own part. Therein exists my autonomy – mine and that of every genuine scientist" (1960: 2).

In other words, the autonomy of any scientific endeavour requires from us not so much a faithful aping of the systems of those who went before us, but a "radical" new start in thinking for ourselves. However, I do not subscribe to his statement that progress in knowledge is ultimately not based on the "scientific community's co-operation", as there is a great deal of evidence that often progress is indeed achieved through a "revolutionising paradigm" of not "thinking as usual"; this has been corroborated by Kuhn (1962). Husserl by contrast starts his own radical (and "autonomous") doubting by not slavishly following Descartes, but states rather:

> "And so we make a new beginning, each for himself and in himself, with the decision of philosophers who begin radically: that at first we shall put out of action all the convictions we have been accepting up to now, including all our sciences. Let the idea guiding our meditations be at first the Cartesian idea of a science that shall be established as radically genuine, ultimately an all-embracing science" (1960: 7).

Do we need any further defence for eclecticism? Husserl gives an unequivocal nod to this form of philosophising when he closes his article *Philosophy as Rigorous Science* with the following remarks:

> "To one truly without prejudice it is immaterial whether a certainty comes to us from Kant or Thomas Aquinas ... What is needed is not the insistence that one see with his own eyes; rather it is that he not explain away under the pressure or prejudice what has been seen" (1965a: 147).

During this essay the question to what extent the "blinkers" can really be put away, how much of our prejudices, or pre-knowledge etc. can be "bracketed" remains open. It cannot be doubted that Husserl would have been the first to applaud the attempt to see in what way and how far we can follow the phenomenological program in a particular field. As Quentin Lauer explained, Husserl was so exclusively involved with his program that he found little time to apply his phenomenological perspective to specific problems as did many of his students (1965a: 169).

So, let us get Husserl "off the ground" by determining the degree to which a phenomenological approach could ideally be put into practice in the social sciences. If we need any further apology for an eclectic interpretation, I would remind the reader of the following remarks by Nietzsche in regard to his own and his predecessor's, Schopenhauer's, philosophy:

> "Every great philosophy ... as a whole says always only: this is the picture of all life and from it learn the meaning of your life. And conversely: read only your life and understand from it ... universal life. And so, too, Schopenhauer's philosophy shall always be interpreted first: individually, by the single one alone for himself, to gain insight into his own misery and want ..." (Kaufmann 1950: 137).

### Husserl's Phenomenological Program

How did Husserl then see his "radical" new start of philosophy? He begins with the discussion of the everyday world given to our consciousness as "natural knowledge". It is from this realm of the "natural standpoint" that Husserl wants to depart radically. He begins with the statement:

> "Natural knowledge begins with experience and remains within experi-

ence. Thus in that theoretical position which we call the "natural" standpoint, the total field of possible research is indicated by a single word: that is, the World" (1969: 1).[1]

The change he envisages is formulated as follows:

> "Instead now of remaining at this standpoint, we propose to alter it radically" (ibid.).

The alternation is brought about by the famous proposition to suspend or bracket our belief in the natural world, or as Husserl says:

> "... the attempt to doubt any object of awareness in respect of it being actually there necessarily conditions a certain suspension of the thesis ... It is not a transformation of the thesis into its antithesis ... we do not abandon the thesis we have adopted ... yet the thesis undergoes a modification – whilst remaining in itself what it is, we set it as it were 'out of action', we 'disconnect it', 'bracket it'" (ibid.).

Husserl aims at the grasping of "essences" through these several steps of bracketing; grasping not only essences of the given objects, but the absolute essence of pure consciousness. These essences are for him "eidetic" absolutes which are cleansed of any contingency of particulars. In his procedure of bracketing Husserl applies the term "epoché" which he distinguishes from its classical usage as follows:

> "If I do this [bracketing] ... I do not then deny this 'world', as though I were a sophist, I do not doubt that it is there as though I were a sceptic; but I use the phenomenological epoché, which completely bars me from using any judgement that concerns spatio-temporal existence (*Dasein*." (ibid.).

Let us understand clearly Husserl's starting point and final goal. He began with his seminal idea of the *intersubjective constitution* of the natural "environing world", stating that in spite of individual differences of experiencing the objective world which includes the subjective consciousness of the indi-

---

[1]  Husserl, Edmund 1913: *Ideen zu einer reinen Phaenomenologie und phaenomenologischen Philosophie*, translated by Boyce, Gibson as *Ideas*, London 1969, par. 1. All citations from *Ideas* are given without the emphasis indicated in that edition.

vidual "we come to understandings with our neighbours, and set up in common an objective spatio-temporal fact-world as the world about us that is there for us all, and to which we ourselves none the less belong" (ibid.).[2]

Yet if we bracket all this, including ourselves and our consciousness of the object-world which Husserl circumscribes with the term *transcendental epoché*, what does remain?

Husserl hopes we gain the certitude of pure consciousness or of *transcendental consciousness* which will then become the cornerstone of an absolutely objectively valid knowledge. As Husserl says:

> "For what can remain over when the whole world is bracketed, including ourselves and all our thinking (*cogitare*) ...? Consciousness itself, ... remains over as a 'phenomenological residuum', as a region of Being which is in principle unique, and can become in fact the field of a new science – the science of phenomenology" (ibid.).

*Limitations of Husserl's Transcendental Phenomenology*

As practical scholars whose realm is the exploration of this "life-world" as it appears in its multitudinous expressions of different groups and individuals, a complete bracketing of that world is impossible; partial bracketing is possible but needs radically expanding. Yet other objections pertain less to the method of bracketing than to his optimistic and naive expectations that absolute validity of objective knowledge could be gained through the application of the power of pure reason which relies on the transcendentally intuited pure consciousness.

The greatest difficulty arises from Husserl's insistence that it is possible to conclude that the object world of which I am conscious could be an illusion; but also that the fact that I have a consciousness leads to the conclusion that it is the evident source of world-constitution. This logical difficulty has been pointed out by many authors who otherwise share the phenomenological perspective. Sokolowski has argued – and Michael Levin agrees with him there – that

> "Husserl does not set before himself the task of showing the relativity of reality; this is not a thesis he tries to justify. He assumes, as something plainly given, that reality receives its sense from subjectivity, and that it is therefore relative to consciousness and constituted by it. If we

---

2 The term "environing world" is used by Quentin Lauer for the German *Umwelt*, following the practice of Dewey; see Lauer 1965: 151.

were to analyse his argument logically, we would have to say that the
relative, constituted nature of reality is an axiom, and not the conclusion of an argument" (1964: 133).[3]

Husserl made a valiant attempt not to be labelled a metaphysical idealist, since
he understood phenomenology to be metaphysically neutral: it declares neither
for nor against extra-mental reality; it is concerned with what things are, not
with whether they are (Lauer 1965: 19f.). He kept open the possibility of the
non-existence of the objective world. Yet, notwithstanding his innovative
method of bracketing, the question of what effect the bracketing of the consciousness of the individual perceptor of particulars leads to in reality has
been left unsolved; the pure transcendental consciousness posited by Husserl
has in fact become a metaphysical, almost mystical, concept.

The dilemmas as well as the advances of Husserl's quest have most recently
been cogently summarised by Leszek Kolakowski:

> "Husserl's monadology is for me another example of the logical hope-
> lessness of all philosophical endeavours which start from subjectivity
> and try to restore the path toward the common world. It is so more sig-
> nificant that Husserl starts with transcendental, not psychological, sub-
> jectivity. His way of arguing for the reduction is first methodical: let us
> suspend belief in the reality of the world, including ego, since we find
> no certitude in it; let us concentrate on the contents of purified con-
> sciousness. However, once we stand on the ground of transcendental
> consciousness, we notice that it always has to do with a world that is
> made conscious" (1975: 79).

Kolakowski goes on to indicate that Husserl's variation of idealism leads to an
"irrefutable because tautological argument" since there is no thing which is
not an object of thought (ibid.). What then is the importance of Husserl's
attempt? Kolakowski aptly says:

> "He better than anybody, compelled us to realise the painful dilemma
> of knowledge; either consistent empiricism, with its relativistic, scepti-
> cal results ... or transcendental dogmatism which cannot really justify
> itself and remains in the end an arbitrary decision ... (human culture's)
> very richness is supported by this very incompatibility of its ingredi-
> ents. And it is the conflict of values, rather than their harmony, that
> keeps our culture alive" (1975: 85).

If we were then to admit that Husserl's final goal of establishing an indubita-

---

[3]  See also Levin 1970: 91.

ble cornerstone for an epistemology of any science has ended with nothing more, and nothing less, than the saying of Parmenides – which is not undisputed in its interpretation – that "existence and knowledge are one" (*to gar hen estin noein to kai einai*)[4], I think that one point of this failed attempt is worth considering in the struggle between empiricism and transcendentalism which Kolakowski perceives as follows:

> "The empiricist will argue that transcendental arguments imply the existence of the realm of ideal meanings, and that we have no empirical grounds to believe in it. The transcendentalist will argue that this very argument, just advanced by the empiricist, implies the monopoly of experience as the highest tribunal of thought, that this privileged position is precisely under question, and that it is arbitrary to establish such a monopoly. The transcendentalist compels the empiricist to renounce – for the sake of consistency – the concept of truth; the empiricist compels the transcendentalist to confess that in order to save the belief in Reason, he is in duty bound to admit a kingdom of beings he cannot justify" (1975: 29).

If we further admit, as Kolakowski implies, that after Leibniz, Husserl's philosophy has been the strongest argument against the possibility of attaining truth in the empirical sciences (1975: 28), it does not yet mean we fall into the abyss of utter relativism, the chaos of unmitigated scepticism and what Husserl would have labelled the "crisis stage" of modern man (1965b: 150). Husserl's very attempt has opened the way to a variety of new approaches in the humanities from hermeneutics to critical sociology; all rely heavily on his "radicalness", even if not all are willing to admit their indebtedness to Husserl.

### *The Attempt of Alfred Schutz*

Alfred Schutz[5] was the first writer in the field of the social sciences[6] who took Husserl's program seriously and developed parts of it into a coherent epistemological foundation. The question as to whether Schutz introduced into the discussion a different form of a metaphysical concept of transcendentalism with his own idea of the paramount position of the everyday world, will proba-

---

[4] Parmenides of Elea, ca. 400 B.C., *Fragment 2*, 344, *Proclus in Tim*. I, 345; From Capelle 1968: 158ff.; contested in its importance for instance by Gomperz, 1964: 205.

[5] English spelling.

[6] The first applied approach is actually by Adolf Reinach 1953.

bly continue for some time to come[7]. It is undeniable that Husserl himself approved of Schutz' program which applied the phenomenological tenets to the world we live in and to the specific world of the scholar[8].

Under the influence of Bergson, G.H. Mead, Znaniecki and others, Schutz developed the notion of different universes of meaning and our maintaining of those different "meaning-endowed" realities. For Schutz all kinds of realities are based on the "unquestioned" acceptance of the everyday world of man as social being which provides the individual in practice with a "stock of common knowledge". Schutz gave the concept of the "subjectively meaningful action" of Max Weber an epistemological foundation with his notion of the maintenance of the meaningfulness of social life-worlds through intersubjectivity. This is established for the individual by agreement through *convention, socialisation and the use of symbols*, to and about the existence and immediateness of the world as object. Schutz saw the *intersubjectivity* established through different forms of *intentionality* which all rely on the *reciprocity of perspectives* (Schutz 1970; Introduction to Gurwitsch 1971).

Schutz agrees that there clearly are realities which are purely subjectively and individually constituted through the specific biographical situation of personal life-experiences. Yet there exist beyond those private realities socially shared universes of meaning for different groups of people. Social action is for Schutz always intentional, directed toward an object and toward the other; the intentionality itself is socially mediated within the individual consciousness. When Schutz poses the question "How does it happen that mutual understanding and communication are possible?", he gives as answer:

"... does not interpretation of the other's meaning and of the meaning of his acts and the results of these acts presuppose a self-interpretation of the observer or partner? How can I, in my attitude as a man among other men or as a social scientist, find an approach to all this if not by recourse to a stack of pre-interpreted experiences built up by sedimentation within my own conscious life?" (1970: 56)

These remarks and concepts show clearly that *absolute relativism* cannot be taken for granted when we stick to the social life-world of man as actor, because man endows himself, his fellow-men and the objects in the world with meaning. For the social scientist's reality and for his dealings with the everyday world Schutz posits the following requirements:

[7]  The argument appears in Alexander von Baeyer's German introduction to Alfred Schuetz 1971: 20.

[8]  See the remarks by Schuetz (German spelling) (1971: 11) in reference to his visit at Husserl's with regard to the first book by Schuetz 1932.

"How can methods for interpreting the social interrelationship be war-
ranted if they are not based upon a careful description of the underlying
assumptions and their implications?"(ibid.)

In other words, there are multiple universes of meaning, and *one of them is
the reality of the social scientist*. What Schutz requires is explicitness of the
procedures and of the shared meanings in each particular universe. As I will
try to show in context of the anthropological reality, Schutz actually goes one
step beyond pure description in the phenomenological sense; he has entered
the field of hermeneutics which I consider as being merely of a different
order, not kind, for establishing validity of interpretation in terms *of communi-
cability of experiences*.[9]

### *The Anthropological Enterprise, its Methodological Assumptions*

Socio-cultural anthropology has made it the aim to study the life-styles of any
existing or defunct ethnic group in order to gather adequate data for comparative analysis of the variety and malleability of the whole species. Anthropologist are looking for similarities and dissimilarities of the self-expression of
man in contemporary and in historical perspective. The whole endeavour has
clearly some underlying *a priori* assumptions; one of these is the idea of the
"unity of mankind" in regard to the species-character of man. Other general
assumptions could be added; for instance, that humans everywhere have
developed a language, a religion, a social structure etc. A further assumption
is that of the *comparability* of *a repertoire of self-expression* or of "culture",
as it is generally called; culture in this context generally denotes the impact of
man on his environment which here includes the social component.
These general assumptions can be gleaned from the following excerpt in
Boas' writings:

"It is possible to isolate a number of apparently generally valid social
tendencies and to study as well the forms in which they express themselves ... Thus a critical examination of what is generally valid for all
humanity and what is specifically valid for different cultural types
comes to be a matter of great concern to students of society" (1968:
261).

Here we find already underlying the general assumptions shared by all mem-

---

[9] Hermeneutics is used here in the sense given by Gadamer 1965 in *Wahrheit und Methode*.

bers of the profession an array of terms and an apparatus of generalisations which are not generally shared, such as function, structure, type, not to speak of specific typologies as clan, matrilineal descent, polished stone-axe etc.

There are clearly no "pure data" or "pure descriptions" involved in this enterprise. As Willis has recently stated with candour:

> "...the anthropologist undergoing the field experience finds himself rehearsing the successive phases of his discipline's theoretical development. His first impulse on arriving in the strange community is to compare his hosts' way of life with his own: consciously or not, he evaluates it against an absolute standard, as would any robust Victorian. Then his interest necessarily turns to an inquiry into how the alien society works, ... he is now willy-nilly a straight-forward functionalist of the 1920's. In due course he may find certain pervasive patterns in the thought and behaviour of his hosts infiltrating from his subconscious and assuming architectural form in his Western-analytic mind: he has become a structuralist, a man of the sixties. Finally, if he is unusually percipient and fortunate, he may succeed in transcending the past altogether and adding something to man's self-awareness" (1975: 23).

This passage elucidates one more general assumption held by many anthropologists. What we find is nothing but a reflection of our own self, or as Boas once said: "Absolute systems of phenomena as complex as those of culture are impossible. They will always be reflections of our own culture" (1968: 311).This should not astonish us for, as I will show, the instrumental apparatus for comparative studies is taken from our own reality and meaning-structure of the specific science which in turn relies on the everyday "stock of knowledge" of Western cultures. Using ourselves as the main "tool" in fieldwork, no other result can be expected on purely epistemological grounds.

### Participant Observation

Yet a further complication arises in the anthropological endeavour. I mentioned above the assumption which rests on the basic assumption of non-comparability; each culture is a unique "configuration of traits". Both assumptions are often mixed within one person's writings. This appearance of a "unity in contradiction" is connected with the double bind of the anthropologist: to satisfy his professional colleagues by using the generally accepted "vocabulary" on the one hand, and to do justice to the self-expressions of the particular group studied. It is a double bind between the cognitive level of having accepted a profession which is based on the idea of "*humanitas*" and comparability and of being existentially involved with an often radically different life-style through participant observation.

This difficulty has given rise to a considerable controversy about the anthropological aim of description. Originally most anthropologists of the last century – and some still today – insisted on the "objectivity" angle by applying concepts derived from our own vocabulary and imposed a rigid so-called "scientific" scheme on a variety of phenomena. These scholars are often labelled "etic" in approach; to this branch belong the evolutionists of the 19th century who saw Western culture as the apex of civilisation (pure and unmitigated ethnocentrism) and this civilisation as a "gift to the poor natives". It is a position which can easily be traced in the Judaeo-Christian tradition of Europe with certain exceptions among the early ethnographers of Greece and Rome.[10]

On the other side we find the so-called "emic" school which insists on the absolute prerogative of the native's model of the world which is to be depicted and described in the native's terms as accurately as possible.[11] This stand is sometimes combined with a strong form of partisanship which can lead to the idealisation of the "native" or "pure" society, in contrast to which the researcher's society is perceived as "degenerate", "deprived" etc. (the extreme of the Rousseau-syndrome or of alienation).

Yet, the ideological positions which can arise from the "emic-etic" controversy and the double bind of cognitive professionalism versus existential involvement are not exhausted with these two extremes of ethnocentrism versus alienation. One variety comes to us from Tacitus who combined his admiration for the prowess of the Germanic tribes with his lamentations about the degeneracy of Roman society, but never disputed the right of imperial Rome to rule the world; he identified in the same breath the Germanic virtues with the original Roman *virtus* of the golden age and thereby tried to teach his fellow-citizens a moral lesson (Koepping 1975).

Another variety is discussed by Lévi-Strauss who imputes – with good evidence, as every member of this profession knows – that some people become anthropologists because they were unsuited from the start for their own society or felt some disdain or resentment toward their own milieu. Lévi-Strauss continues:

> "At home, the anthropologist may be a natural subversive, a convinced opponent of traditional usage: but no sooner has he in focus a society different from his own than he becomes respectful of even the most conservative practices" (1971: 381).

---

[10] The terms emic and etic have been introduced first by the linguist Pike 1969, as derived from "phonemic" and "phonetic"; for typical etic studies see Harris 1964.

[11] Typically emic studies are those of the ethnosemanticists as for instance Conklin 1955.

The existential and cognitive difficulty to which Lévi-Strauss refers in those remarks seems to me to have arisen basically from the requirement of field-work as participant observation[12]. It is only since the end of the 19th century that this form of information-gathering has become a "rite of passage" for every aspiring anthropologist. One of the strongest proponents of this involve-ment in native society was Franz Boas (Rohner 1966). Later it was in particu-lar Malinowski in England who strongly insisted on first hand experience. This proposition is nowadays unchallenged and it may therefore be useful to quote Malinowski on this topic here:

> "We shall have to follow two lines of approach: on the one hand we must state with as much precision as possible the principles of social organisation, ... of the natives. On the other hand we shall try to remain in touch with a living people, ..." (1935: 4).

And in regard to the difference between the casual traveller and the anthro-pologist's involvement he noted:

> "There is all the difference between a sporadic plunging into the com-pany of natives, and being really in contact with them. ... As I went on my morning walk through the village, I could see intimate details of family life; ... Quarrels, jokes, family scenes, events usually trivial, sometimes dramatic, but always significant, formed the atmosphere of my daily life, as well as of theirs" (1922: 7).

One of the first to deal systematically with the controversy of the "emic-etic" distinction in regard to the adequacy of method was Alfred Schutz when he said:

> "... the answer to the question 'what does this social world mean for me the observer?' requires as a prerequisite the answering of the quite other questions 'what does this social world mean for the observed actor within this world and what did he mean by his acting within it?' In putting our questions thus and its current idealisations and formali-sations as ready-made and meaningful beyond all question, but we undertake to study the process of idealising and formalising as such, the genesis of meaning which social phenomena have for us as well as for the actors, the mechanism of the activity by which human beings understand one another and themselves" (1970: 269).

[12] What appears most problematic is the dichotomising of attitudes connected to research procedures, as in reality an inextricable mixture between the extremes seems the more normal result, *between* fascination and disgust (see Koepping 1987c; Kohl 1987).

Schutz then requires a combination of both, and with this most modern anthropologists would certainly agree.

A very similar statement has been made by Karl Mannheim when he insisted:

> "It is clear, ... that every social science diagnosis is closely connected with the evaluations and unconscious orientations of the observer and that the critical self-clarification of the social sciences is intimately bound up with the critical self-clarification of our orientation in the everyday world" (1971: 44).

That means in the context of anthropological fieldwork that the emic and the etic categories have to be taken into consideration together: no amount of pure description can replace the ordering process to which we are committed, but the ordering of pure structures without the content is also meaningless. *Content* and *context* have to go together. I shall try to show what further implications this might have in regard to the distribution of knowledge, implications which have been clearly seen by both Husserl and Schutz and which are implicitly also advanced by modern adherents of the so-called "critical sociology" or "reflexive sociology", as for instance C. Wright Mills, Alvin Gouldner and Jürgen Habermas. The founders of modern phenomenological approaches and the social scientists who derive their impetus from a Marxian understanding of societal conditions and aim at human emancipation have at least one thing in common: both are unabashed elitists.[13]

*Towards a Hermeneutic and Phenomenological Method*

The ideal type of participant observation would therefore entail the following steps or shifts in attitudes and frames of reference according to different realities which are determined by different horizons:

*First,* the fieldworker makes a choice as to the group, the area and the particular problem to be investigated. He chooses his arsenal from his scientific field of specialisation, his vocabulary, his batteries of tests, but ultimately refers back to his common knowledge. His intentionality is directed toward and framed by purely etic categories, impositions from an outside which have nothing to do with the group's self-interpretation.

*Secondly,* as he enters the field, the participant observer tries to get admission to the insider's view. During this time-consuming process several frames of references are in constant interchange: the etical direction of being intent upon entering the native's world of meaning is intermittently *suspended* when the observer participates. Sometimes he is so successful that the native's soci-

---

[13] See among others Mills 1970 and Gouldner 1973.

ety expects similar standards of behaviour and thought as it does from one of its own members and this is made clear to the participant observer when he is subjugated to the native's sanctions. Again, the participating fieldworker retreats daily during his stay to write down in his own framework of meanings embedded in the native's world: with etic categories the emic world-view is recorded. This period is the most difficult for the anthropologist in its cognitive and existential implications. The constant shifts in the intentionality, the frame of reference, of the levels of reality entailed in participant observation certainly require phenomenological skills.

*Finally*, on leaving the field, the participant observer falls back into his typical role of the scholar; he is required to report, to his peers as well as to the general public, his findings in terms which are understandable to both. This brings with it a constant rethinking of the "data" in the light of the experiences of other participant observers from different regions or in the light of new theoretical propositions. Besides this cognitive re-adjustment the fieldworker has to re-integrate himself into his own life-world. This is often not an easy task, for he has been intent upon internalisation of often radically different life-styles for a long time. This process will never be completed, for his horizon has irreversibly been shifted and transformed.

Much of what Husserl has said about a genuine social science in his phenomenological program is indeed contained in the described process of fieldwork. Let us recall some of his statements which pertain directly to the social sciences:

> "A statistics ... gathers valuable facts and discovers in them valuable regularities, but of a very mediate kind. Only an originary social science can arrive at an explicit understanding and a real clarification of them; that is, a social science that brings social phenomena to direct givenness and investigates them according to their essence" (1965a: 93).

If we do not put too much emphasis on Husserl's understanding of "essence" we can claim that anthropologists indeed follow the phenomenological procedure. However, I think we do more than only phenomenological bracketing or suspending the belief in the "taken for granted world"; the anthropologist has consistently to explain and distinguish his procedures and must lay open the steps he has taken; that is typical for what is referred to as a "hermeneutic" or interpretative task.

This mode of bracketing and interpreting is central to anthropology, and by extension to all social sciences. A constant *switching of frames of reference*, of levels of reality, occurs in the various contexts as follows:

(i) the native gives his interpretation of the world (not "raw data");
(ii) the researcher has to find the "typical" in diverse native view-points;
(iii) the researcher is placed in a typical frame of reference by his job;
(iv) the native categorises the researcher in a specific frame;
(v) the native's point of view is given back to the native via the researcher;
(vi) the native's view is transmitted to the world of meaning of the researcher's fellow-citizens.

There are logically many more possibilities and permutations for the interplay of different horizons, since the presence of the participant observer clearly changes the reality-horizon of the native society, and the next researcher will get under item (v) a view-point that is possibly mediated by the earlier researcher and by what the native has made of it. A systematic correlation of all possible cognitive shifts would virtually be impossible.

## The Attitude of Epoché

How then could this complex task ever be approached? I think we can use a term which Husserl interpreted rather differently from its classical meaning: the basic stance of any participant observer has to be one of epoché. I do not mean here only the epoché of bracketing, since the whole process is more than a mere suspension on the cognitive level. Epoché entails the *fragile balance between commitment and detachment*, between passionate involvement and hermeneutic reporting. This epoché, as understood by the Sceptics and Stoics of Greece and Rome is based on pure rationality.[14] Rationality I interpret in the sense Kant gave to it when he said:

> "Voluntarily to preserve one's self in suspension judicii, is testimony to a great intellect, and it is so very difficult, because preferences tend to meddle immediately with the judgement of reason" (Kant cited in Kaulback 1969).

Epoché is a stance taken deliberately in relation to the world and it requires the existential attitude of *ataraxia* ("composure"). *Ataraxia* I interpret not in the narrow sense of *apatheia* ("non-passion"), but in the wider sense of the stand anybody has to take in order to remain "sane" and be able to switch from utter involvement to utter detachment. Epoché is therefore a process, not a static element; it involves a union of practice and theory (Kranz 1971).

[14] On Stoa and Skepsis, among other references, I used mainly Kranz 1971; also Pohlenz 1948.

Epoché, understood thus, seems to me the only practical way of overcoming the feeling of alienation, disorientation or impotence. Only through applying epoché can the fieldworker overcome the constant danger of "liminality", as Victor Turner (1969) called it, of stepping over "thresholds" which constantly endanger existence and sanity. The danger lies in continuous status-reversals or status-shifts, because nobody is quite sure who manipulates whom: the researcher the native or *vice versa*? The danger is then the state of "unease". Epoché in contrast is the process of leading to a state of "being at ease". This is the very point where I would disagree with Alfred Schutz when he said:

> "The attitude of the social scientist is that of a mere disinterested observer of the social world" (1970: 275).

On the contrary, the social scientist is only genuine when he is interested. He has to be interested in order to become the "bridge" between the worlds of different meanings. I therefore claim Montaigne to be the immediate ancestor of the standpoint of epoché. Montaigne was – maybe because of his scepticism and impartiality – a very good "bridge"; his services as diplomat were sought after all over Europe, by Protestants and Catholics alike (Koepping 1973).[15]

### Is the Stranger a Marginal Man of True Knowledge?

What, might the reader ask, is then the result of all this rather involved enterprise? In answering, I would refute two statements, that advanced by Alfred Schutz on the role of the "stranger" and that proposed by Husserl concerning the progression from *doxa* (opinion) to *episteme* (knowledge) (1965a: 167ff.).

Schutz perceives the role of the stranger to be objective. This derives from the fact that the stranger is not forced to worship the "idols of the tribe" (1970: 85ff.). Schutz also sees, quite rightly, the limitations of the stranger's reporting when he says: "... the interpretation of the group by the outsider will never fully coincide with the self-interpretation of the in-group" (1970: 95).

So far I agree fully with him; yet I think he somewhat overemphasised the role of the stranger as "outsider". This becomes very clear when Schutz remarks that the stranger creates a world of "pseudo-anonymity, pseudo-intimacy, and pseudo-typicality" (1970: 80ff.). I think Schutz relies too much here on his requirement that the social scientist be "disinterested". As I have defined the horizon of participant observers, the stranger does not remain an

---

[15] On Montaigne see also Horkheimer 1971.

"outsider", for he is intentionally involved. This involvement is the only way of penetrating the emic side of reality, and it enables the participant observer to become more than a "stranger"; he becomes a "friend".[16]

We must not forget this transition, because it is only through it, through the double role, that the participant observer can surpass his "liminality" or "marginality" by establishing what Turner would call a "spontaneous communitas" or what Buber has labelled the "I-Thou" relationship (1969: 131ff.). The relevant literature is full of those examples.[17] I think Simmel came rather close to the point when he conceives of "strangeness" as a correlation which exists in all social interrelationships as a dialectical process between proximity and distance (1968: 63ff.).

The *second* point is related to the first. Schutz implied that the stranger in his typical role-aspect, has more of an objective point of view because he is disinterested. This goes back to the idea of Husserl that through phenomenological reduction opinion (*doxa*) can progress to certainty in knowledge (*episteme*) (1965a: 154ff.; Schutz 1970: 93). I cannot agree with either point of view. The position of Husserl and Schutz presupposes that the outside view, the one of the observer, is of greater validity, because the outsider has additional knowledge, because he brackets, he imposes the etic dimension on the primary experience. We cannot go that far: no one point of view is superior to any other, the native's is not inferior to that of the participant observer. Both are equally valid.

Each point of view has its own legitimate place in reality and its own frame of reference. This is exactly where the criticism of social scientists of the so-called "developing" countries of Africa, South America and Asia is pertinent. These people conceive of our kind of anthropology as a continuation of "imperialism" in the form of "mental colonialism"[18]: they are quite right in that attack[19]. If I were to take the proposed scheme of participant observation as a hermeneutic and phenomenological procedure seriously, there would be no unequal distribution of knowledge[20]. This uneven "power over knowledge" only creeps into the picture if I evaluate and rank the emic and etic points of view.

The only thing we can state is that perhaps the social scientist has a more rounded and relatively more informed opinion than the native, but he certainly has no unassailable certitude of "truth". It is here where I can take a value-

---

[16] The terms "stranger and friend" have been juxtaposed by Hortense Powdermaker in her autobiography.

[17] See for instance Casagrande 1960.

[18] See for instance Fanon 1967.

[19] See my argument in response to Asmarom Legesse, in "The Ethics of Planning", in: John Western and Paul Wilson (eds.), *Planning in Turbulent Environments.* Brisbane 1977a.

[20] This argument appears in the writings of Schutz (1970: 115), where he admits his indebtedness to Max Scheler; the argument is implicit in Husserl (1965a: 158ff.).

stand: there is no scientific grounding of ends, only of means.[21] It is here that the "critical" attitude can come into the play, and I do not see an unbridgeable gap between hermeneutic and phenomenological interpretation and a critical social science: as a scientist I cannot support my value-judgements, as a human being I am entitled, even compelled, to make a choice between the "struggle of world-views" (Weber 1918/19). Although he defends his stand differently, Husserl has in my opinion left room for a "critical theory" when he states categorically in his *Philosophy and the Crisis of European Man* that through the application of epoché, as he understands it, we gain "... a new kind of practical outlook, a universal critique of all life and of its goals, of all the forms and systems of culture that have already grown up in the life of mankind. This brings with it a critique of mankind itself and of those values that explicitly or implicitly guide it ... to transform (mankind) into a radically new humanity, made capable of an absolute responsibility to itself on the basis of absolute theoretical insight" (1965: 169). Unfortunately, this implies still the Platonic model of the philosopher as ruler which for the participant observer of social life in a diversity of settings remains unattainable and also undesirable, if participation has had any effect at all.

Malinowski put it more humbly and possibly more realistically:

> "To discover what are his (the native's) main passions, the motives for his conduct, his aims ... At this point we are confronted with our own problems: What is essential in ourselves?" (1967: 119)

### Phenomenological Hermeneutics – Past and Future

I therefore think that the example and the description of the process of participant observation show the viability of a phenomenologically tempered hermeneutics. I do not share Husserl's pessimism about a phenomenology which is not grounded in a transcendental consciousness. And I do not share Husserl's negative attitude to the genuine sceptical stand (1965a: 150ff.).

A phenomenology based on our life-world is possible and feasible, if the evaluations which are *a priori* built into the method of participant observation are made explicit. Any such method which involves consciousness, attention, intentionality, carries with it clearly a built-in "bias". Yet, the forms of the "bias" can be hermeneutically explicated; explicated not "from the things themselves", but from the interplay between the world and that consciousness

---

[21] The saying is derived from the works of Lévi-Bruhl who is supposed to have used it first explicitly; see also the works of Max Weber and Roger Bastide on applied social sciences.

which directs its attention to it. That is why we need epoché as an attitude which encompasses both aspects in the same process; conscious and intentional (as well as unintentional) involvement and rational detachment.[22]

As Dilthey once remarked about the nature-philosophy of a Schelling, a Goethe and a Novalis: "We only know what knows itself; therefore the logical conclusion that nature is incomprehensible *per se*" (ibid.: 79). This notion of an incipient phenomenological attitude which involves suspension of judgement as well as passionate involvement in existence has a direct forerunner in Giambattista Vico who advocated as the highest vocation of man the study of history because that is *what man himself made* (Vico 1966). Whatever the link between Vico and the Enlightenment, Ernst Cassirer has shown that there is no gap between the Romantics and the Enlightenment thinkers in these matters; the binding link is the figure of Herder. As Cassirer describes in Herder's historical method:

> "... (it) required a sympathetic understanding of the inner lives of others. This sympathetic insight necessitated not the effacement of self but its enormous expansion and intensification. Herder would never renounce his ego, and he never could deny it" (1969: 224).

I have tried to show that the romantic writers as one source of German historicism – which was so strongly attacked by Husserl – are at the same time those very persons who can be seen as forerunners of a genuine phenomenological approach. As far as the suspension of judgement and the belief in the "taken for granted" world is concerned, we have been carefully following Husserl. It should be clear in what way the social sciences can make use of Husserl's seminal attempt. However, if we do not follow the transcendental reduction which Husserl required, where will a phenomenological approach lead us?

I would like to close with a quote from Heidegger for an answer:

> "The essence of phenomenology does not lie in its being real as a philosophical direction. Higher than reality is possibility. The understanding of phenomenology can only be seen in the grasping of this stream as a possibility".[23]

---

[22] See Koepping 1975.

[23] See *Sein und Zeit* (1927: 38); my rendering.

# TRANSFORMING REALITIES

*Figure 6*: Mrs. Sayo Kitamura – called Ogamisama, during the dance of Non-Ego (1968)

# The Shamaness and the Nation

## Orientations

Shamanism in Japan has possibly never existed as a separate religious practice or system. In historical times it has largely been restricted to local practices and, in its adapted form, both Shinto and Buddhism have taken over a number of features into their rituals, albeit with a formalisation, routinisation or "domestication" of many of its originally ecstatic features of trance and possession states. However, with the rise of some New Religious Movements *(shinko shukyo)* we do not just find a revival of the personal possession experience, in particular in female founders. The innovative "survival" of an assumedly archaic or historical feature of folk-religious practices as individual affliction and its healing have become the legitimising foundations for a messianic and millenarian movement with world wide mission activities aiming at global salvation. While some written testimonies are available from such foundresses as Nakayama Miki of *Tenrikyo* (1838) and Deguchi Nao of *Omotokyo* (1898), it is only with the recent works and activities of the late Kitamura Sayo (1900-1967) of *Tensho Kotai Jingu Kyo* ("Religion of the Ise-Shrine and the Sun-Goddess", founded 1945, registered 1947) that we find detailed proof and testimony of a genuine shamanistic initiation experience.[1]

The group which Mrs. Kitamura founded is also referred to as *Odoru Shukyo* or "Dancing Religion" due to the ritual feature of the "Dance of Non-Ego", *muga no odori*[2]. It has a membership in and outside Japan of perhaps half a million believers with headquarters near the small town of Tabuse in Yamaguchi prefecture.[3] At present Mrs. Kitamura's granddaughter, referred to by believers as *Himegamisama* ("young divine princess", born 1951) is the designated leader of the group, though without having yet received the personal calling by the deity. In the following I shall trace the biographical trajectory of Mrs. Kitamura who is referred to as *Ogamisama* ("Great Goddess") from interviews, the hagiography of her life (published 1954 in English) and

---

[1] On the details of the millenarian, messianic and nativistic elements of the teachings see Koepping 1974, 1977, 1981 and 1990. Japanese names are given in traditional form with family name first.

[2] This designation is not always liked by its adherents as in Japanese it has a slightly derogatory connotation; often the dance of the non-ego is therefore also referred to as "muga-no-mai", the reading "mai" designating traditionally a more ritual dance than the reading of "odori" which has normally the connotation of less formal dancing (though also used in the context of mass-performances such as "bon-odori", the dancing on the occasion of the memory of the dead). I have retained the popular designation in the title as the group is known under this term widely in Japan and overseas.

[3] Here the present author observed and interviewed her and was kindly received by her family during visits from 1966-1967 as well as after her death, last in 1999.

the sermons which are reprinted regularly in the journal *Tensei* ("Voice of Heaven"). These go back to her first address in 1945 which for adherents of the group represents "The first year of the New Era" (*Kigen 1*) when divinity appeared in the flesh on earth in the person of Mrs. Kitamura in order to announce the apocalyptic judgement of the destruction of the world, to be followed by the era of paradise on earth for the elect.

As Mrs. Kitamura has not left an organised body of sacred scriptures and while the group has not yet developed a systematic theology, the sermons of the foundress, understood as "the word of the Universal God" and regularly played on tape at various meetings of the congregations, and her recalling of her life-story, are some of the most intricate narratives on the interaction between a possessing divinity and the "vessel" of the calling. Of specific importance seem the very pronounced somatic symptoms accompanying the calling and the rationalisations for these which appear in a complex internal dialogue between the deity and the foundress. These will be taken in the following as the centre-pieces of empirical evidence to show the transformation of shamanism from the personal initiatory experience to a world-salvation religion, which I. M. Lewis in a comparative context has aptly called the shift from a "peripheral" to a "central morality cult" (Lewis 1971). It is in the dialogue of the narrative between the deity and the foundress that that complex dialectic of parallels and inversions of body and world, individual somatic suffering and collective symbolic identification, emerges, which is of great relevance for the comparative study of charismatic legitimation through individual calling after affliction has been conquered.

Before discussing these issues in detail, I shall give a brief survey on the theoretical framework employed here and in previous studies on the relationship between shamanism and new religious movements.

*New Religious Movements in the Framework of Theories*

The meteoric rise – in terms of numbers of groups as well as of adherents – of so-called "New Religions" (*shinko shukyo*) in post-war Japan has deservedly attracted wide scholarly attention, for this phenomenon provides a fertile ground for testing the applicability of diverse theories of modernisation, secularisation and syncretism in a cross-cultural setting (see early Norbeck 1970; for criticism see Koepping 1977b; Shimazono 1982).

Of the many hundreds of groups which are registered with the Ministry of Education only a handful has retained a consistently high profile within Japan and beyond, either due to their long historical continuity, as for instance in the case of *Tenrikyo* (founded 1838), or because of their sudden rise in popularity, as is the case with such lay-Buddhist movements as *Soka Gakkai* or *Rissho*

*Kosei Kai,* which due to their great number of many million adherents have become major players in the field of Japanese politics. Many groups have also achieved international visibility due to their missionising efforts as is the case, in addition to the mentioned movements, with groups such as *Omoto-Kyo* (known by its efforts to create international communication through using and revitalising Esperanto), *PL-Kyodan* (with strong mission efforts in South America) or the group under discussion, *Tensho Kotai Jingu Kyo,* which has found many adherents in Hawaii and California.[4]

Most writers agree that the rise of religious movements since the 1830's with high points of effervescence in the 1880's and 1920's and particularly big numbers since 1945 raises problems for such sociological generalisations as to the covariance between modernisation and the evolution of societies toward a more secular world-view. While earlier writers argued that modern Japan was on the way toward a "secular, scientifically oriented society" (Norbeck 1970: 106), recent Japanese authors, in the wake of Daniel Bell's adage about "the return of the sacred" (Bell 1977), go as far as to doubt the applicability of the concept of secularisation to the culturally specific difference of the Japanese understanding of "religion" as pertaining to the realm of the sacred as an immanent category, as distinct from the notion of the transcendental in the West (see Araki 1986; Tamaru 1987)[5].

While the discussion on the comparability of secularisation theories has led to a very lively and productive debate in Japan about theoretical preconceptions[6], there is a tendency in the literature on New Religions to concentrate primarily on the doctrinal teachings, attempting to assign these to specific historically identifiable religious traditions and institutions. This labelling of certain groups as "Shinto" or "Buddhist" derivations is inadequate, and it replicates the policy of the Meiji administration which used these classifications for the purpose of controlling religious dissent as well as to bolster the state-cult (for a critique of these see also Koepping 1967 and 1994; Shimazono 1982 and 1993).

Moreover, such typologies are inadequate because they run the risk of simplifying the doctrines by concentrating selectively on a few key-concepts and,

---

[4]  On the overseas expansion of new religions see Shimazono 1993; for the presence of these groups in the UK see Clarke and Somers 1994. In my discussion I am not touching on the new wave of new religions which with the case of the notorious "Aum" group has reached world-wide notoriety. On the latter issue see Shimazono 1995.

[5]  Japanese authors who make this distinction often forget the immanence of divinity within the Christian canon. Nevertheless the notion of a this-worldly orientation of much of Japanese religiosity and of values guiding social life cannot be denied, even if the now largely Buddhist ancestor-cult is taken into consideration: ancestors are only considered as benefactors for the present generation, and while one is obligated to them, the concern with the transcendental world does not seem to be developed in any pronounced way in the popular consciousness.

[6]  As for instance in the special issue of the *Journal of Oriental Studies,* vol. 26/1, 1987 on the CISR Conference in Tokyo.

in doing so, run into the additional problem of being unable to define what is "new" in these religious movements, so that the notion of the "return of the sacred" degenerates easily into the adage about "new wine in old bottles" or "old wine in new bottles". Depending whether one intends to stress the traditional derivation of religious structure or doctrinal content, if some metaphorical allusion be considered necessary or helpful at all, the adage may be rather "fresh wine – blended from classical vintages – may slate unrequited new thirst".[7]

Typologies which attempt to re-align the doctrines of the new religious movements to assumedly "pristine" traditional frameworks deny the uniqueness and coherence of these doctrines and thus fail to come to grips with the very creativity of synthesised traditions. They also give little credence to the self-image of the founders who claim to experience a genuine personal transformation, which only gains the status of a "historical pattern" through its treatment from outside observers. Largely ignored too are the interpretations of participants who, in spite of the objectively eclectic re-combinations of traditional forms of belief and ritual, do insist on the "uniqueness" of each doctrine. In sum, much of the present discussion on Japanese new religions sounds like a recapitulation of the now aged arguments about what one could call the "innovativeness of syncretism" in the anthropology of Cargo Cults between Peter Worsley and Peter Lawrence. (see Worsley 1957; Lawrence 1964).[8]

---

[7] The notion of the traditional garb of new religions was strongly stressed by Kitagawa (1966) by concentrating primarily on semantic features of the teachings. There is no denying the similarity of many new religious orientations along the lines of traditional precepts, if one takes a very abstract view-point of generalised ideas such as the notion of the uniqueness of Japan and its culture. Thus the Nihonjinron debate of the last two decades which seems to hark back to the School of National Learning of the 17th and 18th century, would certainly be shared by a great number of Japanese and seems at first sight very similar to the salvation idea of most new religions. Yet, when put into the context of personal ethics, the salvation idea is far removed from the national identity problem, though it cannot be denied that the shading of one semantic field into the other may occur at a subtle level. Whether the success of the major new religions rests on the unacknowledged merging of the two ideas of Japan as both unique as well as the centre of salvation would be difficult to prove, but it appears from observations unlikely that in the case of the group under discussion the adherents were giving the national identity problem much thought. Most of the believers I encountered over the years at headquarters in Tabuse on their pilgrimages were either attracted by the powerful personality of Mrs. Kitamura or, in later times, were actually going on a pilgrimage either for reasons of devotional duty or to have a present affliction (sickness or accident in the close family) relieved.

[8] The problem of the new religions is often still couched in terms of "syncretism" (see Koepping 1994a). Most debates on cultural uniqueness of Japan as well as on religious groups which combined various features of major world-religions (even as an intentional strategy of proving "superiority" or "modernity") were conducted prior to the debate on hybridity and merged cultural experiences as "third space" recently introduced by literary scholars such as Homi Bhabha (1994). While the Japanese insistence on uniqueness and pristine cultural traditions may sound like the opposite to this debate, the actual content of the Nihonjinron debate is full of references of "superior uniqueness" due to the incorporation of the best of two worlds, the essentialised East and West.

A more promising typology than the purely "denominational" may be established through concentration on seminal features in the self-understanding of the founders as well in the doctrines and ritual practices of the groups founded. Through this procedure we may not get away from such descriptive abstractions as "messianic" or "charismatic" leadership by replacing the outside terminology (the etic level) through a more precise indigenous generalisation (the emic level). Yet the procedure nevertheless enables us to concentrate on the experiential level of founders, followers and other adherents, and thereby take cognisance of individually variable perception while still retaining the ideal-typical terminology for purposes of comparing the possible co-variation with social, economic or political variables as well as the general issue of the mobilisation of mass-support for anti-hegemonial internal and external tendencies in modern states.

As I have shown previously for Japanese phenomena, the self-understanding of the founders could be allocated on a scale of extremes from the position of the belief in the possession through a spiritual entity at one end of a continuum to those founders who rely on a purely rational self-legitimation at the other. This provides a range of charismatic forms which allows internal contemporary and historical as much as cross-cultural comparisons (Koepping 1974 and 1977b). In a similar vein, Arai divided the founders of New Religions into *kami*-inspired shamanistic figures and those who understand themselves not as *kami* but as human beings, *ningen* (see Arai 1996: 104-05). The latter may however still be considered "living deities" or *ikigami* by their followers, a term used in Japan for a variety of persons from the artisan to the emperor, for which the word "genius" in its Roman and Renaissance connotations may not be inappropriate. The explanatory power of this typological dichotomy or, as I prefer it, the range on a scale of opposites within a *continuum* of empirical phenomena, hinges rather strongly on the specificity of the generalised ideal type of what is called *shamanistic form of possession*. To avoid the pitfalls of the above mentioned debate on the "return of tradition", it is also necessary to look beyond the purely phenomenological appearance of shamanistic traits, relating the personal history of revelatory experiences of founders to the goal-orientation, the ethos, of their teachings in both the socio-political context and that of collective symbolic identifications, or the relation between the personality, the social system and modes of historical and cultural representations.

## The Plural Range of Shamanism in Japan
## as Marginal and Peripheral Cult

Various authors have previously referred to shamanistic roots for a number of features of the New Religions (see Hori 1951 and 1968; Blacker 1975), suggesting that we find in the new movements a continuation, derivation or revitalisation of those folk-religious beliefs and practices (*minkan-shinko*) which, while in themselves indubitably syncretistic, are still considered to represent the bed-rock for all forms of Japanese religiosity as well as the sub-soil of the plurality of institutionalised religions (see Miyake 1996).

Without delving into the historical phenomenology of Japanese shamanism, the assumed revitalisation of such features as spirit-possession through its (re)-emergence as legitimating sign for the charismatic calling of some founders of new religious movements is in itself of utmost significance for assessing the vitality of traditional religious practices, as shamanism for the major part of Japanese religious history was a marginal cult in several respects. It appeared either in the organised and institutionalised form of the *kuchiyose-miko* system in North Japan, where to the present day mediums talk with the voice of the dead (see Schiffer 1967), or in its widely distributed but ephemeral form of the village-mediumship (*sato-miko*) where trance-mediums of the locality would divine causes of misfortune or perform healing rituals for individual or communal affliction, a function often performed in combination with *yamabushi*, the mendicant priests of the esoteric and syncretistic Buddhist tradition of *Shugendo*. In addition, shamanism could be considered marginal or peripheral in a third way insofar as it was not only restricted to temporal exigencies and effective in local contexts but, by being incorporated into major institutional traditions, it lost its own cohesiveness, if that ever existed at all.

Thus shamanic practices were incorporated into the folk-religious repertoire, from divination to healing practices, whereby the folk-religious rituals already syncretistically combine Buddhist and Shinto elements with more archaic forms of individual or collective trance or possession states (see Miyake 1993). At the other end of the syncretic spectrum of accommodation and incorporation, shamanic forms of individual "anarchic" possession were "tamed" in elaborate ritual performance styles, such as the refined and sedate dances of female shrine attendants, the *miko*, in the case of institutionalised Shrine-Shinto (*Jinja Shinto*).

Alternatively, these individually variable and unpredictable forces of possession were methodically harnessed and made over into teachable traditions through ritual control in the form of esoteric ascetic practices, as in the case of the already mentioned Buddhist *Shugendo* movement of mountain asceticism, which in turn influenced the folk-religious practices through esoteric and magical ritual gestures during cyclically recurring communal festivals, as can be observed still today during so-called *Shimotsuki-Matsuri* and related forms of end-of-year ceremonies and dances (Köpping 1997). The communal festivals, generally known as *matsuri*, which, particularly at the time of calendrical and cyclical changes, are clearly performed for the purpose of "renewal" (*yonaoshi*) of fecundity in nature and society.[9]

To deduce from the usage of similar terminology among millennial religious groups that we find here a "re-invention" of the traditional past would be a very misleading conclusion. As I shall show, a "renewal" is intended on many levels (personal, social, mental, ethical), but the reference to traditional concepts – while undoubtedly ringing a bell in the "collective memory" and thus probably leading to an easier acceptance of new practices and goal orientations connected with this well-known semantic field – does not tell us anything about the significance of these concepts in their specific socio-historical context.

In order to elucidate some of the changed connotations of shamanic experiences and the use that is made of these for legitimising the aspirations of people living in a modern world, I shall describe how the personal afflictions of the foundress of *Tensho Kotai Jingu Kyo* became remodelled into symbols of national importance through what one could call a semantic slippage which occurs – and this is more or less a speculative inference – only when the conditions which people perceive as oppressive in an unfocussed reflexivity, and when the accompanying anguish or deprivation (real or assumed) are brought into social consciousness through being concentrated and expressed by a charismatic individual with whose suffering, as well as release, a variety of individuals with a diversity of symptoms of material or spiritual affliction can identify.

### A Biography of Afflictions

At the age of four Mrs. Kitamura falls from a tall tree and hits her forehead. Bodily injury, often to the head and with concomitant unconsciousness, an almost "typical" feature of Japanese male and female religious founders, is also reported for Mr. Otsuka of *Shinreikyo*, and a spinal injury after falling from a horse for Okada Kotama of *Sekai Mahikari Bunmei Kyodan* (see Koepping 1967 and 1977b; Davis 1980). In 1920 she is married off to Kitamura Seinoshin, after five prospective daughters in law had been rejected by the extremely exacting mother-in-law. She was forced to carry out extremely hard and long labour in the fields, starving most of the time, losing 17 pounds

---

[9] For a general survey on the variety of matsuri see Plutschow 1996; for an ethnographic account of the matsuri in one Japanese town, see Ashkenazi 1993. On the connection of the idea of world-renewal and new religions see also Young 1989.

in a single month, and later having to sever the umbilical cord when she has her first son (1921). She cares for the mother-in-law until 1940 when the old lady died at the age of 90, carrying her around on her back for the last 20 years. Her reaction: "All my relatives ... tried to persuade me not to return but I did because I had firmly resolved that, once married, I would never leave my husband no matter how difficult my new life might be." The mother-in-law becomes the moral "testing-ground" for her steely character, an example for her/the deities' later moral tenet to "polish one's soul", *migaki*, hindrances and difficulties in life being nothing but points of proof for the individual's resolve to master one's "karma", *innen*.

After a few years, the calamities and tribulations come to a head with the burning down of the family barn with all the year's wood-supply and the only milking cow.[10] A mendicant *yamabushi* priest (a member of the above mentioned esoteric Buddhist school of *Shugendo*) divines that it was done by a jealous neighbour, advising her to take cold-water ordeals at the nearby Hachiman Shrine in order to find the culprit. However, soon after embarking on her nightly rounds of penance which she was to pursue for two years, these "witch-finding" exercises turn into a search for her Self.[11] After having experienced a "hammering in the head" since 1940, Mrs. Kitamura now develops ecstatic visions accompanied by other altered states of perception, such as sound and sight hallucinations, and reaches the state of "inner peace". Finally, she hears the inner voice of an entity which is first identified by the *yamabushi* exorcist as a "snake-spirit", but who resists all attempts at being driven out.

---

[10] This latter accident was taken by Mrs. Kitamura as a major source of blame, deriving from Confucian principles of responsibility as much as from Buddhist notions of the sacredness of all living beings. From the number of terms employed in the teachings, it may appear that Buddhist thought had a major impact in Mrs. Kitamura's thinking. However, the separation of single strands of ideology do not lead to any deeper understanding either of the significance of the merging of life-experiences with several clusters of values as explanatory principles or for the significance of the movement and its attractiveness. Thus the karma concept is here strongly influenced by a personal ethical choice which allows for the severance of its influence in life here, now and forever. In similar fashion, the concept of mappo, the third age in the cyclical theological theory of history developed in Buddhism as era of decline (when relatives kill each other and morals are in decline), is re-interpreted in the light of modernisation and technological progress which is seen as a Western intrusion and a cause of modern warfare.

[11] Witch-craft is not developed as a cohesive religious system in Japan, but the ascription of misfortune to evil intentions and envy through neighbours and the concomitant consultation of mediums to find the culprits seems to point to a similar attitudinal structure as was reported by ethnographic works in a number of African societies; for a collection of essays on witch-finding cults which show traces of millenarian expectations and seem connected to anxieties and real deprivations due to modernisation see Douglas, ed., 1970.

## *The Spiritual and Bodily Initiation*

At this point the entity begins to divulge its plans for Mrs. Kitamura to announce the renewal of the world and the establishment of the divine kingdom on earth through the teachings of its vessel. The apparently male spirit utters the warning: "If you disobey me, I shall have to leave you. I will kick your stomach in to give you an internal haemorrhage." She is advised by the spirit entity to chant *Na-Myo-Ho-Renge-Kyo*, interpreted by Mrs. Kitamura as meaning *"Hail to the humble woman who unites God and Man through the Sutra"* (by changing the *kanji* symbols of *Namu-Myo-Ho* of the Lotus-Sutra (the *Renge-Kyo*) to *na-myo* meaning "small, humble woman").[12] She is also asked by the spirit to address people about the dire state of the Japanese nation and to sing hymns in which the demise and destruction of the world are prophesied, calling the ruling classes "maggot beggars".

Trying to fight the spirit, the entity makes her bleed and vomit, she gets severe stomach disorders and suffers from constant diarrhoea. In explanation the entity in her head says that he has to cleanse her body in order to make it ready to receive the female second deity which is an inseparable part of himself. He reveals his own being as *Kotai Jingu* and his expected spouse *Amaterasu Omikami*, a combination signifying the *Shrine of Ise* and the *Sun-Goddess* worshipped there.

Mrs. Kitamura's spiritual and bodily preparations are finally finished when the spirit entity who originally called itself "controller of the mouth" moves with his spouse into her belly as their permanent abode. While these internal mental and physical changes go on, Mrs. Kitamura also displays a heightened and qualitative change in her sensory abilities, perceiving her husband's smell as "of rotting flesh", telling him that she cannot stand his odour having experienced and partaken in the perfume of the "musk of angels", advising him to move out of her bedroom and to "polish his soul". This episode is of great importance for legitimising the prophetess' later divinatory abilities to foretell the future of the world and for her assessment of the conditions of this world being wretched and run-down, as only with the sure knowledge of true paradise as won by her own sensory experience can the present be judged to be deficient.

However, the most important switch occurs with her later pronouncements

---

[12] Many founders of new religions employ the feature of word-games or puns as a tool for arriving at the "truth" or for legitimating their specific claims to knowledge and thus cater to the famous past-time of Japanese of playing with the shades of meaning emerging from different readings of Chinese ideograms and the resulting confusion through the great number of homophones. This is a rarely noticed feature of the "ludic" aspect of Japanese religion (see Koepping 1967). The category of "play and game", in short the ludic, asobi, is specifically applied to the spheres of the erotic, to studying at University and to ritual activities (see Koepping 1997c; see also a recent collection of articles on ritual in Japan, van Bremen and Martinez, eds.,1995).

that this otherworldly paradise will be established in this world (the millenarian expectation) for which the presence of the deity in the body, the embodiment of the transcendental, is proof. Yet, there remain some ambiguities in the
status of Mrs. Kitamura's body: on the one hand, the Shrine of Ise was the
home of the Sun Goddess, on the other, the deity of the Shrine (*Jingu*) itself
(an image not unusual for the *kami* concept) moved to a new "shrine", the
body of the foundress, so that we find a shrine (incarnated divine power)
within a shrine (the female body). There can be no doubt that Mrs. Kitamura
re-fashioned the Shinto-concepts by making the Shrine of Ise and the Sun-
Goddess a male-female androgyny, while the gender allocation to the Universal Spirit which the voice in her mind designates itself over time is initially
clearly perceived in the beginning often clearly as a male deity. The latter
image would indeed be logically most congruent with the idea of classical shamanistic calling in which a divinity of opposite gender enters into a kind of
hierogamy (sacred marriage) with the possessed shaman/shamaness. Mrs.
Kitamura's experience can therefore only partially be assimilated to a classical
shamanistic model which is admittedly a scholarly construction from a diversity of heterogeneous materials (see Eliade 1951; Hori 1968; Blacker 1975).

After this event, Mrs. Kitamura begins her preaching career with fierce
attacks against the government, speaking with the voice of the deities (one
deity) who talk to her in the following manner:

> "Osayo[13] the Emperor is good for nothing and he is not a living god
> (*ikigami*). If he were a living god, why should he not be able to detect
> the many traitors who surround him?",

or on February 4, 1945:

> "I burned down Ise Shrine, which had been my house, because I
> detested it. And now I have moved into Osayo's body ... I will punish
> the Ise priests who earned meals and money by selling my name and
> deluding my people"[14]

And again the divine duality says:

> "Osayo, isn't it funny that the silly Ise priests are quite ignorant of my
> absence from the Shrine? But go and see it at present. You will never
> feel the inspiration now that I have left there."

[13] In this typical form of the 'internal dialogue' she is only addressed by her personal familiar through
the deity.

[14] The internal dialogue shifts during sermons to an address to the audience, often imperceptibly and
quite unpredictably.

But there are also hopeful images of the future utopia:

> "Japan will become the leader of the world. The leadership I refer to does not mean occupying other territories. I mean that Japan will become a country looked up to spiritually by other nations."

The most remarkable ambiguity about the notion of the independence of the *persona* of the foundress is apparent from these dialogues which shift constantly between addressing her as independent agent to the direct address by the deity through her to the audience: for the listener it was not always clear who was speaking. While the believers usually seemed to presume it was the divine voice, the foundress often insisted that she was only a passive agent, like a radio-set. Instead of speaking of "trickery" in this context, as did many traditional ethnographies of Northeast Asia when referring to auditory manipulations such as ventriloquism, I would prefer the model proposed by Leiris after experiencing possession cults which he situated "half way between life and theatre", adding the analytically important distinction between played and lived theatre (Leiris 1934).

### Shamanistic Experience and
### the Embodiment of the Symbols of National Identity

Without further elaboration of the moral teachings of Mrs. Kitamura who introduced the notions of the overcoming of individual *karma* through the achievement of the state of *magokoro* or "sincerity", of a "clean heart" through the mental exercise of "polishing the soul" *(migaki)* and the ritual action of the "dance of non-ego" *(muga no odori)*, it seems clear that the spiritual initiation of Mrs. Kitamura, which proceeds to the deities taking possession of her *persona*, is accompanied by those very specific bodily changes which make the comparison to shamanistic initiations compelling. The most telling examples are the "dreams of dismemberment", as reported for Northeast Asia (see Czaplicka 1914=1969; Eliade 1951), in the case of Mrs. Kitamura manifesting themselves in the "cleansing", or "re-arrangement" of the body, accompanied as much by states of bodily dissociation on the subjective level as by objectively observable symptoms such as the spitting of blood. Of further comparative importance is the fight of her *persona* to stand up against the spiritual entity which leads to a worsening of the bodily symptoms. Giving up her "personal identity" to the spirit leads not only to a changed personality but also to a body at peace though, as the sermons show, she never is without her own subjectivity. While a dialogue does ensue with the deity during sei-

zures and often in direct speech, she also addressed her believers about their
individual problems, clearly indicating that she herself was speaking, the difference often only recognisable through the voice level.

There also exists – and this is a very distinctive feature of Mrs. Kitamura's
initiation which deviates from the "classical" shamanistic calling – a very pronounced correspondence or parallelism between her bodily changes and the
social and religious teachings of the deities. The mental and spiritual initiation
goes hand in hand with a symbolic and symptomatic "gestation" period, after
which the "birth" is on the one hand the revelation of the true nature of the
double deity (a male-female unit which actually constitutes a trinity with the
host-body), and on the other the onset of the teachings of the deity through
Mrs. Kitamura as the "mouth-piece" or "radio-set" of divinity, indicating the
mentioned ambivalence between human and divine *persona*.

*Comparative Issues*

Mrs. Kitamura has become a living kami in somatic reality, a feature which
connects her with other historical female founders of new religious move-
ments such as Nakayama Miki of *Tenrikyo* (1837), or Deguchi Nao of *Omoto-
Kyo* (1898) whose tribulations and reactions are very similar to those of Mrs.
Kitamura, further examples being the possession experiences of Kotani Kimi
of *Reiyukai* (see Hardacre 1984), Naganuma Myoko of *Rissho Kosei Kai*.
Male founders also report possession states, as is the case with Munetada
Kurozumi of *Kurozumi Kyo* (1814; see Hardacre 1986), Kawate Bunjiro of
*Konko-Kyo* (1857-58) and more recently of Okada Kotama of *Sekai Mahikari
Bunmei Kyodan* (1967; see Koepping 1967, 1974, and 1994a).

The difference between Mrs. Kitamura and other female founders is the
feature that all other women are accompanied by or chose as male co-founders
as interpreters of the divine teachings and as spiritual mates (see Arai 1996),
and in contrast to the male possessions she undergoes the decidedly somatic
experiences of "gestation" and "birth", though the sexual opposition or com-
plementarity of the divine spirit to the bodily vessel assumed for many shamanistic phenomena does not occur here as explicitly as reported for Northeast Asian shamanism. Yet, a number of ancillary features point to a greater
than apparent similarity: the original possession spirit is identified as a male
entity, and Mrs. Kitamura is referred to and refers to herself as an exceptional
personality with decidedly "male" behavioural traits of demeanour and attire
so that the suggestion of a "cross-gender-relationship" between spirit and
human vessel may be present here as well.

In contrast to established shamanism as main morality cult in classic ethnographic areas, Mrs. Kitamura's initiation and maturation shows also some

extraordinary features when compared with the functions or goals of other more peripheral cults. Foremost among these is the inversion or dialectic occurring between the giving up of her own personality and the taking over of the divine mentality: when her body is out of kilter, her spiritual maturation becomes complete (which would be typical for the classical code of shamanism). However, when her body is re-fashioned, she is out of kilter with her social environment, so that the outside considers her odd. She in turn perceives the political and social conditions of her time as a decline of human spirituality which is overpowered by materialism and scientific striving for control.

She/her spirits not only attack the main symbols and activities of the nationalist government of the war-time, but go to the core of the national identity of Japan, the shrine of Ise and its priests. Since the inception and re-invention of State-Shintoism as national "cult" (the label "religion" being explicitly rejected by the Meiji administration), the Ise priests have been the guarantors of Japan's ethnic identity, merging of the body of the Emperor with the "body politic" of the Japanese nation in direct blood-descent from the Sun-goddess *Amaterasu Omikami*, giving it historical somatic continuity ("embodying the nation") and being worshipped symbolically at Ise. This is where the sacred mirror is kept, one of the three "sacred regalia" symbolising the descent of the Japanese ethnic group from the gods, and where the emperors worship their own lineage descent. Ise is thus the epitome of the "spirit of the nation" (*koto-dama*) of Japan (*yamato*), as well as of the people who worship there and at its substitutes, the other "imperial shrines" of the "National Cult" or *kokka-shinto* (see Holtom 1943; Sansom 1958-69).

Worship of the emperor is the paramount ritual act of *Shinto* as *Kan-nagara-no-Michi*, meaning *The Way of the Gods*. As the spirits in Mrs. Kitamura indicate, the Shrine as deity itself and the highest national symbol, the Sun-goddess *Amaterasu Omikami*, have abandoned the national abodes and moved into the body of a peasant woman. The body of Mrs. Kitamura has thus become the living vessel of the national identity of Japan. This is why the spirit can also announce the future utopia will spring forth from Japan, as in this nativistic conception Mrs. Kitamura and the headquarter of the religion of *Tensho Kotai Jingu Kyo* will become the centre for the anticipated "paradise on earth".

While many of these expression do sound like a repetition and revitalisation of the slogans of the war-time national and jingoistic chauvinism of *saisei itchi* ("Religion and Government are one"), or of *hakko-itchi-u* ("The Eight Corners of the World under one Roof") of the imperial cult of State-Shinto, the goal-orientation is in fact the opposite and points to a further layer of "inversion". No more conquests for Japan's imperial aggrandisement are anticipated, indeed on the contrary Japan is to be destroyed and humiliated;

Mrs. Kitamura goes so far as to identify McArthur's troops as *kamikaze* (*divine wind*). This epithet normally refers to the saving of Japan from foreign invasion by a divine storm and is politically first used during the Mongol invasions of the 13th century and as such endorsed even then by the messianic fervour of Nichiren upon whose teachings the new religious group of *Soka Gakkai* (*Value Creating Society*) rests theologically. The Atomic Bomb which Mrs Kitamura observes from a distance (Tabuse is about one hour train-ride from Hiroshima) is interpreted by her as the beginning of the apocalyptic "cleansing" of the world from "corruption", but Japan will be a spiritual centre for the world civilisation which will start when the great apocalypse has finished.

Mrs. Kitamura thus advocates and embodies a "world upside-down" in several respects. A woman becomes the spiritual leader of the nation and the world; the present conditions are rotten and the future will be paradise on earth; the national symbols are not in Ise but in her body; a value-revolution has to be initiated which includes the abolishing of hierarchical differentiations of sex and rank, colour or ethnicity. In short, as she/the deities put it: "When I say black is white, it is the truth." Her legitimation is also supported by the anecdote or legend that in 1945 before she started to preach a messenger arrived from Izumo with the prediction that a peasant-women in Yamaguchi prefecture would be the ultimate living deity.

This anecdote has relevance for the legitimation of Mrs. Kitamura in the traditional view of State Shinto, as Izumo was considered the second highest sacred centre of the Imperial rule since the time of the writing down of the Imperial line of descent in the mythical histories like the *Kojiki* of 712. Thus, surprisingly in the light of the normally assumed self-legitimation of charismatic founders through personal experiences and afflictions or merits and through behavioural traits, Mrs. Kitamura reverts to traditional symbols of national legitimacy to endorse the truth or veracity of her message.

*Significance of the Shamanic Experience:*
*World-Renewal and Bodily Rebirth*

While there can be no doubt that Mrs. Kitamura represents the paradigmatic sequences and experiences of a true shamanic possession, the dialectic of her initiation has to be seen in the interplay between her and her spiritual in-dwellers as well as between her somatic experiences and her/the spirits' message. In the same way, as the deities rebuild her body after destroying the old body and thus effected a transformation, so do the teachings advocate a turning upside-down of the existing *status quo* of the values of the world, by first destroying the old order (the leaving of the Ise-shrine and the apocalyptic war-occurrences, the defeat of Japan), in order to rebuild it. Mrs. Kitamura/the spirits rebuild her body, and so will the deities/teachings rebuild the Japanese nation and the world as a spiritual world. The conclusion for believers and followers is tantamount to a "re-living" or replicating of this rebuilding process on the individual level by "cleansing their soul" (destroying the old ego, aided by the ritual action of the *dance of non-ego, muga-no-mai*) in order to live with a clean heart. For this the traditional *karma*-concept is invoked insofar as the attachment to the "sixfold roots of desire", *rokkon shojo*, is to be severed, as it says in the daily prayer-song: *"... wagami wa rokkon-shojo nari ..."*, (*may the six roots of desire be cleansed in me ...*).

*World Salvation from the Womb:*
*the Move of the Divine from Symbol to Soma*

While a great number of traditional Japanese concepts from various religious traditions do appear, their symbolic significance takes on quite a different hue when seen in the context of the somatic and spiritual re-organisation and transformation of the *persona* of the foundress, especially when this re-organisation of the body as originally shamanistic feature par excellence is put into the context of the symbolic transformation of the social and political world in the form of inversions of the status quo. This is more than the classical "ritual rebellion", being rather, as I have argued previously, a genuine revolutionary attitude to the world (Koepping 1980b). In a similar way, the normally purely ritual activities (such as the cleansing which goes on at every shrine-visit, or the chanting of sutra-like formulas, as occurs in all Buddhist services) as much as the ritual orientations (such as the *yo-naoshi*, meaning *world-renewal*, festivities of dancing and prayer which occur in folk-rituals at the ending of an old year and the beginning of a new one) are re-interpreted as forms of inner conviction which should lead in the followers to an inner change of personality, surpassing the "magicality" of the outward ritualistic performance. The ritual process for the believers is practically inverted by being moved from the outside to the inside of the body, or rather from the body to the spirit, from performance to attitude.

As far as traditional Japanese attitudes toward the sphere of the religious are concerned, the experiences of Mrs. Kitamura are indeed revolutionary. To put it in Christian terminology, it is the inversion of the spirit into flesh, whereby the flesh is remoulded into a tool of the spirit (the *logos* becoming *sarx*), while the life of believers in the world (the realm of matter) has to be remoulded into a life "in the spirit" through active involvement and internal "return to origins", aided by the ritual action of the body in the "dance of non-ego", so that the spirit can enter the "empty shell".

On the level of a transformation from a personal shamanic experience of a peripheral kind to a main morality cult, the inversion of national symbols finds expression in the shift from the symbolic and metaphoric level to the level of the somatic presence of the deities (as "embodied symbols") in the body of the foundress who – and this may be the specific female element of this initiatory sequence – had to undergo a gestation period of somatic re-organisation before the deities could be re-born and the nation and the world could be "renewed". The abstract symbols of nationhood and the world, instead of residing in the bodily activities of priestly male rituals, are finally at rest in the womb of a peasant woman from which world-salvation will spring forth. Abstract symbols have become concrete flesh in performative transformation.

*Figure 7*: Stele for the Commemoration of
the first revelation by the late Mrs. Sayo
Kitamura at headquarters of the religious
group in Tabuse

# The Dreaming among the Ungarinyin

For their religious life as well as for everyday practice the concept of the Dreaming is until today of crucial importance among all groups of Australian Aborigines. The concept, becoming known through the 19$^{th}$ century ethnographic works, encompasses not only the time-concept of a mythical past and the activities by divinities and divine ancestors creating all forms of life and giving the earth its features. It also refers to those activities through which present-day members of social groups continue the creative work of the ancestors in constituting reality and supporting the order of things, including the laws governing social life, into the future: individual acts of dreaming and collective performances of rituals.

The Dreaming therefore has not only deep significance as an ontological concept but alos ongoing relevance as a legitimation for claims for those tracks of land by different social groups on which their ancestors travelled and performed their life-creating activities. While the creator ancestors have removed themselves into the sky or underneath the earth, they left "marks" of their creative powers in geographical locations such as rock-pools or as imprints of their shapes in rocks. It is ritual duty of the living descendants to renew or re-animate the life-giving powers through repainting the rock-imprints or to partake int the life-essence deposited in rock-pools through individual acts of dreaming through the conception dreams.

The Dreaming encompasses therefore a time-concept of the mythical creative past (often referred to as Dream-time) as well as the notion of the life-essence deposited in places, people and substituting sacred paraphernalia (such as boomerangs or bull-roarers) and connects the life-essence of individuals and groups of humans with that of other species whose prototypical forms have been deposited in the same sacred places. The multiplicity of meanings has understandebly led to considerable confusion in the literature, as concepts which we differentiate – such as time, past, present and future, as well as ritual performances, social laws and life-essences of different species – are inextricably interwoven in this extremely complex notion of the Dreaming. While the concept in its different shades of emphasis seems distributed among all groups on the Australian continent, its particularity is therefore best illustrated by reference to a specific group and region. In the following I am concentrating on the ethnographic evidence from a particular linguistic group in the Northwest of Western Australia in order to show the multiply significant-connotations connected with the Dreaming among the Ungarinyin.[1]

---

[1] On the general concept and merger of the terminology of Dreaming and Dreamtime in different ethnographies, see Ronald Berndt, The Dreaming. In: *Encyclopedia of Religions* (edited by Mirca

*The Ethnographic Region of the Ungarinyin*

To speak of the religious system, rituals, and beliefs of the "tribal" or language group that carries the label Ungarinyin (Ngarinyin) is to deal with the intellectual and spiritual culture of an Aboriginal group that, as a coherent traditional unit, has all but disappeared. It was, for instance, reported to the researchers of the Frobenius Expedition in 1938 (among them the main authors of the ethnographies of these groups, Helmut Petri for the Ungarinyin and Andreas Lommel for the Unambal) that ceremonial and ritual gatherings in 1928 could still draw several hundred adults; by the time of the expedition, however, only about one hundred people came together for an intergroup ceremony involving five major language groups of the Kimberley area in Northwest Western Australia (Petri 1954: 8).

The Ungarinyin inhabited the vast territory between the King Leopold Ranges and the lower Prince Regent River. Among the different people with whom they shared many aspects of their material and spiritual culture were the Unambal, who inhabited the northern and north-western parts of the Prince Regent River area, and the Worora, who inhabited the region between the lower Prince Regent River and the Glenelg River. Between 1940 and 1955, this culture, this worldview, all but ceased to exist, either through the impact of European culture upon the Aboriginal value system – which led to a breakdown of the social structural arrangements and to consequent abandonment of the traditional knowledge and classifications that tied social structure to the natural and social environment (the whole of which was legitimated by myth) – or through the impact of cult innovations which have for a considerable time intruded into the Kimberley Plateau from numerically stronger and possibly more resilient language groups (movements such as the Kurangara).

This second phenomenon, the supersession of the traditional beliefs of the

Eliade), New York 1987 vol. 4, and Ronald Berndt, Australian Religions. In: *Encyclopedia of Religions*, vol.1. The following account relies on the ethnographic records of my mentor Helmut Petri, as it was my privilege to accompany him on his fieldwork sessions in the Kimberley region, in particular on La Grange Mission Station. Petri's accounts are exceptionally clear while sticking to the culturally specific, though his publications are rarely cited by specialists on Aboriginal religion. For a general overview on theoretical issues revolving around the data from Aboriginal ethnography, see Koepping, K.-P., Religion in Aboriginal Australia. IN: Religion, vol. 11, 1981. The centrality of ethnographic reporting on the Aborigines for theory developments in general anthropology see also Patrick Wolfe, *Settler Colonialism and the Transformation of Anthropology*, London 1999. On the continuity of the importance of the concept of Dreaming and its changing connotations in this region under acculturative pressure, see Koepping, K.-P., Nativistic Movements in Aboriginal Australia. In: Deborah B. Rose and Tony Swain (eds.), *Aboriginal Australians and Christian Missions*, Adelaide 1988. In the same volume appeared the English version, translated by Erich Kolig, of the treatise by Helmut Petri and Gisela Petri-Odermann: "A Nativistic and Millenarian Movement in NorthWest Australia". This was written during a stay in La Grange in 1963 and first published in the *Festschrift für A.E. Jensen* (editied by E. Haberland, M. Schuster and H. Straube), München 1964. For similar phenomena in the adjacent region of Fitzroy Crossing see Erich Kolig, Mission not Accomplished. In: Deborah B. Rose and Tony Swain (eds.), op.cit.

Kimberley people by foreign ones, gives the observer an insight into processes of acculturation and assimilation, as well as syncretion of world-view, that might have been a feature of the whole region. The traditional system of Ungarinyin religion is certainly a mixture of diverse cult innovations with several older strata, the syncretion of which is not always coherent. Added to this problem is a greater one: religion here, as for other Kimberley peoples has to be seen as a whole, for each local group has its own cult centers and specific mythic personnel. Since European occupation, many clans have died out, and with them has gone the knowledge of their local cult and myths, which they alone had the right to activate and transmit (the spiritual heritage of of a local group). In these circumstances it is not always possible to understand the finer details of a system.

This region was known to the outside world through George Grey's *Journals of Two Expeditions of Discovery in Northwest and Western Australia* (London 1841), in which he published an account of the famous rock paintings of *wandjina*, discussed below. The first systematic report, however, was written by A.P. Elkin (1930) after his research in 1927-1928. The only in-depth study of Ungarinyin culture appeared when Helmut Petri (1954) published his data, gathered during the Frobenius Expedition of 1938. The following description of the Ungarinyin religion relies on these two ethnographic reports, concentrating first on the general analysis of the creation during the Dreaming, or Dreamtime, as the period of cosmogony and anthropogony has been known in anthropological literature since the work of Baldwin Spencer and F.G. Gillen at the turn of the 20th century. This term is applied to all Australian Aboriginal conceptualisation of events believed to have taken place at the beginning of time but to be of continuing relevance to contemporary belief and action. Second, I shall describe the origin of major social institutions as reflected in Ungarinyin cosmology through anthropomorphic spiritual beings, *wandjina*, which are of supralocal importance.

### *Spiritual Universe*

Like many other Aborigines, the Ungarinyin believe in agents who, during a primordial period, shaped the natural environment into its present configuration and instituted the laws governing natural and social life. This creation by spirit beings, heroes, and deities is a constant and ongoing process. It is manifest on two levels. First, the reproduction of all fauna, flora, and human beings depends on the power emanating from the Dreaming characters: life ends without them. Second, human beings can participate in the power of the Dreaming through the ritual actions and also through ordinary dreams, evoking the spirit beings and ensuring fertility of mankind and the environment.

While all persons are able to contact the Dreaming, some are in a special position to do so through their ritual status and because of their direct linkage with
specific spirit beings. Such persons are considered to be the vehicles through
which these spirits can exert their power. In Petri's terms, these are medicine
men (*banman*, Aboriginal doctors).

The Dreaming of the Ungarinyin is called by the term *Ungur* or *Lalan*, and
all items belonging to or originating in that period are labelled by the possessive suffix -*nanga*, as in *Lalan-nanga*. Some items that derive from that
Dreaming are rock paintings, stone arrangements, sacred places, water holes,
bull-roarers (used in sacred ceremonies and also in trade between different
groups), and dances and songs. Another term that connects the primordial
Dreaming with the broader concept of the eternal Dreaming and that focus on
personal power is *yayari*. This word designates a dream or a dream experience
and also a vision. It refers to a life force inherent in a person (as one aspect of
his or her soul) and is connected with that state of feeling and thinking, as well
as with the procreative force of sexual excitement. As one Aboriginal doctor
said, "*Yayari* is the *Ungur*-part in myself" (Petri 1954: 99). In particular, the
Aboriginal doctor in trance is able to contact the powers of the Dreaming,
sending his *yayari* to the creative powers, the source of which is the Rainbow
Snake (Ungud). This is done by singing to his penis, which becomes Ungud-
like, resembling a raised snake with two eyes. During erection, a thin thread
rises from the penis of the Aboriginal doctor on which his *yayari* can ascend
to the otherworld, the "world on top".

Although the Aboriginal doctor has a specific gift of sending his *yayari* on
trips over land and into the realm of the creator spirits and thus is a "living
*wandjina*", everybody has *yayari*. It is received during dreaming from the
creator spirits that reside in sacred places, rivers, water holes, and billabongs:
every father receives the spirit children during a vision or dream and transmits
the essence, the *yayari*, in a dream to his wife. In Aboriginal thoughts, much
stress is placed on the spiritual component of human life, but those psycho-
analytically oriented Western authors who presume that Aborigines are
unaware of the physiological basis of procreation should distinguish between
theological and physiological discourse; the strong emphasis on the connection between "soul substance" (*yayari*) and the sexual excitement related to
visionary experiences should have cautioned them against facile deductions.

The Ungarinyin see a close connection between the creative actions of
Dreaming spiritual powers and the dreaming action of living human beings:
the connecting link is established through the thought system that become
known under the term *totemism*. The Dreaming heroes, foremost among them
the Rainbow Snake, Ungud, and the *wandjina* of tribal importance, as well as
those of the many local areas of clans, traversed the world and not only created the landscape with all its present features but also, as shall be shown,

instituted the rules for social and ritual life. At the same time, they were anthropomorphic beings, the ancestors of the existing animal species of the tribe's territory. Many carry the names of the species they represent, such as the saltwater crocodile, the night owl, the emu, or the crane.

As they finished their creative work in primordial time (*ungur* time), they landed on rocks, left their imprints or shadows (the *wandjina* rock paintings), and disappeared into places of permanent water to become *ungud* spirits (Ungud Snakes). It is at these sacred places (*ungud* places) that both people and animals can receive, while in dream states, the progeny incessantly produced by the *ungud* spirits of the particular place. Such locality is therefore the ancestral place of both a local human group and a particular animal species, creating a bond between humans and animals and between the spiritual essence of all existing living beings and the primeval creative forces. For this reason the Ungarinyin sometimes say, "Ungud, *ungur*, and *wandjina* are all one and the same". This does not imply that they are unable to make conceptual distinctions, but rather that they are aware of the participation in a life force that surpasses species differentiation. Man is only one participant in the process (animals also find their progeny in dreaming), not master of it. The only superior form of action that human beings can (and must) fulfil is the ritual retouching of the rock paintings to ensure the continued fertility of man and nature. If this were not done regularly, the powers and forces would cease to be active.

This explains, to a degree, the disintegration of the social and religious culture of these tribal groups when because of decimation of population the ritual action can no longer be performed. It explains the Aboriginal perception of the running down of the world, and why Aborigines are often prone to slide into states of utter despondency, inactivity, and apathy when the visionary states of ecstatic or trance dreaming cease. According to Aboriginal self-perception in the region under discussion, this has occurred increasingly over the last forty years. If there are no more dreams, there are no more creative acts in nature and, concomitantly, human fertility decreases. This seems a vicious circle. The acculturative pressure of white society makes the Aborigines – by their own admission – unable to achieve dream states, which in turn leads to a lower fertility rate, which then results in the loss of more and more local and general traditions (since these are neither reinvigorated nor re-created), so that a general run-down of the Aboriginal world ensues.

Psychologically and intellectually, this is causally explained through the decline in re-creative powers of man as his own sacred agent. Rarely do we find a religious system with so close a connection between individual and communal survival, and so concerned with the survival of the natural universe itself and the act of creation in *illo tempore*. It is one of the aspects that cannot be emphasised enough, as the general fragmentation of Aboriginal culture –

indeed its very loss – cannot be explained purely from the mechanical process of cultural change. The Dreaming ethos is so strongly tied to the psychological and mental structure of individuals and communities, to every aspect of social action, that the weakening of links in the chain of tradition affects individual psychological or emotional dispositions to such degree that even biological survival might be threatened.

### *Cosmogony and the Origin of Social Rules*

Within the mythical framework of the Ungarinyin, Ungud, the Rainbow Snake, plays without doubt the major role. It is said that she emerged from the primeval ocean, took a boomerang (not indigenous to this region), and threw it across the salt water, making land emerge from wherever the boomerang hit the water. Ungud then travelled across the land, depositing the innumerable eggs from which all *wandjina* hatched. In other versions, Ungud herself (who can be of either or both gender) created salt water by urinating and fresh water by drawing it from the body of a long crab. In this version the *wandjina* are self-created, emerging from the earth. This is not necessarily incompatible with the Unglued creation, since Unglued is also seen as earth: "We walk upon her back", say the Ungarinyin. The category of primordial creative beings called *wandjina* includes some whose special significance derives from their introduction of major rules governing social relations. The most important of these culture heroes are Wallanganda, Ngunyari, and the twin brothers Banner and Kuranguli, who shall be presented in turn.

Wallanganda rivals Ungud in his power of creativity: in some versions the spirit children of all species are created by him through rain, when called upon by Ungud. He is also considered, together with his substitute Ngunyari, to be the bringer of the "blackfellow law" (i.e., marriage regulations and rules of ritual action). As such the symbols and meanings of the deeds of these two *wandjina* are dealt with specifically in the instructions that young men receive in the bush schools over a period of several months, accompanying the two main initiation ceremonies of circumcision and subincision (Kuramede).

Wallanganda represents the prototype of the great hunter, who invented some of the major hunting weapons, such as the spears with quartzite tips and spear-throwers. After his creation deeds, Wallanganda retired to the sky, concretely symbolised by the Milky Way, where he is coiled up as a giant Ungud Snake and where he continues hunting with other *wandjina* in a paradise full of water, grass, and animals.

Wallanganda and other *wandjina*, as well as Ungud, share the trait of a certain incompleteness: all are described and depicted without mouth and ears. As the Ungarinyin say, if the *wandjina* had mouths, a great flood would occur and drown the creation. The *wandjina* can sing only through their noses: that is the noise of thunder. This relation to rain as the main agent of the fertility of nature is strengthened by the Aboriginal belief that only half the body of a *wandjina* is made of blood, while the other half is made of water. As for the incompleteness or handicap of Wallanganda, he shares one trait with Ngunyari: he got into a fight with another powerful *wandjina* during which one of his legs was crushed. From the broken leg originated the famous bull-roarers, the *mai-angari*, the most sacred items in the male initiation ceremonies.

In other versions the origin of the *mai-angari* is adduced to Ngunyari, who is supposed to have made them from his elbow and his blood. Ngunyari is also the *wandjina* who introduced circumcision with a quartz knife and who is called "the boss of the young man". When Ngunyari fastened the bull-roarers on strings and whirled them about, he could hear his own voice, the voice of thunder. He decorated the sacred woods with the sign of lightening, which he himself had painted on his chest. These *mai-angari* are kept in secret store-houses, to be seen only by circumcised young men and not by women or old men. From the myths of the Ungarinyin, as well as those of their neighbours in the Kimberley, it becomes apparent that the bull-roarers are introduced from a country outside their tribal territory; the design and shape of the bull-roarers also point to outside origin. Nevertheless, the Ungarinyin have incorporated them neatly into their concepts about Dreaming creativity: all bull-roarers belong to different classes of food items, and they control the food category after which they are labelled, which means that they affect the supply of the natural food. They thus fulfil a function equivalent to the totemic increase centers of the Dreaming. They are received and given away as trading objects and thus circulate constantly, and the exchange always involves food.

Men who have reached the age of which they put on the colour of red ochre (the symbol of the blood of the *wandjina*) and are undergoing the second initiation ceremony (the subincision ritual) must take their *mai-angari* and trade them with the neighbouring Unambal, Worora, and even the Nyigina of the Kimberley Downs. Such trade seems to have been well organised in former times. The Ungarinyin speak of a former historical "great boss" (*djoin-gari*) of trade relations, Balinar, who sat at a central location in the tribal territory, collecting the *mai-angari* from diverse local groups and redirecting their exchange.

In the myths concerning Ngunyari, about whose fate we are not informed, the importance of women in social as well as ritual life seems to be touched upon. Although no female ceremonies are known to have been held among the Ungarinyin, the role of women must have been important, if the transmitted myths are taken to be significant. It is said that Ngunyari made only his own bull-roarers (or received them in a far country from Wallanganda) and that his two wives made different ones: while the "male" bull-roarers are oblong, the extant "female" bull-roarers tend to have a more convex shape (see Petri 1954: 118-122).

The probability that women were ritually important is strengthened in some myths about female *wandjina*. While the majority of *wandjina* (of male or ambisexual gender) seem benevolent and only concerned with the increase of fecundity, one specific category of female *wandjina* appear terrible. They are the Mulu-Mulu, who live at the bottom of certain wells and capture children and adults wandering alone. They take these abducted people to their abodes, pull out their hair, skin them alive, then roast and devour them. However, these figures are ambivalent, as shown by their creation of new springs, since wherever they put down their digging sticks during their journeys, springs were formed. They thus support fecundity as well as destroy life through their cannibalistic voraciousness. The meaning of these female *wandjina* in Ungarinyin religious thought is not clear. It is possible that the behaviour of these female *wandjina* can be compared with the southern Arnhem Land Kunapipi complex (see, e.g., Berndt 1951: 146-152).

Another line of comparison would offer itself were the data more explicit: the actions of the Mulu-Mulu resemble the initiatory visions and dream experiences of apprentice shamans as reported from other parts of the world. Among the Ungarinyin too, the Aboriginal doctors undergo an initiatory ordeal through Ungud that shows traces of the treatment the female *wandjina* mete out their captives (see Elkin 1945; Petri 1952-53).

Before discussing the last set of culture heroes of supralocal importance, it should be mentioned that the ceremonies connected with the bull-roarer myth and the accompanying circumcision have been largely abandoned in the area and superseded by new cult movements from other groups (such as the Kurangara cults; Petri 1950). The last of the Dreaming culture heroes, who finish the creation of natural and social life that was begun by the actions and powers of Ungud, are the twin brothers Banar and Kuranguli (and their doubles Wodoi and Djungun), who become the initiators of a dual organisation (patrilineal moieties) which permeates all aspects of life of the Ungarinyin and adjacent Kimberley groups and categorises a society into two complementary but contrasting parts, which are exogamous.

According to the myth, men and women used to cohabit indiscriminately until Kuranguli and Banar went into the bush to seek wives other than their own: Banar ("wild turkey"), as representative of the Yara ("grey kangaroo") moiety, took a wife of the Walamba ("red kangaroo") moiety, of which Kuranguli ("native companion bird") is the representative. The clever brother Kuranguli lived with his daughter in the more fertile country that represented the inland (sweet) water moiety, but he did not sleep with her. However, his slower brother, Banar, lived with his own daughter as his spouse in a harsher environment associated with the salt water of the opposite moiety. In order to persuade his brother to follow the "correct" form of marriage, and for Banar to arrange that Kuranguli's daughter should marry Banar's son, Kuranguli deflowered her and took her to Banar.

Banar and Kuranguli are therefore the originators of the incest prohibitions (while Banar is given credit for introducing the mother-in-law avoidance rule). Although it would appear from many myths that Banar and Kuranguli are often opposed (and even engaged in mortal combat), they always resolve their differences harmoniously, and indeed their rules for social life do stress mutual interdependence rather than antagonism.

Generally, the Dreaming spirits belong to different localities and are identified on the one hand with particular natural species and on the other with specific human collectivities, conforming with the rule of moiety exogamy. Whether the religious, ritual, and mythological system reflects social relations and social classifications, or whether the mental categories involved can most usefully be seen as means of legitimising the social order through myth, is open to question. What seems to be of paramount interest in the Ungarinyin system is the strong mythic and ritual basis of social relations and the tying together of individuals through descent and locality with the environment of natural species. The spirits of human beings and other species are eternally interdependent: their position in the natural order exists only as long as they can re-create or reproduce the basic Dreaming events and can follow the injunctions or exhortations expressed by these Dreaming beings.

# The Festive: Structure and Contingency

Ethnographic and historical writing on festivals has always highlighted two *paradoxes*. The *first* of these relates to the behaviour patterns of those concerned and to the course of events. It is about the clash of contradictory attitudes during a festival: the mood may swing from the sublime to the ridiculous, ceremony may lead to parody, prayer be followed by exuberance, or fasting by feasting.

A *second* paradox would seem to supplement these contrasting attitudes. It is that contradiction I would call the temporal ordering of the festival between *periodicity* and *liminality*. The festival is actually designed to be a calendar hiatus, separating normal working time from periods of rest and cultic activity. Hence it divides the ordinary from the extraordinary, the profane from the sacred. On the other hand, a festival is precisely time that is *outside* chronology, historicity and periodisation. More pointedly, a festive period is time that actually legitimises, justifies and sanctifies normal time. It does so by recalling and repeating the deeds of primal or non-time (*illud tempus* understood as "ever-lasting" or "without duration"). In mythical terms we could say it commemorates Creation.

So festive time is liminal time in that it enables historicity through periodisation and makes units of time distinguishable, while thereby remaining itself outside and before time. Festive time therefore initiates the differentiation of time, but it only does so by remaining outside chronological historicity: *in festive time non-time (uchrony) breaks into history*, a time in which behaviour conjures up a lack of difference, a *communitas* of utopian social relations without normal rules – thanks to actions involving excess, transgressing borders and breaking taboos.

Le Goff (1980) termed medieval festivals "cataclysmic", i.e. catastrophic events like a great flood breaking into life. It is therefore no accident that early ethnographers paid particular attention to those periods which fell between, before and beyond historical time. One example is James Frazer who, in his monumental work, *The Golden Bough* (1913), concentrates on the *Saturnalia* and related inter-calendar festive periods. Only if you connect the two paradoxes do you get an indication of a rationality behind those ambivalences that surface in festivals in the form of the required – contradictory – guides to action. Since festivals constitute liminal periods of time normally taboo behaviour is allowed, even *de rigueur*. In other words, *excesses* of various kinds are permitted, from acts of violence to erotic licentiousness, by analogy with liminal periods in initiation and other rituals – even if these actions are represented theatrically and not always acted out in real life. However, all excess always remains confined by the time limit set on the festival – although, paradoxically, the festival substantively corresponds to non-time – and also by the ceremonial nature of the staged representation. In this latter case the paradoxical element is that what is being acted out is non-ceremonial, that is, excess.

Like liminal rituals, excesses are curbed by a framework: it consists of ceremonialism and form, or etiquette, or again of different kinds of preparations, from ascetic, physical and spiritual exercises to sexual abstinence. In the *Thesmophoria*, the festivals to recall the mourning of Demeter Thesmophoros, the obscene joking of the women was preceded by chastity and physical castigation in the temple (Détienne 1972; Devereux 1981; Koepping 1987a). In this sense theatrical representation itself can be understood as formalised, dramatically curbed excess, since the representation of excess already means distancing (after all, it is rehearsed or *staged*, not always spontaneous). There is always a risk of the blurring of borders when excess is acted out: spectators become actors and both can be carried away in real life or metaphorically (by *catharsis*). In the thick of carnivalesque parodying and other outbursts of aggression they can quickly come to blows.

It is not always easy to keep a balance between exuberant participation in excess and distanced, staged ceremonialism. This is shown, for example, in the lamentation when someone dies in traditionalist regions of Southern European. Distance to the horror and violence of death and the intolerable pain of mourning is created by wailing women, yet the exaggerated actions themselves often turn into uncontrolled destruction. Often the observer cannot distinguish the "overdone" playing from emotional reality on the part of the participants (for a complex form of exaggeration, in which death is equated with excrement, but participants consume excrement in order to avoid madness, see Monica Wilson on the Nyakyusa (Wilson 1957: 53f.; 80, 151) and the resolution of this paradox by Mary Douglas (1966: 176ff.).

The following account will focus on the way these paradoxes interlock in an approach drawing on history, cultural comparison and the history of ideas. It will highlight the shift of weight to one or the other extreme position as reflected particularly in the rejection of excessive exuberance in European festival history since the Reformation. We should not lose sight of the two paradoxes since it is the liminality of festival time [which should be understood as a break into the history of *uchrony* (primal time as eternity and non-time)] which supplies the reason for the liminality of excessive action in the festive context.

One of the earliest references to this contradictory constellation of attitudes is to be found in the work of Karl Kerényi, who pertinently describes the festive as the combination of the "light-hearted" and the "serious". He does this in a ground-breaking essay in the first volume of the journal *Paideuma* (1938), starting from research and analysis regarding the religious corn-plant-ing festival among the Mexican Cora Indians. Drawing on this work by Preuss (1912, 1933), a now almost forgotten German anthropologist, he moves on to portray the feeling of Greek and Roman festivals, also attempting to define a general concept of festival (Kerényi 1938/40). Almost at the same time then, drawing on the work of Kerényi and similar indications in the writings of Frobenius, [who laid emphasis in playful and cultic actions on the attitude of "being moved" (Frobenius 1932, 1933)] Huizinga also adopted this approach and worked it into his paradigmatic definition of playing in "Homo Ludens" (Huizinga 1956; Jensen 1960).

For Huizinga, playing in its purest form is related to the consecrated action of the cultic, for which the festive is the indispensable precondition and side-effect. Here Huizinga includes the occurrence of bloodshed and violent, terrifying rites, yet the main feature of the festival, as of playing, is the shutting out of ordinary life, the temporal and spatial limitedness and the "combination of strict determination and genuine freedom". After all, "ordinary life has been silenced. Meals, feasting and all kinds of exuberant activity accompany the festival" (Huizinga 1956: 28f.).

Particularly this last requirement, which stresses the cultic connection between playfulness and exuberance and resting from normal working life, points to the link with the etymological concept of festival. It is derived from the Roman contrast between *dies fasti* and *dies ne-fasti*. The days when people were not allowed to work, which in this case meant trade and legal business, were considered "holy days", "*dies [ne]fasti*", described with the word "*feriae*" (the older form being *fesiae),* including days on which cultic acts were performed by order of the state (Pauly 1979: II, 518; 536). In short, *fasti* or *feriae* were the calendar names for festivals in Roman law, particularly in the official and festival calendar. It is significant still that in contrast to religious calendars (Jewish, Christian and Islamic) the Roman annual calendar did not derive from the founding of the city but, until the Justinian reform in the 6th century, was structured according to the reigns of the Consuls, i.e. the political sphere enjoyed higher status than the religious (Price 1993: 4).

Historically speaking it is interesting that these approaches from the 30s – bringing out the paradoxes of the festive in its mixture of gravity and gaiety, ceremonial formality and anarchic exuberance, cruelty and sacredness, and which thereby indicate the relatedness of all those ways of acting described as the *holy,* the *cultic,* the *festival* and *playing* – had hitherto played only a minor role in comparative cultural studies, particularly in anthropology. Both Kerényi and Huizinga regretted that anthropology, particular in the English-speaking world, had not taken up this issue of the festive and the playful (Kerényi 1938: 65; Huizinga 1956: 28). Kerény blames a certain "style" of anthropology for this, that is "primarily typical of large Protestant cultures". By that he means the one-sided concentration on biologist and mechanical-positivist explanations of the festive, e.g. by R.R. Marett, who like the classicist Jane Harrison, saw in it the principle of that "primal feeling" of religion which was necessary to sustain and foster life and survival, health and wealth (Marett 1912; Harrison 1921). Kerényi sees this as a reduction of the significance of the festive to the functional side of biological survival and critically protests: "The inadequacy of this principle only becomes clear if you want to explain a religious phenomenon – in our case a festival – exclusively in terms of a hungry ... human being" (Kerényi 1928: 66).

By contrast, Kerényi develops a phenomenology of the festive based both on classical sources and on ethnographic data on the Australian Aborigines, which shows great similarity to the definition of the "holy" given by Rudolf Otto. Back in 1917 he had brought out the paradoxical mix of fascination and disgust that constituted the attitude to the sacred (Otto 1963). Otto also pointed to the contradictory inter-penetration of rational and "irrational" forces, or of sensual elements from human drives and instincts, which infuse the rational aspects of religious feeling and bring the numinous-holy very close to the erotic (Otto 1963: 62). Kerényi similarly locates the festive between ceremonial obligation and "immediacy and freedom". "But anyone who surrenders to this compulsion (of holy tradition) will find themselves suddenly in the middle of the free play of the gods, and will through partaking of it become divine" (Kerényi 1938: 71).

Kerényi was here concerned to regain an understanding of the festive, which had largely disappeared from the European canon of ideas since Romanticism; the "holy duty" to perform cultic actions is linked here with the playful freedom of joyful participation. This also removes that division into participants and spectators typical of the modern secular festival, since *all* are participants and feel *moved by the play*. Festivals do not just become a decorative element for the working world but help to constitute it; everyday life receives its very meaning through festivals. This largely removes the contrast between the *sacred* and the *profane* but the festival is not consigned to irrelevance, something which always happens when enjoyment and religion are regarded as fundamentally opposed.

It is therefore not surprising that Kerényi resorted to a Nietzschean concept of festival, without specifically referring to his accolade of the *Dionysian*, of ecstatic participation, when he recites "that the everyday seems absolutely new and attractive, indeed new-born through the power of enchantment and experienced now for the first time" (Kerényi 1938: 72; from Nietzsche's Basle inaugural lecture *Homer and Classical Philology*). It should be stressed here that Kerényi does not equate festiveness with gaiety, nor with the sanctification derived from duty; he sees it as a "light-hearted" yet "serious" way of acting that is closest to free play.

When Kerényi questions the classical Anglo-Saxon explanations of the festive it is striking that he does not name the most prominent and best known "arm-chair anthropologist" of the time, who had compared festivals at great length, namely James George Frazer. The latter had actually described the paradoxes of the festive pretty accurately when focussing on the contradictions of the Roman *Saturnalia*, those festivities at which social order was reversed and whose main features he compared with the carnivals of southern Europe. He also thought they were closely related to the festivals of Twelfth Night in northern Europe, writing: "Feasting and revelry and all the mad pursuit of pleasure are the features that seem to have especially marked this carnival of antiquity" (1913: 207).

At the same time Frazer points out that these excesses of carnivalistic Saturnalia take place in a period followed by a time of fasting and abstinence, in the European context the Lenten period before Easter; he makes a more than metaphorical connection between the contrasts by relating precisely birth and death, fertility and drought, excess and abstinence (ibid.: 345ff.). While Frazer's scheme is still rooted in a traditional explanatory theorem of *sympathetic magic*, it is unmistakable that he already connects the contradictions of the festive with calendar irregularities arising from the discrepancy between the lunar and solar cycles for the year (ibid.: 339ff.). With the aid of the *Saturnalia* and related phenomena he cites vicarious sacrifices, "fools" playing rulers, the parodying of sacred acts by "jester bishops", the rule of the "bean king" and so on.

Generalising about this discrepancy brings us much closer to a modern concept of festival and ritual, where the contradictory character of the festival falls precisely in that time which lies outside of time. It is a period of danger in which normal rules (taboos) are suspended, in order through the invasion of anarchy and chaos to recreate and legitimise the existing order, *ex nihilo* so to speak; as in the mythical time of origin *in illo tempore*, this is a primordial time which makes temporal time possible at all through festive periodisation. The main feature of religious and secular festivals is the "remembering" *(anamnesis)* or repetition of deeds from a founder period, ultimately Creation, so that festivals of all kinds can be understood as mnemonic means of remembering, written down through theatrical-ritual acts (dance, pantomime, recitation).

Kerényi's description of the festive as a creative act and an act of remembrance still shows the way to a possible intercultural definition of this concept since *the festival as a mnemonic ritual act and reiterative act* can certainly be universalised. Although Kerényi's criticism of early anthropology therefore appears somewhat one-sided and fragmentary it is undeniably true that the theoretical level of knowledge about the significance of the paradoxes concerning the festive (and also of the sacred, ritual and playing) – above all of the significance of the excessive and the anarchic elements of gaiety and exuberance as constitutive elements within the reverent, holy framework – only came to the forefront of ethnological and literary historical studies from the 1960s.

We cannot here explore all these approaches, which are primarily located in the theory of ritual. However, the following may be useful pointers, most of them owing much to the preparatory work and stimulus of Frazer. That applies, for example, to the introduction of the concepts of "ritual rebellion" (Gluckman 1954), of "liminality" within ritual processes (Victor Turner 1969), of the "impure in the sacred" (Mary Douglas 1966), the "excessive" in sacred acts (Caillois 1950) and, finally – going back to Freud's definition in *Totem and Taboo* that "a festival is a permitted, indeed required excess, a solemn breaking of a ban" (Freud 1913) – the concept of "transgression" (Georges Bataille): "The profane world is that of prohibitions. The sacred world is open to limited transgressions. It is the world of the festival, the rulers and the gods" (Bataille 1979: 63).

The most productive concept for all fields of cultural studies, from literary theory to semiotics and classics, has probably been the rehabilitation of medieval carnival culture by Bachtin. After reading Rabelais he endeavoured to rehabilitate it as a popular culture of laughter and thereby as paradigmatic for festivity (Bakhtin 1968). He thinks the most prominent feature of carnival festivities is the literal and metaphorical use of uncontrollable bodily functions: The gap existing between anthropological and literary approaches to the culture of laughter has still not been fully explored (Radin et al 1979; Babcock 1978; Pelton 1980; Apte 1985; Hillman 1992)[1].

It is appropriate then to look more closely at the development of the *concept* of festival, which is bound up with a *social transformation* of festive events. The separation of the sacred from the profane and the relegation of the excessively exuberant to the profane sphere seems indeed to have its roots in the Reformation (Bachtin 1990: 20). A clear indication of this change from Catholic to Protestant asceticism can be found by comparing the actions of Catherine of Sienna, who consumed suppurative wounds, with the "inner" asceticism of Lutheran penance. The ideological distortion of religious festivity, from which emotional and sensual components were eradicated (the anarchism of chaotic corporeality), is here accompanied by a *de-sanctification* of the profane festivals which thereby threatened to become purely ceremonial and formal. A differentiation emerges between profane and religious festivities in which the former lose their religious legitimation.

In order to balance our historical generalisations, however, we should add that despite the enthusiastic identification of the Middle Ages with the festive par excellence, as found in Michelet (Michelet 1861), there was naturally a tendency in medieval Catholicism towards a restriction of popular festivity by

---

[1]  See chapter on the Trickster in this volume.

clerical culture with its rejection of enjoyment (Le Goff 1980, 1985).
Recently, however, there has been conceptual and real-life resistance to this,
for example with the recognition of Christian liturgy as festive play, or the
surfacing of emotional ecstasy at such festivals as modern rock concerts, not
to mention devotional events at the "shrines" of past heroes of pop culture like
Elvis Presley. Jakob Baumgartner argues for a new concept of worship as
playing: "Playing a game before God, not to make or achieve anything but just
to be, that is the innermost nature of liturgy. Hence the strange mixture of
deep seriousness and divine gaiety" (quoted by Koch 1995: 15).

This discussion is basically being conducted in theological circles. It cannot be understood, however, without the influence of recent theoretical
approaches such as those put forward by a number of different cultural disciplines after observing phenomena in foreign cultures and describing them in
ethnographic studies. The whole discussion sprang primarily from a reformu-
lation of the concepts of the sacred, ritual and play, whose affinity with the
concept of festival is indicated above.

As shown by the above literature, the paradoxes of the festive relate to the
contradictory behaviours that are caused by or are meant to accompany it. One
of these contradictions appears in the descriptions of the Old Testament and
the one-sided conclusions drawn from that by Luther. To quote Leviticus:

> "The Lord spoke to Moses and said, Further, the tenth day of this sev-
> enth month is the Day of Atonement. There shall be a sacred assembly;
> you shall mortify yourselves and present a food-offering to the Lord.
> On that same day you shall do no work" (Lev 23: 28-28).

Shortly afterwards the following demand is made of another festival, the
week-long Harvest Festival, after the reference to the people assembling and
their duty to make sacrifices and vows:

> "On the first day you shall take the fruit of citrus-trees, palm fronds,
> and leafy branches, and willows from the riverside, and you shall
> rejoice before the Lord your God for seven days" (Lev 23: 40).

In contrast to the first festival, gaiety and sociability are called for here, not
castigation. We see a fundamental contrast, with the latter case calling for
light-heartedness and exuberance and the former for solemnity and ceremony,
and also for the rites of abstinence and repentance, those oppositions to which
the closeness of carnival and pre-paschal fasting bear witness in the Christian
calendar. These contradictions are also reflected in bourgeois, secular under-

standing of a festive occasion, with its demands of etiquette and formality, on the one hand, (festive dinner, festive garb) and of light-heartedness, a good atmosphere, entertainment and exuberance, on the other.

The same contrasts can be found in most festivals with a ritual or cultic significance: from royal coronations and civic ceremonies (e.g. laying foundation stones) to the festivals celebrating the seasons and the cycle of life, from birth to marriage to funerals. Festivals seem to be characterised by a stage of mourning, of separation, abstinence or fasting followed by unrestrained celebration, over-eating, exuberance, with previous or interim stages marked by ceremonies of purification, of driving out bad luck, disease, evil and dirt (Gaster 1987). The basic ritual structure of festivals – related to the trio of segregation, liminality and re-integration, and postulated by van Gennep and Victor Turner – will not be enlarged on here (van Gennep 1909; Turner 1969).

The above-mentioned contradiction in both cultic and secular festivals only remains puzzling if festivals are defined by only *one* of the modes, either by castigation or revelry, or if – frequent since the Reformation – it is argued that everything secular, all joy, all enthusiasm, in short the pleasures of the flesh, are not appropriate to the religious festivals, which are the only true celebrations. Luther himself suggested in 1520 that all festivals (except Christian worship on Sundays) should be abolished as they only involved "abuse with drinking, playing, idleness and all kinds of sin (and) we only anger God on holy days more than on others" (Luther 1982). Besides a very one-sided interpretation of action pleasing to God there is a risk, he thinks, of people eating and drinking too much, and the danger of being kept from their work. Church anniversary festivals should be completely abolished, he continues, as they are just "fun-fairs and playgrounds", highly detrimental to God's glory and the good of our souls (Luther 1982).

German Protestant and English Puritan hostility to the pleasures of feast-days were certainly partly due to the rejection of the feudal way of life by the rising bourgeoisie. This can be seen from the dislike shown by Richard Burton in his classical work *The Anatomy of Melancholy* for the aristocratic culture of idleness. By contrast, all those aristocratic sports and pastimes were now claimed for the rising middle classes; he used them as medical and natural remedies for the disease of the soul, melancholy, be it hunting, gardening or fishing. In principle Burton, in 1651, was also opposing the Puritan rejection of all festive pleasures as defined in the 1600 law on Sabbath observance. He supported the rehabilitation of traditional Sunday pastimes undertaken by the King in 1618 in his *Book of Sports*: "Dancing, singing, masking, mumming, stage-plays, howsoever they be heavily censured by some severe Catoes, yet, if opportunely and soberly used, may justly be approved" (Burton 1993 part 2, sec. 2, mem. 4: 349).

By contrast with the aristocracy and the lower classes, the bourgeoisie had a problem with festivals from the beginning. It esteemed hard work, which was as far from aristocratic luxury as from the festive joys of the people (Aleida Assmann 1989: 237). Puritanism was well adapted to a class based on achievement and increasingly rationalist in its guides to behaviour; it was one which did not only want to subject the sphere of work to the primacy of functionality and rationality but also the sphere of leisure. It even made recreation into a new kind of work, which may end up in what Ernst Bloch called the "furnished despair" of Sunday at home for the lower middle classes (1977: 274) or what Horkheimer and Adorno called the "manipulation of pleasure" where festivals become "events" (1969: 275; Schmid 1995).

The grounds for this in Protestantism are clear from Luther's polemics: unresting activity is pleasing to God and a person should use the permitted Sabbath rest period to meditate, examine their soul and conscience, and thereby try to please God not just through work but also through fasting and prayer, and through collecting their inner forces (for more work). If festivals have to be, they should serve no other purpose than to increase human strength to better endure everyday working life, focus people on their final goals and place the reward for their toils and tribulations in a higher sphere.

This is an attitude that runs through all rational utopian world designs, from Plato to Rousseau, and which is coupled with a certain disdain for the plebeian working classes, but also with a fear of their getting out of hand if they gather in large masses. Plato thought that all theatrical performances, particularly comedy, were uneducational and harmful to the soul, as they weakened the virtues. Speaking of the function of festivals he said that the gods ordered out of pity that mankind should interact with the gods during festive times during which their edification would be ensured by the intercourse with the gods (Plato, *Nomoi*: 653c and d).

Festivals are just as instrumentalised here; they help to teach patriotism, on the one hand, but also compensate for hard work or are an incentive to continue to work hard for the common good. Rousseau takes a similar line, when he lauded Geneva as a city where people could obtain all the necessities of life because they had renounced everything superfluous, adding: "Give them festivals ... so that they learn to love the state" (Rousseau 1981: 428 and 464).

These statements undoubtedly point to the *cynicism* that was to lead to Marx's belief that religion was the opium of the people. Yet they are only understandable on the basis of a decoupling of festivals from the sacred. By dissolving the close connection between *festiveness* and *piety* that still occurs in the Old Testament, and by linking the sacred festival to the piety of etiquette, good behaviour and propriety at the formal level, and to internal contrition, abstinence and castigation at the substantive level, everything connected with exuberance, people have relegated joy and enthusiasm to the arena of "secular" pleasure. This particularly applies to drama and the performing arts. In the early modern age this delinking of leisure from religious action in the festival and thereby the differentiation of the festival itself into secular and religious forms was certainly due to a new Protestant attitude to life. It did not just understand idleness as such as an aristocratic, feudal vice, leading, according to Burton, to the spread of melancholy (the remedy being those very worldly, "distractions" of aristocratic times!). It was also afraid of all physical experience and uncontrolled behaviour.

Protestantism had at least a sceptical, if not hostile attitude to playing, as can be seen from the statements of Rousseau that the theatre was a way of *passing the time*, and that idleness and *superfluity* (of time) were wrong for a person whose life was so short and whose time so valuable. Idleness and leisure are here subordinated to the new work ethic. Festive time should likewise be used to edify the soul on its hard road to salvation. *Renunciation of drives* was the highest ideal, and turning away from the pleasures of the world was to be legitimised as part of a *plan for salvation*. It is thus not surprising that Luther could not make much of the holy humour of Erasmus of Rotterdam. While Erasmus worked on the same premise as Luther that the world as such was only a way-station on the road to eternal station, a *pilgrimage* to true bliss, he disguised this truth in the dialectically complex depiction of Lady Folly. She rejected all worldly things, above all the desire for fine clothes, extravagance and pleasures and praised those who in this life, expectant of the eternal bliss of the resurrection, behaved "as if drunk", and were then considered crazy: yet it was those who said this of people filled with the Holy Spirit who were the real fools.

From the Renaissance and the Reformation onwards the European bourgeoisie had a problem with the festive mood of popular culture, which in the view of the spiritual and worldly leaders always entailed the danger of getting out of control. This exclusion of anything orgiastic or festive, of the exuberance of the soul and feelings, marked the beginnings of the modern dichotomy between work and the sacred, accompanied by that loss of ecstasy in religious ritual that is such a problem for modern churches since the "meaninglessness" of ritual certainly goes hand in hand with the negation of emotional extravagance.

This foreshadowed modern sociology, notably Durkheim with his distinction between the sacred and the profane. It also took the meaning out of the very concept of festivity, which nowadays, liberated from the sacred, looks likely to disappear into the hedonism of a leisure culture. This development was noted by Jakob Burckhardt in the festivals, processions and self-representation of 15th century Renaissance culture. Both spiritual and worldly performances, masques and parades only demonstrated the meaningless of the symbolism (Burckhardt 1939: 236ff.). With this loss of meaning of symbols and their arbitrary associations they became free to be filled with all kinds of content and could be used just as much for totalitarian control as for the induce-ment to indulge in infinite pleasure. Through the separation of the *excessive* from the religious festive framework, or, to use the language of Nietzsche, through the rejection of the *Dionysian* in the sacred, the Reformation was cer-tainly responsible for the loss of the magical, playful and mysterious – in other words for that disenchantment of the world perceived by Max Weber, both within the religious festival and in secular pleasures. Equally responsible was the subsequent Enlightenment that sought to ban all things irrational from public life, even religion itself from life in general.

Perhaps that which Horkheimer and Adorno called the negative dialectics of the Enlightenment, the spawning of totalitarianism from reason, the grace-less rationalisation of the world, is only *Dionysos* having his revenge, and get-ting in again through the back door. Was he just having his own back when Reason, raised to the status of divinity in the French Revolution, spawned such bloody orgies of killing in the aftermath? The ecstatic merging of feeling was now to be expressed in mass movements that were no longer religious. In their fascist and communist embodiments "surplus energies" and "emotion extravagance" were directed towards destruction and self-annihilation.

It was also the fear of the destructive force of surplus energies that lie in any festivity through extravagant actions, or the fear of the uncontrollability of feelings, which caused the distaste of Reformers and Enlightenment philoso-phers for this aspect of festivity. After all, any religious funeral could degener-ate from a mood of orderly, solemn mourning, followed by a still orderly meal, with the observance of strict etiquette, into a wild punch-up. Rousseau describes being at a court event and withdrawing as soon as a young man started throwing gingerbread around causing boys and girls to scramble for them.

Jean Starobinski shows in his large-scale study on the gift that the distribu-tion of gingerbread was only a matter of the traditional gesture of *largesse*, the "gift", the strewing or *sparsio* of luxury, of surplus or abundance, which had been carried out since the Roman Empire on coronation days and the like, dur-ing processions and at festivals staged with the aim of renewing, was designed to destroy or distribute wealth. It was a continuation of the equivalent idea and custom of renewing fertility through the pouring out of goods (also of sacri-fices) familiar to us from many fertility festivals and which were depicted alle-gorically by the symbolic figures of the *cornucopia* or the goddess *Fortuna* as a variation of the goddess of love *Aphrodite*. (Those apples that Rousseau gave the children recall the first erotic fertility symbol, the gift of the apple by Paris to Aphrodite: Starobinski 1994.)

Many different historical sources enable Starobinski to show that this *sparsio* – intended to safeguard the rule of a new emperor in Rome, and in the late Middle Ages to bring fertility, happiness and wealth, including the happiness of the ruler's subjects – ended up in a battle among the recipients. Entertaining in itself, this was also an essential part of the festive ritual of coronation (one is reminded of Frazer's explanation of the myths of the regicide at the annual renewal festivities). Starobinski goes so far as to claim that the signs of degeneration, the negative turn things took when the scattering of gifts led to campaigns of plunder and war, were all tied up in this gesture.

Despite all personal perversions by rulers the reaction of the masses who enjoyed the *sparsio* points to a deeper and more fundamental structure of festivity, to that necessary interlocking of existential opposites. They present the simultaneity of death and rebirth, of destruction before re-foundation, or of *orgiastic* celebrations, of *obscenity* in the sacred, or to use Mary Douglas' phrase, of *pollution in the holy* (Douglas 1966), or of the erotic anarchy at spring festivals, of the penetration of the orderly by the disorder of chaos. The accompanying ritual and other acts only contribute to establishing the regeneration, the conquest of structure via the liminal phase of *communitas*, to quote Victor Turner (Turner 1969).

One can thus understand the imaginary reconstruction by Antonin Artaud (and the writings of de Sade) in the "Theatre of Cruelty" as a structurally apt sensing of the genuinely festive that appears through its perversion. On the occasion of a *sparsio*, Artaud has the Emperor Heliogabal, whose perversions are as historical as those of his predecessors Caligula and Nero, throw down from a tower sacks of wheat and chopped sexual genitals into the crowd: "He nourished a castrated people" (1970: 102).

It should be said that the priests in fact castrated themselves for *Cybele*, the mother godhead, which was as hard to accept for the 19th century interpreters as were certain Greek customs around the Demeter or Hermes cults: this open obscenity and explicit sexuality was relegated to the area of pornography or dismissed as *dirty rites* which could only have come from the East. It is the problem of the excess of the festive which bothered the early interpreters so much, since from Reformation times this lack of inhibition had been incompatible with the holy (Douglas 1966).

Festive extravagance and debauchery was not just a problem for Protestantism but had also bothered the Greek philosophers, who suspected it could lead to anarchy and be a threat to society. As shown by Jean-Marie André, there were attempts in all philosophy schools in Athens to write a *sociology of the festive*, Aristotle making a distinction between the idleness that leads to cultural enrichment (*paideia*) and a mere pastime, or distraction (*paidia*). As there were two types of audience, the educated upper classes and the lower working class, this latter group had to be provided with mass entertainment; André argues that Aristotle developed an elitist and authoritarian concept of leisure (André 1994: 103).

While Aristotle thought absolute idleness was utopia and anarchist idleness harmful, he saw festivals as a contrast to the world of work, necessary relaxation for the human psyche. Like Plato, however, he considered professional acting and singing philistine activities with the exception of when they were practised in ecstasy or festive performances put on for the gods (André 1994). Despite the rationalist and pragmatic development of an elitist concept of education, and the theory that festivity and playing were only "distracting", "entertaining" pleasure, Plato and Aristotle still believed in the divine inspiration of the festival. After all, Plato thought all good things had arisen through divine "madness", including rites, festivals and other arts (depending on whether they were inspired by *Apollo, Dionysos, Eros* or the Muses). So the *excess of ecstasy* was recognised in its *Dionysian* and *Apollinian* form – at least when ritually defined, albeit uncurbed and dangerous – as basic ontological conditions of life.

For Plato as for Aristotle, however, there was a limit to the obscene: the "dirty speeches", the *Aischrologies*, which, as we know from Aristophanes' comedies, occurred among women at the Thesmophoria festival, but also at the *Eleusinian mystery cults* and the processions of the virgins with baskets of flowers containing phallic loaves, at the *Anthesteria* or spring festivals, or at other *Demeter* rituals at harvest and sowing time. These were ritual acts which were no longer understood and tolerated by the official Establishment philosophers (Burkert 1985; Koepping 1987a).

Although in antiquity people thought that festivals and games were held not just for their recreation but above all for the pleasure of the gods themselves (see the early ritual sources and late philosophical epigones of Epicurian teaching; see Veyne 1994: 328f.; 482ff.), different philosophical schools from the 5th century B.C. (including the Stoa) had already distinguished between festivals and holy rites. In particular, the secular festival was regarded as an expression of idleness; in other words, leisure was largely separate from holy time. Idleness and leisure and its distractions were always regarded with scepticism, and mixed feelings, since they were seen as a road to gluttony and licentiousness in the style of oriental potentates. Largesse and generosity were therefore shifted into a close and rather suspect relationship with extravagant luxury (*tryphe*).

In connection with a theory of festivity, which in the field of religious legitimation strongly overlaps with the concept of ritual, Gluckman asks a key question. In our modern society there are few public rituals expressing such protests in this tamed form. Is it because we settle conflicts, such as those between the sexes or political rivals or age groups, in a secular context? This is also the case with Bantu peoples like the Barotse, but not with the Zulu and Swazi who express conflict in *ritual rebellion*.

Following from this Gluckman speculates that a ritualised acting out of antagonisms can only occur in societies possessing an unquestioned value structure, while this is probably not possible in fragile relations. It is precisely the strength of the army that enables officers to serve their inferiors once a year while, for example, a family in most societies is such a structurally vulnerable arrangement that parodying the tensions arising there would not seem appropriate – it would expose the family to the danger of collapse (1994: 132-135).

Independently of this criticism of the strongly functional structural approach these insights of Gluckman have opened up new avenues in the assessment of festivals and their courses. At a similar level Bachtin, independently of ethnographic surveys, has proposed a similar interpretation of the popular culture of laughter as expressed in carnivals. For him, too, festivals in which existing order is turned on its head or parodied in other ways are, although limited, an expected protest, necessary in the form of "legalised ... licentiousness", in order to legitimise order (Bakhtin 1968).

Bakhtin goes beyond functional structuralism in identifying the earthiness of the culture of laughter as a metaphor and reflection of the cosmic (1968: 334ff.). He remains within this approach, however, when he speaks of the significance of that laughter called forth by a grotesque body: "The feast-day temporarily suspended the whole official system with all its prohibitions and hierarchical barriers" (Bakhtin 1990: 33). The fact that in reality the temporarily utopian freedom he evokes did not always last is shown by the examples of carnivalesque *charivaris* in French cities of the Renaissance, studied by Natalie Davis (1965). In addition some of Bakhtin's premises have to be questioned. He rightly draws a parallel from the fairground to behaviour at the "festive table", where the serious tone was put down like a mask and another truth began to sound: "laughing, foolish, unseemly, cursing, parodying, travestying" (ibid.: 39).

Nevertheless, it should not be overlooked that the festive table remains determined by social rules despite freedom of speech and action. Richard Seaford proves in a study on Homeric festival culture that the excesses of the Penelope's suitors at the festive banquets were so overdrawn for Homeric thought that the only response to it had to be seen as Odysseus coming and killing them all off. Hence the norm of reciprocity was upheld, i.e. the subversion of mores met by counter-subversion (1995: 25ff.). It is clear that above all in the literary canon [Bakhtin's main work being on the way it was turned over to the carnival (Bakhtin 1989)] there is "production of meaning through its disruption", as demonstrated by Richard Hillman in his work on trickster figures and other subversive characters in Shakespeare's plays (1992: 13). However, the power of the subversive should not be underestimated: there is no guarantee of a resolution of conflicts with a new social or mental equilibrium. The philosophical literature on the subversive power of laughter-related festivity, irony, sarcasm and cynicism, has since antiquity emphasised the sheer destructiveness of these forms of expression. The German Romantics, and then Nietzsche and Kierkegaard, drew attention to the positive and negative consequences of Socratic irony and, above all, of the cynicism of the legendary "dog philosopher" Diogenes. Their subversiveness was a remedy for dogmatism through the combination of *spoudogeloion*, i.e. the mixture of the moralising and serious with the ridiculous and witty. Human regression to their animal nature often provoked a radical hiatus, which in antiquity led to the Christian "revolution" (Niehues-Probsting 1988; Pieper 1963; Hyers 1969; Lynch 1969; Berger 1969; Cox 1969).

Screech gives a similar interpretation to those statements of Rabelais on whose work Bakhtin builds his argument that medieval festival culture was a culture of laughter. He points out that precisely the travesty of sacred texts suggests the existence of a profoundly Christian attitude on the part of the protagonists of the epic *Gargantua and Pantagruel* and also of the humanist Rabelais, himself an admirer of Erasmus of Rotterdam (Screech 1979).

Some theoreticians have raised the acting out of excess in *transgression* to a paradigm of the festive, culminating in Bataille's phrase, "religion calls by its very nature for the transgression of prohibitions" (Bataille 1979). They too agree with the classical functional structuralists and Bakhtin's view of the culture of laughter that ritualised transgressions still follow rules in the spirit of Marcel Mauss. The implications of this view for the discussion of ritual and violence cannot be further pursued here – suffice it to say that René Girard also takes the line that a *sacrifice* still constitutes a murder (Girard 1972; Burkert 1985).

In conclusion let me quote Roger Caillois, whose work is a clear continuation of Mauss's anthropology and who, besides Leiris, was perhaps the most stimulating thinker, in anthropological terms, among the Paris *surrealists*. In his *L'homme et le Sacré* (1950) on the theory of festivals he refers to ethnographics observations about excessive violence at the death of rulers in traditional Polynesian cultures, in this case Fiji, with the adage: "Sacrilege belongs to the social order. It occurs on behalf of majesty, hierarchy and power. ... These transgressions are nevertheless sacrileges, but sacrileges of a higher order" (Caillois 1950: 151).

This shows the limits of the idea and reality of *transgression*. In conclusion one may only speculate as to whether a revitalisation of the excessive, or of transgression – as a permitted, essential condition for full festivity – might contribute to an avoidance of real violence, for example, the outbreak of war. Or could it cathartically heal the consequences of such violence? This would be a field of investigation for the philosophy of violence and a practical one in respect of the social and psycho-hygienic effects of performance and drama, with Burton's *Anatomy of Melancholy* of 1651 representing a beginning for modern times.

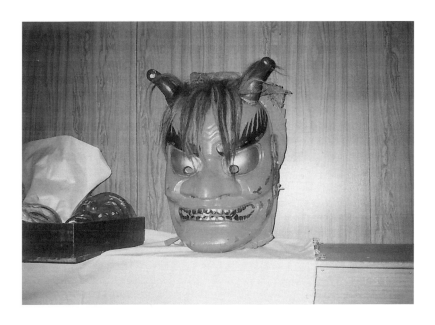

*Figure 8*: Mask of Mountain God for a *Hana-Matsuri*

*Figure 9*: The Mountain God in performative posture

# Japanese Festivals: Theatre and Ritual

*General Questions*

Researchers into ritual performances seem to encounter considerable difficulties for when it comes to proving the transformation that is said to take place in relation to perception on the side of performers as well as audience or participants. They find themselves up against a position that seizes upon the formality, repetitiveness and redundancy of ritual as an opportunity to discover its lack of significance or to assert that rituals always support existing structural arrangements. These problems do not just turn up in the theoretical discussions of academe, they are part of the cultural discourse in a diversity of societies and among different social groups during events.[1] In the following I will deal with the problem from a Japanese angle[2], supplying a description and interpretation of ritual events and relating them to the historical discourse about the practices of Japanese theatre performances. Through this inquiry about forms of transformation we will find ourselves focusing on the body as a sphere of experience.

First we need to clarify the concepts underlying my specific inquiry. In my consideration of ritual, focusing on ideas about bodilyness, I am primarily

---

[1] A good example of the sensitivity to problems was given to me by a participant at those festivals that will be the focus of what follows. Many of these festivals have been raised to "intangible cultural assets" (*mukke bunkazai*), which theoretically means that they should not be changed and must be preserved. For many Japanese these ritual dance festivals have become symbols of a past "authentic" culture and so attract large crowds of tourists every year. In the view of a member of a dance group, the festival should die out if it is no longer held for religious reasons and only because it is of historical and cultural interest. This dancer rejects the "museum" status of the allegedly authentic, an attitude that reflected his status as a "spectator" that year. He had not been allowed to participate due to a death in the family – ritual dance was taboo for him. Rituals could only be effective in one way, by keeping strictly to the "rules", which for him included the goal and traditional intention of the ritual. If this intention was missing, the ritual changed into a performance in the minds of spectators and if this was its only justification it was not worth continuing. This position may be considered extremely traditionalist, clinging as it does to what used to be. I see it differently though: this position is that which makes a ritual what it is (according to the very restrictive definition of Humphrey & Laidlaw 1994) while those who only want to keep it up as an authentic cultural heritage are the genuine "traditionalists", wanting to freeze a tradition for exogenous reasons. The informant was someone who could be called a "modernist". His position seemed to be: if a tradition is no longer maintained in its intention by the performers then it should be dropped and the change in culture accepted as given. This is an unusual attitude in modern Japan, in a society that wants to cling to everything that is "disappearing" (for a post-modern critique of these practices see Ivy 1995). For a critique of nationalist restoration efforts see Harootunian 1988.

[2] Research on dance rituals took place from 1996-99 and was supported by the German Research Council (DFG) in the context of its special Research Program "Theatricality" (coordinator: Erika Fischer-Lichte).

concerned with the connection between perception and performance. This raises an immediate paradox. While performances are required to have a reflective aspect in that the actor has to be consciously aware of them, it also turns out that articulation in ritual – precisely when the medium is the body – is largely involuntary. Ritual and the transformation it engenders is therefore both produced actively and brought about involuntarily.

The question of transformation is rarely raised in relation to the body. It is postulated that ritual calls up emotions, attitudes, guides to action and worlds of ideas, and then gives them form and at times reorganises the structural principles. But the reorganising of concepts is only consciously realised when they are discursively unpacked and negotiated (see also Richard Bauman 1986). In such analyses the body is perceived as a transformative agent but it is not given due significance when we consider aspects involving reflection alone or when the meta-level of discursive reflexivity is taken to represent the actuality of experience.

By contrast, I think that the idea of transformation can only be upheld when the context of bodily experience is accounted for. True, if transformations are to be effective they will always be traced back to a new attribution of new levels of significance, implied through discursive means in the negotiations during the staging or rehersal or in judgements after the event. But this attribution must not remain on the level of pure speculation or the kind of social game in the sense of Simmel where you act as though you see things differently (or see what you are supposed to see). If, therefore, we are talking about a genuine reshaping of the understanding of reality this will only work *via* experience, the locus of which is always the body.[3] In the following I do not want to speak of a primacy of experience over conceptualisation. Rather, I will opt for defining changes in the way we perceive the world in terms of how we experience the world through our senses. How this bodily experience is formulated will be illustrated through the medium of the Japanese discourse about it.

---

[3]  Theatre practitioners like Grotowski espouse the idea of transformation through body training of actors (Grotowski 1986) and drama therapists shift empowering and self-empowering agency into the sphere of reflective bodily performance. Sue Jennings, for example, describes the process of drama therapy as a practice allowing patients to create a balance between internal experience and external reality, through "re-experiencing" in the form of embodiment in a "personal theatre" and in a "healing theatre" of group interaction. She does this, like many practitioners, with reference to anthropological research on ritual processes (see Jennings 1995: 188). Here we find the domains of therapy, ritual and theatre closely connected via the practice of embodiment of experiences.

*Figure 10*: Consecration of drum

*Figure 11*: Consecration dance for drum sticks

Following in the theoretical footsteps of Foucault and Bourdieu[4] all discussions of performative action have given much attention to the idea of embodiment – both in theatre practice and in the analysis of rituals. The body is treated as an inter-communicative, inter-active factor tied up in a network of social relations (Giddens 1984: 36). Embodiment, however, is mostly understood either only as a form of representation of social ideals (Douglas 1970). Again, the body may be seen as a place for exercising social practices such as disciplining or the acting out of power relations (Bourdieu 1977: 14; Bloch 1982; Asad 1992).

Yet such arguments remain caught up in the Durkheimian mode of the compulsive replication of structures where the performer is only regarded as the bearer of inscriptions. The repetition of gestures can never correspond completely uniformly to the model of the symbols that have been handed down but the performer is not completely free to interpret them either. If we are not interested in abstract structures, however, and only in how ritual practice creates "power over the sign" (Comaroff and Comaroff 1985: 196) – in the contest between social context and existing symbolic structures – then it is important to get away from the image of the body as a passive "consumer", otherwise the implied empowerment of the performer's agency – his competence – remains neglected.

The line I would like to take is one of emphasising the body as a generator of emotions and attitudes (for a review of the literature see Csordas, 1994). The body seems to me a pre-linguistic, and extra-linguistic medium of articulation that experiences, or suffers things, and to which things happen. It is a medium of sensory experience to which it can abandon itself, to which it involuntarily opens up and to which, in brief, it can react extra-conceptually, acting out these experiences non-reflectively in the momentum of movement (or non-movement).

Such a concept of the body does not mean playing with the idea of the unstructured body. It must always be borne in mind that *embodiment* implies a culturally marked concept of the "natural" bodilyness since the body is always socially determined, even in its own sequence of movements. In this sense I follow Terence Turner's distinction that the body is an individual, sensory entity and also a material substrate for interpersonal action, or a medium for inter-somatic interaction (Terence Turner 1994).

In order to be able to trace precisely this effect of *structured involuntariness*[5] of the body in ritual we should clarify the concept of gesture. It is

---

[4] Bourdieu presupposed that it was necessary to concentrate on the "socially informed body" in order to grasp the principles underlying all practices as those contextualised human actions that show *habitus* as an arsenal of dispositions and attitudes expressing "structural practices" (Bourdieu 1977: 72ff.).

[5] See Lock for a review of similar approaches in recent anthropology of performance (Lock 1993: 173; with specific reference to studies by Devisch 1985).

unhelpful to describe the "gesture" as a "frozen attitude" which, according to Langer, is supposed not to call forth feelings but to point up their "articulation". It seems questionable whether ritual performances would be "effective" if they only demonstrated an "ideal" emotive attitude as expected from the stock of cultural standards. It seems to me, rather, that the performance of a dramatic liturgical act can lead to the unforeseen experiences that arise through the involuntariness of the receptive and perceptive body undergoing transformations. It is precisely the repetitiveness and redundancy typical of ritual gestures that can be used here as a means of snapping us out of other ways of perceiving the body and the world (Marglin 1990).

The predispositions appealed to by bodily performance are doubly determined: *first* by available thought structures, *secondly* by contextual, personal aspects. What happens with these predispositions after going through the black box of ritual performance is then just as doubly determined: the result is dependent, *first*, on the performance itself and, *second*, on the attitude of expectation given by the disposition. We face here a *double contingency*: *firstly*, the openness and indefiniteness of the expectation that need not necessarily correspond to the standardised attitude of the "cultural capital". *Secondly*, we confront an openness of experience and the judgement of it by the recipients (spectators) whether the performer produces the culturally standardised resonance remains an open question. After all, the multidimensional character of the predispositions with which spectators approach such an event brings different expectations into play. Both, the normative statement and the predisposition, can be changed. One can even go so far as to say that the expectation – of the unexpected, shown in bodily involuntariness – can itself become part of the cultural repertoire (see Handelman 1979).

This openness of outcome is directly connected with the cultural concept of embodiment referred to above. Whether there has been a *transformation of identity* can only be understood by referring back to the idea of embodiment in the respective performing culture. This is not just connected with the universally human constitution of the body, i.e. that we *have* a body and that we also *are* a body (Plessner 1974: 41ff.). It also depends on the culture-specific ideas about the body as to whether a transformation of perception through performance is allowed, possible or to be expected. Only in relationship to certain cultural values can we ascertain to what extent the body – *via* a performance following rules and duly staged, i.e. reflexively thought about – is a means of achieving the transformation desired.[6]

---

[6]  This is the sense in which I use the work "embodiment", inspired by the theoretical statements of Bakhtin about the historical construction of the carnivalesque body (Bakhtin 1968). Bakhtin showed how the late Middle Ages used the "natural" body as a subversive instrument to express joy in life, because it lent metaphorical expression to the idea of freedom from social pressure, through the "grotesqueness" of its extensions and openings. The physiologically given involuntariness thereby serves as the expression of the cultural idealisation of an everyday state of emergency.

The following description of Japanese ritual practices and theatrical dis-cuorses is hence of special significance for our consideration of the body. *Firstly*, it gives an insight into the lively discussion in Japan about embodiment and performance and their merging in the religious and theatrical field, whose beginnings reach back to the 15th century. *Secondly*, they particularly refer to the discussion that began after the Second World War in the face of modernisation and which raises provocative questions about the meaning and role of rituals in a rapidly changing society (see Jansen 1965; Maruyama 1965; Koepping 1974; Koepping 1999; Davis 1992).

### *The Ethnographic Framework of Village Dance Rituals*

The phenomenon of embodiment – involving the risk of the openness of the body to expected but unpredictable possession or rather loosing of conscious control – can be observed in Japan during rituals still held in dozens of villages in the alpine border region of the three provinces of Aichi, Nagano and Shizuoka between early December and late February. They are staged under the heading of *Hana Matsuri* and *Shimotsuki Matsuri* (*harvest festival* and *frost month festivals*), sometimes also called *Fuyu-Matsuri* or *Yuki-Matsuri* (*winter* or *snow festivals*).[7] These are dance rituals lasting up to two days and nights, organised by the village population with meticulous care in richly decorated halls (formerly in private homes). By contrast with the Shinto rituals conducted by priests the protagonist at these festivals is the population itself. People perform up to thirty dance sequences that can last between 30 and 90 minutes. These dance sequences are largely laid down in advance – particularly in the "ritual" (liturgical) parts – but do not only vary from village to village but also from year to year.[8] The "non-ritual" (non-liturgical) parts, nonetheless limited in space and time by the ritual framework, are relatively open to negotiation. I have chosen to describe a few typical sequences in order to illustrate performative embodiment as observed over several years and in different villages. These ritual festivals are chosen to elucidate the question of the desirability as well as expected potentiality for the transformation of experience as well as the world in the light of a belief in cosmological order.

It is not just given room to let itself out "naturally" – this involuntariness and uncontrollability deliberately used this grotesque bodilyness ritually in liminal phases in order to act out an ideal of life that transcended the indicative world, not representing it in images but making people aware of its boundaries through the fact of crossing them.

7   Similar experiences of possession naturally occur at other festivals in Japan, e.g. the *Hadaka-Matsuri* (naked festival).

8   The rituals (*gishiki*) are highlighted by two formal criteria: *first*, the lay priests perform their actions on a raised "stage", the altar area and temporary seat of the divinity; and *second*, the dancers perform on a mat laid out on the dance-floor below.

The dances relate to fragments of local and national collections of myths without the exact context being completely understood by performers. The centre of the dance festivals is a mud-brick stove set up every year in the middle of the room, below which the leader of a group of lay priests[9] lights a fire by the ancient ritual method of rubbing two stones together to keep the water in the kettle placed above it on the boil till the end of the festival. At the end it has to be splashed violently over the spectators to preserve them from illness in the coming year, as part of securing general well-being of nature and people. Although the ritual sequences in the *Shimotsuki-Matsuri* are much longer and more extensive than at the *Hana-Matsuri* (with a frequent stirring of the water to invoke a host of divinities), the sprinkling of the hot water is seen as the main way in both types of festivals how everyone can participate in the holy power of the gods (*kami*), since their power is said to accumulate in hot water. The gods climb down to join in the festivities either *via* the flue or the paper canopy installed above the kettle, or *via* a special paper streamer called the "navel".[10]

The second – but no less significant – focus for the effectiveness expected from the festive ritual (at least for the villagers among the spectators) is the appearance of masks. *Hana-Matsuri* features as main mask the mountain god (*Yama-no-kami*). There are a whole lot of divinities in the *Shimotsuki-Matsuri*, including the *Tengu* who protects the borders of the locality and who possesses the same qualities of natural wildness as the mountain god. They guarantee thereby the fertility and welfare of nature and human beings in the coming annual cycle.[11]

Before going into the bodily transformation and related ambivalence of dancing as a ritual performance I should note that the effectiveness of ritual itself can be the subject not only of negotiation but also of contestation. In one instance, the village Shinto priest had accompanied the aniconic patron spirit to its temporary seat in the festive hall. When I asked him about the function of festival he replied that only his own ritual action was truly effective and could call forth the divine presence. The dances of the villagers under the guidance of the music ensemble of lay priests was only "entertainment".[12]

[9] The office of lay priest is mostly hereditary. It is to be distinguished from the office of Shinto priest, responsible for the village shrine of the patron divinity.

[10] Here lies the agency of the lay priests, who also call the power of the Kami into the water with their ritual acts. The concept of *hana* (flower) with the *Hana-Matsuri* is supposed to relate to the bubbles of hot water which metaphorically designate the power of the gods and their real presence. A similar role to that of hot water is played by the canopy over the kettle, which is torn up at the end of the festival in a kind of charivari and then taken home by different families as protection against misfortune.

[11] The Tengu – with his long nose – is identifiable in the collected Shinto mythology as *Sarutahiko*, who can be considered as a Japanese Hermes, the companion of the grandson of the sun goddess when he came down to earth to found the Japanese imperial dynasty.

[12] On the morning of the first ritual dance evening this group of lay priests conducts the invocatory

After the roughly hour-long entertainment the Shinto priest left the ritual room – as on all such occasions. The members of the lay priest group and a few dancers, plus the "producer" of the festival – a former charismatic leader of the lay priest group – explained to me that the Shinto priest had to adopt such an attitude in order to represent his office, while it was clear that they as priestly representatives of the village called up the gods for the festival through their ritual actions as only they, not the Shinto priest, knew the right way to do things, and the proper rules and prayers.[13]

The view expressed by the villagers through participation or non-attendance was even more radical. They showed a complete lack of interest in the liturgical actions of both the Shinto priests and the lay priests. Only when there was an opportunity to look at the masked mountain god and dance with him did they turn up in droves. There was such a crush that the mood they themselves call festival fever arose, "Matsuri madness" – helped along by constant sipping of sake. Then they open themselves to transformation – over a hundred people, crammed into a small ritual area of about seven by ten metres, turn into a heaving crowd, shouting out to the dancing god or joining in the singing of traditional refrains.

These differing views and interests in ritual illustrate elements of a historical argument between high or state religion and popular religion about ritual power and the exclusion of transgressive behaviour from rituals in high religion. At the same time they illustrate a demotic reflexive discourse about the efficacy of ritual. While the Shinto priest insists on ritual "correctness" and attributes the effectiveness of the ritual to his knowledge, for the villagers the rituals work as a performance, regardless of whether they understand the texts, can make sense of the names of the gods or know the stories in their "authentic" mythical connotation.[14] In the following I will concentrate on the dance elements emphasised by the villagers. They will help us to better understand bodilyness and embodiment as part of the Japanese cultural repertoire.

and reassuring ceremonies in the woods, fields and house, staying during the whole festive time in the ritual area on a raised altar stage, carefully unwinding the masks of the main divinities, making signs of reverence and rubbing them down with sake in order to place them in the changing room of the dancers (the "room of the gods", *kamibeya*), even keeping some of them covered with cloths until the end of the festival; during the ritual dances they do not just provide the musical accompaniment but in the interval perform sacrificial rituals, songs of praise and supplication, and purification ceremonies; finally, they conclude the festive ritual by "sending away" the gathered gods and enshrining the village patron god. Averbuch, an ethnographer participating in the dance, reported that when learning the kagura dances she had not been allowed to perform the *Yama-no-Kami-Mai*, the dance of the mountain god, it was too sacred.

[13] These are syncretistic formulae and hand movements, mantras and mudras, communicated through Buddhist esoteric wandering priests, *yamabushi*; they were disseminated in these mountain regions centuries ago in a kind of "Buddhist mission".

[14] Whether a ritual is performed to the left or to the right is crucial, according to the rules, since turning the wrong way led in Shinto mythology to an abortion for the first couple. When the villagers discovered it had been performed the wrong way in 1999 they agreed to let it go.

## *Bodily Performance in a Liminal Festive Period*
## *as Dramatic Freedom*

The body is featured directly in the dance parts of the festivals. They demonstrate a behaviour that is extremely unusual in a normal Japanese code of conduct. Here actions are no longer controlled, but "informal", "wild" and based on "feeling". Under the influence of alcohol and in a thronging "crowd" there is uninhibited body contact, otherwise completely prohibited. Drunkenness and chaotic, wild dancing are only two facets of a relatively "uncontrolled" bodilyness that involves a loss of individual control.

To understand the change in behaviour the role of masks needs to be discussed. When asked about the significance of the dances, people say, for example, that the dances were organised to please the gods, or that the event is about watching the gods dance. The ambiguity of the masks is shown here. On the one hand, it is the actors that have to play a "role" to entice the gods, while, on the other, they hope to see the gods themselves appear in these masks and thereby that they will not just be represented but be present directly, immediately, unmediated and tangibly. This double relation of the masks to the gods is shown in the fact that the masks are put on and taken off again before the shrine of the village patron god in the changing room (also called *room of the gods, kamibeya*). This is accompanied by bowing and formal prayers.

*Figure 12*: Childrens Performance with typical head-dresses as conduits for divinities

*Figure 13*: Typical introductory dance-performance
during *Hana-Matsuri*

The expectation is that the god will overwhelm the wearer in order to perform through him. The dance starts calmly and sedately with "ritual" steps, but the more wildly and rapidly a masked dancer twirls around the boiling kettle (to a rhythm beaten out by the drummer, the leader of the lay priests) the more the god is regarded as present. It can happen that the gesticulating dancer hurts someone with the long-handled axe when he starts swinging it more and more quickly. Just putting on the mask changes the dancer's persona. The god represented in the mask takes possession of the dancer and he becomes "god-like", a "living *kami*". This change is expressed in the chaotic (but still rhythmically controlled) dance fever; since the mask cannot express feelings or attitudes. These are to be interpreted into and read off the changed bodily performance of the dancer.

Yet while the dancer becomes a "god" he also remains a person. This is shown by a girl pushing a slice of orange through the mask into his mouth to refresh a "mountain god". The dancer imbibes a sip of water from time to time and he is fanned so as not to collapse in the mask that is up to 10 kilograms in weight. And yet there are often attacks of asphyxiation and almost fainting so that the co-organisers and "conductors" of the mask dances – mostly four to six young men – are available to help at any time.[15]

While the dance continues the crowd encourages the *dancer as a person* to put on speed. Many older, drunken men join the "mountain god" and start doing a wild dance. Although they mostly stumble around more than dance they are not felt to be "nuisances" and called to order. They, too, are considered to be possessed by the "festive spirit" and are thus accepted in their changed state. Groups of young men and girls arm-in-arm move in a phalanx up to the dancer and then back, with ever increasing speed, until the escalation is brought under control again by the drummer by toning down the rhythms. The repetition of such *ad hoc* performances can drag on until the dancers are exhausted. The working up and calming down of the dance is not necessarily part of the ritual regulation but it is still expected or at least much applauded. It is largely what makes the dance so attractive.

The sequences of masked dancers are even more unruly in the *Shimotsuki-Matsuri*. After dressing up before the shrine god the "masks" enter the place of ritual, but then begin to leap more and more quickly from one side of the room to the other. They run forward and then jump backwards into the waiting crowd. After about ten minutes of this, up to six strong men have to go at the masked dancers to throw them on the floor and force him to end the dance

---

[15] The ordeal is, however, accepted by the performers for various reasons that illuminate the meaning of the social context. One dancer in a mountain-god mask told me that although he was about fifty he could not give up this difficult dance until his son, a lad of about five, had grown up (the grandfather stood by as the former leader of the lay priests). Similarly only certain families could provide the dancers for certain masks. These socio-structural components are relevant to the performance, of course, since skilful dancers are covered in glory.

since he ("the divinities") does not want to stop. He has to be dragged before the altar and held fast until the mask is stripped off. Then you see a face that is hardly perspiring, breathing normally and with an almost remote expression. The dancers claim not to know what they have been doing during those "mad leaps".

At such festivities the mood reaches its climax when a dancer is led to the kettle and after a rhythmic dance to start with suddenly stops and with his bare hands sprays the hot water onto the packed crowed – many men having stripped down to a loin-cloth. Then his hands are inspected to see whether they have been scalded or not. If not, the believers assume that the god was present and took possession of the dancer.[16]

In all these examples it becomes clear that people here become vessels of the otherwise aniconic gods. What is invisible and hidden is brought out, and made present, through embodiment. These mask dances are thereby different in quality from the others performed by the festival. While it is usual for dancers to be decked out with a lot of paraphernalia – swords, fans, bells, flowery hats – the masked dancers use no other objects. That can be interpreted such that the normal access to the gods take place *via* props that serve as "the gods' antennae" and – as with the paper streamers over the kettle – are themselves a way for the god to come down. The masked dancers do not need this paraphernalia. They do not need any "antennae" as the gods become present through the body.[17]

Yet the ambivalence of the idea of a person and a mask, the changing between human dancers and divine presence also has a meaning pointing to a perhaps specifically Japanese concept of bodilyness and also to a universal component of bodily performance under a mask. Napier shows that masks are always zones of transition and therefore also of transformation. They are

---

[16] At the ritual festival taking place every seven years in the city of Suwa this concept is expressed metaphorically by "sacred tree trunks" which after being felled are considered the home of the divinity, and then dragged several dozen kilometres over steep slopes to the town. Due to the unpredictability of their falling down the mountainside the "spirit" of the god is thought to be "wild". The men in the city show their physical skill and closeness to the divinity (whose wildness they control) by sitting on the trunks with which they slide downwards not hanging on. The divinities, i.e. the trunks, are months later set up as god trees at the shrine, after secret rituals, and now show their "peaceful", protective sides. This undoubtedly corresponds to the traditional idea of the double-sided soul of Japanese Shinto gods, which have a "soft" and a "rough" side (*nigi-mitama* and *ara-mitama*). What seems important for our discussion of embodiment, however, is the presentation and "transference" of these aspects to the human body which makes them both really present in its performing act.

[17] The *torimono*, like many complex sequences of steps of ritual or "sacred" dances (the *kagura* dance sequences) are just as full of symbolic magic-religious meanings as the mantras and mudras (see Averbuch 1995: 21 and 100ff.) although there are here often differences in esoteric nuances (the "hidden" and often secret levels of meaning) between performances by "professional" groups like the kagura dance groups that wander from village to village and those of the villagers themselves.

transformers of the highest order in that they frequently indicate the transitions of death and life. They raise up what is hidden and at the same time hide what is visible (Napier 1986; see also Koepping 1989). Masks reveal gods but hide *personae*. The paradox can be even extended by arguing that the hidden element expressed in bodily performance is not analogous to that which the mask represents, but to that which is normally hidden by the face, namely the inner self, what one would like to be but is not allowed to become. In the case of our ritual dances we see what is hidden by the cultural whitewash of good behaviour and etiquette, i.e. the wild, "natural", "instinctive" nature of the person, who wants to be carried away by their desires and inner cravings, which are still culturally conditioned as to what is to be expected as "wildness". According to Napier the mask protects the person in this state from remaining in a state of possession, since it can be put aside, thereby paving the way back to normality.[18]

This approach to interpretation probably corresponds fairly well to the Japanese understanding of human behaviour. Normal life consists of orderly "face behaviour".[19] In the transition spaces and during the transition times – e.g. after work or at a festival – one can show one's "true nature"; excesses – whether through erotic transgression, silly behaviour or induced by wine or fury – cannot be held against the person in their normal state (that would really be loss of face). The feeling of being able to let oneself go, of being allowed to cross the barriers of mores, creates a liminal space corresponding to the liminal ritual room of interaction between gods and human beings. In this state the latter can develop the *hara* or stomach feeling, which is mostly seen as a pre- and extra-linguistic way of communicating well-being or one's frue self, including one's rage.

It seems to me indicative that the non-linguistic communication of well-being is expressed by means of the body metaphor. After all, the stomach is also regarded as the seat of life force, feeling and emotions. The mask allows a person to show "stomach", whether their "true nature" or the appearance of the divine. On the basis of the numerous body metaphors in ritual it would not be too far-fetched to suspect a relationship between the two – as the way the gods gain access to the festival *via* the paper-streamers is called the "navel". Napier comes to a similar conclusion.

---

[18] The paradox reaches its climax in the Japanese theatre form of *noh* when the mask of the first part of the play is taken off to reveal the person underneath in the second part, only to reveal a further mask.

[19] The face, *kao*, is also called the "outside" or *omote*, sometimes *tatemae* (standard behaviour), in contrast to *honne*, the "true inside", the *ure* which is the backside, equivalent to *kokoro*, the heart (for which the notion of *hara*, belly can be substituted).

> "Masks are ... a means of describing transitions in substance and in idea, a way of expressing selected modes of both natural and supernatural classification" (Napier 1986: 22).

Before I go into the theory of theatrical practice that has taken up the topic of this ambivalence of double *personae*, its embodiment, and then its resonance with the audience, I must refer to a typical phenomenon that seems extremely important in the indigenous understanding of embodiment. Frequently during the festivals men – who had travelled long distances to their villages of origin especially for these rituals – were asked out of the blue to perform certain mask dances. On asking how these inexperienced people could learn so fast I was told that it was learning by doing, through the body or the skin (*karada de* or *hada de*). In the initial phase, the first rounds of the performance, these novices were frequently taken by the hand or slapped on the hip to show them what to do. Anyone who has ever wanted to learn one of the classical "arts" in Japan will know – whether it be water-colour painting, floral arrangements or the martial arts like Kendo, Judo or Aikido – that it is not a matter of discursive, reflective learning, on the basis of understanding the principles. Instead it is about "copying", a *mimesis which is mimicry and suffering* together, learning through performative experience and action/passion.

### The "In-Between" of the Puppet Membranes or the Liminal Role of the Skin

The fundamental question behind this phenomenon of embodiment by and with masks relates to the old argument about the theatrical in ritual performances, to the appearance before or after the being and *vice versa*. This was precisely the problem dealt with by the dramatist Monzaemon Chikamatsu (1653-1724) in his work on the role of the skin, or rather the membrane between appearance and being. He wondered how to play with the *jōruri* puppets, which only consist of a wooden head and below it a piece of cloth, animated by up to three actors who move the limbs and head with their fingers.

   Chikamatsu had the goal of executing movements with the puppets in order to express feelings better than living actors. He developed the art of performance in the "in-between" space of the membrane (the fabric). In order to illustrate the requirement that art use different means in order to uncover reality he compared the puppets with the *Kabuki* male portrayers of women, who in his view perform the role women differently, and better, than women could. Chikamatsu was convinced that the imaginary world of the play did not remain mere appearance when it was filled by the flesh of the actor. The "membrane" of the puppet and the skin of the person fulfilled the same function of mediating between outer and inner world. The skin-membrane is neither an exterior nor an interior, it is both, and mediates between them. So, according to Chikamatsu's philosophy, there is also an interstice between appearance and being that is neither one nor the other.

This sophisticated philosophy of theatrical practice was, according to Ohashi, anticipated by *Noh* actor and theoretician Zeami in the 14th century in his work *Fushi Kaden* ("The Teaching of the Beautifully Shaped Flowers"). He spoke of a "thick" and "thin" theatrical art.[20] A "thin" performance tries to imitate reality, while a "thick" art expresses, through human gestures, aspects of things hidden in everyday life and "becomes flesh" in a higher sense (Ohashi 1998: 155). When actors are young they are beautiful like a flower, but when they have lost their beauty in old age they must be able to portray the flower that never fades.

I have deliberately cited these ideas about theatre by way of comparison as they form a direct analogy with embodiment in ritual dances – particularly those with masks. The transformation that emerges during the danced performance through the momentum of the body is made possible by the mask. Dancers can only be possessed by the invisible god when their intentional self is hidden so that the Other can take effect from inside them. The mask is here a "membrane" between the outside world and the dancers, and also a "skin" covering their inner world. The divinity is slipped onto the skin of the dancer like a template that comes to life in connection with the person's life and strength. The precondition for the transformation is the "animation" of the dancer's body with reality, the "being" of what looks like "appearance" in the mask. The dancer is the link and thereby himself a skin between the representation and reality of the divine. Ritual dances can therefore be understood as multivalent. They are both ritual and performance. The participant is prevailed upon to join in the dance by divine power but also applauds the acrobatic feats of the dancer.[21]

[20] I shall not succumb to the pleasure of comparing this with the portrayal of thin and thick description in ethnography given by Geertz. Zen philosophy of the perfection of emptiness to be achieved by non-desire, then animated with the fleshly spirit, would contradict Geertz's idea of thick description. After all, bringing researchers into their ethnography would mean overestimating their own achievements; instead of holding back he would actually point to his own agency as the ethnographic creator and thereby often of the subjects described. That would be anathema for a Zen stance, that – almost like a phenomenology – wants things for itself and to let them speak by themselves.

[21] The many-facetted modern reality of Japan has blurred many boundaries regarding religious and theatrical forms of performance. Within many New Religions almost the same argument takes place as that regarding the contrasts between the practice of official Shinto rituals and popular religious performance. Many of the religious groups founded since 1945 insist on the performative execution of liturgies through dance, prayer, song, pilgrimage and voluntary service, while a number of recently successful groups project a spectacular multimedia show by way of worship or liturgy, the faithful only constituting a passive "audience" (Shimazono 1995).

*Inter-Corporeal Experience: Mishima and Richie*

The popular religious practices dealt with here, and drawn from ethnographic observation, clearly give priority to participatory bodily involvement. The *inter-somatic* contact plays the main role in *intra-somatic* transformations and experiences. There are two fine examples in the literature, describing this experience of the "haptic"[22], or inter-corporeal experience. The *first* experience is recounted by Yukio Mishima, known for his almost obsessed refinement of the body. The *second* experience is given by the American film historian and journalist Donald Richie. The two stories concern participation in *Matsuri*-rituals where the portable shrines, containing a non-iconic divinity, are normally swung back and forth on the shoulders of their bearers. Consequently they not only rub the skin off their shoulders through the heavy weights and swaying objects, they also push the shrines into the crowd, claiming to have been possessed or made drunk by the divinity whose essence is contained by the portable shrine.

Mishima[23] once related the feeling that overcame him at such a procession of gods when he felt the ecstasy of bodily effort, fatigue, perspiration and the joyful plunging into the crowd (Mishima 1958: 38ff.)[24] Yourcenar describes him on a photo, still very young and this time with a beaming smile, his cotton kimono open at the chest and in every respect like his fellow bearers (Yourcenar 1985: 12).[25] The topic of being overpowered turns up later in an essay by Mishima when he is striving for knowledge from his "stomach" and "muscles" through hard body training. He writes that training his muscles illuminated and explained the myths that the words had brought forth, and that physical exercise opened the way to flashes of spiritual insight, like the acquisition of erotic knowledge. Yourcenar makes the insightful remark that Mishima followed the philosophy of *"ou mathein, alla pathein"* ("do not explore, just experience") (Yourcenar 1985: 77). It is an experience that implies openness to suffering.

A similarly impressive report is also given by Richie, who took part in a procession of thousands of young men. He felt a strange transformation taking place in himself. After he had lost his shoes in the jostling of the many bodies, torn his shirt, and feared losing consciousness in the crush of bodies a sudden change came over him. He seemed to feel his limbs mingling with those of the

---

[22] The "tangible" as something that one can grasp through the skin, which has led some philosophical anthropologists to speculate that the German word for "concept" (*Begriff*) is derived from the haptic (through touching).

[23] Participation in such a procession is described by Mishima in his autobiography *Confessions of a Mask*, 1958, interpreted in turn by Marguerite Yourcenar (1985) in *Mishima or the Vision of Emptiness*.

[24] He later worked this into a novel (Yourcenar 1985: 11).

[25] *Taiyo to Tetsu*, (Sun and Iron), 1967.

bodies pressed up against him. In the dark and utter silence of the square before the shrine he had panicked but now, as the typical refrain is struck up by the crowd:

> "I felt my fear depart. It lifted slowly and I thought no more about our differences. We were now a single mass crammed into this narrow vessel, and there was no telling us apart. Cradled, we were slowly merging ... losing all feeling in arms, in legs, smelling the hot rice odour which was now mine as well. I, the man I thought I knew, was gone, become a thousand others. What had terrified me now consoled me. How secure, how safe, how warm, those bodies moulding mine, those several near, those hundreds farther off. This was as it should have been" (Richie 1991: 22-23).

The inter-somatic power of physical contact, that cancels out all social and individual differentiations in the performative activity, is certainly one of the motives that runs strongly through Japanese ritual practice, in so far as it has remained popular and participatory. The emotions aroused here in Mishima and Richie have been allayed by the time they are recounted in that they both contain reflection about the experience. In ritual dance the communication lies not in words but in gestures that become an invitation to articulation for the involuntary body and at the same time can bring about a transformation of the participants. The experience of transformation may always be an ephemeral phenomenon, but what remains is certainly another attitude to reality, regardless of whether this is now perceived and interpreted as the presence of gods or as an experience of "authentic" Japanese tradition – or again, as in the last two cases described above, as inter-somatic non-differentiation.

A transformation had certainly also taken place when one of my students, who had attended such a village *matsuri* for the first time in her life, said, "I'll go back next year. I felt alive." Another student, on seeing the dancing crowd in the ritual space, said, "That is paradise."[26] And everyone from the village agreed that this was the only festival to which they simply had to return

---

[26] With this comment the student hit upon two interpretative systems: *firstly*, his own perception that intuitively grasped the utopian, timeless dimension of the ritual act, the out-of-time-and-space and the performers and participants being "beside themselves". In addition he (unconsciously?) hit upon an interpretation that speaks of the mountain god as a Buddhist-inspired figure who opens the way to the Western Paradise to the souls of the dead, metaphorically indicated by his striking the kettle with an axe; in the geographic area where the dance festivals take place one of the highest mountains of this alpine region is called *Shirayama*, the White Mountain, which is protected by the mountain god. But it is more than just a geographic name; it is also a statement about the entry to paradise in Buddhist folklore, a mythical place, that is in turn equated metaphorically with the mud-brick stoves (according to the statements of different villagers in this region, in which the *hana-matsuri* is still performed in seventeen places).

(which they did not even do at New Year or for the O-Bon festival, in memorial of the dead, that otherwise constitutes the highest ritual family duty in the annual cycle).

Independently of personal intention, whether participants come back to be healed or to have an authentic experience, in this case there is commitment to the ritual framing and to attending a performance (even if the "purely" religious "ritual", *gishiki*, is something hardly anyone is aware of except for the lay priests). The desire to participate is already a result of the resonance called up through experience of earlier performances, which is linked with the cultural coding of modes of behaviour and attitudes. It is known that there will be a bodily performance and behaviour that would be disapproved or banned in ordinary life. However, whether the transformation will really take place is still not certain. Many visitors withdraw from a lot of dance sequences because they are repetitive and boring. But those who have been so captivated as to watch the whole performance are "seduced" by the reaction of their own body to come back again and again, so that they believe they cannot do without it. That is the transformation that counts for Japanese.[27]

The charismatic founder of a religion with participatory liturgy once told me, "Don't be silly, don't ask any questions, dance with them then you will get a feeling for the truth."[28] Here too the redundant performance of a dance, the dance of the "non-Ego" was considered the dramatic aid to reaching that state of emptiness (*muga*, non-Ego) that was supposed to enable a filling with the awareness of the god.

### *Ritual Resonance as Structured Involuntariness*

In this paper I have examined Japanese dance rituals – of a certain, clearly defined geographical region – with respect to its effectiveness in changing perception and awareness. This has been both by describing and interpreting performances I have observed and referring back to a historical discourse about theatrical performance. It turned out that performative ritual behaviour led to

---

[27] I was told by many visitors from cities, who travelled long distances every year to attend these dance festivals, that they felt this was the only right way to begin the New Year. Among these visitors there were some who watched several festivals in the course of a week, so that I came across a group of *aficionados*, always seeing the same faces, without being able to call them "tourists". This group feels genuinely suffused by a religious feeling of participation and many of them can perform the dance perfectly themselves. A few have become close friends with villagers without having any connection to these festivals from birth.

[28] That was Sayo Kitamura, in 1967. The religion she founded (one of the many that have sprung up since 1945) was called *Tenshō Kōtai Jingū Kyō* (Teaching of the Sun Goddess and the Holy Shrine of Ise), better known as the "dancing religion" (*Odoru Shukyo*) because of her "dance of the non-Ego" (*Muga-no-Odori*); cf. Koepping 1999). See the chapter on shamanism in this volume.

different forms of change of consciousness that all contained a form of "over-powerment". For example, there were performers who were carried away by dancing, there were participants and spectators who got involved in the performance – as in the case of Mishima and Richie – and there were observers, like townspeople or photographers, and students, who began to understand that it was a matter of "ritual" not of show. They suddenly understood that at this place and time the differentiations and mores that otherwise applied in society had been more or less cancelled out and that the performers and participants were in an extraordinary condition.

Related to the different groups there are several paradoxes here:

(1) The dance ritual meant that the lay people who performed it were empowered, indeed overpowered by other powers;

(2) The participants merged with their individual feelings into the crowd. Through the direct tactile, haptic experiences they achieved undifferentiated bodily community;

(3) The spectators, starting to clap after a performance, suddenly paused when the dancers bowed before the shrine of the god. They suddenly understood that something different, and more serious was happening. At that moment they were – like those who had an experience with their bodies and worked through it afterwards – at once reflective spectators and involuntarily moved, people who were "amazed" to note the new dimension of the festival.

These observations give rise to a number of important points for the theoretical discussion of performance. Taking up Bourdieu's concept of the "structure of practice", Kapferer insists that ritual performances, by virtue of their expressive qualities, call forth a transformation of significance and experience through the dynamic qualities of aesthetic modes (Kapferer 1983: 178) In his latest work he describes ritual as a "generative practice" that is characterised by generating a "virtual" reality. This virtual reality is characterised by its "determinedness" and "repeatability" and contrasts with "actual" reality, that is "indeterminate" or contingent (Kapferer 1997: 179).[29] If, however, as he has formulated in the past, ritual performances so to speak release the values of a society for inspection (Kapferer 1979a) and contribute to the constitution and

---

[29] This is certainly a remarkable phrase, recalling Victor Turner's appraisal of theatre as "genuine" reality that, since it can be virtually played with, reveals the "indicative" world as the "semblance" of the "non-genuine", while the "subjunctive" world of theatre conjures up the "being" as the "genuine" – albeit only potentially (Victor Turner 1989: 135). This attitude, however, forgets the contingency of ritual events, which is also a reality. Kapferer is certainly right when he points to the relative uselessness of defining ritual via the conventionalisation of behaviour (1997: 178). But this conventionalisation takes on another status when it can cause that "emptiness" that makes a "filling" with new potential meaning possible (Tambiah 1979).

reconstitution of self, society and cosmic order (Kapferer 1997: 178), then the experiences of overpowerment – as I have shown in my ethnographic examples – are of precisely the quality that would testify to a transformation of experience (this way criticism of epistemological circularity – as Scott (1992) put it – could be avoided). But then we cannot keep to Langer's concept of "gesture" that through the articulation of feelings is intended to evoke more or less "normative" experiences. Instead, we must expand the concept to the involuntary.

Nor can we then postulate a "determinedness" of ritual performance but must take account of the contingency of the unexpected and involuntary – also and precisely in ritual. After all, without such a reference it would not be easy to explain the effectiveness of potentially subversive actions within a ritual framework, which – if they do not lead to real social restructuring – can at least raise awareness of the artificiality of all cultural codings.

The overstressing of the determinedness of the "virtual" world goes hand in hand with an underestimation of the effectiveness and significance of repetition and redundancy for the evocation of the unexpected. The problem remains one of theory design: how can one regard performances as reflective and stereotyped actions while still remaining open to the unexpected, the unconscious "event"? I believe that there is the possibility of a link *via* the concept of *habitus* as a core concept in practice. This is because the structuring practice for which it stands takes place, according to Bourdieu, in part unconsciously. If we apply this not just to everyday unthinking behaviour but also to the concept of embodiment, which leaves room for an involuntary element, the contrast between the structuredness of ritual performances and transformative experience could at least be harmonised, if not resolved. If we presuppose that people in their everyday practices show an "unconscious mastering of their systems" (Sahlins 1998: 51) then reflexive ritual performance can be understood as "regulated improvisation", enabling the "unintentional" appearance of the unexpected so that the unexpected and involuntary dimension is a downright result of the regulation of ritual redundancy and formality.

However, for the social mediation of this experience there naturally only remains the gesture, in part consciously executed and culturally standardised, which – like the narration of an event – enables and requires a structuring of the unexpected and involuntary in a communication situation. But again it is not certain whether it will be able to call forth a resonance and, if so, what kind – there lies precisely the potential of empowerment for the performers and the spectators. Neither the experiences during the performance nor the interpretations of what happens with the performers in dance rituals are free from culturally coded preconceptions – like the fact that there can be surprises at such festivals at all. Whether there are expressed, however, and how they are expressed, can only be discovered in the act of performance itself.

# The Trickster: Boundaries and Ambivalences

*Introduction: Ambiguity and Inversion in Language and Ritual*

When Alice in Wonderland says, "I can see nobody", and the admiring response to this linguistic ambiguity is, "My, you must have good eyes", we all immediately understand the joke of the absurd play on words as well as on structural principles and see beneath the even deeper level of lampooning general principles of logic. All of us, irrespective of cultural background, seem to enjoy this kind of play with logic and structure, which enables us to escape the prison of the cut-and-dried rule-governed realm of deductive principles: yet we can only escape the prison by applying the rules of paradox through acknowledging these rules. In other words, we use the rules in order to show that a strict adherence to them leads to absurdity. Playing manifestations of the Trickster around with negativity or with inversion and reversal of symbols in word or action, which is in itself potentially inherent in the rules of language, reveals a hidden truth, that of the absurdity of the close adherence to them, while acknowledging at the same time the existence of the rules without which even the game of negativity could not be played. That means even negativity is rule governed.

Many forms of rhetoric have made use of this antagonism, which is not one of simple opposition but one of intertwined complementarity, where one entails and encompasses the other. In simple linguistic games we find this inversion game in the grammatical figures of anastrophe and antistrophe, in more literary works as parody and paradox, as irony and persiflage, as high and low comedy.

Ancient literary satire is one of the main forms of literature dealing with such paradoxes of social life as the covering up of violent urges through the mask of politeness. As Michael Seidel's penetrating analysis has shown, satire may in one sense be intended to cleanse society of its hypocrisy, but in that process the satirist incurs the risk of transferring the disorder, dirt, and pollution to himself: the job of any cleanser, whether satirist or garbage collector, may take on itself tile taint of others' dirt.[1] The "satiric dispensation", as Seidel has called it, is characterised by the danger that even if the author distances himself (as he does in the typical autobiographical introductory denouement that is a formal sign of the genre of the *picaresque*), the satirist "more often than not ... suffers the contamination of his own subject" (Seidel 1979: 14).

---

[1] The metaphor on the garbage collector is taken from Heinrich Böll, *Group Portrait with Lady* (1973: 390).

This ambiguity within all forms of violation and transgression – here of the author and his subject matter – or intrusion from one bounded sphere into another sets such literary devices formally close to the structure that governs those central social and religious forms of action such as sacrifices. As Hubert and Mauss show, these forms present, virtually as a generic type, the identification of sacrificer and sacrificed (Hubert and Mauss 1974). This ambiguity may be seen in the Germanic concept of *sjalfr-sjalfrum*, where the actor becomes the victim (von Ström 1975), or in the case of Greek mythology, where the hunter becomes prey, Pentheus being substituted for Dionysos. Indeed, as Kott has so clearly proved, this motif suffuses the *Bacchae* of Euripides (Kott 1975). The violence (whether rape or murder or even cannibalistic devouring) inherent in such acts places them in an ambiguous and ambivalent category, which may, as René Girard has observed, be codified in a "ritualisation of violence" in the socio-religious sphere of marriage and sacrifice (Girard 1977).

The literary as well as the ritual ambiguity and ambivalence both point to deeper paradoxes of experience and existence, to certain value precepts whose bases are often irrefutable by normal social logic: I only have to remind the reader of the catch-22 embodied in the giving of alms to which Marcel Mauss has alluded. On the one hand, many cultures consider generosity praiseworthy and also endorse the virtue of compassion; yet on the other, when following such compassionate values by giving alms to the poor, the donor will rarely be thanked and will frequently be hated by the recipient.

The ambiguity and ambivalence of which I am speaking find literary expression in the symbolism of worlds upside down or topsy-turvy, which tests the boundaries of logical discourse or indeed shows the limits of discourse in general, but social discourse also displays similar built-in devices of criticism, of rebellion, of protest against existing structures, against boundaries, against the seriousness of order; and these devices are socially and ritually acknowledged. They are manifestations of the chaos on which order depends and over which it must reign supreme (Gluckman 1955; Turner V. 1969). The other paradox of inverted social action, of chaotic topsy-turvydom, is that it remains a beacon pointed toward the positive, for with its constant attempt to create an antistructure, it cannot avoid structure or even deny it because, without it, chaos would not be possible. Such social figures of antistructure, which surpass the boundaries of the controlled, irreversible, perfect delineation of the world we find in the clown and the transvestite and in customs like the backward acting and reversing of speech at festive occasions (of what Victor Turner called, following van Gennep, "liminal" periods) (Turner 969: 94ff.).[2]

---

[2] Relying on Arnold van Gennep, *The Rites of Passage* (1960); Turner states that "the attributes of liminality ... are necessarily ambiguous, since [they] ... elude or slip through the network of classi-

### The Anomalous Trickster – Theoretical Comparisons

The particular form of ambiguity and inversion I am concerned with here is that of the figure of the trickster, as he appears apparently world-wide in primitive mythology and in classical antiquity as well as in modern deritualised and more secularised form as the fool and jester in the prankster tales of the time of the Reformation (the so-called *Schelmenromane* or, to use a widely applied literary term, the *picaresque* novel) with close connection to the focal ambivalences of the dramas of Shakespeare.[3] The devices the trickster figures seem to use have a lot in common with the formal genres of rhetoric, though I am here more interested in presenting the two forms of action which seem to designate the trickster across all cultural variations, namely, his cunning form of intelligence and the grotesqueness of the body imagery used to indicate the inversion of order. To use a comparison with rhetoric studies: the body images and the forms of reasoning applied are either already expressed in metaphors or in turn become metaphors for something different, namely, the protest, the sometimes serious, sometimes laughable attempts at creating a counteruniverse, a very utopian counterworld, that shows the real world off as what it is or seems to be.

My main examples will be the figures of Prometheus, as he emerges from the accounts of Hesiod in the *Theogony* and in *Works and Days*, and the Winnebago Trickster of Wakdjunkaga, as he is reported to us by Paul Radin, a connection that Jack Lindsay has hinted at (without developing it; Lindsay

---

fications that normally locate states and positions in cultural space" (p. 95).

[3] The term Schelm connotes the Middle High German "carrion, hangman, knacker, dishonorable man"; the Schelm has appeared in the figure of Reineke Fuchs since 1150 (Nivardus's *Ysengrimus*) and merged in 1515 with the figure of the "wise fool" in *Till Eulenspiegel*, a folk book of collected episodes (cf. Frenzel 1976: 608-11). The term *picaro* appears first in Spain in 1525 with the meaning "kitchen boy" and is later defined by the dictionary of the Spanish Academy of 1726 as "low, deceitful, dishonorable, shameless" (cf. Parker 1967: 4). The equation of "picaro" and Schelm is introduced by the translation of Paul Radin's classic *The Trickster: A Study in American Indian Mythology*, with commentaries by Karl Kerényi and C.G. Jung (1956) as *Der göttliche Schelm* (1954). Because of these connotations of the terms Schelm and *picaro* the literary genre has been extended to encompass works such as *Moll Flanders* and *Gil Blas* as well as the whole field of literature of roguery, including Thomas Mann's *Felix Krull*. This is a result of the one-sided emphasis on the "criminal" character since the work of Frank W. Chandler (1898). As Blackburn points out, the genre should be restricted to "the art of the picaresque novels, not their subject matter", whereby he opts for a formal criterion that (in contrast to *Gulliver's Travels*) "subordinates satiric perspectives to a novelistic perspective" (Blackburne 1979: 18). I take a different perspective, being convinced that the subject matter and content cannot be divorced from the form of the novel (following closely linguistic paradigms about code and message or content and form, as expressed by Benveniste and Jakobson). The dependence of the German Schelmen-Motiv of *Simplicius* (1688) on the Spanish *picaro* is indisputable (see Parker; and Bjornson 1977). The suggestion of the picaresque element of the trickster goes back to Radin's *Trickster* and also earlier to his *The World of Primitive Man* (1953: 337). In this comparison I am much indebted to Barbara Babcock's study *"Liberty's a Whore"* (1978), which relies as well on linguistic paradigms.

1965). These two trickster figures will be followed up by one example of cunning intelligence or verbal madness as it appears in Shakespeare's *King Lear* and reference to the grotesque body imagery in the tales about Gargantua and Pantagruel by Rabelais to show the enduring appeal and irrepressible as well as inexhaustible optimism and assertion of the joy of life (positivity against the negativity of "Thou shalt not") that permeates these figures, even if their exploits might lead them to defeat, shame, or even madness and death. As Denise Paulme in her study on African trickster tales has cogently remarked, "When the Trickster's temerity does not cost him his life, he loses face and runs away disgraced. But he is known to be incorrigible, and after a success story in which ruses and dishonesty triumph, an audience will in the course of the same evening willingly hear another story with an unfortunate outcome" (Paulme 1977: 64).

Ambivalence is vividly shown in the ritual murders and rapes of epics and sagas, where the hero treads the narrow path between killing and being killed. Less violent, but just as ambiguous, is the appearance of the fool, as has so ably been shown by Enid Welsford in her study of this figure when she says, "The fool is an unabashed glutton and coward and knave, he is – as we say – a natural: we laugh at him and enjoy a pleasant sense of superiority." She immediately adds the paradox of the fool, who not only shows society up for what it really is or seems to be behind the mask of surface pretence, of status and role, and of social game playing but also infers that the fool is at the same time perceived by every kind of audience as the alter ego of the spectator: "He winks at us and we are delighted at the discovery that we also are gluttons and cowards and knaves" (Welsford 1961: 322).

A similar point is made by Elisabeth Frenzel when she asserts that the medieval theme of the fool (the *artificial* as against the *natural* one who is unpredictable) revolves around the position of the figure as outsider (of the play or in life, the "marginal" in the widest sense of the word) who mediates between the happening of the play and the audience, who on the one hand stands apart from the unfolding story but on the other hand is a part with which the audience identifies most closely: one delights in the stupidity of others but also in the fool himself, which in turn means a joke on the *alter ego* of the listener or viewer (Frenzel 1976: 557).

I think it appropriate at this point to summarise some of the theoretical and methodological points that govern this essay. I am not aiming to create a new theory of the trickster or to debunk any of the existing theories of this figure.[4] I am rather trying to point to two facets of the universal figure of anomaly and ambiguity, those of crooked thinking and of a grotesquely extended body, pointing to them as the possibly paradigmatic expressions of the experience

---

[4] Summaries of the extant trickster theories can be found in Mac Linscott Ricketts 1965 and in Robert D. Pelton 1980.

and perception of absurdity, in social arrangements and their governing values or in the logic of rules of language and symbolism. I am not claiming that the two expressions of anomaly/ambiguity always have to occur together, but I do claim that they are the restricted repertoire pervading most of the trickster figures in sacred narrations as well as its secular extensions, without implying that there is historical continuity provable between tricksters and such secular phenomena as jester, fool, and picaro. I restrict myself in the following two examples that show the two forms of ambiguity/anomaly either alone or combined in exemplary fashion, extracting the formal characteristics or topoi, to use Ernst Robert Curtius's terminology, as structural foci from the respective narrations (Curtius 1953). Methodologically, this extracting procedure in many ways resembles a structural analysis, yet I try to avoid that form of structural analysis that engages in the rational manipulation of mental binary oppositions resulting in cognitive structures devoid of meaning and affect, to use Eric Wolf's apt description of the results (Wolf 1974: xii).

A case in point is the treatment of the trickster by Lévi-Strauss. He treats the apparently indissoluble paradoxes of existence and experience as allowing resolution through replacement by other oppositions that admit a third term as mediation. Thus the opposition of life and death in Zuni creation myth is in his opinion symbolically encoded by another opposition, that of agriculture versus warfare, which permits hunting as mediator, with a second homologous relation between herbivorous animals and beasts of prey and their mediator of carrion-eating animals, such as raven or coyote. Though this second triad in which the trickster makes his appearance is a beautiful construction of the mediator who does not hunt what he eats, this construction becomes difficult in culture areas where the animal representation of the trickster does not conform to such a middle position, as Stanley Diamond has shown (Lévi-Strauss 1967: 220-23; Diamond 1974: 312ff).

The crux of the matter seems to lie in the contention of Lévi-Strauss that "mythical thought always progresses from the awareness of oppositions toward their resolution" (Lévi-Strauss 1967: 221). This, I maintain, is plainly fallacious or at least unproved and, as far as the trickster figure is concerned, more than doubtful, in particular, if one takes the above-mentioned ambiguity between potential audience and trickster figure into account, which always (through laughter) shows the tension between identification and distancing. Besides, anomalies and ambiguities, the paradoxes of life within set boundaries of language and custom do not admit true resolution but rather need expression. Thus the trickster might in my opinion be not a figure of resolution of paradoxes but merely a signpost pointing out these paradoxes, bringing them to the conscious mind, which then is able – in the most favourable case – to laugh about them (resignedly or defiantly or both at the same time).

Speaking of theoretical approaches, I should point out that the way I perceive the trickster in this essay does not therefore accord with the image of pure contraries, as could be mistakenly inferred from my introductory references to worlds upside down, to topsy-turvydom.[5] I do not want to deny that this feature is prominent in some trickster tales, as in the meaning imputed to Prometheus from the structural and semantic analysis. In European consciousness Prometheus becomes the symbol for man's never-ceasing, unremitting, and relentless struggle against fate, against the gods, unrepentingly defying the laws of the Olympians, though (and this again shows the continuing absurdity) never being successful in this endeavour, which, however, is necessary for the origin of civilised life (the ultimate paradox of rule breaking as a rule).

The audience, aware of the futility of the revolutionary urge both to challenge sovereignty and to regain the utopia of the paradise lost, presents us also with the spectacle of the impersonation of hope against all odds. Though we laugh about the antics of the trickster, we too seem to say through our laughter (less derisive than conspiratory) that we shall probably always try to violate boundaries. To use an idea of Max Gluckman's that has become seminal for many studies on the dialectic interplay of structure and antistructure, of hierarchy and *communitas*: though we know about the futility of successful revolution, we do not cease playing at ritual rebellion. Through seasons and life cycles, we revive the symbol of rebellion, in tales told, in plays staged, in ritual persons re-enacting the same sequences (or adding new ones). By forgoing the narrative structure in its diachronic patterning and unfolding, by concentrating on the synchronic "deep" level of the unconscious, and by forgetting about the audience, much of the meaning of the trickster gets lost in the Lévi-Straussian analysis. Besides, as Rodney Needham has recently suggested, we might not get at the roots of some distant symbolic systems if we rely too strictly on a monothetic form of classificatory hierarchies, grouping together in best Aristotelian fashion those things that to us share a common property and thus reinforcing binary, oppositional thinking in categories. A more useful tool might instead be some form of polythetic symbolic classification that puts items into categories, which for those trained in the hierarchical trees of Porphyrius or Linné, do not seem to be categories at all (Needham 1980).[6]

I therefore find my analysis here more in tune with such suggestions as Girard's that murder can under certain circumstances (in ritual) become sacrifice (permissible, atonable, and, be it through a reverting to the persecution, real or symbolic of a *pharmakos* or scapegoat), that rape becomes permissible (in marriage), or that incest does not count (in certain rituals in Northern Arn-

---

[5]  On such worlds, see Babcock 1978.

[6]  Earlier exposition is in his "Polythetic Classification", *Man*, n.s., 10 (1975: 349-69). The diverse levels of distancing between trickster and audience through the channel of the story's and narrator's implicit structering cannot be pursued here, as they belong properly to literary discourse. For the model on "metacodes", see R. Jakobson 1960.

hemland, for instance).[7] It is for such reasons that I do not quite follow the strict binary argument that the trickster is a rebel who might have similarities to the social rebel of modern times, as Babcock-Abrahams has proposed, or that his deeds are just the breaking of taboos in order to show the existence of boundaries (true enough), as suggested by most writers on "symbolic inversion" or by those who speak of the dissolution and reinforcement of boundaries as has Laura Makarius (Babcock-Abrahams 1975; Makarius 1974). The qualities of the trickster personality seem to me to comprise not the opposition to any specific symbolic code that distinguishes and hierarchically classifies good and bad, high and low, power and submission, but rather the one in the other, the complementarity of symbols in a given classificatory scheme. It is therefore not always easy to escape the elegant conclusions that Lévi-Strauss's formalism has been able to reach: Lévi-Strauss shows that the trickster is of an ambiguous and equivocal character since any mediator has to retain something of both sides of that duality that he mediates (Lévi-Strauss 1967: 223).

We may look to the arguments of those neo-Durkheimians, like Victor Turner and Mary Douglas, who perceive the poles of sacred and profane not as antithetical but as permeating one another. Turner sees society as dialectic interplay of structure and antistructure (*communitas*), of hierarchical organisation and egalitarian aspirations, in line with Nietzsche's notion of "the power of the weak" (Turner V. 1969). Mary Douglas in turn pointed to the ambivalence and ambiguity of dirt, "a matter out of place", which in rituals of pollution, as, for instance, the example given by Monica Wilson of the Nyakyusa death ritual, includes behaviour of "insanity" in sacred ceremonies (Wilson 1957). This permeation of the sacred with things and actions belonging to the sphere of the profane indicates the conquest of that which would otherwise threaten normal life, namely, insanity in its true form, not its ritual dramatisation (Douglas 1966: 208). I am therefore in full sympathy with the description of Handelman's that the ritual clown (*koyemci* of the Pueblos) is a "dissolver of structure, indicative of its in-between or transitional state of being", strengthening the earlier argument by Ortiz, who defines sacred clowns as "permanently equivocal and liminal characters" (Handelman 1981: 333; Ortiz 1972: 155). However, I cannot agree with Handelman's specious distinction between ritual clown as dissolver of boundaries and the trickster who brings boundaries into being (Handelman 1981: 333): he follows the distinction of medievalists like Welsford and Willeford between festival fools as ritual characters and the blustering court fools. It depends very much on the viewpoint and the level of analysis whether certain phenomena become comparable. Thus, as I indicated, every trickster might be a rebel, yet not every rebel is also a trickster. Not all substantive traits, such as thieving or rebelliousness,

---

[7]  Compare R. Berndt 1951; for a survey on the religious concepts of the area and anthropological literature, see K.-P. Koepping 1981a.

are carried through all cultural traditions or diverse genres through time, and therefore not all jesters, fools, or picaros are tricksters, while the trickster might contain properties common to all.

Each property, that of "hiding the truth" and that of "overstepping the boundaries of the body", is culturally ordered. There is, though, an almost universal sameness in body imagery, for all must play on the same basic body and its same functions, and this sameness may be seen as a universal topos. Wherever it appears to counter the well-ordered classification of things, bodily imagery concerns the obscenity of sexual and excretory organs and their function and the play with such obscene connotations, for, as Bakhtin has clearly pointed out, "the body of the non-official speech is always a ... drinking, eliminating, sick body, a fertilising-fertilised, swallowing-swallowed entity" (Bakhtin 1969: 23ff.).[8] The surpassing of the boundaries of the body always occurs where there are extrusions, and as the body is always in a state of becoming, we should not be surprised about the boundary transgression at points at which new life originates or is sustained: in the sexual organs and their substitutions, the alimentary openings.

Contrary to this sameness of body imagery is the variability of expression of "hiding the truth", of feints, deceits, and illusions. This may appear in the mode of sacrifice (as a code about sovereignty) – as with Prometheus as Titan, possibly in Loki (also with emphasis on sovereignty), or with the Vedic Indra – Garuda and the Puranic gods, churning the ocean (both as a mixture of sacrificial and alimentary code and, as with Loki, as strong on the code of immortality as is the case in Greece) – in divinatory and thus random playing – as among the Fon with their trickster Legba (with faint Indo-European comparative hints in the Mahabharata in the game for the female partner of the Pandava brothers and in the riddle games of Odin and Loki or the knucklebones of Hermes in Greece) – or in the mode of "translator of languages" – as with Ananse of the Ashanti (with echos in Hermes, mediating heaven and underworld, or in Loki as spokesman between gods, giants, and dwarfs).[9] In the Christian tradition, the truth of God might appear in its courtly surrounding of the twelfth century as the awakening of spiritual chivalry for the divine (the search for the Grail, the "dumbness" of Parcival), while in the medieval folk culture as well as in comedies since Aristophanes the derision of the masks of the powerful might find expression in the fool's horseplay.

Tragedy, the other side of comedy, is likewise a vehicle for hidden para-

---

[8] I would tend to deemphasise the epithet "non-official" of Bakhtin's, as far as trickster tales in the realm of the sacred/secret are concerned.

[9] On the trickster problem in Germanic myths, see, among others, Georges Dumézil 1959; one of the first scholars to endorse critically the view that Loki may be labelled a trickster is possibly Jan de Vries 1933: 253-81). On Hermes as trickster, see Karl Kerényi 1944; and Norman O. Brown 1969; criticism on the latter by Karl Kerényi in Radin (1956: 182). On the West African Trickster figures, see Pelton 1980. For early comparisons of the theft motif, see Georges Dumézil 1924.

doxes: the mythical prototype for the "insanity" of Hamlet has recently been traced to a trickster figure by Giorgio de Santillana and Hertha von Dechend.[10] That the Christian image of folly-wisdom appears in the picaresque journey of *Simplicius Simplicissimus* as a cautionary tale (though not as pronounced as in Sebastian Brant) about the sanity of a hermit whom the world considers a fool should not prevent us from comparing the Titanic mode of suffering with the mode of the "suffering messiah", as proposed by Laura Makarius (though denied by Pelton as provable; see Makarius 1969: 17-24; Pelton 1980: 246-47). This formal similarity should not, however, obscure the great difference that exists in the world orientation between a culture hero as trickster and transformer who does not seem to be able to change the world and its natural laws as designed by a demiurge or sovereign deity and a messiah who aims at radical transformation of world and man with the implied hope for the audience that has faith that this will be accomplished: the difference is between an ideology that permits rebellion and one that aims at revolution.

Might it be also that cultural traditions such as the Indo-Iranian that rely on a clear linguistic division of binary forces shaping the world, with dualism reigning supreme (whether through thought categories or through social organisation), make it so difficult for us to identify mediating tricksters that encompass the world of chaos and through their chaotic actions bring boons to mankind because the major expression of the final resolution of antagonistic forces is brought about by a messianic figure embodying the god-man unit (as we find in Christ, Buddha, and Zoroaster)? This is one of the problems that has plagued Indo-European comparative studies from its inception, so that Dumézil finds the closest analogue to Loki, who has all the attributes of the deceiving and of the body trickster, only among the Ossetes (with Syrdon), though attempts at finding other parallels such as between the Hinduist Siva and the Greek Dionysos have begun to emerge through O'Flaherty's research (1980). Again we find the problem that most tricksters may be mediators (though the mediated opposites might change from culture to culture), but not all mediators may be seen as tricksters, some being messiahs (in the Indo-European tradition the complexity of the problem of *messiah* versus *trickster* has not even come near to any solution, though the early German works on the culture hero speak of *Heilbringer* or "saviours"; the difficulties can be envisaged if I hint at the comparability and dissimilarity of the "saviour" Krishna, in his childhood so similar to Hermes – full of trickster horseplay – and the trickster Loki, who does not save the world but brings about its final destruction).[11]

[10] Giorgio de Santillana and Hertha von Dechend, in *Hamlet's Mill* (1970), trace the motif to Saxo Grammaticus and finally to Amlodhi's quern, with crossreferences to the Finnish trickster of the *Kalevala-Epos*, Kullervo: they alss throw new light on the astronomical meaning of the story of the churning of the ocean of the Puranic literature.

[11] The term *Heilbringer* appears in Paul Ehrenreich's critical appraisal of a book by Kurt Breysig

To these methodological and theoretical strictures under which I pursue the following comparison I would like to add that I do not intend to locate the trickster figure in any particular evolutionary layer of thought formation. It should through this introductory discussion as well as through the following examples be abundantly clear that the distinction between "archaic" and "pro-gressive" cultures is a rather futile one: we can only say that the expression of the paradoxes of life in such multistranded symbolism as that of the trickster-culture hero certainly points to a highly developed form of reflection on cul-ture and nature (either one being understood as rule-governed or not). Despite their laughable aspects, the narrations and actions reported about tricksters clearly place them in the same sacred-secret sphere as the "fools for Christ's sake", which Syrkin has recently elaborated for the Byzantine and Russian Orthodox forms of Christianity (Syrkin 1982). Besides, the trickster figures of the Australian *Dreamtime*, that is, of early hunter-gatherers, are figures as developed and complex as any Greek or Germanic mythical hero.

I also do not share the distinction between folk-religious buffoonery and priestly shamanistic religion, the former then being opposed to the latter, as the very features of many tricksters, as for instance the magical aspects of shape changing and of sexual inversion (as they certainly appear in Wakdjunk-aga, in Loki, in Hermes through Hermaphroditos, and in Dionysos and his Indian counterpart Siva) pertain essentially to shamanistic ritualism (besides the rarely mentioned trait of smithing, which is the trademark not only of Eurasian shamanism but also of the trickster, if one were prepared to prove and corroborate the inclusion of Hephaistos among them).[12]

The dimensions of crooked thinking as well as of the body grotesque are therefore only two formal facets pervading very complex paradoxes of thought and existence. These touch on the sacredness of rules; the breaking of boundaries of social taboos; the mysteries of creation and transformation pow-ers; the destructive forces that become creative and creative urges that turn to dust; the question of freedom and chance (divination or dice playing) versus preordination and the power of natural laws; the quest of hope for a paradise

1905 und 1906, where the trickster character of the culture hero is not noticed; however, early interpretations by Paul Radin, dating from 1914 onward (see 1914: 335-73), are influenced by Ehrenreich's critique; see Radin (1953: 307); this line of influence in the historical perspective of anthropological works on the trickster, which goes from Brinton to Ehrenreich and then back to the United States with Boas and Radin, has been left out in Rickett's appraisal.

[12] The archaism of the trickster is stressed by, among others, Radin 1956; and also by Karl Kerényi in Radin. The opposition of folk and shamanistic religion is also to be found in Radin's "Religion of the North American Indians". The soundest methodological view on the question of the euphemerisation or its opposite, on fallen gods or risen heroes, comes from Dumézil's historical structuralism; in this essay I follow Dumézil's lead to a degree (see Dumézil 1970). The question of shape changing, bisexuality and smithing in relation to shamanism cannot be expanded here (see Koepping 1983). The suggestion for Hephaistos as trickster has been put forward by Karl Kerényi in Radin.

lost and the threat of the conflagration of the world; the eschatological battle brought about by adherence to laws and oaths, which have to be broken, to retain eternal life (for the gods), as shown through the actions forced on the half-god Loki, that trickster-demon of the dark whom the Ases and Vanes need to do their deeds of lawbreaking, whom they, however, refuse to let share in divine drink, who through apparent boons that the gods delight in (and which they do need) usher in the final annihilation of the cosmos. If these are the problems of the pole of highest sacredness, then the trickster belongs here.

On the other pole, that of the purely profane, the battle of deceiving and deception is played out by the classical picaro, who does not fight to transform the world (as do the "foolish" saints) but rather cocks a snook at the society into which he himself wants to enter successfully; he adapts to it by the very tricks he denounces, often finally deceiving himself and half believing that he "has made it", though, being the classical type of a "marginal" character, who conforms, he knows that he really remains outside (see in particular the first classical pieces of the genre, *Lazarillo* and *El Buscon*).[13] He too attempts a "ritual rebellion" but does not succeed in reaching salvation (which the awakened chivalrous hero whom the picaro lampoons by satiric imitation always does reach through following his true unspoiled and unsocialized nature which however – as typical sign of paradox – has to be tamed or "sanctified" after all). The picaro does achieve outer, worldly success, but at the expense of his inner values because the ritual of societal rules defeats human nature, a nature that can only be given free rein during those times that Bataille labelled as times of permitted violation, the time of festivals (Bataille 1957).

### The Crooked Thought of Prometheus

If we take the account of Prometheus first, in the analysis of which the structuralist Vernant has paved the way (Vernant 1980), the story yields from semantic content as well as from lexical word usage a threefold structure that I would summarise as follows.

Prometheus is engaged with Zeus in a battle of wits that he wants to turn to the advantage of mankind, whose advocate he plays. He thus agrees to divide things that are for the gods from those that are for mankind in order to establish some clear boundaries for the exercise of authority over which, as we know, Zeus will finally hold sway and reign supreme. Prometheus divides the sacrificial ox into two heaps. On one he puts the bones, covered by the fat of the animal, on the other he puts all the meat, covered and enclosed by the stomach of the sacrificed beast. While the first heap looks large and appetis-

---

[13] The anonymous novella *Lazarillo de Tormes* was first printed in 1554, and *El Buscon* by Francisco Gomez de Quevedo in 1626.

ing, the second hides the goods under an unpleasant outside. The main deception of Prometheus's form of *metis* of intelligence of resourcefulness (like that of the later Odysseus, who is called *polymeteis*, "one who knows a lot of tricks") lies in the act of gift giving that conceals the truth: the shiny outside hides the truth of the inside.

Zeus, although all knowing (since he is helped by true foresight of everything, by the goddess Metis herself), nevertheless accepts the deal and chooses that which he is expected to choose: the large amount of bones. He becomes angry and withdraws the divine fire from mankind, so that people are threatened with a return to the savagery of animals. In much the same way as the sacrificial parts hid the good under the bad and the bad under the good, so both, Prometheus as well as Zeus, are hiding something beneath their smooth smiles and amiable negotiations. Prometheus is a descendant of those Titans who challenge the sovereignty of Zeus, and Zeus, though having all-knowing foresight, lets himself be cheated, which implies deception on his part.

After this stand-off Prometheus steals the fire, takes what is not given. The gods now reciprocate with a gift for mankind as a return for the first act of giving (and because they are angry about the theft) by devising the woman Pandora. She again hides the truth: on the outside shining and attractive, full of charm she is truly a "belly", like the stomach that the humans chose the first time, a belly that is, as the myth says, always hungry and bitchy. Moreover, Pandora carries with her a jar that hides all evils, like diseases that cannot be seen or heard, and this is the very opposite of the entrancing woman, sweet voiced and endowed with all pleasures. This gift (which Epimetheus was not supposed to accept because Prometheus expected that the gods would reciprocate his first deceitful gift to them by a countergift that was really a poison) bestows on mortal humanity, in spite of its hidden evil, the blessings of civilisation in the form of marriage and procreation.

All the gifts that are bestowed on mankind after the fall, after the separation from the gods, have two aspects: they are pleasant and necessary for life, but they are also unpleasant and difficult to obtain. For example, sacrifice through its very structure enables and re-establishes the lost communication, but communication reasserts the gap that exists because it shows that the gods can live on the inedible fragrance of burned bones, while man needs meat for his stomach. The fire that is necessary to open the communicative channel to the gods has to be tended from sparks (*sperma*, in Greek) that are "hidden" in a fennel stalk. Cereals that grew formerly abundantly and without labour in the lost paradise have to be tended from seeds (*sperma*) that have to be buried ("hidden") in the ground by labour (*ponos*) in the fields, just as women who will ensure procreation have to be plowed like the fields in order to bury a seed (*sperma*) that will germinate.

What is of interest for the present topic is not so much the verbal and lexical equivalence and logic of the threefold steps of the story as the reasoning behind the outcome: the inexorableness seems to stun even the modern listener with the ruthless inescapability of fate, a fate that the Greeks interpreted as expressing the mixed blessing that I outlined above, the pleasant and unpleasant side of the items necessary for civilised life: fire, cereals, marriage, and sacrifice. The Greeks held that since these early times evil was inextricably mixed with good, a view that at least leaves place for man to hope – hope (*elpis*) being the only and last thing that did not escape from the opened jar of Pandora – because man does not have the divine foresight to know how things will turn out.

A central point of the myth is the use of cunning intelligence in the competitive struggle between Zeus and Prometheus: Prometheus employs his wit, but it is an intelligence that likes to gain the upper hand; it is a competitive wit, yet, however hard he struggles to gain a better fate for man with his first apportioning, he cannot escape his own deception, which has been seen through by Zeus. He knows that, by the rules of gift giving (as of sacrifice), the return gift will and must be dangerous. A poisoned gift cannot go unreciprocated, and the inexorable hidden evil takes its toll. The shrouded goods of the sacrificial division are reciprocated by evil enveloped in the charms of Aphrodite and Peitho (the goddesses of erotic charm and verbal persuasion assisting Zeus in fashioning Pandora).

The intelligence of Prometheus is from the start a deceiving one: he intends to work not only for the good of mankind but also for a different purpose: to challenge the sovereignty of the gods. Although Prometheus is the "fore-seeing" one, with foreknowledge (as much as Epimetheus, his *alter ego* is the one who thinks after he has acted, the daft one), his hatred of the gods gets the better of him: his own intelligence deceives him and in turn is deceived. The paradox, which is known as a folk-tale motif as well, has many ramifications, yet the main point seems to me to be the paradigmatic delineation of the eternal trickster and his mind: he is a *deceived deceiver*, a cunning person shown up for what he really is, namely, a fool who should have known better than to try to outwit the gods (or the rules of the game for that matter).

Yet the trickster's paradox extends further: although his deed, which from the start was to benefit mankind, through its hidden intent (the attempt at deceiving the gods) brought evil to mankind (though disguised by charm), this very evil, which is connected with death, labour (in the fields and with women), and diseases, is finally the origin of all civilised, truly human life. The blessings of marriage, cooked food, and religious rituals take man finally and irrevocably out of the state of raw-eating, cannibalistic, promiscuous, non-thinking animality. This is then the paradigmatic character of the trickster: though he wills good, the result might turn out to be evil, yet the hidden evil he wills is reciprocated by unintended blessings. The trickster is the culture hero who, though his cunning intelligence goes awry, mediates between gods and men; his intended actions bring unintended consequences, and vice versa. It is noteworthy that the Greeks use the term *ankylometes* for the intelligence of the trickster, as Kerényi has pointed out. Prometheus uses an intelligence that is knotted like a sling for trapping animals, which implies that the Titans are too smart for their own good, that they possess an intelligence that traps itself in its own snares.[14]

This Greek version of the trickster seems to lay bare the deepest abstract level of the trickster's personality in a solemn epic tone that leaves little space for laughter (the possibility of perceiving in Hermes, in Dionysos, in Hephaistos, and even in Herakles other facets of a split trickster I have to forgo).[15]

*Laughter and the Grotesque Body: Wakdjunkaga*

Other tricksters, the funny foolish prankster, for example, show the same trait of cleverness that defeats itself while still being funny. Before tracing some of the paradoxes of cunning intelligence within the serious fool who speaks the hidden truth in modern drama, I want briefly to introduce the laughable fool who is also the culture hero: Wakdjunkaga of the Winnebagos is a person who starts with a number of pranks that are connected with his initially lacking awareness of his body. His left and right hand fight over a killed beast (Radin 1956, episode 5); he then orders his anus to watch over another killed prey (episodes 13 and 14). When the anus is deceived by the thieving fox, he burns his own anus as punishment and then eats his own intestines, which have fallen out on the road. One day, when he awakes, he sees his blanket floating above him and wonders what is happening, then realises that his penis is holding it up. He wraps the overly long genital up and carries it in a box over his shoulder (episode 14), uses it to have intercourse with a chief's daughter, and finally loses it to the jaws of a chipmunk who reduces it to normal size. Eventually he fathers a family, but before that he is uncaring and unknowing, inad-

---

[14] See Kerényi's 1959, where he elaborates also the notion that Prometheus and Epimetheus are two sides of the one personality and thus anticipates much of the wisdom-folly argument.

[15] The aspect of the seriousness of myths and epics has also been noted by Dumézil for the Indian materials (see Dumézil 1924) as contrasted to the German myths. The question of the diverse trickster culture heroes of Greece would have to include not only the mentioned characters but alos the repetition of the Promethean deed by a cannibalistic sacrificial meal through Tantalos. If one takes the culture hero as boon bringer for man as given, the question arises whether the female culture heroes like Pandora or Demeter should be included in the quest for the trickster; I judge the potential for finding in the Demeter-Baubo mythologem a tickster-like constellation great, as I have recently shown in a critique of the Baubo interpretation by Devereux (see K.-P. Koepping 1984; ct. Devereux 1981). The problem of the intelligence of Zeus and of *metis* in Greek thought, as shown to be possessed by deities of the crafts, like Athena and Hephaistos, would need to be assessed in the light of the trickster problem as well (ct. Détienne & Vernant 1978).

vertently killing other people's children, indeed, even changing his sexuality, marrying a chief's son and giving birth to three children. He flouts all religious and social conventions, breaks every possible taboo, and creates havoc by not being able to control his sphincter muscle, having eaten a laxative bulb: the world is almost choked by his excrement (episodes 23 and 24). Many of these phantasmagoric deeds of Wakdjunkaga remind us, as Radin rightly remarked, of the great satire and buffoonery of Rabelais's characters (Radin 1956: 138). The crucial point of the whole trickster cycle of the Winnebagos, which excited Karl Kerényi as much as it did Carl Gustav Jung, is its developmental aspect: Wakdjunkaga grows from, as Radin puts it, a purely "undifferentiated and instinctual" being to maturity, and in the course of his physiological and mental maturation, his gaining of self-awareness, he becomes the bringer of culture (Ibid.: 133). First he introduces the domesticated food plants (growing from the bitten off pieces of his penis; episodes 38 and 39), later the Medicine Rituals (episodes 41-43 and 47-48 ).[16]

To show his mental awakening, and the absurdity as well as paradoxicality of language and knowledge about the self, I single out two episodes: in episode 11, Wakdjunkaga, after having been frightened out of his wits and almost having died, shouts, "That such a thing should happen to Wakdjunkaga, the warrior! Why, I almost came to grief." Besides conveying the pedagogical message to the audience, which Radin refers to, this scene shows the culture-bound incidence of fright leading to consciousness, common to Winnebago symbolism. After a further stupid action, mistaking a tree stump for a man pointing at him, he exclaims, "Yes, indeed it is on this account that the people call me Wakdjunkaga, the foolish one. They are right." After having burned his anus, he explains, "Ouch. This is too much. ... Is it not for such things that I am called Wakdjunkaga? Indeed, they have talked me into doing this, just as if I had been doing something wrong." After he has eaten his intestines, he

---

[16] I follow here Radin's interpretation of maturing from undifferentiated to responsible, though critics have pointed out that actually Wakdjunkaga regresses from a chief to a simpleton; (see Layard 1957: 106-11). In the line of my argument, the "regression", i.e. the giving up of social responsibility by a war chief as well as the parting of company of men, could also be interpreted as the heroic act of antihero, an imitation parallel to that of the picaro, who imitates the medieval knight-errant. Without psychologising the trickster, I would at least like to entertain the idea that he has to part the company of societal life in order to fight the battle for a transformation of the cosmic order. On the other hand, he imitates also important stages of initiation, by going into the dangerous state of liminality, being closer to animals than gods, a reversal to the "natural state" from which he has to emerge again. In the same way, initiands, male as well as female, have to "experience nature" in order to become fully social beings again: typical are, for instance, the women's rituals of the *Thesmorphoria* in Greece in honor of Demeter (see Burkert 1977; Détienne 1977). The analogy is very close if one follows the states and methods of awakening as well: suffering and pain bring on the reflective awareness of being "the supid one", a formal element that accompanies not only the trickster as well as the picaro (at least very typically in *Lazarillo*, whose head is pushed hard against a stone) but also the suffering of every initiand, in particular of priests and shamans. In spirit, Radin seems closer than Layard to the formal principles of the narration.

reiterates, "Correctly indeed am I named Wakdjunkaga, the foolish one. By being called this I have actually been turned into a Wakdjunkaga, a foolish one" (Radin 1956: 18; 135).

### The Dialectic of Wisdom and Folly

We can readily recognise that this character relates closely to the medieval and early modern novel of fools in German tradition: *Simplicius Simplicissimus* develops from a country dolt through hard experiences during the Thirty Years' War. He realises that the world is terrible and vicious and becomes a hermit. Though Simplicius is as much coloured by Christian thinking about stupidity and wisdom as the main figure of the Roman de Romance, the chivalrous fool Parcival, as both exhibit similar physical and psychic development after immersion in the sinful world, wherein they committed the most atrocious crimes against humanity (men as well as women). The difference between Winnebago and Christian fools is that Christian thinking sees stupidity not as true innocence (about which one can joyfully laugh) but as an indication of guilt and sinfulness, of man's fall from grace; stupidity was seen as impeded mental faculty that was due to and a sign of being far from God: daftness was not an inborn trait but was wilfully acquired and therefore evil and sinful. In this respect there has been a change between the Middle Ages and the early modern time in so far as it is now not stupidity that is sinful but sin itself that is seen as stupidity. This idea that sin was foolishness and reducible to a defect of the mind is the innovation of the post-Reformation novels (Konnecker 1966: 15ff.).

Yet to return to the similarities of Parcival and post-Reformation literature of the "ship of fools" genre to the mythological trickster of the Winnebago, it is noteworthy that the Christian dumb hero Parcival is foolish because he adheres to the letter of the law, in this case the code of chivalry. Just as we still admonish children with the saying, Do not speak until you are spoken to, Parcival actually "sins" by following this precept too closely and not asking, even when human pity moves him. That is, in terms of the Promethean problem of knowledge, he hides his human knowledge, his natural compassion, behind the screen of politeness driven to an absurd extreme. The fools of the post-Reformation period, by contrast, show more of a pedagogical interest in mirroring the world as bad and anybody who follows worldly pursuits as a fool, with the result that any person who renounces the world, though he might be considered a fool in general, becomes the wise one. Most of these stories are informed by the image of Christ the fool as well as by the logical impenetrability of the story of the Fall of Man, for the interpretation of which in this context I would agree with Eco, who said:

"Adam has arrived at a comprehension of the system at the very moment in which he is calling the system into question and therefore destroying it. Just as he comes to understand the rigid generative law of the code which had governed him, so he realises that there is technically nothing to stop him from proposing a new code. ... While bent on destroying the system, he comprehends its full range of possibilities and discovers that he is master of it" (Eco 1973: 173).

Indeed, the problem with *stultitia* and *sapientia* is that in innocence man is depicted as "daft", while with knowledge he becomes sinful. He cannot escape the dilemma, a dilemma made more difficult when the Renaissance made the search for knowledge the prime distinction man from animals while at the same time declaring that this very search is foolish. With this, the distinction between fools and wise men becomes reversible at any turn.

The complexity of the relationship between natural wisdom and status position in the world is another point that shows the dilemma of early modern man. This conflict is exemplarily dealt with in the so-called *Lalebuch* of 1597 in which wise men (who had been advisers to kings) are founding a utopian kingdom, playing at being peasants, which in itself is a contradiction between inner nature and outer status. In order to heal the breach of order, they think of a way to combine both wisdom and their love of farming; they devise the trick of playing the fools, behind which facade wisdom could be hidden. They are not naturally daft but play consciously at it. While they conceive of the most outrageous things, they actually turn into morons themselves, a state of mind concordant with the status of peasants, so that in the end the rebellious utopia of the preservation of low occupation in combination with high status is turned around, asserting the originally ordained order of things and of social relations.[17]

---

[17] *Lalebuch* (1597; reprint, Stuttgart 1971). It should be noted in passing that a number of picaros are female, as the most celebrated pendant to *Simplicius, Mother Courasche* by Grimmelshausen (see n. 15 above).

## The Paradox of Knowledge

Such contradictions between true nature and surface appearance, between mental state and occupational status, between persona and mask, leads us into the problem of the fool in Shakespeare, where truth lies hidden in foolish persons and utterances while stupidity appears behind the mask of high standing. The lines of the fool in *King Lear* are most telling:

> "I marvel what kin thou and thy daughters are: they'll have me whipped for speaking true, thou'lt have me whipped for lying and sometimes I am whipped for holding my peace. I had rather be any kind o'thing than a fool".

As Jan Kott has interpreted it, the fool who recognises himself as a fool in the service of a prince ceases to be a fool. The world is divided between fools and nonfools, knaves and kings. But the philosophy of foolishness rests on the precept that the greatest fool (all of us being fools anyway) is the one who does not know that he is a fool (or that he is human). Therefore the fool has to show the others up as fools (Kott 1980: 166). Hiding and subterfuge are apparent at every turn since truth is hidden behind the mask of a fool: yet the turning of the world upside down is in its absurdity only finished when the fool disappears from the stage, after the king himself has truly become a fool. It is the inversion of Beckett's saying (in *Waiting for Godot*) that, while all are born fools, some remain fools. The fool, however, who has become aware of his position – indeed because he is aware of it, as otherwise he could not play the role – tries to renounce his role. Yet if he did that truly, there would be a really foolish and absurd world left, one of totalitarian negativity, one of dogmatism, without laughter, joy, play, or the potential chance of sanity. As Nietzsche said, "Objections, digressions, gay mistrust, the delight in mockery are signs of health: everything unconditional belongs to pathology" (Nietzsche 1966: 90). When kings are idiots, we have an undifferentiated, mad world. To perceive the world as a stage, as has been done since the Renaissance, since Shakespeare and Calderon, and, further back, since the Stoic philosophers, leaves at least the hope that fools turn out to be sane and wise men to be fools.

At this point we are back to the paradox of the Fall of Adam. A deity who forbids knowledge is absurd, as he wants to keep man at an undifferentiated stage at which classifications, sexuality, and language are unknown. This same deity creates dire punishment when man gains knowledge of differentiation and, through transgression, knows the law, a knowledge with which – if I enlarge on Eco's statement – he can play the game of deconstructing the social and linguistic order by rituals of inversion and rebellion, by negotiation between men and gods and among men, by dadaistic games, by riddles, mockery, and jokes, by profaning the sacred, even by making profanity the ultimate form of sacrality. As Freud observed, "By the help of the symbol of negation, the thinking process frees itself from limitations or repression" (Freud 1950: 5; 182ff.).

*Conclusion: Unruly Nature and Social Rules*

A final point to be discussed is the problem of the use of grotesque body imagery in trickster tales. In Wakdjunkaga we easily recognise the themes of the trickster-creator and hero who transgresses. Among the Winnebagos he commits incest, and his sexual organ is of huge dimensions; among Australian Aborigines the creator-heroes also have genitals that are too long and drag on the ground (Berndt 1951). The transgressions are described as images of over-functioning of the bodily orifices: Wakdjunkaga puts excrement on the world (a parallel exists in Australia as well) (Buchler 1978), and both Wakdjunkaga and the trickster of the African Zande, Ture, violate the greatest taboos, those of sexuality and religion (Evans-Pritchard 1965b). The imagery and the deeds, in spite of cultural differences as to what particular kind of taboo exists, seem incredibly repetitive and of a similar kind. Modern forms of Gulliver's encounter with the culture of excrement and of Gargantua and Pantagruel's "impenetrable city-walls" (the vaginas of women) and indeed the very process of extraordinary birth among animals and feces (their mothers possibly being female tricksters as well) are well-known devices that show the modern grotesque satire as a distant cousin of the trickster myths of old.

As Michail Bakhtin remarked, "The themes of cursing and of laughter are almost exclusively a subject of the grotesqueness of the body" (Bakhtin 1969: 26). Bakhtin interprets the use of what he considers a universal theme in a way similar to that taken by Freud: it is the victory of laughter over the severity and seriousness of taboos, thus the victory over fear, especially over moral anxiety, and therefore it is an affirmation of man's freedom (Ibid.: 35). There can be little doubt that such images express social protest through the use of body imagery. As Mary Douglas has shown, many societies perceive and conceive of the "social body" [*sic*] as analogous or as equivalent to the physical body: caste pollution is so framed, as are transgressions from within and without. There is the metaphor of germs attacking the body or things that leave the body and thus as "dirt" contaminate the environment, social and natural, cultural and political, thereby erasing the clear boundaries between inside and outside (Douglas 1966: 208). In the same way we use metaphors like "heaping shit on somebody" for derision and mockery in social interaction (as do Australian Aborigines when they refer to old women who are permitted to joke sexually and otherwise with young men). I would therefore tentatively suggest that the inflated use of body images, in particular of emissions from the diverse orifices, reflects our understanding of the irrepressible forces of nature, of those somatic processes that are the most difficult to contain and control through rules, and whose infringement is therefore in most societies a central focus for taboos and harsh punishment, toilet training being an obvious point.

We realise that we cannot by custom control the very processes themselves, for they are, as we might say, automatic, involuntary, beyond control of the mind, a universe separated from the thought processes. We can dress the body, we can physically separate the toilets, we can constrain sexual life through marriage rules, and we can devise table manners, but we cannot deny the urges, we can merely channel them. To put it more bluntly, we can do little about the noises, the stench, and the outpouring of effluvia. What better image then is available to show transgression, rebellion, the *mundus inversus*, but that based on metaphors taken from the most uncontrollable element of human existence? The question remains, Why does this appear to us as ridiculous, as laughable? Perhaps we are really laughing not about the body but rather about its unruliness while at the same time delighting in it. We laugh about the fabricated rules of social life that attempt to bring this unruliness under control. We can interpret the woodblock print of Till Eulenspiegel's first prank in two ways. His first act is to bare his ass to the world when riding behind his father on a horse. Maybe he wanted to tell the world, I shit on You. Or does he want to say, This is what you are?

To sum up, the intellectual Greek trickster Prometheus shows us the operation of thoughts that hide deceit under the surface of smiling negotiation, and the earthy body trickster shows us the hidden dimension of the naked orifices under the clothing of civilised and rule-governed life. Both reveal a hidden truth, and truth might be a cruel joke. But by laughing about the cruelty (the absurdity) of natural and divine laws, man has truly reflected on them, and the reflection frees, as Gadamer put it, because it makes us free from that which, if not seen through, would oppress us (Gadamer 1975: 296).

I do not want to imply that the games of reflection played on the metaphoric level of tricksters and picaros would get rid of true oppression. The very absurdity of these figures is contained in the paradox of attempts to overthrow an order that not only becomes transparent through the attempt itself but also seems irreversible, which every audience attending this spectacle knows in advance. But then there always existed and continues to exist the possibility of turning the metaphor into actuality, as did the cynics like Diogenes with their philosophy of the body, thus pointing to the absurdity of pure philosophical speculation. This cynical impulse, as Sloterdijk has recently labelled it, always entails the hope and potential of turning a mental or ritual game of rebellion into a true personal, social, and semantic revolution (Sloterdijk 1983).

# TRANSGRESSING BOUNDARIES

# Satire: Anthropologists as Tricksters

*"My young friends, you should learn foremost the art of this worldly consolation – you should learn to laugh ... Laughter is sacred said Zarathustra, the Dionysian Trickster."(Nietzsche)*

## Forms of Laughter

Laughter and humour seem rare virtues among anthropologists. Perhaps they are laughed about in the halls of academe or by readers of their treatises, and certainly some anthropological self-revelations indicate that informants often laugh about the stranger in their midst, yet, given that the majority of readers of ethnographic texts are themselves anthropologists, we rarely hear the joke. True, some intraprofessional jesters ridicule other practitioners in writing and in public, but generally exclude themselves, for theirs is the laughter of vengence. Australian academic audiences were treated to such a display by the new guru of a millenarian cult (to borrow Jarvie's, 1988, apt phrase for the anthropological profession) of deconstruction/destruction, Clifford Geertz, when he presented the ancestors of fieldwork anthropology, Evans-Pritchard and Firth, Malinowski and Lévi-Strauss, in such a way that the non-anthropological audience roared with delight at the debunking of sacred figures; yet the magister's thick brushstrokes left himself untarnished, even though a dash of tint could have redeemed the performance by making the clownerie a conspiracy between speaker and audience which recognises itself in the deeds of the fool.

It is this particular form of laughter which is missing in anthropological discussions about its own history and its goals, that sacred laughter of Nietzsche which reconciles that perfect communication with others with the much needed distance to our own idiocies.

Our field though has certainly in North America, if not everywhere, a streak of messianic conversion built into its rhetoric of the relativity and uniqueness of cultures; the very phrase "science of mankind" in all its universality and totality implies that hubris which, if taken seriously, should lead to incredulous laughter. We are almost by definition more serious than humorous, for missionaries do not like to joke about themselves to others. However, if we take Dionysos the trickster as our metaphor, the messianic impulse itself contains a source of laughter par excellence: when Pentheus ignores the demands of the new god, his body is torn asunder, and the god stands laughing on the roof – but I am jumping ahead here, for Dionysos and his tricksterhood must wait a while. Whether we recognise any affinity with that particular trickster image must be left to the imagination and self-reflection of my colleagues.

*Dilemma of Anthropology? Whose Dilemma?*
*A Note on Disembodied Texts*

The anthropological vocation is painstakingly described by those whose shoulders sag under the seriousness of the business: anthropologists live with a "dilemma" or "predicament" even overshadowed by a "crisis" which may end in our unmourned demise.

While these writers correctly identify the source of the dilemma in the mongrel provenance of the method of participant observation, they end up talking about textual practices and the "scratching of other pens" (so Clifford's 1988: 24ff.), thus dismembering the mongrel as they emphasise product not process and, smoothly forgetting the participation of the body, lean on the crutches of the minds (and experiences) of others. This creates the fog of a meta-discourse which seems to bury Otherness ever deeper in the recesses of footnotes. Neither Dogon, Trobriander, nor Tikopian speak forth from the page as its hero, for instead we have the self-referential circus of a mutually adulating "salon" as the panoply of the world is reduced to a puny flight-corridor in the United States between Princeton and Rice (except that the center of attention are not anymore learned ladies of the 18th century who bathed in morning robes in the adulation of the savants like Rousseau).

These (unacknowledged) trickster qualities in the new authorities of detexting have been cogently criticised by Sangren: "the assertion that among prominent intellectuals Lévi-Strauss and Derrida are the textual stylists most 'pleasurable to read' and lacking in 'pedantic labouredness' is not only amusing but also the rhetoric of power; it communicates the message that what most readers find difficult the writer finds pleasurable" (Sangren 1988: 408).

While I will refrain from pointing to the logical contradictions inherent in the enterprise of the new "texters", for Sangren has done this sufficiently, I must emphasise that the new authorities in their infinite regress of debunking ("I show you how time-bound EP was": who will show us how time-bound CG is?) hoist themselves on their own petard: the hurt feelings of one author of textuality who is the butt of the attack by Sangren on the "logical insanity"(p. 415) of the self-referential vanguard, "a group of insiders against the wider community of scholars who have inexplicably failed to get the 'new' ..." (p. 409), are rather revealing. Rabinow makes the self-pitying yet self-congratulatory comment about the "momentary visibility and success ... of a few", adding in brackets that "all of whom were hired for their previous ethnographic and theoretical work" (Rabinow 1988: 430).

For him, as for others, "we have been there, therefore we may debunk" or, as we may put it as well, "we are deconstructing our ancestors, but we really are fieldworkers". Is such self-designation enough?

Jarvie has probably put his finger most cogently on this wound by pointing out that "Established and tenured scholars who attack the ancestors are feigning radicalism ...", a group of people whom it suits best as a "bureaucratised academe controlled by the regime of paper" to proclaim their gospel, "the 'deep' insight that what is on paper does not represent the world but is the world, so to study the world all one needs to do is study the paper, the texts, the processes of their production ... The Postmodernists have produced the ultimate argument for armchair anthropology" (Jarvie 1988: 428). The trickery of paper-tigers, indeed!

Yet what is particularly bothersome seems to me to lie in the humourlessness of the new authorities, their preference for extruding more meta-bodies of disembodied literature, rather than letting the body incarnate speak. In this regard, even the reference to the authority of Derrida sounds a bit precocious: if the self-appointed deconstructionists would have read him with understanding they would have realised that he is one of the foremost tricksters who refers to his own writing as a form of grotesque frame, whereby the category of the in-between of grammatology is the space of licence.

They remind us of Munchhausen, trickster Baron, who tries to pull himself up by his own hair for they say that while the barons of the past were all liars, we can tell you the truth, forgetting not only that the Baron-trickster rises ever again in new guise but also that with their statement "all anthropologists before us are liars but we tell the naked truth", they fall into the trap of the Cretan who wants to be taken seriously yet who cannot save his own scalp.

Besides, who wants truth naked? What is it? We can enjoy the exploits of the Baron as we do those of so many tricksters, without having to ask "what does that really mean ..."? Does not all social life rest on lies, on roles as masks of the self? Did not our illustrious ancestor Gluckman point to rumour, hearsay and truth-embroidery as the very oil to smooth the wheels of social interaction? Did not Schuetz point out to us the empirically incontestable fact that we write in typifications, twice removed from "the world out there", based on the common-sense life of people? Why do all known paintings of the Middle Ages and the Renaissance depict truth as female and with a veil, as is the convention also for Venus and of all things sacred? What about Plato's cave-men? Did not Schiller write a poem that indicates the blinding of truth by a veil? Did not Nietzsche say:

"Maybe truth is a woman ... and perhaps her name ... Baubo?"

Debunking the ancestors, telling the truth or our present truth, can be a dangerous business: instead of deconstruction we find destruction, instead of a pinch of humility, a heap of hubris. If truth is a woman (the German-writing Nietzsche would not doubt it), do the deconstructionists not commit rape by her unveiling?

I suggest that it is the negation of the bodily experience which leads to the lack of laughter. But then Nietzsche put truth together with shame and laughter: Baubo makes the weeping Demeter laugh through a shameful act never described clearly until her brutal public exposure by George Devereux. The connection between shame and laughter is seen clearly by Roman poets who considered *pietas*, or reverential shame for the divine, to encompass laughter during festivities. Maybe we cannot or dare not laugh about the postmodernists, and they are unable to laugh about their own folly, because *pietas* is dead. Telling the truth about ancestors is certainly "not done" in refined society. How did Rabinow answer the scholarly attacks against his own authorial status? By stating: "The work in *Writing Culture* is the product of years of discussion and debate among friends, Scientific ... debate does imply civility ..." (1988: 430). Whose civility indeed!

A paraphrase from Nietzsche may put things into perspective again: "Mother, does God see everything? Yes, my child! But mother, that is indecent!"

Transgressions, perhaps. But, the reader will reply, as you are aiming to show us that anthropologists are tricksters, are not tricksters transgressors by definition? True, and we do transgress for we try to tear down boundaries, those between us and others, for example. In trickster-tales either the transgressor reflects, saying "this predicament I do deserve for I did foolishly transgress", or the taleteller leaves it to the audience to acknowledge the fact through their delighted laughter as they ambivalently acknowledge the pleasures of sin. In short, the transgressors laugh about themselves or/and we laugh about them (and us): nor are laughs for the victims.

## A Plea for the Return to the (Language of the) Body

What the excess in detextualization seems to miss is the most important leg on which anthropology has rested in the past, that of the body-experience of participation which, while steered by the mind, provides the authentication for the writing of texts as well as the legitimation for the invasion of privacy, a transgression similar to those of tricksters.

It is this dimension which I want to throw into relief in the present essay by recourse to the metaphor of the trickster, because as ideal types tricksters and anthropologists have a lot in common. The body's solidity encapsulates that which cannot be seen, the mind posits itself only as it is objectified in the body, that fragile, perishable surface covering the non-substantial and non-perishable inside: only through this medium can the mind even grasp and conceptualise the world. Yet detextualisers forget or ignore the body, this source of pleasure and pain and of the mental ability of humour expressed in laughter, as well as the body as boundary against the world which is at the same time the only opening to the world which the mind possesses.

It is deeply disturbing to see recent postmodernists standing speechless and puzzled in front of a "body of writing" by one of the leading fieldworkers of this century, Michel Leiris, in which he describes in meticulous detail his actions and feelings, in particular about his body, while on the French expedition ("mission") to Africa. Thus the presumably sympathetic interpreter Clifford says: "it is incredible that Leiris keeps on writing ... every day the journal's scrupulous entries appear each promising that something will somehow happen and that soon we will see what the relentless series is leading to. We never do" (Clifford 1988:172). Maybe the point which Leiris wants to make is that the bowel movement he describes, or the dream, is both end and integral part of the report on experience: maybe it is (involuntarily) a parody on ethnography as well, not to be dismissed as self-indulgent surrealism: maybe Leiris actually has the guts not to glorify the experience of fieldwork as he eliminates the romantic from the morning shit! Perhaps he was a precursor of Kurt Wolff, who later published as class exercises on phenomenology and anthropological fieldwork the meticulous expression about bodily sensations (see Kurt Wolff's *Surrender and Catch*, 1984).

Can people like Clifford not find the body in the text? One great trickster, Rabelais, did much better by letting his protagonist search for the best arse-wiper: maybe the elusive Don Juan of Castaneda answered our textualists well when he indicated Castaneda's many pages would serve as loo-paper. Power of words versus power of bowel movements? I have little doubt – I hope – where the sympathies of readers will lie: laughter for Rabelais, yawns for textual meta-body emanations.

Let us go back to the beginnings then: participant observation. What creates this much bemoaned dilemma which is clearly a proud badge of honour, judging form the number of publications devoted to it? Another unacknowledged trickery which, when properly deconstructed, or decomposed, may make the reader smirk if not laugh? Is the anthropologist really a masochist by choicc? Why do what seems hopeless to achieve? Utopian transgressions? Principle of hope? Naive self-deception? Or even self-deception as intentional act?

*A Sure Recipe for Cultivating a Split Personality*

Self and Other, nearness and distance, commitment and detachment, are some of the typical opposing terms used to describe the method of participant observation, supposedly still the paramount tool of anthropological work, expressing the split consciousness of the researcher while at the same time asserting the unity of two attitudes where one cannot be accomplished without the other. In order to say something about Otherness, the Self is presupposed at least since Malinowski's and Boas' time and teachings: earlier, Bastian chanced on the metaphor that a rare flower has to be picked by chaste hands, the collecting of ethnographic data being equated with Jacob Grimm's notion on collecting folk tales.

The final aim is declared to be the mediation of two world-views, that of Other's through the words and interpretations of the researcher's Self which has freed itself from its own prejudices (and principles) to the degree that it may communicate the experience of Otherness to the life-world of the Self.

It will not surprise us that the term used for this endeavour to desire participation in oneness while upholding the aim of rational objectivity is taken from the language of religion: "alienation" was first used by Calvin to describe the separation of man from God. What is surprising is the relative silence of anthropologists about the religious roots of their own undertaking, by rarely referring back to the basic dichotomy between mind and body which, according to both philosophy and Christian thought, lies at the roots of alienation.

*Religious Metaphors*

One source for the roots of alienation was given by Plato in his notion of the body as the grave of the soul, which, driven by desire (*eros*), strives to regain the dimly remembered realm of divine ideas. The other source is given by the Christian theme of the fall from grace through the desire for knowledge, which is redeemed by divine intervention. Only through recollection of the religious roots of anthropological thinking may we be able to recover the purpose, not the solution, for the continual search for the meaningfulness of research. The search for truth in objective reality will not do (the 19th century excuse and legitimation), nor will the debunking of ancestors satisfy; in both cases, Otherness hid itself even deeper, and so did the Self, the body of the researcher, who through its interaction with other bodies (and minds) created the image of that Otherness. We should learn more from religious language and from theology: the search for the ultimate Other is legitimate, say most religions, but whether the Other is revealed or not is not guaranteed by the search. The Other may appear if we surrender ourselves but, believe Christians, He too took on the body of man. To what, then, should we surrender to as anthropologists? And in which body will Otherness show itself? Where may redemption be sought?

Another religious image: If Christians believe we are strangers here in this world, with our home elsewhere in paradise, heaven or the body of Christ, and if Christians are, or should always be, as Erasmus of Rotterdam saw it, on the road to the homeland, why do anthropologists make the stranger their emblem? Where is their home? Or does it suit us better to use the secular version of the Christian image, to declare ourselves cosmopolitan citizens of the world, at home everywhere? Does that not imply faith in the utopia, in the paradise of the faithful, in the ultimate homelessness of the rootless individual who has no allegiance to any culture?

Is it this which we have to sacrifice in order to redeem the anthropological terminology: are we supposed to be guides, interpreters, witnesses to Otherness, and then to spread that message here? Are we then really missionaries, as are Christians who are called upon to be witnesses of the wholly (holy) Other and the embodiment in the Flesh of the Word? Who called us to be such witnesses? I think we will not find the answers for this perhaps most European of the humanities, if we cover up the religious roots of our profession: but if we were to acknowledge that this root feeds our search, it would not then be seen as science, but theology and a matter of faith.

## The Metaphor of the Trickster

In order not to impinge on the sensibilities of any particular faith I shall try in roundabout way to consider the anthropologist *via* the metaphor of the trickster, that born deceiver with split mind, divided consciousness and divided loyalty, whose voracious and sensual appetite leads him, despite all his cunning, into constant strife. Some cultures emphasise the grotesqueness of the mental manipulations which through pure logical analysis leads to constant impasse, while other cultures stress more the hilarity of the grotesque, ungainly and gigantic body. European imagination and tradition has made some remarkable contributions to this latter genre, which permeates modern social imagery. Whichever version is stressed, stories about the trickster abound from all times and places, and they are told and retold with great delight, as everybody seems to like them and laugh at them, for while the trickster comes to a disastrous end, he is eternally reborn in new guise. The main trickster characteristic is the one which seems to create the problem of the metaphor: while his deeds and thoughts are laughed about, few seem to laugh with that same happy hope about the anthropologist, least of all anthropologists themselves. Yet they also delight in their body-exploits, and we wonder where the body has been left in anthropological work: we do find as we say a "body of literature" called ethnographies, and a further "body" of secondary literature, of the kind produced here by myself, which is a metabody on the possibility of the method or of the comparative kind called the discourse of ethnology.

But where is the body of the researcher and where do we find the bodies of the researched subject? Barthes once called writing the science of desire and voluptuousness; if this is so the many tractates available on ethnography and on Otherness seem to be rather the results of the need for writing, imposed by a canon of conventions about scientific work, than by lust; instead of the pleasant results which Montaigne finds in Rabelais, we seem to receive the decaying odour of dead bodies or of the death of boredom through seriousness[1]. Whoever dares to write pleasantly for the public is quite suspect, and those who don't write, burn their fieldnotes, or go native incur the scornful wrath of the profession.

I think the only redemption for anthropology lies in the recovering of the dimension of the humorous, of the laughter of the trickster, and to discover in ourselves this source of laughter, admitting, as the Winnebago trickster does at several occasions, the foolishness of our enterprise without ever giving it up.

## Sources of Laughter

Laughter of and about the trickster has two sources; one the grotesque body imagery, in particular the sphere of sexuality, the other the heroic-tragic component. While the *first* is relatively easy to discern in a variety of tales, such as the losing of the penis by the Winnebago trickster or the drowning in piss in the trickster descendants Gargantua and Pantagruel, the *second* form is not as easily unravelled: the cunning trickster Prometheus, as many other Titans, may deceive the gods for some time, but he ends up the deceived one, punished for his impunity and impiety. Having been too slow-witted, he ends up snared in his own logic, nothing but the butt of the jeers of the deities or, as Kerényi (1962: 194) once put it: "before Zeus, the laughing onlooker, the eternal human race plays its eternal human comedy".

The identification of the Titan's slow-wittedness with human character is also given in Greek myths, for from the ashes of destroyed Titans mankind is fashioned, and we have thus inherited their nature. When the gods laugh, they laugh also about our own deceptions, our everlasting play at trying to be

---

[1]  A typical recent publication with an indeed dry meta-discussion on the bodily involvement of researchers in the field see Don Kulick and Margaret Wilson (eds.), *Taboo: Sex, Identity and Erotic Subjectivity in Anthropological Fieldwork*. London 1995.

somebody different from what we truly are, a feint which fails through our betrayal of ourselves. Yet the eternal rebirth of the trickster in ever new stories implies the other side of the message: we should be able to laugh about ourselves.

As Elenore Smith Bowen put it once: "we ourselves are the only ones to see ourselves as what we think we ought to be or what we would like to be thought" (Bowen 1967: 290). By his failure to dupe the gods, Prometheus becomes the ancestor of our present human life with its tragic pain and mortality, its one source of laughter in sexuality, and of immortality in procreation.

This leads us to another facet of the trickster figure: the body, the grotesqueness of which is often connected with the anal and sexual orifices, becomes the paramount locality of rebellion. Starting with the mythical figure of the sacred and secret deeds of the Winnebago trickster or Loki mounted by a stallion, moving on through the demythologised form of the Athenian comedy, to the Medieval plays of the *risus paschalis*, the asses mass and the *charivari*, to the literary figures of the Renaissance with their Rebelaisian derision of authority, we encounter over and over again the expression of anti-authoritarian thought and action through the employment of the bawdy and obscene imagery of the bowels and genitals, often in juxtaposition to sacred imagery. In early myths the relation was direct: what is bawdy and obscene is often most sacred, a dialectic of thought which cannot easily accommodate the sacred-secular opposition.

The myth of Demeter, mourning for her abducted and raped daughter Persephone the eventual queen of the underworld, contains the key episode of Baubo who through her indecent manipulation of her genitals makes Demeter laugh. The message, or at least one message, seems clear: the return of fertility through the liberating gesture of obscenity leading to that laughter which frees the mourner from the constraints of abstention and infertility. In like manner does the goddess Uzume in the Japanese creation myth induce the hiding sun-goddess to peep out of the rock-cave as Uzume is performing an obscene dance in order to ascertain the source of the other gods' uproarious laughter. It is this mythically embodied truth of the sacredness of obscene laughter to which Nietzsche referred in the enigmatic statement about Baubo above.

What seems of interest here in our metaphor of the anthropologist's dilemma goes beyond the pure play of surface and deep structure, of deceiving and being deceived: the trickster is the communicator par excellence, and is often explicitly endowed with this office, as is Hermes. He is a translator, a guide between different worlds and different orders of classification, and the paradox lies in the fact that he himself is the one who tries to break the rules, to muddle the classifications: he intends not merely to straddle boundaries, but totally to erase them by whatever available device. In trying to achieve this, he actually establishes the boundaries in our minds and in eternity though, for example, the sacrificial order of burnt offerings. This paradox becomes even stronger: the very figure which tries to re-create the dimension of chaos, or at least to overturn the established order, becomes the guarantor of that order and the mediator between classes in the order of things.

### The Resemblance between the Trickster and Sacrifice

It is interesting (and fun) to compare these two basic paradoxes: anthropologists declare that the alienation of the researcher is the precondition of the virtue of the hermeneutic guide, the messenger, the bridger of the two worlds. The split personality which becomes the tool of reconciliation, translation and mediation between two worlds of perception and living, as well as between the subjectivity of experience and the objectivity (or at least objectification) of description, puts the anthropologist on par with the figure of the trickster, the chaotic rebel who is also a mediator and guide between different worlds. Put in this context, the second metaphor, that of sacrifice, arises naturally. Prometheus introduced the sacrificial order and became the first sacrificial victim, a self appointed scapegoat, while the anthropologist potentially sacrifices sanity, or at least prejudices, in order to become a hermeneutic guide. Before pursuing these metaphors further, as serious discourse or playful debunking, let us see whether we can recognise foolishness in anthropologists or some hint of their basic trickster nature.

While few anthropologists may see themselves in the forms of tricksters referred to so far, others may see similarities to less amusing more serious tricksters, to those very figures, indeed, which are closest to the notion of sacrifice. Some structural correspondences may therefore be called for.

Prometheus, while a deceiver towards the gods, is only the beginning of a story. He finds his counterpart in one of the twelve Olympians, the stranger in their midst, Dionysos, who institutes another form of sacrifice, of himself, as well as of his double, Pentheus. Those who follow his missionising road and teachings will be possessed and experience the blissful union; those who oppose him will go mad (vide the mother of Pentheus slaying her son). True followers must abandon themselves, being possessed and filled with divinity in order to be united with the wholly Other: self-sacrifice is thus indispensable.

Similarly, the original sacrifice in the Old Testament of a son through his father is repeated in the suffering of Christ in the New Testament, when God sacrifices his son. The followers of Christ are the "fools of God", "filled with a new wine" (the divine spirit); but of course they are not really fools, as they know the truth, while the fools are actually those who laugh and jeer at them in their supposed madness: the divinely inspired are in truth sane, while those who consider themselves sane are the truly mad. A message of and for anthropologists? To what should he surrender?

Nietzsche answered in the Dionysian mode:

> "There exist people who – for lack of experience or due to dumbness – recoil from such phenomena as if from 'popular diseases', in derision or with pity, convinced of their own health: these poor ones! They do not suspect how corpse-like and ghostly the colour of their 'health' really looks, when the glowing life of Dionysian revellers passes them by".

### The Limping Mind

The leading mind of structuralism in anthropology, Lévi-Strauss, at the end of his first foray into the world, comes to the dismal conclusion that there are only two mental attitudes possible in the interplay between Us and Otherness: either we stick to our own culture, and then all others arouse in us no more than ephemeral curiosity, or, he says, we have to give ourselves over to another culture, but then we lose our objective stance forever. This must surprise those who have followed the paragon of structural myth-analysis: that all contradictions and anomies find their resolution through transformations is Lévi-Strauss' credo and he proves it through the analysis of the trickster motif through the four volumes of *Mythologiques*.

Why did he never apply the tool to the basic dichotomy of Us and Them and instead posit an impermeable opposition, why did he not play with the transformations of one into the other in good dialectic spirit?[2] While the answer is not easy, one suggestion fitting the criticism implied in my essay is the overemphasis of the scientific attitude: in order to be able to compare and to classify diverse worlds of meaning, in order to "translate" from one to the other, immersion in Otherness can really only be seen as a fake, Lévi-Strauss seems to imply; and if it were possible, we would have in good faith to throw overboard any aspirations of scientific objectivity. Maybe Lévi-Strauss has seen through the possible deceptions of anthropology, and does not like us to play the trickster in real life. But we should not let him get off this easily! On another occasion he refuses to come down on either side, that of pure ethno-

---

2 Lévi-Strauss overcomes this problem by invoking the structure of language according to the adage "it thinks in me", going back at least to the essays of Lichtenberg (see Koepping 1983, Introduction to the Works of Adolf Bastian who also used this reference). However, he gives it a particular direction by claiming that it does not make any difference whether the myths think through his or the native's mind.

centrism or of alienation, when he admits that as far as politics in his own country is concerned, he cannot take sides, cannot be critical, because he feels like a cripple in his own backyard.

Does this not imply that he had become alienated from his own society through the knowledge of other cultures to the degree that he does not feel ethnocentrically committed, for he does not feel compelled or able to approach his own society with fresh eyes: the anthropologist as speechless individual? Yet we know this is not so, for elsewhere he perceives the intrusions of Western industrialised society into the outside world, the world of the Pacific for instance, as pollutions which we have brought. Is it not then a form of deception, even self-deception, to deplore the contamination of other societies, while not at the same time taking a critical stand towards one of those societies whose politics does contaminate the world?

This attitude is one of a crippled mind indeed, and it may be that the oeuvre of Lévi-Strauss shows his own perception very deeply: the first myth theme upon which he hoists his analysis, is after all Oedipus the "Swollen Footed" whose self-deception has become proverbial.

But this cripple is also part of the "autochtonous" original human being, a fully ethnocentric being with crooked mind who does want to discover the truth about himself, and has a relentless urge toward disaster in order to uncover deception as both victim and perpetrator: deep structure at play? Does Lévi-Strauss the invalid with crippled critical faculties want to say: I, the anthropologist, am a part of the pollution of the world outside?

### *Split Heads*

Before discussing the dialectics of dirt and pollution, let us look at another example of a crooked mind. Clifford Geertz once mockingly asserted that those anthropologists who see the tears in the eyes of their informants when leaving the field may suffer from an inflated sense of their own importance: they deceive themselves. Considering what we know about his own approach to the field, we may entertain some doubts about who is the deceived one here.

It is well known that Geertz treated his informants in a rather cavalier, even magisterial, manner, leading to a break-down of communication with an aspiring informant as poet who wanted to borrow the researcher's promised typewriter. Obviously, no dialogue between two writers was initiated for the communication broke down. Thick description? Maybe, for it is an excellent cover of the meagre heart by the agile mind. CG, as he advertises himself on bookcovers nowadays (the new JR of pop-anthropology or maybe the founder of the Dynasty of self-referential American anthropologists), falls into the trap of what the Romans would have called, that agility of the tongue, which, together with the *gravitas* of ponderous spirit is the opposite of the poetic ideal of *perpetua festivitas*. For the Roman poet, the antidote for gravity was openness to humour and, as the saying goes, whoever has humour is a religious person.

Instead of a Hermes as "leader of souls", we get the pomposity of a thief who covers his tracks with thick brushes. While CG makes audiences laugh about the silliness of previous anthropologists with their romantic notion of finding Otherness, thus playing the devil's advocate from the inside, he is shown up for what he really is: somebody who, never having achieved the dialogical encounter of the heart, must perforce revert to the monologue of the fast tongue.

Maybe a trickster after all: Hephaistos the limping smith was cuckolded by the war god Ares, but got his revenge by catching him in bed with Aphrodite and publicly exposed his own shame as well as the duplicity of Ares to the scornful laughter of the assembled gods. Any message here? After all, the story does not end there: Hephaistos is called upon to assist in the birth of Athena, the fruit of Zeus and Metis the goddess of knowledge, whom he swallowed in an inversion of intercourse: Zeus head is split open as Hephaistos, the limping smith, swings his hammer freeing the infant Athena. The limping trickster as midwife for the fruit of mental abilities, with inverted gender, bodily functions and nature; however, with the cerebral liberated by the hammer, he uses a very appropriate tool, if we follow Nietzsche, to demolish bourgeois bigotry, while the anthropologist seems to find thick description appropriate to paint miniatures on small canvas!

### The Self-Reflective Mind

Since I have used two examples of ethnographers as deceived deceivers who do not reach the level of self-irony through liberating laughter, this being left to those who – like the present author – analyse the meta-play (a dangerous play of deconstruction which so often ends in destructiveness), it may be useful to show two counter-examples.

Michel Leiris commented in the expedition's ethnographic survey:

> "Intense work, to which I give myself with a certain assiduousness, but without an ounce of passion. I'd rather be possessed than study possessed people, have carnal knowledge of a 'zarine', rather than scientifically know all about her. For me, abstract knowledge will never be anything but a second best" (1934: 324).

Leiris was one of the few who saw that dangerous poison which lies behind the demand and aim to publish about lived experience, that which Susan Sontag has called the revenge of the intellect upon art, as each interpretation implies that the original is not good enough: such hermeneutics is not only aggressive but also impious: "From the start, writing this journal, I have struggled against a poison: the idea of publication" (1934: 215). He adds also a melancholic note: "In the year 1933 I returned and had at least destroyed one legend: that of travelling as the possibility of escaping oneself" (1939: 202f.). However, there is an answer to Clifford's question, for Leiris did explain why he eventually produced a text, saying, "I liked very much what Genet told me when we met first: 'I write in order to be loved' – that seems to me of unconditional sincerity". While wishing to embrace the research subject, he ends up yearning to be embraced by the reader: from the impossible to the potential. Segalen put it similarly:

> "Exoticism is not an adjustment; hence not the perfect understanding of what is outside the self, embraced by that self, but the acute and immediate perception of an eternal incomprehensibility" (1987: 60).

I referred previously to the Christian language underlying much of our research procedure and its discourse as an unacknowledged sub-stratum and here we find it expressed clearly in Leiris, with the faint voice of a church-father: "*amor, ut intelligam*".

The other example of the self-reflective mind which looks back on itself and discovers through laughter its own foolish position, comes from Elenore Smith Bowen. In one instance, the fieldworker is confronted with a pantomime by the informants about her pestering queries and writing activities, which culminates in a satire on the whole approach of the white man in Africa; the informants play to her the game of the missionary who talks about that brotherhood of mankind, implied by common descent from Adam and Eve. As soon as the African, fascinated by the discussion of kinship which is one of his own themes of expertise, sits down to engage in deeper discussion the missionary rebukes him for sitting in the presence of superior humanity. Hilarious laughter follows the story.

The implication here is not so much the daring of the writer to show how foolish the anthropological enterprise looks to informants, or even the crypto-message about the researcher's involvement with the imperial powers, but the very fact that they expected the researcher to laugh with them at herself. That one does not expect from strangers, but it is the highest compliment, taking the Other into one's own sphere of affect in a mutual conspiracy borne from love and esteem: in short it is true dialogue.

Bowen clearly perceived the difference between her own shared laughter and that laughter in which she cannot participate, the laughter about the misfortune of others (a pantomime about a blind man), stating: "In an environment in which tragedy is genuine and frequent, laughter is essential to sanity" and later, "These people know the reality and laugh at it. Such laughter has little concern with what is funny. It is often bitter and sometimes a little mad, for it is the laugh under the mask of tragedy, and also the laughter that masks tears. They are the same" (Bowen 1964: 297).

Here then is humour as the art of balancing between self-enjoyment and sympathy for the suffering, a sign of true humanity, since Roman times. As Schlegel wrote:

"Irony contains something of and creates a feeling for the insoluble struggle between the impossibility and at the same time the necessity of complete dialogue. With irony one surpasses one's self" (*Lyceum Fragment* No. 108)[3].

### Trickster-Anthropology as Parody: Conventions of Scientism

The stance of irony may provide us with some answer to the insoluble folly of trying to combine dialogical participation and the search for objectively valid knowledge, but before doing so, examples on the dangers of anthropology's reliance on a scientific status may be in order. The problem seems to be that anthropologists have rarely seen the precariousness of the position which arises when they make the experience of dialogical communication into a scientific tool; incredible follies arise in written work through inattention to the form of authentication of knowledge which can only be achieved through participation, as metaphoric statements out of context become proofs for scientific pronouncements on other people.

It is exactly those conventions which make the anthropologist into a trickster who, as Crapanzano put it, cannot enjoy his alienation by playing the puckish Hermes in our own world, because we lose our critical edge through our recourse to conventions and the "anaesthetizing fashions" such as empiricism and realism (Crapanzano 1987). Let us look at some cases and results of delusions by conventions. We may recognise our own faults in the folly of others, or as La Rochefoucauld said: "Si nous n'avions point de defauts, nous ne prendrions pas tant de plaisir à en remarquer dans les autres" (If we had no faults we would not derive so much pleasure discovering them in others); what puckish delight!

A marvellous example of not understanding the reflective discourse of research subjects and thus declaring them as pre-scientific, is given by Ashley

---

[3] Original source in German: *Friedrich Schlegel, 1794-1806 – Seine Prosaischen Jugendschriften* (ed. J. Minor). Vienna 1882. The Fragment is from 1797. See for translation Szondi 1986: 66.

Montague, who wanted to prove that Australian Aborigines do not know the physiological causation of pregnancy. As proof (!) he cites a woman with mixed blood children of lighter colour than herself, who explained the cause of this as "I have eaten white man's flower". Implying that the woman in question did not know physiological causation suggests that the scientific mind of the researcher is out of balance, for Ashley Montague obviously did not understand the saying as a comment on the social and economic conditions of a dependent society where women pay with their bodies for survival rations. A researcher who can scientise such statements is not only ignorant of context, but one suspects also has not had very close authentic contact with those whose discourse he has been part of. Besides, as the long-standing controversy on virgin birth in anthropological journals has shown, not only was the hypothesis taken seriously, but nobody noticed – until Leach pointed it out – that the discussion mixed two forms of discourse, theology and physiology (for a recent appraisal of the importance of this particular form of "nescience" see Wolfe 1999).

Lest the reader think that only Western scholars have perpetrated such atrocities on mankind, it should be pointed out that similar idiocies have been proposed recently by Japanese scholars who argue from the trickster logic of the following kind: a) foreigners say they cannot understand Japanese people easily; b) Japanese say, no foreigner can understand us, because no outsider has the right "feeling"; c) both are right, because Japanese brains are different from those of other people (and of course superior according to the full panoply of pseudo-science): therefore let's not try to understand one another. Well, the German fascists also had a science (an uncanny mixture of measurements of race, phrenology and ideological metaphors of blood and soil) to prove their racial superiority.

One could satirise these seriously believed forms of nonsense in the way of Andrew Miller (1982), who heaps scorn on such evil drivel. The trouble is only that millions of people buy such books, because they reassure the individual that he is a special, superior being, and serve as an ethnocentric cushion for the paranoid who believe themselves to be persecuted by the world: millions believe such fascist rubbish because it has the trappings of science.

It would be healthy to remember what the grandfather of deconstruction, Lichtenberg, said about the image of mankind in the works of academics, if mankind were to be like that, God would have to be considered mad. Erasmus once put it in an attack on the Stoics: "we do not only leave all human measure, we also build a new deity – a picture of man in marble, dumb and without any human feelings".

*Sacrificial Journeys*

A number of metaphors, stressing the dimension of fieldwork, have previously been used to point to the problems of anthropological work between fieldwork and scientific description. I.M. Lewis likened anthropologists to shamans in their voyage of initiation to other cultures, their obsession in getting into the mode of perception of Others and their exorcism of the object which possessed them through the act of writing texts at their desk (Lewis 1972).

Other metaphors offer themselves from this religious vocabulary, most, even if appropriate in individual cases, making anthropologists' occupation a very serious business: the research endeavour is an act of sacrifice, the anthropologist the scapegoat. Whether by sacrifice is meant the objectivity of the scientific endeavour during the field-encounter with Otherness, or inversely the sacrifice of the chummy dialogical nature of being "one of them", or whether we mean more concretely the sacrifice of one's bodily integrity, is a moot point.

Have conventions of writing ethnography already become so slick that even professionals can be so fooled that they cannot make up their minds whether Casteneda did plagiarise other writers as meta-plagiarist, not the normal plagiarism of all other ethnographers who, bracketing the researcher's self, re-write in their ethnographies the lived experience of others (see the controversy about Castaneda 1971: De Mille 1976; see also Mary Douglas 1975; Koepping 1977c).

It is not quite clear which trickster the anthropologist represents best, or where the trickery really lies: only in our own society? Let us return to the other metaphors for a while: the paradigm of the initiatory journey of the anthropologist has been since Malinowski deeply ingrained in our canon of requirements.

This demand has deprived itself of some of its best potential acolytes by denying people who want to work in libraries the entry to the sacred order of the profession. In the case of Jarvie we might say luckily so, for otherwise one of the earliest critics of anthropology may never have begun work on the epistemology of cargo-cults as a disenchanted anthropologist, showing us another kind of millennarian salvation cult: Oxford at the time of Jarvie's PhD attempts must have been full of little Malinowskis who, like Maurice Freedman, could not envisage anybody not going through the trials and tribulations of fieldwork (see Jarvie 1981). Getting his hands dirty, his liver ruined, or losing his "innocence" would have possibly made of Jarvie another convert to the fraternity, that brotherhood which presides as priestly class over the young initiates and at the same time over the dissemination of knowledge about what the brotherhood of mankind is. The trickery should be apparent: not the subjects in the field decide on the admission to the fraternity of mankind, but the masons at home.

That is a very one-sided understanding of sacrifice. Most theoreticians subscribe to the basic paradigm that one of sacrifice's functions is the opening of channels of communication between the human and the divine whether through burned offerings or through the spilling of blood, that transgression which, according to structural interpretations, shows us our own place in the classification of being: we down here eat meat, they up there need only smoke and ambrosia for immortality.

What channels, we may ask, are opened by the anthropological fieldworker's sacrifice? From practical experience we may answer that the initiate gains access to the sacred robes of the PhD which is a union-card to teach and convert others to the same enterprise: if young adepts can convincingly dupe old codgers into believing they have suffered with and for the humanity of Otherness and convincingly show that they have gained through that suffering the knowledge and right to say something profound about the *conditio humana* in the preordained framework, they have supposedly pleased the gods of the scientific fortress of Anthropodunum, that city of mankind fenced by the canons of scholarly discourse. Whether we please those Others with whom we may indeed have suffered together (in the mud and poverty, the mental and bodily anguish) is not the point in this game whose rules must have been designed by one of the most cunning tricksters imaginable. Is the fortress of anthropological science unconquerable? If we follow the shameless trickster Pantagruel and his fool Panurge there is only one way to make fortresses unconquerable: to raise walls of vaginas. A trickster's invitation to bring the body back to power?

*Power Games and Jesters*

Our "burned offerings", the ethnography, with its smoke-screen of scholarly jargon, are not directed toward the acceptance by the gods of life out there, but to gain admission to the city whose rulers we hope to be ourselves one day, perhaps with a view to repaying our debts to those who have suffered our curiosity and our pestering. In order to be able to do so, the members of the anthropological fraternity have however to get access to the true rulers of the fortress, the political and financial powers that permit us to talk and write about that very humanity to which we all presumably belong. It is here that the catch of conventionalism really shows up: while the experience in the field authenticates us in the eyes of co-conspirators in anthropology, it has to be couched in scientific terms, denying the experiential component when it comes to teaching, writing or grant-grovelling. Anthropologists then end up not sacrificing just themselves or their conscience on the altar of power, but also, and more insidiously, they sacrifice as high priests themselves the experience of the life of others and therewith the authenticity of Otherness itself.

To play the games of power in the courts of the world, the anthropologist may do well to remember the role of that late descendant of the trickster, the court-jester of emperors and kings: he may be permitted to show power up for what it really is, but the rebellious and critical impulse does not permit him to exercise power. He is there to be laughed at, and there can be no doubt that the jeering authorities play this game in the secure knowledge of their power, thus displaying the cynicism of power itself. If we cross this boundary from jester to power-broker, we irrevocably contaminate our own aims: perhaps we should instruct our students of anthropology less in the dangers of the dirt of fieldwork, and more in the dangers of the dirt of the corridors of power.

While we have gained access to power and knowledge in our own world by the sacrifice of the authenticity of Others which legitimises our own authenticity (or that of the alienated meta-frame of ethnography), we negate at the same time our own authenticity by recourse to the conventions of the game of science. It would be healthy to recall the role of the jester. As Kolakowski said, we have enough high priests in academe, but what we lack is the court jester (Kolakowski 1976).

### Hermes as Prototype of Anthropological Trickery?

Given the many variations of tricksters, which is the anthropologist to follow? Crapanzano refers to the image of Hermes, baby and thief, who gains admission to Olympus by reconciling himself with his angry brother Apollo appeasing him through the invention of the lyre, finally becoming the messenger of the Gods and leader of dead souls, the archetypical psychopompos. How close is this metaphor?

Well, we could wax lyrical about the final reconciliation of cunning and thievery which gains a serious office: the anthropologists rob the secrets and sacred knowledge of others, conning the grant-giving authorities into believing that they are the producers of knowledge. Instead of leaving footprints which lead back to the sources, to these Others who told what life was all about, they pretend that the shoes lead back to their own cradle. One trick is performed with the home-fraternity: "look, see how clever I am, I have proved that lineage systems do not operate in New Guinea, I have exposed Malinowski or other deities". Having gained access to Olympus, our luminary can now say to the Others in the second trick: "I really have tried hard to convince my tribe that you are human too (pity the piece is only available on microfiche), so I am really a good translator, bridge builder: I am a hermeneutic (sic) agent, not a spy."

However, trickster metaphors invite many interpretations, and that is the ambiguity of the figure: if we follow the Hermes image, then we have to ask when and where do we become the leader of dead souls? As a good bridge-builder, incorporating, as is now fashionable again, the words of Others into our discourse, we could say "when we lead the dead souls of our informants into Hades". If we reflect and still have a conscience, we may admit that we also lead our own soul upon the same path.

But there is another problem: Hermes invented the lyre: how good a singer is the anthropologist? Well, we can always excuse ourselves by claiming that we are not Apollo, and after all, Hermes did not really become the singer of the gods. Yet if we are asked to sing, we do so with the voice of Others: the epic poetry of the Samoyeds and of the Aranda are now available for English readers, who can sing them loud as they can the Edda of the dead Vikings, as the world resounds with the voices of dead cultures, courtesy of Anthropology Inc.

Since we have long ago declared the death of the author, these texts will resound with the splendour of Otherness and will thus, hopes the sly anthro-pologist-trickster, seduce people in our cultures to yearn for the beauty of this decomposed yet cleansed Otherness. We would then be perfect hermeneuti-cians, for the final interpretation is in the heads of the readers as they make them authentic again.

What a splendid vision! But an ironic one, for which professional has not laughed or become angry as the joke hit home: maybe some lack the insight of the trickster. Self-deconstruction has the will to do what Lichtenberg referred to as thought experiment in the mode of the subjunctive. It is that type of experiment which is, as already Bacon realised, most deficient at academic institutions which insist on the reproduction of received knowledge through adherence to methodological canons. But without such experiment in thinking the potential of utopian thought (that the world could be different, and maybe better, than it is) does not even surface; without such experiments, the is becomes the ought, as Adorno and Horkheimer resoundingly criticised run-of-the-mill academic practice.

### The Vomiting Trickster of Orality

There are not many vomiting tricksters around in the literature: one that comes to mind is the picaresque figure of *Lazarillo de Tormes* by Francisco de

Quevedo who liked to trick his blind master by gorging himself on food, only to be made to regurgitate it when the master pokes his beaky nose (the inverse of the penis) into his throat.

A really good trickster does not vomit: he fills the world with shit, from the right opening of digestion, vomit being the result of indigestion, an "unfinished internal body-cuisine" (see Buchler 1978). The scientific enterprise, though, does a good job at that, for the determining feature of science is discrimination, analytical dissection through classification and concept formation inductively, deductively, or in any combination: to discern, to cut, to dissect being closely related to eliminations, *Ausscheidungen* of the body, *Scheisse*, the German derivatives from the Indo-European root *skei*.

One cannot avoid the notion that many writers nowadays have verbal diarrhoea, and that means that the things which should have been eliminated below, come out through the wrong orifice, improperly digested. The main issue is not that the readers have indigestion, but that professional writers are bad writers and themselves have indigestion, lo and behold, not where indigestion belongs, in the gut, but the head: inversions upon inversions!

What would the fitting answer of the true trickster be to this? "Cut the crap"? Or would he acknowledge with a soft smile his co-conspirators, who are "heaping shit" on the world? The aspiring vomiting deconstructionist should have remembered better the adage of the arch-trickster of modern grammar, Derrida, who once referred to his own work as parody and *collage*, to be carried out "as gaily and scientifically as possible", and should have taken note of his discussion of orality which includes vomit (as disgust) as a key-term of his ontology of the senses. That is gay science indeed, as Nietzsche envisaged it.

What are the objective boons for mankind from anthropological work? Even if all practitioners were to hope that we help intercultural communication in the developing global society, there would be much doubt whether that is really true. Maybe the fertility of our eliminations lies somewhere else. If it is true that through writings we learn more about the author than about the things described, we may come to the liberating insight that anthropological writings unintentionally portray the true sham of deception of the whole field and with that of a large slice of the mental make-up of Western culture.

What exemplary insight into tricksterdom could be gained by applying the image with which Kott illuminates theatre. In reference to Genet's convention that lets white actors play black roles in masks, Kott comes to the conclusion that the best portrayal of whites would be that of black actors putting on white masks (Kott 1965). That is exactly what the minstrel tradition has done, with the result of a persiflage and parody of reality as imagined by white audiences. Are anthropologists playing such a game? Is Malinowski wearing only the white mask under which the true persona is a Trobriander? Or is he through his ethnography only putting on the role of a Trobriander who is really Malinowski?

Does this fit the notion of the sacrificed sacrificer? Or do we end up as fence-sitters between worlds of inversions which we can no longer handle? Let us remember that the most famous fence-sitters in modern history were the witches, the medieval *hagazussa* who were thought to have introduced the other world as contaminating agent into this world. Are anthropologists doing both? If such separate worlds do indeed exist, the fence-sitter has to be careful not to sit there too long lest he lacerate his behind, in true trickster style. Let us pursue the dialectic of pollution to gain an oblique answer to the questions posed.

## The Dialectic of the Rhetoric of Pollution

There are two approaches to gaining knowledge. One says you find knowledge through abstemiousness, through suffering, through restraint, in short through the ascetic idea of cerebral abstraction for which penance and abnegation of the body is the first demand. This ancient image finds its final expression in the modern scientific canon of positivism, empiricism and restricted discussion, the main method of which is still the abnegation of life, laughter, and the body. This is the line which runs from Plato via Hegel to Max Weber: purify yourself so that the mind can rise and the soul re-unite with the divine truth. It shows clearly the close connection between religious zeal and the origins of scientific methodology.

With this picture we regain the notion of the cripple, the limping invalid, and we are entering the dialectic of dirt. Originally the European mind declared the outside world, that of barbarians, savages and monsters as contaminating and dirty. We now continue with this practice in a cunning way, for we have inverted the paradigm and labelled Western civilisation as that which contaminates the world. Not surprisingly this reversal of insight nicely reflects the image of that science which ends at the collar of the neck: the body is denied and ascetically punished, while the mind soars in the realm of pure ideas.

It should be no surprise that Western consciousness has transferred the negation of the body first onto the body of Others, and then upon itself in disgust, as is so well expressed by Lévi-Strauss in his reflection upon his travels.

The roots of anthropology which is often labelled "xenology", go back to curiosity and the search for the uncontaminated outside, the noble savage, for we see that we are contaminated. The parallels to internal European social history are very revealing: Elias has pointed out that the European history of etiquette is one of increasing restrictions of the body through manners, nature being denied and imprisoned through the corsets of clothing codes and hidden eliminatory practices, with tools for eating instead of body-appendages.

But history is cunning, as Hegel would have put it, for the outside brings that very pollution which we have banished back through other doors, one being the anthropological import of exotic ways of life. Another way is the intrusion of the dirt through the dirty joke: hygiene in outer appearances and the well-oiled machinery of public life hides the truth of a crooked mind which enjoys the pleasures of the body in foreign places (such as sex-tourism).

If we believe that cleanliness is next to godliness, we declare the outside unclean and therefore ungodly, the attitude of traditional mission and colonisation ("the civilising mission"). But with that mission to tame the outside, "dirt" penetrated the inside in various forms: anthropological writings have certainly led to a whole trend of alternative life inside "civilised" society (a different form of revenge of the colonised outer world), or to put it more positively, they have contributed to a revival of utopian visions, thus undercutting the very foundations of the ruling paradigm of Western instrumental rationality.

There is hope then for a deception to which the trickster-anthropologist may unbeknownst have contributed: aiming for the pursuit of objective knowledge and classification of the world of mankind has enabled the creativity of chaotic reality of multiple worlds to invade the fortress of science and administration.

The notion of contamination, and everything from the outside as polluting is not unique to Western thought. It has always been the stock-defence of totalitarianism which uses the language of medicine, disease and images of vermin, as the recent events in China show, students being labelled rats to be killed. The vocabulary of pollution, dirt and contamination is always that of power and conservatism (a political party in Germany got into power through its slogan "no experiments", while Lichtenberg considered the French Revolution a political experiment!). It is the language of those who want to fence themselves in against any change, the means of inoculation being modern propaganda.

Anthropologists should therefore be very careful using this vocabulary, or its counterpart of "cleansing": the Greek *katharsis*, applied up to the Classical Age to the effect of staged drama upon the soul of the audience, is nowadays used by political conservatives to disguise purges and persecutions (whether in South-Africa, Iran or China), to "rid the body politic of foreign diseases". It is thus doubtful whether the *kynic*[4] trickster can cope with the cynicism of the language of power. The anthropological trickster's ritual rebellion in the form

---

[4] The spelling is intended following the distinction made by Sloterdijk 1983.

of "denigrating" (blackening, *sic!*) ourselves as polluting agents leads only to the political inertia of which Lévi-Strauss' early melancholic conclusions in *Tristes Tropiques* give evidence. If we do not deny the bodily experience in ourselves, we do not need the expiation of guilt through the rhetoric of pollution and cleansing; as Segalen put it:

> "Those who have transformed the act of the flesh into an act of hygiene have lost everything in the process ..." (1987: 60).

The plea for the recovery and integration of the experiential body in anthropology is not to be misunderstood as the adulation of the ideal of naked beauty, as this would be nothing less than falling into another trap of the aesthetics of fascism, so well analysed by Susan Sontag in her essay on Leni Riefenstahl (e.g. the sacrifice of beauty for victory etc.). What this essay tries to stress is the body of the trickster: unrestrainable, bawdy, dirty, not cleansed and perfect, but grotesque.

The acknowledgment of the dirty and sexually charged body as unrepressed creative vessel has been early emphasised by one of the ancestors of anthropology, Adolf Bastian, who in 1860 castigated the one-sidedness of the cerebral emanations as follows:

> "A normal connection exists between the brain and the genital system, though it is important to recognise that the brain is not always the predominant factor in determining the relationship to the genital nervous system, for a reverse influence is possible ... any deviation ... in either of these two polar systems leads to a battle in the organism ... where these forces (the genital ones) are gradually ... instilled into the brain system, the awakened consciousness will be stirred and reach unbounded heights of fantastic creations of genius" (Bastian 1860, in Koepping 1983: 197ff.).

We in turn do not have to pretend to like outside what we hate inside, as Lévi-Strauss seems to think; this only leads to self-disgust, as a recent fieldworker in Japan has clearly expressed (Moeran 1985: 2). Fieldworkers, having been out there, having intentionally as well as involuntarily shed their prejudices, will also have found out about the boundaries of their tolerance (or their inviolable values). To denigrate everything outside, or to adulate indiscriminately, is not a form of alienation we can afford to embrace, because in this way, we make the Other into devils or deities, and in both instances deny Otherness its humanity. How do we then find a balance? Let us return to the stance of irony.

*The Freedom of the Buffoon and the Power of Irony*

The statement by Friedrich Schlegel that

> "as long as an artist is still inventing and is still inspired, he finds himself in an illiberal state at least with respect to communication" (Fragment 37)

seems to express the dilemma both of the trickster and the anthropologist, torn between the desire to communicate and the preconditions for such communication such as translation and materialisation in the text. There is the need to experience, to act, to live, but also to think at that particular point of time, with a constant reflection about the ultimate aim of the experience. Yet, and this is the nub of the problem, such a stance may negate the very experience as a fountain for reflection, if by distancing the naive sensation of joy, passion or pain is destroyed or even worse, if these are mere illusions for the sake of "information gathering". The only safeguard against such fake experiences is to keep faith with one's own humanity: keeping faith with science, as Burridge suggests, would not help. In other words, we must guard or restrain distancing through our underlying desire for sympathy, tact and empathy with a humanity which we perceive, albeit in strange guise, in the very same naked condition as our own.

Friedrich Schlegel, critic and commentator, saw behind the artistic, creative impulse of Romantic poetry the impulse of the buffoon: he described the inspiring force behind poetry as "divine breath of irony", permeated by "truly transcendental buffoonery" (fragment no. 249). This attitude of what we now more prosaically call participation, observation and communication is not one of effacement of the self or renunciation of one's ego, but rather an "enormous expansion and intensification" (Cassirer 1969 on Herder's notion of sympathetic understanding).

Without these experiential dimensions the critic becomes a hollow wordsmith, and there cannot be a redemption of the analytical attitude without submission to experience in otherness. Just as the trickster gives himself to the insatiable demands of his body, or follows his destiny to another self-inflicted trap because he is "too clever for his own good", his mind being enmeshed in its own "loops" (*ankylometeis*, from *ankylos*, sling), so too is the anthropologist with his "reservatio mentalis" close to poetic irony with its inbuilt buffoonery, not to fool others, but rather to be aware of the precarious vulnerability inherent in the desire to experience the totality of an ethnography.

The researcher, in order not to be enslaved to the surrounding world needs what Schlegel called the paramount dignity of man, that self-restraint through which "we must rise above our own love and be able to destroy in thought that which we adore, otherwise we will lack a feeling for the infinite and with it a feeling for the world" (Schlegel, 1798).

Schlegel refers to the grasp of the "universal" as a state of *hovering* (*Schweben*) and with this he reaches perhaps the most concise description of the freedom of play, that form of play which Caillois referred to as the fourth form or *ilinx*-rapture, possession, participation in ecstasy for which George Bataille used the analogy of eroticism in which boundaries are transgressed, just as they are in blood-sacrifice, in the carneval spirit of blasphemy, or in Leiris, who yearned for bodily union with a *zarina* while still holding his pen to record the vision of these possessed women.

While Schlegel's romantic metaphor of the hovering intellect finds an echo in Karl Mannheim's often misunderstood idea of the "free-floating intelligentsia" (*freischwebende Intelligenz*), its roots go back to Kant who defined this hovering or free-floating as the precondition for the judgement of reason: "voluntarily to preserve one's self in *suspensione judicii*" (Kant 1792 in Kowalewski 1924)[5].

Such free-floating between inspiration/commitment/illiberality and detachment/freedom/communication always, even for Schlegel, depends upon the primacy of the experiential. His 1798 lines, "It is fine and necessary to abandon oneself entirely to the impression produced by a poem ..." precede his demand to rise above our own love (in his essay on Goethes *Wilhelm Meister*). While it may be true that the ironic stance and that of self-irony as a form of self-consciousness may be a rejection of "pure experience", exchanging the negativity of the bound slave for that of the disenchanted analyst such as Max Weber, I do not subscribe to Peter Szondi's melancholic remark that the subject (the isolated man who has become his own object) "cannot overcome the negativity of his situation through an action leading to a reconciliation [of the contingent and the necessary]" (Szondi 1986: 68).

The image of the solitary man maybe misleading here, for the experience of Otherness makes me aware of self, as Schuetz as well as Malinowski saw, though it is true that our method of writing which liberates us from the immediacy of unmediated experiences may be seen as a flight from anxiety through method (as George Devereux, 1967, aptly put it).

Searching for unity in oneness, which is both enemy and source for the reflexive mind, permeates all philosophies based on a dichotomy of mind and body. For Plato, the rational mind together with the anamnetic faculty of the soul and its divinely inspired madness of Eros, was the tool to achieve such reunification. The later renunciation of Eros by the Christian negation of the

---

[5] Compare the early reference by Montaigne to the same attitude: "is it not better to suspend one's judgement?"; see Horkheimer 1971: 96ff., and J.S. Slotkin 1964: 54ff.

body was not complete, for in their yearning, mystics experienced bodily union with the divine, a union sanctioned by the Church fathers, not least because the body was after all the receptacle and dwelling place of God's incarnation.

Embracing otherness may be a difficult and daunting prospect but, as Burridge pointed out, it cannot be understood without recourse to the Christian moral imperative to love one another, which can only come from the self-conscious and articulated perception of our animal nature. Burridge sees the dichotomy with which we grapple as one between knowing and embracing, and while he admits that some of us anthropologists have stuck to knowing, few have not engaged in the dialectic between both (Burridge 1973: 84).

Yet it is perhaps only when the rebellious Promethean spirit can say with Goethe in defiance "here I sit, forming mankind in my image, to suffer, to weep, to revel and to enjoy themselves, without regard to you", and can do this from incomplete inner awareness and self-originated irony, that we can enter into the dialectic.

The trickster's self-consciously ironic insight into the futility of human life and striving (as of his own), is a "nevertheless", an assertion based on a strong faith not in the gods but in the self's ability to bear exposure, ridicule and alienation. It is not the power of hatred but of love which emerges as the foundation, a love which realises that perfection is unobtainable, but still aims for it, as Goethe's Prometheus says: "Did you think I should hate life and flee into deserts only because not all dreams came to fruition?" A recent plea for a Promethean social action is given by Kolakowski who states categorically that true revolutions happen only when the initiators cannot be sure about the success of the challenge: self-ironic insight into the possibility of failure is the definition of the *conditio humana* of the trickster.

May the gods laugh, may the reader laugh about the anthropological attempt to bridge life and write science: no reader laughs about the authentic attempt at experiencing Otherness to find Self, because in the very defiance of the canon of science lies the basis for regained naivety, the divine fool's intoxication with the objects being captured like a child in the play of mimicry by true possession, like the mask wearer who is finally filled with the deity, spirit, ghost.

Denying the authenticity of the experience of being taken over by the object in research inevitably leads to such surprise and suspicion as this comment: "what remains most inexplicable [in Leiris' work] is the strange child-like innocence emerging somehow, each time, after experience" (Clifford 1988: 172). Clearly Clifford does not understand that his insistence on deconstructing a text is a vicarious alienating enterprise for dead knowledge while the process of writing for Leiris is achieving the composition and decomposition of his own identity. Leiris knew that the trip through Africa did not free

him from his self, but he certainly knew that he had to do it, follow his
impulse. It is both inadequate and inappropriate to label Leiris' style as the
inability or unwillingness to "speak without artifice or from the heart"; as
Leiris put it, staying "as eternal prisoner of relevances and laws". Leiris
chooses two ways: dealing with phenomena of possession and of the occult is
one, writing about bowel movements in his expedition diary is the other. Both
are transgressions, the latter being close to the grotesque embroidery of the
frame for the former: the surrealist enhances the strangeness effect of the
Other's spirituality through overly meticulous attention to the Self's body.

    We try to approach the absolute, which reveals itself in the miraculous,
through a reversal of the fames of relevance, and a "condition of intensive
chaos". Schlegel sees both that "Irony is the clear consciousness of eternal
agility, of the infinitely full chaos", and that "Only that confusion out of which
a world can arise is a chaos". As Szondi points out, in raising his chaotic existence to the level of consciousness and living it consciously, Schlegel adopts
an ironic attitude to it. This understanding of the dialectic of irony indeed
raises the problem of the re-evaluation of the paradigm of anthropology, particularly the question of what the final end of research is supposed to be, and
where Otherness ultimately resides (Szondi 1986: 66ff.).


### The Kynic as Philosopher of the Body

Fieldwork, understood as an existential search for what is human in all of us,
including the researcher, does not deny the body. This ideal has been seen and
clearly expressed by a number of writers in philosophy and literary theory: I
am thinking primarily of Nietzsche, the iconoclast, and Bakhtin the analyst of
the modes of carnival as semiotic system. The living philosophy and practice
of this stance goes back to the impulse of the dweller in the tub, the anti-
Socratic Diogenes, whose influence has recently been polemically re-assessed
by Sloterdijk (1983). Anthropologists have so far rarely shown in their writing
any awareness of this dimension into which they fit so perfectly, indeed they
have also rarely shown traces of humour or laughter and irony, the very traces
of the great dog-philosopher.

    It is the attitude to social rules and regulations of etiquette and the control
over the body, which find their mythic representation in tricksters, with a grotesque body imagery, and in the rebellious impulse in jesters, fools and the
carnivalesque cosmos of Rabelais or the ironic scatology of Swift, which are
combined in this early philosopher who "pissed against the wind".

    Diogenes was the paragon of anti-Platonic philosophy: instead of leading
the opponent to a pre-envisaged point of truth through dialogue, and then trapping him in his own logic, the maieutics of Diogenes is one which was to

remain unwritten, for the philosopher as midwife used his body and practical life as both tool and an argument. Diogenes intentionally lived in a barrel and, as it says in the sources, conducted the business of Aphrodite and of Demeter in public, which means that he loved and defecated on the streets with many a high-class Athenian prostitute.

Plato called him the "Socrates gone mad" (*mainoumenos*). The last epithet, meant as devastating judgement, we can only take as the highest compliment from the idealist protagonist: the materialism of the body was given its due.

In all his crassness, Diogenes is not a fanatic, but a comic, a jester, showing the powerful up for what they are, bringing the private into the public.

Some parents still try to diminish the fear of authority in their children: imagine your teachers sitting on the loo! Such body language liberates from the fear of the constraints and shows the constraints up for what they are, like the trickster in the mythical age showed the existence of law through transgression. The message in the Kynic philosophy is less that of the futility of surpassing the boundaries, and more of the resurgence of nature against civilising practice.

The enduring message of the dog-philosopher was never completely suppressed by pure mental idealism, though at times, if we argue from a functional point of view, it was misappropriated by the power-holders who give freedom to temporary rebelliousness and the carneval spirit. This should be seen as cynical masters coming to terms with the natural cheekiness of the kynics: "let the rabble have its day and spend its energies, then we can go ahead with our rule for the rest of the time!"

Diogenes' counter-cosmos found its late expressions in the bodily folk-culture: it is considerably different from satire, in which the laughter is negative and where the writer places himself above the object of his mockery.

### *Anthropology as Joint Folly*

Purely satirical laughter can contaminate the author as well ("dirt sticks"). The laughter we are talking about is participatory and does not distance from humanity: it is a joint folly. Ideally, when anthropologists do fieldwork they are participating in the counter-cosmos of the ribald, the grotesque, the absurd, and while not expected to commit those same obscenities which permeate the figure of the incontinent trickster with his elemental urges, we can at least expect the anthropologist to be committed to the enterprise of Diogenes.

*Firstly*, the participating researcher is a pretty good fool who does not know the way about or the rules of the place and inadvertently commits all kinds of taboo breaches, although where genuine commitment to the place (without subscribing to all its values), is clearly shown, informants will take researchers seriously by involving them in a counter-dialogue: Elenore Bowen's description of the farce the research subjects play to her being a perfect example.

*Secondly*, the returning anthropologist can indeed become the trickster who enjoys his tricks with puckish delight by pointing to the idiocies of our own institutional power-arrangements, by being a gad-fly for the education system, the cheeky jester who does not join the power-game but jeers from the sidelines. It does not matter for this purpose how subjective the accounts of the field-endeavour are, for a new self-awareness about the fads and foibles of our own societal arrangements is created by the journey from the Other to the Self. When Habermas speaks of true dialogue free from domination, I think the field-encounter is at least as good an example as the one he gives about psychoanalysis. We may have to sacrifice the positivist notion of science, but still not be thrown in with novelists.

The writing of ethnography is as creative a process as writing novels, but the point of departure and the authentication of the characters derives from other sources than our own imagination or the encounter of people in our own backyard (though those may be as far from the researcher's mode of life as any foreign culture and therefore often serve a similar cathartic purpose).

This may be seen as the inversion of the Kynic's point, but Kynic philosophy and early Christianity had a lot in common, which was the very point Erasmus in his *Encomium Moriae* (*In Praise of Folly*) wanted to make, as institutionalised Christianity abandoned the kynic attitude, succumbing to the cynicism of corrupt power games. Diogenes, however, made his point with his body, while Christians did it with their hearts; while both renounced the head , it being the seat of true natural insanity, Christians referring to the eating from the tree of knowledge as the first evil deed, and Diogenes depending on his insight into the convolutions of the mental strategies of sophistry.

### *Consolation for the Cerebral Anthropologist*

As consolation to the very cerebral trickster who would like to wallow in the living reality but cannot overcome his own nature, we may look at the limping Lévi-Strauss who at first did not see how he could be a critic of his own society. In his last work, he overcame his oedipal lameness by killing off one of his mental fathers, Freud, and giving psychoanalytic insights back to the Amazonian Indians, having first walked the cosmos of the shitting trickster, from the Birdnest thief to the coyote over the whole American continent (Lévi-Strauss 1988). It is a long way around to origins, but then that is our heritage of believing in the globe-like picture of our world. On a flat earth we would have to think from the centre (ethnocentrically, as all normal people do), travelling up and down on the *axis mundi*, down to the sources of knowledge, where we might lose our eye sight or be taken apart by the smith, or up to where we encounter the blissful *unio mystica* which again renders us speechless.

*Anthropology as Possible Dialogue – From Irony to Love*

So far I have stressed the body as a metaphor for the return to the participatory enterprise of anthropology. However, the body grounds us in experience, in the mode of the carnal and carnevalistic which always has the potential for social undifferentiatedness and human surrender to the world, united by the bond of Bakhtin's "cultic brotherhood". Yet there are other ways of countering the alienation of the mind in the world: the tradition of silence, for example, which goes well with the "cultic brotherhood", despite the fact that it is directed not toward the immediacy of the body or toward surrender with other bodies in carnival spontaneity, but rather toward a totally different Otherness, the Otherness of the sacred. The merging of these two forms comes through the embodiment of the deity, of the Word, in the flesh of the body of mankind, (theologised into the *ecclesia*, the female body of the Church as institution).

One feature which is paramount for the laughter of the body which may not suit the anthropological drive toward communication has not been mentioned: laughter of the body and the carnival cult are modes of forgetting. True dialogue enables the Platonic notion of recollection (*anamnesis*), for it is through social interaction that the soul is stirred to remember its true home of the ideas. Anthropological writing aims for just that: recollection and memory of the encounter as recreated in the ethnography which becomes a sign or pledge of continuity between the discontinuities of researcher and researched. If the encounter is based on the desire (*eros*), on love for the Other, which cannot be enacted without love for the Self, the text can repeat the creative act of the superseding of individualistic alienation.

The anthropologist therefore has to move, if we use Bakhtin's semiology, from *monologue* – with its dead memory and self-circulatory reasoning of everything which is rule-governed – through the *carnival encounter* – with its moments of spontaneity and forgetting driven, perhaps, by curiosity, *eros*, for the magic of the world of people, that magic which Max Weber saw engulfed in bureaucratic structures – in order to arrive at the continuity and memory of the *dialogue* inherent in the written text.

Where anthropology must part with Plato is when the Platonic and later Augustinian philosophy gives the inner word of the monological soul pre-eminence over the outer word, for anthropology needs the Otherness of others, because monologue is pre-conditioned on dialogue, the Intersubjective prior to the Subjective or, as Plessner put it, in order to perceive one's own strangeness, one must "know" Otherness (which does not necessarily imply that one has to like it). Only our texts can suggest whether we have found Otherness in ourselves, and such texts could not be considered "plagiarism" of lived reality, as we rely here on the creative encounter of Self with Otherness in dialogue (ideally free from domination) based on the yearning of Self for exoticism (understood in Leiris' terms) which is reciprocated by possession through the object after surrender to it. We do not have to rely on a representational (nor representative) depiction of reality, but with that claim we have to relinquish the status of replicable science and the traditional understanding of objectivity.

The tradition of *silence* may be appropriate for those who find the mystical union with divinity, the protest mode of Diogenes may be sufficient to liberate us from authoritarian demands and pressures, the trickster may wake in us the awareness of our conventionality, but the ethnographic text of the anthropologist is the culminating communication to both the inside and to the outside, words being double-directed as our ancestor Steinthal noted in 1855 after the insight of Thomas Aquinas: *"vel ad se vel ad alterum"*.

Burridge labelled this the "faith in the rationally objective" which he sees as the antidote to "the inertial human drift toward a viewpoint based wholly on participation and interrelatedness" (Burridge 1973: 12). Yet, I cannot agree with him that we should still be looking for rational objectivity, for I would set the creative text in its place: the writing of ethnography should not degenerate into the mere technology of translation, but must be a creative act. It can only be so if there was true corporeal dialogue before and that indeed means transgression: it thus means the introduction or acceptance of liberating eroticism in anthropology rather than philistine hermeneutics.

The act of surrender to persons, tasks, and objects (Otherness), as symmetrical act to the yearning (curiosity) to know Otherness, is thus absolutely necessary; we need surrender to the chaos of the world rather than to the canons of methodology. If this permeates our texts, we will no longer sit ingloriously on the fence, but slip through the lattice of the multiple forms of lived reality. As a great trickster author, Christian Morgenstern, put it so aptly about fences:

| "Es    war    einmal    ein Lattenzaun, | There once was a fence |
|---|---|
| mit    Zwischenraum, hindurchzuschaun. | with    space    between, through to peek. |

Ein Architekt, der dieses
sah, stand eines Abends
ploetzlich da

Suddenly one evening,
there came an architect,

und      nahm      den
Zwischenraum heraus

who took that space,

und   baute   draus   ein
grosses Haus."

and built a mansion.

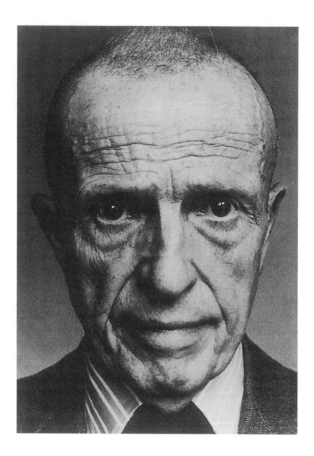

*Figure 14*: Michel Leiris

# Leiris – "Sinister" Aesthetics

*From the turn of the century, European artists have taken "tribal art" pieces,
in particular African sculptures, as inspirational to revolutionise those stylistic conventions that they perceived to be obsolete. The whole movement of
"primitivism" focussed on the exotic forms of tribal art, which were taken out
of their context of creation and usage as well as meaning and imputed with
values considered to be lacking in Western civilisation. Exotic art production
was perceived as being close to the origins of human creativity and a direct
expression of emotive and psychic states. Pieces which were usually used in
their indigenous context in religion and ritual were now re-interpreted
according to European aesthetic needs. In 1937, however, Michel Leiris, who
followed most of the European artistic innovations, approached the corrida,
one of the surviving "primitive" mass spectacles of Europe, in an anthropological spirit. While imbuing it with his own notions of eroticism, he developed in his Tauromachia a genuinely innovative theory of ritual which found
strong resonance in the ideas of other members of the surrealist movement
around the unorthodox "collège de sociologie", such as Georges Bataille and
Roger Caillois. All three concentrated on the idea of ritual as transgressive
mode in relation to the normative social order. Through his analysis of the
corrida as a transgressive ritual that in his opinion combines notions of death
and the erotic, Leiris also developed a particular notion of the aesthetic as
being inherently and necessarily connected to the presence of a "blemish", a
transgressive rupture, an idea which, as this essay argues, has affinities with
the artistic understanding of Picasso as expressed in a number of productions
which culminate in the "Guernica" of the same year (1937). The essay closes
with a tentative connection between the European search for re-invigorating
artistic expressions through a return to the "imagined primitive" and Leiris'
attempt at ethnographic work that puts the researcher's self into focus.*

In 1937 Michel Leiris finished the manuscript of *Miroir de la tauromachie,
précédé de Tauromachies*, for which André Masson had designed illustra-
tions[1]. As so often among the works of Leiris, it is an inextricable mixture of

---

[1] As reference I am using in the following the bilingual edition published by Matthes und Seitz in
1982, which follows the French edition from *Editions fata morgana* of 1980. A criticism of the
presumed misogyny of Leiris has appeared in Torgovnick 1990. The shallowness of Torgovnick's
views and her superficial acquaintance with anthropology as well as with surrealism, not to speak
of her censorious attitude that requires everyone to pursue a politically and morally "correct" line
for which she herself is the judge, has fortunately been challenged by Marjorie Perloff (1995). She

ethnographic observation with highly evocative literary allusions about the pan-human predicament located in the interstices between basic drives and their cultural negotiation. The work therefore provides an excellent example for the discussion of the interplay between ethnography and that European artistic consciousness now labelled "primitivism" or, to put it in a wider context, between the development of an aesthetic theory of modernity in relation to anthropology and the uses to which each field has put the notion of the "primitive". In the widest sense, discussing *Tauromachia* by Leiris, which surprisingly has never been considered as an "ethnographic" text, allows us to relate the often heated discussion about "primitivism" that ensued around the time of the First World War to current concerns about the hybridity of cultures and the problem of innovation through borrowing. It also allows us to consider whether art and art-theory appropriated the "primitive" in the same way as anthropology.

Leiris uses his almost structuralist description of the Spanish bullfight, perceived as a sporting and an artistic activity, yet surpassing both on the level of a dramatic ritual performance, to address the problem of human awareness of, and coping with, death. The measured ceremonialism as well as the bloody excess of the *corrida* serve as metaphors for the game of eroticism. His *Tauromachia* of 1937 is particularly important because it is one of the first works which tentatively set down a new theory of ritual that gained importance in the later publications of other members of the *Collège de Sociologie*. This institution was founded in the same year by people such as Georges Bataille and Roger Caillois as a secession from the circle of surrealists around André Breton.

What are we to make of this project of Leiris? He takes the bullfight of Spain as a paradigm of the "festive" that modern Europe has otherwise forgotten and replaces the artistic search for the "primitive" through recourse to living "survivals" (as the anthropologist Tylor would have called it in the 1880s) in folk-customs. In doing so, is Leiris not following the footsteps of Gauguin who, first in Britanny and then in the South Seas, tried to locate the "paradise" of original creativity? Does Leiris's approach not fit neatly into the surrealist passion for rejuvenating European art-forms for which the *avant-garde* – from the Fauves, Picasso and the members of the German *Brücke* group to the Expressionists – had worked since the turn of the century? They expected this rejuvenation to come from the well-springs of creativity embodied in the art, in particular in the sculptures, of the primitives, as well as that of children and the insane. Did Leiris, just as these surrealists, follow the same lines of reasoning as every "primitivist" movement and make use of that return to the "primitive" as a means to break through the stifling conventionalism of a

thus puts Leiris's work on ethnography in a more appropriate frame which at least gives the reader a chance to locate Leiris in his cultural and publishing environment. A balanced view on Leiris' life in German has been published by Hans Jürgen Heinrichs (1992).

spent, even bankrupt, European idea of art? Does Leiris fall into the trap of their eurocentric obsession with novelty which ignored the meaning of primitive art in its ethnographic or cultural setting? Or is he rather pursuing what James Clifford's critical assessment (1988: 142) of Leiris's autobiographical ethnographies such as *L'Afrique fantôme* (1934) has labelled the inversion of the classical ethnographic research paradigm by targeting his investigations at the Self rather than the Other?

The latter point raises important questions about the ethnographic method and its results. After all, the most widely accepted mode of the ethnographic enterprise follows the participant observation requirements of Malinowski as stated in his seminal work, *Argonauts of the Western Pacific*, of 1922, which aims to describe the lived reality of others as they perceive and interpret it themselves. The final result may be, as Malinowski put it, that "through realising human nature in a shape very distant and foreign to us, we shall have some light shed on our own" (1961: 25). But this is a serendipitous result, while the aim of ethnographic work is "to grasp the native's point of view, his relation to life, to realise his vision of his world", a feat achieved through a plunging "into the life of the natives" (ibid.: 25; 22). Clifford sees Leiris making the Self rather than the Other the target of observation.

In *Phantome L'Afrique* (1934), Leiris sharply questioned certain scientific distinctions between "subjective" and "objective" practices. Why, he wondered, are my own reactions (my dreams, bodily responses, ...) not important parts of the "data" produced by fieldwork? In the *Collège de Sociologie* he glimpsed the possibility of a kind of ethnography, analytically rigorous and poetic, focussed not on the other but on the self, its peculiar system of symbols, rituals, and social topographies (Clifford 1988: 142).

Whether the two approaches are really as far apart as they first seem will be discussed later, after a closer reading of *Tauromachia* has shown how tightly and almost inextricably interwoven the ethnographic and the observations are.

Leiris starts with the observation that in other cultures, rites, games, and festivals are used as a means for people to express their feelings of having briefly achieved a pact with the world through the release of feverish emotionality. Were it not permitted in these forms, this emotionality would be externalised through explosive aggression or utilitarian and rational disguise. Our society, argues Leiris, has no ways of letting these emotional urges run free, so we live out the boredom of a mutilated life, boredom which leads some to be beguiled by the most hideous atrocities (Leiris 1982: 389). So far we have reached but a traditional anthropological analysis of the role of ritual to which any good structural-functionalist, in best Durkheimian tradition, would subscribe.

However, these detailed statements about modernity and its disenchantment (to use Weber's expression) could only be made *after* experiencing and analysing the *corrida*. When writing, however, the separation of influences from a general theoretical preconception and the observed and experienced reality is not easily achieved. Thus, while dissatisfaction with modernity may have been present in Leiris' thinking before, it certainly was the experience of the bullfight in Spain which brought this disenchantment to a focussed awareness through reflexivity ensuing from the opposite impressions of the life normally lived and the life experienced in the altered mode of a "strange" culture. The bullfighting atmosphere may have been just the answer that Leiris was looking for as a "genuine" expression of what was "pre-modern" or missing in "modernity", containing that "immediacy" of the "authentic" which he discovered in the mode of the festive. Festivals in this sense are occasions to which people submit or by which they are taken over, not that mimicked or orchestrated form of organized joy that characterizes many modern, "re-invented" festivities of collective groups in Western European cultures to which much of the "memorial culture" of modernity belongs. This is at least the interpretation indicated by the use of both the terms "transgression" and "festival" in the works of Leiris, Caillois and Bataille. (See also Bataille's review of Roger Caillois's *L'homme et le sacré* [originally 1939]; reprinted in Bataille 1994b: 113-22).[2]

When writing, though, generalisation precedes the ethnographic analysis, which indeed could indicate that in Leiris's thinking the disenchantment with modernity antedates the search for more "genuine" forms of cultural expression. As I shall show, things are not as easy as this. Leiris likens the dramatic scheme of the *corrida* to an antique tragedy, and then deduces an analogy to eroticism from his own understanding. The *corrida* "unveils" those "dark spots" of our nature, holding them up to us like a mirror in objectified prefiguration. More than a sport, the *corrida* is actually an execution, full of danger for the life of the actors. For Leiris, it is loaded with discontinuity and incoherence. On the one hand the bloody sacrifice of a noble creature (the bull as semi-divine) in combination with the spilled blood of the gored horses contrasts with the splendid clothing and attire of the actors. On the other, the artful "toing and froing", the ballet of seduction, the game between intelligence

---

[2] The close connection between Leiris and Bataille is vouchsafed by the recounting of their 1924 meeting in Leiris's accolade following the death of Bataille in 1962. Leiris's homage was published as *De Bataille l'impossible à l'impossible 'Documents"* (1963), originally having the title *Hommage à Georges Batailles*. In it, he sympathises strongly with what he refers to as Bataille's search for the impossible, when the above and the below merge in Dionysian ecstasy, when the distance between the whole and nothingness is eliminated. On the other hand, Bataille had approvingly referred to Caillois's notion of comparing the festival with war, as war gives rise to "monstrous and formless explosions that serve to break up the monotony of normal existence" (quoted from Caillois's French edition of *L'homme et le sacré*, p. 169, Bataille, 1951, in Bataille 1994b: 121).

and brute force that Leiris describes (the reputation of the matador being measured by the skill with which he can entice the bull to follow his choreography) – is tainted through these factors by what he can only call "cheating".

*Tauromachia* is thus a typical example for Leiris of that aesthetic pleasure which only the transgression of rules of orderliness can instill (op. cit.: 77ff.). His analogy to the game of eroticism consists in the playful activity of coming together and detachment between two people, that rhythmic pendulum swing signified by coitus and completed by penetration, which he likens to the thrusting of the sword by the matador. The inversion of the gender of matador and bull that is implied here through recourse to the game of eroticism is clearly indicated and displayed in the accompanying drawings by André Masson (see Fig. 15). The bull is shown as an open vaginal wound into which the horn of the matador is thrusting. The repetitive steps of the matador, the "pases", lead to such giddiness that the antagonists seem to merge, much as in a love game.

In both games, in the *corrida* and in the erotic encounter, Leiris is intrigued by the impossibility of fulfilling the yearning for merger, which implies total communication that only death can bring. Both games entail a "fissure" which he labels the "left" or "sinister" element, without which no true beauty is possible (Leiris 1982: 89-93; 59). Leiris interprets the erotic as the art of consciously taking into account and incorporating the "gauche" (left) element that breaks established normative rules through excess. This places both games, the *corrida* and erotic play, close to the artistic notion of creativity which needs the lucid perception of romantic irony: the impossibility of complete merging leads to the renewal of desire out of despair (op. cit.: 97-9, clearly following the notion of irony by Friedrich Schlegel).

The most intriguing aspects of Leiris's interpretation of the *corrida* and its analogy to the erotic are his notions of the left element, the element of dissonance, of lack, of deficiency, of blemish. Much as only the awareness of death gives life its colour, so does transgression contribute to the beauty of the normative, because it makes the normal into an actively appreciated part, and the normative element in turn is necessary to let the left element of transgression bloom. Thus, transgression is the necessary element in the aesthetic, as much as in the erotic, sphere, where the left is entering either through feelings of Christian guilt or the notion of excess and wasteful squandering (Leiris 1982: 79).

Irrespective of the "ethnographic" nature of the description of the *corrida*, we find here the anticipation of ideas typical of Leiris, in this case concerning the ambivalence of the festive, of the sacred, and of religious ritual. These ideas would later be expressed in a much more systematic and coherent way by Bataille, who dedicated his 1957 work, *L'érotisme*, to Leiris, who had dedicated his *Tauromachia* to Colette Peignot, Bataille's erstwhile companion.

Bataille's long-standing view that violation is a function and meaning of a taboo (which may go back to a remark by Marcel Mauss) was in turn influenced, as he freely acknowledges[3], by lectures delivered by Roger Caillois. Caillois's lectures on "festivals" were given at the Collège and attended by Pierre Klossowski, Alexander Kojève, Walter Benjamin, Bataille and Leiris, and were condensed in Caillois's work, *L'homme et le sacré*, of 1939. As James Clifford cogently pointed out, the orientation of the members of the Collège de Sociologie toward the left-handed sense of the sacred must be seen not so much as an opposition to their teachers of the Durkheim school but rather as an extension of those teachings. While the sacred – that moment when the non-normal erupts into normal life – was of the greatest concern for Durkheim because it established collective solidarity expressed in social order, the members of the Collège concentrated on the "regenerative processes of disorder" found in ritual (Clifford 1988: 141).[4]

While *Tauromachia* remains one of the literary masterpieces of Leiris, it is clear that many of his suggestions about the importance of the intrusion of the left-handed element into ritually controlled performance, of impurity, excess and exuberance have proved seminal for the development of a cross-cultural theory of ritual. This theory takes into account the transgressive as an expected behaviour within the sacred, a theme which was independently developed by British social anthropology in African studies and generalized in the paradigm introduced by Victor Turner in his work of 1969, *The Ritual Process*. Influenced by van Gennep's scheme of ritual stages of 1909, Turner put forward the rites of separation, of liminality and of reincorporation as universal phases in ritual processes. The liminal phase became the main stage in which the world could be turned upside-down, initiates reverted to the stage of nature and pre-birth, obscenities could and must be uttered[5], structure was abolished and the "communitas" of equality and brotherhood ruled (Turner 1969: 95-97).

[3] The acknowledgement can be found in a footnote in the German edition of *L'homme et le sacré* (Der Heilige Eros) of 1979: 61.

[4] It certainly is also suggestive that one of the closest members of the Durkheim-Mauss school, Robert Hertz, had published an eminent work on *Death and the Right Hand* in 1909 (engl. translation see Needham 1960), where the connotations of left and death or pollution and of the correlations of right and the sacred were extensively discussed in a world-wide ethnographic comparison as basic principles of social organization and collective thought. When Leiris uses aspects of the sinister in his work *Tauromachia*, he seems to allude to this concept in a purely metaphorical way. Connotations of the left suggest the awareness as well as the intrusion of dissonance and death in life, or a circumscription of what existential philosophy would label "to be thrown into the world", or existential fear. In fact, Leiris also uses the "sinister" in a non-metaphorical way when he refers to the left-handed use of the muleta, which fools the bull and which is requested by the audience with repeated calls for "La izquierda" (Leiris 1982: 123).

[5] This idea was anticipated by Max Gluckman (1954) through his notions of "rituals of rebellion" and "licence in ritual" and by Evans-Pritchard's functional analysis of prescribed obscenities (1965a/1929).

The idea of transgression within ritual, within the sacred, became the seminal concept of the anthropology of religion, making it possible to make sense of many features of the ritual behaviour of almost all religious systems encountered. Leiris seems to anticipate much of anthropological theorizing now current about rituals and religious festivals which, as I have summarized in other writings, combine two paradoxes. Festivals could be seen to embody the paradox of ceremoniousness and excess on the one hand and of liminality and periodicity on the other. Liminality in this context establishes the interphase lying outside of time and space, while periodicity, in its variations of the continuity or cyclicity of historical awareness, is only established through the very interstices of liminality itself (Koepping 1997b: 1049).

The innovation anticipated in Leiris's work concerns the role of violence, unpredictability and the left element as an indispensable feature of the sacred ritual. This approach contrasts with the one-sided view of ritual as a "culturally constructed system of symbolic communication", a form of communication which, as Tambiah succinctly puts it, is characterized by "conventionality, rigidity, fusions and redundancy" (1985: 128). As Bataille would later express it: "The world of the sacred is that of limited transgressions" (relying on Freud's definition of 1913 in *Totem and Taboo* that "a festival is a permitted, even required excess"). Indeed, there is an interdiction, a taboo, there are boundaries of propriety, there are staged forms of theatrical performative actions, circumscribed minutely; in other words: there is ritual. But there is also within that ritual the indispensable aspect of danger; there is transgression in the form of plunder, violence, mayhem, and that these are "expected" does not negate the notion of transgression. As Caillois was to point out, "these transgressions are still sacrilegious ..." (1950: 151).

*Figure 15*: Drawing by André Masson, 1938 (in
Leiris 1982: 74), © VG Bild-Kunst, Bonn 2001

For Leiris, too, the harmony of contrasts, to use Rudolf Otto's terminology, is the main focus of the *corrida*, where geometrical beauty and aberration, tension and release, come together. The *corrida* is a sacrificial rite within a communal festival which aims at the paroxysm of a ceremonial transgression, symbolized by the execution of the bull, which is followed by de-sacralization and the departure of the deity. Just as sacralization increases during the ritual, so too does the "sinister" element gain in importance. The torero is increasingly in danger of being gored to death, but the death of the bull finally restores order (Leiris 1982: 111ff.). Yet the main emphasis of Leiris's argument lies in the key notion of the liminality of the boundary where the left and right elements meet in suspension ("point de tangence, limité vers laquelle nous tendons mais que, comme le torero, finalement nous evitons ..."; op. cit.: 78). The torero and the bull are only a few centimetres apart, and the *muleta* tricks the animal into coming as close as possible. The audience holds its breath in anticipation of disaster, releasing it only in a great public sigh of relief after a particularly dangerous *pase*, a vocal release which Leiris compares to the ejaculation of sperm (op. cit.: 91).

How ethnographically reliable is this account of the *corrida*? There can be no doubt that the structural elements and the process of the bullfight are meticulously observed and rigorously analysed, but the whole account can also be construed as metaphysical and philosophical musings. These do "make sense" of the whole and of parts of the bullfight, but they seem to arise from Leiris's own questions about modern life and its emptiness. The whole meaning of the *corrida* is informed by the analogy to the game of eroticism which, while accorded the status of the dependent variable, suffuses the entire description and analysis of the bullfight itself. Eroticism here is without any "ethnographic" base other than personal experience.

The thread of Ariadne in the myth of the Minotaur often seems the starting point of the *corrida* analysis, not the end. Moreover, the analogy becomes difficult when the male bull is equated via the thrusting sword (the "penis") with the deflowered or penetrated woman.

Can we get around this apparently intractable problem with the answer given much later by Victor Turner about the "multivalence" of symbolic systems? Or with that given by Aborigines in Australia to the question of how the rainbow-serpent can be both symbol of male generative power as well as of female fecundity or of voracious mothers, which is that in ritual, things are done "the other way around"? Is Leiris's *corrida* analysis merely imaginative or even imaginary male-oriented ethnography? Whose interpretation are we getting? Certainly not that of the actors, the matadors, the spectators, or the average Spaniard. Leiris's whole *corrida* ethnography is part of his quest for the answer to three larger cosmological questions: God as *coincidentia oppositorum* (Nicolaus of Cues; Leiris 1982: 31); pan-human emotional needs and dispositions; and the basis of aesthetic judgements on beauty.

Let us consider the last point. There is enough evidence in *Tauromachia* to make it more than a simple ascription of aesthetisation which indeed may have informed many other non-ethnographic artists and authors of the same time. There is indeed evidence that Leiris's interpretation is not so far off the mark either in regard to the perception of the bullfight by Spaniards, or in regard to the mythological and ritual complex that may once have permeated the whole Mediterranean area.

The latter conclusion can be made judging from such divergent images as the elopement of Europa and her seduction by Zeus as a white bull, the vase-paintings of Knossos showing young men and women somersaulting over the horns of bulls, the myth connecting the bull of Poseidon with Pasiphae, as well as their offspring the Minotaur with Ariadne. Ariadne was once consort to Dionysos, whose bull-epiphanies and general traits as sacrificed deity may come closest to the meaning-complex of the *corrida*, Dionysos being invoked by the sixteen matrons of the city of Elea: "come, Dionysos, into the temple ... rush in with the steer's hoof" (cited in Détienne 1995/1986: 105).

As far as "inversions" within the same ritual frame are concerned, we do find cross-culturally the common feature of the transformation of one role into its opposite, in which the hunter becomes the hunted. An example is the famous story of the goddess Artemis being voyeuristically observed by Actaeon, who is transformed into a stag that is hunted down and torn apart by the dogs of the goddess. (The tearing apart of Pentheus is another of the many examples that structuralists love to analyse.)

It is this very notion of the change of subject and object, or rather from active agency to passionate suffering, in a narrative or performance which gives the framework of tragedy as well as of ritual its flavour. This flavour is what Leiris calls a "left" turn, and it provides power for reflection as well as cathartic shock. It is the very ambiguity of roles, the danger of their being inverted, and the paradox entailed by such roles which gives them the power of transformation, as can be seen in the figures of the "wise fool" or the trick-ster as "sacred fool" or the "suffering redeemer".

What Leiris's essay points to is the notion not of opposition, but of com-plementarity of opposites within a categorical unit such as the *corrida*. As far as the connotations between the bull and Spanish self-perception are con-cerned, Leiris's suggestions may not be so far removed from the lived reality of the bull as symbolic icon for "Spanishness" and/or the Spanish male. For this we can turn to that other great *aficionado* of bulls, Picasso. In the same year when Leiris finished his manuscript, Picasso chose the *Guernica* as his painting for the Spanish (Republican) pavilion at the Paris World Exposition of 1937. Besides the gored horse from the entrails of which Pegasus is born, the most prominent feature of this picture is the bull. Despite the then current interpretations, ranging from "Spanish totem" to "symbol of violence", from "representation of fertility" to "symbol of fascism"[6], Picasso's *Guernica* can only be interpreted, as so many of Picasso's iconic pictures, in relation to his own perception of his role as artist.

Picasso's interest in the ethnographic exhibits in the Trocadero, in particular the sculptures of *"l'art nègre"*, was negligible as far as those exhibits' ethnographic content, context or meaning were concerned. Instead, he used the examples merely as pointers for his search for new forms of expression in modern art. Yet his image of the bull seems to point in the direction of Leiris's interpretation of a closely felt connection between the ethnic icon and the artist's understanding of his own Spanish "descent", as well as his role as male artist *vis-à-vis* the female model. Concerning the bull as an identity icon for Spain, we have the quote from the unpublished manuscripts of Picasso which reads "the beautiful steer who gave birth to me, the steer adorned with jasmine"[7]. This approach makes sense of the variations on the theme of the Minotaur which Picasso repeatedly juxtaposed and substituted for his own person as artist in his many "painter-model-relationship" images from at least 1926. As Spies has perceptively pointed out, Picasso often transforms the *atelier* into the *agora*, the festival, the bacchanal and in particular the *arena* of the *corrida*, using the paint-brush and palette like a matador uses his *muleta* and sword (1988: 110). In particular the 1927 etching for Balzac's *Chef d'oeuvre inconnu*, which replaces the painter with the bull and the model with the horse (before it is gored in the fight) is a clear pointer to Picasso's perception of the atelier as equivalent to the ritual space of *Tauromachia*. As Spies remarks, the theme of challenge and destruction is the key for the second reading, which relates the artistic ritual and the rules of the atelier (taken as rules of the erotic game), to those governing the ritual of the *corrida* (op. cit.: 108).

But what are we to make of the following observation by Leiris in *Tauromachia*: "The capas are robes which have been ripped off the Maenads (who nakedly scream elsewhere) and dipped in wine" (Leiris 1982: 17)? For "empirical" evidence we may turn to a classicist and structuralist who has devoted his entire *oeuvre* to problems of Dionysian epiphanies, sacrifices and symbolic interpretations. Détienne defines the power of Dionysos in a threefold manner. Dionysos is carried in processions as phallos, and he is the deity who makes the Maenads jump as well as the wine foam.

---

[6] A particular misreading by Anglo-Saxon authors which Leiris and Spanish authors tried to correct by referring to the bull as a symbol of steadfastness: see Spies (1988: 92-94) for other examples of socio-political and folk-psychological readings.

[7] May 4, 1936, quoted in Spies (1988: 94) as evidence against establishing too readily a narrative causal link between *Guernica* and the historical destruction of the city by German bombs.

His power is the power of the heart, of the foetus, of the growth of nature and the cycle of the seasons and of life, and it is he who makes organs, especially the heart and penis, pulsate autonomously without the intervention of the intellect. When rejected, Dionysos uses his power to delude people, as reported in the tragedy of Euripides, the *Bacchae*, where Pentheus (also the double of Dionysos) is made to spy on his mother dancing with other Maenads in the forest. Being discovered, he is ripped apart alive by her, for she is deluded by the god into believing that she was ripping apart an animal.[8]

Wine, blood, sacrifice, death and fertility, madness and the return to nature for womanhood, phallic public processions and intoxicating rituals, dancing steps and the bull iconography, the god who is slaughtered and cooked by the Titans to be reborn from the thigh of Zeus: all these represent solid evidence for Leiris's ethnographic interpretation of the bullfight.

Judging from his style of argument in his other ethnographic works, apparent in his meticulous observations about theatrical aspects of possession cults in Ethiopia, Leiris would not have been averse to using such supporting evidence for his ethnographic credentials. However, a pure empiricist or inductive approach to the observed reality was not his major method for finding the structure of meaning in events and social processes. "Realism" for Leiris is a most suspect category as is a logical "hypertrophy" because both lead to an unnecessary split of our self (1982: 36). He tends rather to see events like the bullfight as privileged occasions which give us the illusion of decoding our "true nature" through a "secret analogy" or some other kind of "affinity", so that the intense experience of these occasions become "revelations" (op. cit.: 34).

It could however be argued from the work under discussion that Leiris supports "primitivism" insofar as he, just as his colleagues at the Collège, considers certain forms of action – like the category of the festive and the behaviour and ideas manifested therein – to be more basic, primary and indispensable than other forms of cultural channelling of drives. For him, love and eroticism are so grounded in the spontaneity of life itself that their "savage-original state" can rarely be constrained by such a ritualized mastery of the left element as shown in the *corrida*. The element of the sinister is indispensable for capturing the essence of the sacred, which at its deepest level is characterised by ambiguity.

The sacred is also the razor's edge, the dividing wall which engenders the polarisation of all things. As Leiris says at the end of *Tauromachia*, the basic problem of all religions is to neutralize the wretchedness of the human condi-

---

[8] For the custom of the *sparagmos* as the non-cultural return to nature - the dancing women who had to eat their meat in the raw, *omophagia* - see Détienne (1995: 114ff.).

tion of death and suffering (a similar argument permeates the sociology of religion of Max Weber), and therefore, so he argues further, we invent ideal projections (1982: 133) such as "the primitive" or the search for the "natural":

> "To ban death or to hide him behind the architecture of timeless perfection, that is the senile occupation of most religious founders and philosophers".

On the contrary, Leiris continues, including death in life, constructing it in a "voluptuous" way, is the task of the "mirror-inventors". A term with which he describes those who, through artistic or other means, become craftspersons shaping our cognition. The mirror-inventors can only achieve this if the mirror (a spectacle, erotic performance, poetry, or a work of art) is made in such a way that a "hue of poison", something vice-like and "sinister" ("left") shines through (Leiris 1992: 132-33).[9]

This notion of the arts, of emotive events, of the festive and the sacred is indeed far removed from the image of the "primitive" pervasive when Leiris wrote his *Tauromachia*, or of the primitivism movements since the turn of the century. Leiris's idea is particularly powerful because he uses the image of the staged performance, far away from the idea of "naturalness". It is this interest to which I referred to in the beginning, this interest in the interstices between basic human drives and their cultural negotiation. It is a paradigmatic vision of the theatricality of social life, in particular of the sacred and of rituals, including those of apparently unmediated possession states (Leiris 1934).

Lest the reader assume that Leiris advocated some *conscious mimetic construction* of social processes which would make the whole of society a deliberate ruse and a sham of deception, let me point out that he differentiates between "played theatre" and "lived theatre", cultic events being counted among the latter (Leiris 1934: 226). Leiris comes close to the notion of the sacred as being framed by performances which are *ludic*[10] in the sense of what

---

[9] A similar approach is later taken in the last published work of Georges Bataille when he interprets the cave-paintings of Lascaux as a manifestation of the closeness of death and the erotic, closely connected to the sacred by the notion of "awe" as well as the historical introduction of interdiction. In this interpretation, the erotic is for Bataille the calculated surrender to lust, a game or play which is opposed to the world of work, the major feature that makes it so different from animal sexuality. Artistic creativity, eroticism and death-awareness are closely linked in Bataille's interpretations, which interestingly focus on representations of bisons (see Bataille 1981/1961, the work being conceived in 1959, as letters to Lo Duca indicate; see Bataille 1981: 15).

[10] In English the linguistic usage of "ludic" is comparatively recent. It derives from the notion of "ludus" in the French and German editions of the works of Huizinga and Caillois, and has as such been used in recent anthropological literature to denote the two modalities of play and game (see Koepping, ed. 1997c) through a combined term. "Ludic" covers the ambiguities of certain forms of collective behaviour that contain elements of both the more rule-governed game and "free" play. With this meaning the term was used by Don Handelman in relation to the behaviour of the Iatmul group of New Guinea, as described in the classic ethnography, *Naven*, by Gregory Bateson (1936),

I call the constant shift between the messages of the frame and the framed, making the ludic such a powerful transformer and dissolver of boundaries. In the purely ludic, ambivalence and ambiguity are intentionally used to subvert, the frame indicating "this is only a play", while in the religious realm the frame may indicate "this is how life really is", even if the performance within the frame is a burlesque or a game of dice (Koepping 1997c).

Leiris looks at the *corrida* as both a cosmic game of love and death and also as a staged game with loaded dice. Life itself is more amorphous, unpredictable, chaotic. While orchestrated, the bullfight nevertheless contains the idea of liminality in the risk of death for the protagonist, the matador, instead of the predetermined and expected victim, the bull. This game has rules, but it is still a play with danger and loss. A performance lacking this element of risk would not be a game – and it may not be accidental that the later major autobiographically encoded lifework of Leiris is called *La Règle du Jeu* (1948), with ambiguity and contrast built into the title.

There is ambiguity in the game with frame and rules, for it may take over the player's consciousness, carrying him away as a lover possessed. The arena of life is thus quite different from the stage, being closer to an altar without the sacrifice being fully determined in advance.

It is at this juncture that Leiris' whole notion of making the Self the object of the ethnographic search begins to make sense. Instead of the Malinowskian strategy of hiding his person in a private diary, he proceeds to make the self available to the public by confronting it as Other, a well-known strategy in an intellectual tradition that is traceable from Montaigne through Rousseau to Lévi-Strauss. Lévi-Strauss' interpretation of the *Confessions* of Rousseau brings this point most clearly to the fore: in order to discover the Self in the Other, the Self has to deny itself, or rather the Self has to be perceived by the subject as Other (following also Rousseau's, and later Rimbaud's, saying "*Je est un autre*").

This is not the notion of "collage" of surrealism, as Clifford intimates (1988: 146), but the well-known method of establishing the "we" over the institutional inscription, the "empathy" of passion and suffering over ascrip-

---

for the relaionship between mother's brother and sister's son (see Don Handelman 1979). In reference to the works of Huizinga and Caillois as well as to the mentioned anthropological discussions on ritual, the present author organized in collaboration with Bruce Kapferer an international and interdisciplinary conference in Heidelberg in 1992. For this conference, the two organizers coined the title "*The Ludic- Forces of Generation and Fracture*", and the resulting papers appear in Koepping, ed. 1997c. With this term, both organizers referred explicitly to Victor Turner's mentioning of the Vedic Indian notion of the "play of the gods" as creative "work" of the gods. Turner's formulation is quite explicit and encompasses almost all "performative" aspects: "Modern Bhakti movements still have the spontaneous, 'performative', ludic quality – where Eros sports with Thanatos, and not as a grisly Danse Macabre, but to symbolise a complete human reality" (Turner 1977: 41).

tions of roles, of life over culture[11]. Leiris would have had no problem fitting into the category of the "hybrid" person advocated by postmodernists like Homi Bhabha, recognizing the cultural space of the in-between, of transgression of boundaries and the desirability of the liminal state:

> "For a willingness to descend into that alien territory ... may reveal that the theoretical recognition of the split-space of enunciation may open the way to conceptualising an international culture, based not on the exoticism of multiculturalism or the diversity of cultures, but on the inscription and articulation of culture's hybridity. To that end we should remember that it is the 'inter' – the cutting edge of translation and negotiation, the in-between space – that carries the burden of the meaning of culture" (Bhabha 1994: 38).

Leiris thus seems far removed from the aims of early primitivism since the beginning of the century, though he is without doubt deeply indebted to the surrealist movement that wanted to make the familiar strange and discover the sacred under the veneer of humdrum everyday activities (see Jamin 1980; a well-worn strategy of teaching anthropology). After all, Leiris makes the Self strange, not the Other. In order to perceive the difference, a short look at a range of primitivist movements may be instructive.

In his seminal work on *Primitivism in Modern Art* of 1938, Robert Goldwater makes the important distinction that the "primitive" and "primitivism" are separate categories of analysis and perception. Accordingly, he clearly perceives that jumping from primitivism as a European mode of artistic orientation to an appreciation of the art production or aesthetic sensibilities of the "primitives" would be totally inappropriate. "Primitivism presupposes the primitive, and an artistic primitivism assumes the knowledge of an interest in arts that are in some sense considered primitive" (Goldwater 1967: 51).

Goldwater expresses here the important distinction between the primitive as a mode of life different in quality and experience from the European consciousness, coupled with the glib ascription of such states of experience (deduced from material objects and other forms of objectification), and a world labelled "primitive". This is especially paltry if neither the context, content nor meaning of the object are known. In contrast to anthropologists at that time, the artists who labelled themselves primitivists or were given this epithet were generally not interested in the social and religious context of the products of non-European cultures ascertainable through empirical research on the life-style of such groups. Instead, they were interested in the state of mind or consciousness such products expressed or aroused in their own imaginations.

---

[11] See Lévi-Strauss (1973: 45-56; 48f.) in commemoration of the 250th birthday of Jean-Jacques Rousseau).

The "primitive" functioned, and was variously interpreted, as the formal stylistic qualities or underlying psychic powers assumed to be expressed in the "simplicity" and "directness" of the form itself. A number of European schools of art developed out of Gauguin's vain search for the "savage" in Polynesia and the prefiguration of stylistic reductions such as those of Cézanne and van Gogh, which had led away from the then despised naturalist notions of mimetic imitations of reality. The great diversity of non-European art-forms were taken as guide-lines as well as proofs for the legitimacy of the European artistic search for new forms of expression. The ancient Orient with its monumental styles, the decorativeness of Polynesian designs, the recently discovered prehistoric art of the caves of the Dordogne, African sculptures and Oceanic masks: all were nothing but vehicles for the intellectual and artistic circles of Europe in their search for more "original", "simple", "basic" forms to express states of mind and psyche.

Anything went in the search to avoid "academic" ways of producing a piece of art in the European tradition. All the schools reverting to or inspired by non-European art-forms were apparently looking for new forms of aesthetics. From the followers of Cézanne such as Vlaminck and Derain (whose 1905 collection of African sculptures Picasso visited), to Matisse and the Fauves, from the much debated *Demoiselles d'Avignon* by Picasso to Macke and Marc – all were searching for new vehicles to express what they believed art should express: inner states of mind or pregnant comments on reality. As Goldwater put it: "... for the modern artist the primitiveness of these different arts lay in the common quality of simplicity attributed to them. More psychological than formal, it was a quality read into the objects rather than objectively observed ..." (1967: 252). On the whole, the diverse movements of primitivism in European 20th century art seem to have used the notion of the "primitive" only as what anthropologists like Kroeber would have labelled "stimulus diffusion" or what Goldwater called a "catalytic", "which ... helped the artists to formulate their own aims because they could attribute to it the qualities they themselves sought to attain" (Goldwater 1967: 253).

European primitivism of *avant-garde* art may thus not tell us anything about primitive art but a lot about the notion of primitivity prevailing in that time and the desirability of such a state for its protagonists. The avant-garde seems on the one hand to have inverted those stereotypes which existed during the 19th century in imperialist-colonialist circles about the backwardness of primitive societies, in particular when measured by their material production (as did much of early anthropological theory; see Kuper 1988).

On the other hand, the *avant-garde* today still firmly relies on these evolutionist notions about the autochthonous states of societies and their material expressions, societies which are removed in time and space from the European cultural present. Of course this attitude is dressed in different clothes today and is further nurtured by a new wave of despair about the degeneracy, empty formality and rigidity of social conventions of the European present. These conventions are assumed to stifle all affective, emotional and intuitive impulses of the unconscious as well as the "true" natural drives of humanity. Yet the *avant-garde* still adulates these "natural" drives perceived in the creations of primitive art only to pursue its own aims of re-invigorating Western art and civilization. They are thus little more than a replay of that European imagination which constructed its own alternatives through the projections of better – meaning more natural – forms of social life and artistic expression onto the past or the outside world.

Primitive meant and means the original state of mankind, the utopia of a lost Eden in which social and artistic conventionality had not yet stifled an immediate, direct response to the world. The primitivist avant-garde of the 20th century is thus descended as well from the intellectual heritage of Montaigne, Rousseau and even Marx, as Leiris. Yet, where the avant-garde posits the artistic self to find a new self *via* the detour of the vicarious perception of the other, Leiris posits the reflective self as alienated from the subject in order to find it in the other, letting the other into his self.

At least, this is the theory of the genre of "confessions"; in his ethnographic reality, the "blemish" lies somewhere else, when he revels in the participation in a sacrificial ceremony or writes that "I would rather be possessed than study possessed people, have carnal knowledge of a 'zarine', rather than scientifically know all about her" (1934: 324). But in reality, he goes on to take notes! His "gauche" wins?

The only theoretician of the aesthetics of modern art who observed the conundrum of the inability to relate to the "consciousness" of the "primitive" seems to have been Kandinsky. Already in 1912 he perceived the European consciousness as one "which has a crack" (Leiris' notion of the "blemish" of the "left" side comes to mind here), but who nevertheless believed in the inner, empathetic affinity of modern artists with primitive consciousness (see Kandinsky 1952: 21-22). The primitive as lived social reality, however, always stayed outside the horizon of the European narcissistic, self-occupied search for otherness, for difference. (Leiris too only discovers the structural violence inherent in the relationship of inequality between the European and on-European world at a much later stage).[12] The primitive may be "good to think

---

[12] The interphase between European primitivism and notions of modernity and its feed-back to the "world of the primitive" has scarcely been investigated. For first attempts in this direction within the framework of the whole primitivism debate, I am indebted to suggestions put forward by Dr. Lydia Haustein in an unpublished manuscript (1997). The problem of the reception of various artistic, religious or aesthetic products, artefacts and values in different cultural environments has largely informed the recent debate on the interplay between globalisation and localisation. Thus, Signe Howell has in particular addressed their process as a bi-directional one in the field of the movement of art products, stressing that the politically and economically powerful First World has "borrowed extensively from Third World knowledges in domains that affect cultural categories and

with", to modify one of Lévi-Strauss's sayings, but if, as Stanley Diamond has stated, intellectual insight is not followed by "a concretely political transformation", then all knowledge about the "primitive" remains the futile search for "lost paradises or savage nobility", both of which are "straw constructions" (Diamond 1974: 174-75).

individuals at a deep level" (Howell 1995: 179). She rightly points to the difficulty of assessing the value of the global availibility of diverse knowledge products. In regard to the question of the "primitivism" to which I alluded in the beginning of this essay, it remains indeed an open question whether the de-contextualisation of aboriginal art forms can be labelled a form of "inauthentication", or whether one should rather look at the re-contextualisation in the receiving cultural milieu as a form of creative enrichment of existing ideas and values. Should it bother us, as it apparently does Goldwater, that primitive art-forms have been put to use by European artitst according to their own agenda? From the vantage-point of taking any cultural idiom as equivalent in value, it would not matter, as local and regional contexts re-fashion "borrowed" icons and ideas according to their own perceived needs. This occurs even if historical or ethnographic scholarship or the "originators" consider these developments as "misrepresentations" or "misreadings", for which Picasso's words may be typical: "They (the tribal artists) were against everything – against unknown threatening spirits ... I too am against everything ... I understand what the Negros used their sculptures for ... all were weapons" (quoted in Foster 1985: 45). Looking at it from the vantage-point of the power of definition, however, such global borrowings do seem to still leave Third World positions at the mercy of those forces which, through their economic power, also have the power of defining what for instance accounts for "art" (for the context of moving Australian Aboriginal art from the ethnographic museum to the art-galleries, see Morphy 1995), besides the problem that the Third World communities, while re-contextualising products and knowledge of the First World, do not always have a "choice" (see James 1995).

*Figure 16*: Georges Bataille ca. 1939

# Bataille: Excess and the Erotic-Sacred

As is shown by anthropological reports throughout the world, transgressive actions appear to always take place in a period that has definite time limits, and which is marked as an exceptional situation, as for instance during festivals. Transgressions are thus those peculiar forms of social behaviour in which everything that is otherwise considered to be taboo, at least as a public act, is allowed and in fact even expected, especially the portrayal of sexual acts, uttering obscenities, destroying objects, and engaging in violence and aggression that, even if is not really carried out "concretely" is at least performatively or mimetically enacted as a drama or ritual or both. This festive period is for Caillois and Bataille initially understood as a direct contrast to the normal working routine as a time of recreation and leisure, with the additional definition as recuperation and re-creation that legitimises a sacred order or even that by virtue of its sacredness establishes order. This gives rise to a paradoxical combination of sacredness and disorder. Bataille put the contrast as well as mutual constitution of the world of work and of the festive in the following words:

> "The world of work and reason is the basis of human life but work does not absorb us completely and if reason gives the orders our obedience is never unlimited. Work ... demands rational behaviour where the wild impulses worked out on feast days and usually in games are frowned upon" (1986: 41).[1]

In an inversion and at the same time a confirmation of Durkheim's proposed contrasts between sacred and profane and, in continuation of Caillois' idea that "blasphemy belongs to social order" (1950: 151), Bataille tersely points out that chaotic debauchery as transgression has nothing to do with a return to or the freedom of an animalistic life, but rather:

> "Transgression ... opens the door into what lies beyond the limits usually observed, but it maintains these limits just the same. Transgression is complementary to the profane world, exceeding its limits but not destroying it. ... The profane world is the world of taboos. The sacred world depends on limited acts of transgression. It is the world of celebrations, sovereign rulers and God" (1986: 68).

---

[1] All citations are taken from the English translation of Bataille's *L'Erotisme* of 1957 through Mary Dalwood, *Erotism*, San Francisco 1986, while the first English edition dates from 1962. See imprimatur of 1986 City Lights Books.

The development of what is probably the most comprehensive theory of transgression as "overstepping the boundaries" throughout Bataille's work on eroticism is only conceivable if close references are made to the thoughts expressed in his earlier work such as his extensive comments on his sources of inspiration. For example, he says that Marcel Mauss' lectures on the earliest impulses through the "absurd" formulation, "the taboo is there to be violated" as rendered from lecture notes and extended through Roger Caillois' "theory of the festive" helped him to develop his theory of taboo and transgression as foundations of the social, with specific focus on the sacredness of the erotic.[2]

This relationship between the sacred and the erotic is not obvious, and this poses a challenge for both the academic field that tries to compare cultures and for the individual dealing with this question. The connection between the sacred and the erotic does not become clear until the concept of transgression comes into play: the other forms of it are all acts of violence, of war and of death, and the erotic shares its features. This is naturally completely intertwined in all of collective and individual life but appears to be put off limits by the social rules, in particular those prohibitions concerning acts of violence extant in all cultures in some form[3]. As it is especially during "celebratory" periods in the broadest sense of the word that sexual acts as well as those of violence take place which are usually under taboo, that the very legitimate question arises as to whether and to what extent the limits of experience of the two domains, i.e. of the erotic and the sacred can be perceived as closely linked, if not to say "logically" connected, as this theoretical proposition certainly negates the notion of the sacred as it exists in Christianity and many other so-called "high" religions (as well as priestly elite-theologies)[4].

In the field of comparative anthropology, we are not likely to find a more personally committed representative for the developing of a theory of transgression, linking the domains of the "sacred" and of the "profane" than

---

[2] See the chapter on the "Festive" in this volume.

[3] The whole question of where the taboos are in our own society, after sexuality and – to a lesser degree – also the sacred have disappeared as prohibited domains (for instance through laws against blasphemy), has engaged theoreticians from Weber to Elias. Foucault in his accolade to Bataille's L'Erotisme too raises this question in a wider philosophical frame with reference back to the philosophy of Nietzsche. Thus he asks the pertinent question what transgression in terms of overstepping the limits means. Does transgressing mean to enter a region of the limitless? It depends here very much on the linguistic connotation of notions of limitlessness, which can either be understood as infinity or, as unboundedness, as a realm of the undifferentiated. Is language then able to express this which is beyond the boundedness of structurethis, which is beyond the boundedness of structure, or are we then at a loss for words? Or is the only answer that of Bataille as well as Leiris to consider speaking and writing about the sacred, about eroticism and about violence as acts of a revolt of transgression as well as of forcing language to convey what cannot be conveyed, the immediacy of the sensuality of bodies? At the end of this essay I touch upon this question through Bataille's own words, which however leave ample scope for further discussion.

[4] See the chapter on Japanese folk-religious festivals in this volume. See also Koepping 1997a and 1997b.

Bataille, who in his writings, be they academic or works of fiction, had a tendency towards consciously formulated and performed transgressions and who is as much known for a number of "obscene" pieces of fiction as for his theoretical writings. In the following, I am therefore presenting a part of his "system" in which he combines the historical and anthropological re-construction of the connection between taboo and transgression as necessarily intertwined in the domain of the sacred with reflex ion about the personal transgression involved in the writing about eroticism as constitutive of the sacred.

The justification for this is the fact that it puts in question the taboo limits of the modern social sciences – which Bataille on the whole perceived as unable and unwilling to cope with this thorny issue - especially with his open references to personal experience. The relevance of these issues for a universal theory is precisely what continues to make Bataille's thoughts so stimulating because he calls upon researchers and writers to "unmask" themselves as integral part of developing a theory the "scientistic" treatment of which is anathema for him. Thus, the questions that are posed below are meant to be taken as an overview of the framework in which Bataille looks for answers and they give an impression of the totality with which he pursues the dual nature of human beings in their biological and social dependence. In addition, they explore the way in which Bataille explains the basic structure of the revolt against both natures, which in his opinion arise from the power of desire that is shared by all human beings. He considers this revolt to be futile and yet indispensable for the human being's feeling of *sovereignty* and his or her self esteem.

The questions posed below and the solutions which I have selected to discuss later on in this essay do not presume to present a complete picture of Bataille's thoughts but rather are an attempt to illustrate an approach that for me, with its combination of concepts and presumed affective attitudes, has as much a startling as an unsettling significance for the interpretation of societal processes from a "total" and comparative point of view. Bataille's approach is optimal because it neither allows the user to be satisfied with analysing a tiny chip of the reality he or she wishes to examine nor does it lapse into pure introspection. This approach seems therefore congenial with and well suited to anthropological fieldwork, that other form of an ideally total involvement which makes the self the major "tool" of experiencing as well as transmitting experiential levels of otherness without erasing the self. But the other overflows into the self, and the transformation is pre-programmed as form of contagion.

The writings of Bataille on the sacred – primarily of so-called "archaic" societies with a view on the conditions of the present – and its openness for the sacrilegious, his very insistence on the sacred as the focus of required sacrilege is repeated by his own writings: he carries the sacrilege onto the page.

As Bataille – as well as Leiris who closely followed him here – put it, it is the duty of the writer in order to remain close to humanity to put the most dirty or "nauseating filthiness" on to the page because dirt is the most human attribute.[5] As Denis Hollier put it in a perceptive reviewing of the aims which Bataille consciously embraced: "Everything can be said. But throughout Bataille, there remains something unmentionable. To say it, one must expose the taboo and, in exposing it, expose oneself... the forbidden is reintroduced into science" (Hollier 1995: 144). Bataille is as author and researcher interested in that same rupture of the social which fascinated Leiris in his *Tauromachie* which he there called the element of the "sinister". Bataille too embraces consciously the contagion of the "dirt" which he more so than Leiris deals with in his investigations and writings, thus fitting those traits which make the trickster as much as the satirist part of what they perform by having the "dirt stick", as the folk-saying expresses it ... [6]

[5] In contrast to the following quotes it should be pointed out that Bataille as well as Leiris show a considerable ambivalence toward the notion "that everything can be said", as Foucault in a perceptive review of Bataille's work pointed out. For both, Leiris as well as Bataille, there are limits to language, though for both writing is indeed the primary transgression of going beyond these limits of twhat can be expressed in language; see Michel Foucault 1977: "A Preface to Transgression". In: *Language, Counter-Memory, Practice*, edited by D. F. Bouchard. Ithaca. Some of the comments at the end of the present essay make clear the position of Bataille. One could add here that Leiris considered his writing not so much a transgression as a constant fight, a form of Tauromachie.

[6] See my comments in the chapter on the trickster in this volume and the discussion on the blemish in the chapter on Leiris. There is a striking similarity to the concept of the "left" as "sinister" side between Leiris and Bataille. Thus Bataille refers to the *sinister* side (the left or flawed, as Leiris would have put it) of eroticism in the work under discussion as follows: "Erotic activity is not always ... overtly sinister ... it is not always a crack in the system; but secretly and at the deepest level the crack belongs intimately to human sensuality and is the mainspring of pleasure" (1986: 105). It is noteworthy that the only "serious" anthropological study on the notion of "dirt" as disturbance of conceptual systems by Mary Douglas does not refer to the earlier writings of Bataille or the group of dissidents from the surrealistic movement of Andre Breton. Hollier picks out the intellectual climate among the surrealists whose impact became so important through the mixing of ethnographers, museographers and art-historians in publishing the *Documents* which advocated the concentration on an anthropology of the quotidian, a turning away from the formality of beauty as hygienic idealizations (see Hollier, op.cit.,. p. 141ff.). This defamiliarising technique fits very well with the Malinowskian request not to look for the extraordinary in the field. However, the concentration on the sacrilegious and the taboo-braking customs through the *avant-garde* of surrealism in ethnological writings is more than a rehabilitation of the mundane. Clifford therefore identifies as sacrilege the article by Leiris and Bataille on spitting in the *Documents* of 1929 when he congenially interprets: "Spitting indicates a fundamentally sacrilegious condition. According to this revised, corrected definition, speaking or thinking is also ejaculating" (Clifford 1981: 52). The notion of spitting as sacrilege has been explicitly stated by Leiris in that article: "Spitting is the height of sacrilege" (Leiris, *Crachat*, in *Documents* 7, 1929: 381), thereby however inverting the reference to Marcel Mauss for whom spitting was a bodily technique of hygiene (it dates from 1934; see Mauss "Les techniques du corps", in *Anthropologie et sociologie*, Paris 1960: 382). The notion of shouting as ejaculation is also derived from Leiris, see the chapter on the Tauromachie in this volume.

For me, in line with Bataille's perspective, the following questions arise implicitly from his works:

If, as we assume, one of the biggest taboo areas, namely, sexuality, can be violated (superseding all incest prohibitions)[7], of all times, during sacred periods, what then is the connection between sacredness and eroticism? If the breaking of these taboos is a global phenomenon, does some sort of human experience underlie this, which justifies such a uniformity of the representation in the same structure? How do we distinguish transgressions from other types of acts of overstepping boundaries and from everyday criminal acts? What is the difference between a criminal act and a legitimate act if the same act is treated both as illegal sometimes and as legal at other times? What are the particular characteristics of eroticism and how do they distinguish this domain from the physiology of sexuality? Why is it this very sphere, which universally has so many taboos attached to it, and is so private that practising it outside of a celebratory ritual is not tolerated – unless it is carried out as a "polite social game" that Simmel once used for his definition of the "playing of sociality" to which he affixed the label "coquetry" (cf. Simmel 1992[1902]).

What exactly are the connections between sexuality and violence or eroticism and death that we as representatives of modernity do not perceive until we are confronted with them as terrifying events in the context of violence between religious or ethnic groups that are enemies? We are rudely awakened when we hear that the foe can be particularly successfully brought to its knees by brutally raping its women, as was the order of the day for years in the war between the Serbs, the Croatians, and Bosnians and more recently during the unrest among the Chinese minority in Indonesia.

Or, to present perhaps "more lofty" connections, how is it that on the one hand all of the great love poetry connects eroticism with images of death and transitoriness, while the deepest experiences of the mystics are formulated in images of sexual ecstasy? This not only puts Christian theologians on the spot when it comes to the Song of Songs but has led to huge misunderstandings concerning the poetry of Sufis such as Omar Khayyam. Why do so many governments either censor this type of literary form of religious experience or at the very least consider it to be an anathema in today's view of what is sacred? If most peoples whose culture includes rites of initiation or renewal use sexuality in performative and other forms of representation, in accordance with the accepted meta-

---

7   Bataille is quite aware of the literature on the topic from Freud and Malinowski to Lévi-Strauss, yet interprets the exchange of women in exogamous societies as a Maussian *potlatch* of gift giving excess.

phor of maintaining life and growth, then why are the corresponding "natural" acts, be they symbolic or real, not permitted in public or in some cultures and religions even negated within the concept of what is sacred?[8]

What is the basis for viewing the sexual subversive, that not just during periods of renewal such as New Year's celebrations sexuality is the very symbol of the chaotic element, or, using the term from the Old Testament, of the "tohuwabohu"? This also gains particular strength in the so-called rituals of rebellion (Gluckman 1956) or in the expressions of animosity such as curses. It even appears to serve to subjugate the power of the rulers, despite the fact that political power is usually the very domain that allows itself to break its own rules (as the French anthropologist Marc Augé so succinctly formulated recently, cf. Augé 1998). Finally, why do we use the term "victim" in a language of love such as that used to describe rituals most frequently in which one domain usually has a negative connotation and in the second one it is an unconditional precondition for getting access to the sacred, and yet in both spheres it has the association of "sacrificing" one's self to a beloved person, or the highest possible value, death (or suicide)? If love and sacrifice are connected to the idea of giving one's life as the most precious possession, then why are real acts of love covered up and hidden from the eyes of the public under threat of sanctions that otherwise only applies to human excrements and thus to products that normally evoke disgust?

This and related questions appear to share a basic structure, that – by radically simplifying Bataille's theory of "sacred eroticism" – could perhaps be paraphrased as follows: Two milieus are delineated from each other. One is the

---

[8] For an empirical example see the chapter on Japanese festivals, *matsuri*, in this volume. At many other occasions of such festivals the sexual was still performed as grotesquerie, as mimetic performance of the real act through puppets, and in some instances performative imitated by participants and sacred masked actors in a free-for-all ribaldry. Yet, since Meiji times (1868) these folk-religious practices have been more and more restricted and banned as "pernicious" customs which impeded, so the *Charter Oath* of Emperor Meiji, Japan's modernization or being on par with the advanced Western powers. It would lead too far at this place to disentangle the complex historical changes in festive practices in modern Japan, but it should be pointed out that it seems more and more the case that people cannot identify the sacred with excess, the urban mind-set having taken on an almost puritan streak of shamefulness invading from the rational world of work into the sacred. This raising of the rules of etiquette, in the sense of Elias, is a rarely commented phenomenon which in turn may have been strongly influenced by internal mass-tourism where "secret-sacred" activities cannot be performed any more in "traditional" style due to its dissemination by the media to an "unauthorized" public which does not belong to the village community's boundaries. Whether the well-described behavioral patterns of after-work entertainment in Japan are the secular functional equivalent to the former sacred debauchery, cannot be discussed in this context. For corroboration of the observed increase in the stringency of behavioral codes during festivals which I observed over the years see also Ashkenazi 1993 and Plutschow 1996.

profane everyday milieu and the other is the sacred. They differ from each other depending on whether or not the transgressions of sexuality and murder are allowed or are forbidden. In other words, the acts that have the strictest sanctions attached to them, the sex act and that of the destruction of life, are intertwined in the hierarchy of these milieus, since they represent the biggest violation of taboos and yet at the same time are the "most sacred" acts[9].

For Bataille, the connection between the acts of permitted "murder" in the rite of sacrifice (a problem to which René Girard, in particular, dedicated a lifetime of research, cf. Girard 1972) and the act of sexuality lies in both acts' proximity to death, especially between the experience of death in eroticism and in religion. Both eroticism and sacredness can be subsumed under the terms excess, exuberance, overflowing, all in all, licentiousness, to which intoxication, ecstasy and rapture belong (of course, so does the word "offering", whose excessive and in turn probably "purest" form is identified by Bataille in the custom of the potlatch as one form of excess.[10]), since, so he quotes the Marquis de Sade:

> "There is no better way to know death than to link it with some licentious image" (1986: 24).

First of all, human eroticism can be distinguished from animal sexuality, as it "is also an affirmation of life up to and including death" (1986: 11). According to Bataille, the source of the emotional goal of eroticism lies in the awareness of the frailty of life. While it is true that sexual reproduction means the continuity of existence, while life is frail, it is in fact human desire, not just to ensure the continuity of life, but also the desire to produce (the) continuity with other discontinuous individuals, and this implies violence. The overcoming of this discontinuity of individual bodies is only possible by the conquest and sacrifice of one body by and for another individual. The most violent discontinuity that can be experienced by the human being is death. For this reason, experiences of death and eroticism are just as tightly connected through violence as eroticism and religiosity are interconnected as expressions of the yearning for a lost or impossible continuity (1986: 15).

It is true that the sensuous union leads to suffering, without which sex

---

[9] I shall skip over Bataille' discussion of obscenity, pornography and other forms of "debasement" of these urges that are considered to be disruptive to the working world, cf. also Koepping 1985 and 1987a. Two caveats should be kept in mind: Bataille considers the erotic an act of mental imagination to be distinguished from the physiological urge of sexuality; and in this sense, the pornographic imagination is not really considered a "debasement" in Bataille's system, as the erotic only can exert its power through the existence of taboos and thus through the socially conditioned response of the desire to overstep these boundaries, whereby anxiety as well as desire are parts of man's second nature, not naturally given.

[10] See Bataille 1967 *La Part Maudite*, where he deals extensively in Part I with the economy of consumption; see the English edition *The Accursed Share*, vol. 1 of 1991: 63-80.

would be reduced to routine and habituation. Yet the essential element of the definition of the term eroticism is that it cannot contain normality. Habituation would lead to a new discontinuity, because in order to overcome discontinuity "ecstasy" is required. Otherwise routine, which is part of the world of work, will quickly turn into absurdity:

> "Only in the violation, through death if need be, of the individual's solitariness can there appear that image of the beloved object which in the lover's eyes invests all being with significance" (1986: 21).

Thus, for Bataille the two poles of the simultaneous experience of desire and pain serve as the basic elements of both eroticism and mysticism, quoting St. Theresa as follows:

> "The pain was so sharp that it made me utter several moans; and so excessive was the sweetness caused me by this intense pain that one can never wish to lose it..." (1986: 224).

It is especially the striving for dissolution in continuity that brings disorder to the human organism, that the world of work does not permit. It does not allow eroticism as a free game of energy that looks for the conquest of discontinuity but only allows eroticism in the organisation and control of sexuality in marriage.

Thus marriage is according to Bataille to be understood as a form of "permitted transgression". However, the social order is never truly successful in achieving this, because eroticism will never give up its sovereignty. But even the greatest tenderness contains the potential for violence:

> "The violence of love leads to tenderness, the lasting form of love, but it brings into the striving of one heart towards another the same quality of disorder, the same thirst for losing consciousness and the same aftertaste of death that is found in the mutual desire for each other's body" (1986: 241).

In this context Bataille uses the term "sovereignty"; I will be discussing this term in more detail below. At this point, however, I will focus on the comparison of eroticism with sacredness *via* the concept of waste, fusion, violence and excess. To prevent any misunderstandings about the equivalence between eroticism and sacredness, at this point I would like to point out that Bataille in no way considers these two domains to be equal to each other, even if mystic states appear to most closely approach erotic states. He does see a similarity between the two, however, in that both domains reach the most extreme limits of normality in their intensity through their proximity to death. Just as eroti-cism includes the awareness of overcoming discontinuity, the following is valid for the sacrificial victim:

> "The victim dies and the spectators share in what his death reveals. ... A violent death disrupts the creature's discontinuity: what remains, what the tense onlookers experience in the succeeding silence, is the continuity of all existence with which the victim is now one" (1986: 82)

Treating the two domains in this way only makes sense if it is done with the paradoxical configurations of emotions in mind, in which desire and fear are intermixed, as Rudolf Otto, using the succinct phrase *"mysterium tremendum et fascinans"* describes sacredness in the religious context[11], which for the erotic Bataille confirms thus:

> "The inner experience of eroticism demands from the subject a sensi-tiveness to the anguish at the heart of the taboo no less great than the desire which leads him to infringe it. This is religious sensibility, and it always links desire closely with terror, intense pleasure and anguish" (1986: 39).

At this point we are talking about two new types of transgression. When dis-cussing this subject, Bataille never fails to emphasise science's refusal to deal with them. The first is a postulation of universal and human emotional funda-mentals and states (that are brought so close to each other by mysticism and eroticism). The other one is the way we call on our own inner experience.

The *first* transgression, the affect of desire (*désir*), has led to the establish-ment of various institutions within human society. Bataille shares this view with a number of French intellectuals ranging from the group that formed the *Collège de sociologie* (founded 1937 by Bataille, Leiris and Caillois as seces-sion movement from Andre Breton) and which was closely connected to the surrealist avant-garde, influencing in its search for a theory of the sacred later developments, to structuralists around Lévi-Strauss, theorists such as Girard and modern cultural philosophers from Foucault to Baudrillard.

The *second* transgression places him in the company of Michel Leiris, to whom Bataille feels indebted as a trailblazer for his ideas, because he acknowledges that Leiris in his *Le Miroir de la Tauromachie* "envisaged [eroticism] as an experience wedded to life itself; not as an object of scientific

---

[11] Bataille was quite aware of Otto's work, see his review of Caillois' *L'Homme et le sacré* of 1950 in *Critique*, no. 45 (1951), translated into English in Michael Richardson (ed.), *The Absence of Myth*, London 1994, p. 117.

study, but more deeply, as an object of passion and ·poetic contemplation"
(Bataille, p. 9 of the Foreword, as dedication of the volume to Michel
Leiris)[12]. Besides rejecting any quantitative study as well as qualitative comparative investigation of the erotic, he finally considers the process of writing
as the ultimate excess:

> "Thought itself, reflection, that is, is only fulfilled in excess. What is
> truth, apart from the representation of excess, if we only see that which
> exceeds the possibility of seeing what it is intolerable to see, just as in
> ecstasy enjoyment is intolerable?" (1968: 268)[13].

Georges Bataille ends his treatise with these comments that at first appear to
be a type of personal "confession" (not in the sense of a humiliating confession of sins, but rather a self-revelation of the creative roots of the thinking
process). But besides the hint at the problem of writing and reflection, another
key term of his system appears here, that of excess, to be understood as one
form of transgression – as is reflection, is writing and ultimately speaking
about things tabooed, surpassing the limits of language -, as wasteful consumption, but also as free spending or expenditure of energy in profligacy, as
a form of free squandering, borne from a plethora of overflowing production
or abundance of available goods, energies as well as emotions. As the term
has again, as so often in Bataille's thought, an ambivalent connotation, an economic as well as one applied to human emotions and to eroticism as well as to
the sacred, a closer look at the all-embracing system of a philosophical anthropology may be in order. Before looking at this notion of excess a short summary of the tenets of a philosophical anthropology may be appropriate, as they
shine through partially in the previous quotations. It is an approach that views
the human as a biologically determined being but at the same time as a culturally determined totality both on an individual basis and in humankind in general.[14] However, it does not see the human as limited by this but views it as a
being that while it overcomes the sphere of the animalistic through its socio-
cultural renunciation, remains unable to completely escape it.

    Philosophical anthropology attempts to see these poles, the biological and
the sociological, as a synthetic unit despite the existing range of variation. It
also attempts to portray the relationship between the forces of biology and
society that determine the individual, considering the level of reflection of

---

[12] Leiris had previously dedicated his *Tauromachie* to Bataille's companion.

[13] Thus, Bataille would certainly frown upon or consider futile such works as Giddens' recent discourse in intimacy, see Giddens 1998. His attitude would however mesh rather well with recent
experiments in writing ethnography as poetic endeavor.

[14] The only equivalent philosophical anthropology in its total reach und range was probably developed by Helmuth Plessner ranging from the social and biological foundations to an aesthesiology of
human perception, embodiment and cognition.

"culture" through which this dual foundation (*"the two natures"*) of human existence is always objectified as a symbolically broken notion in both individuals and in collective representations and at the same time can always be subjectively "understood" otherwise (as Augé put it recently, anthropology is also always a portrayal of the anthropology of the other, cf. Augé 1998).

Thus, philosophical anthropology will always seek to view the human being as a totality, yet in so doing makes a special effort to trace those fracture points at which the biological and socio-cultural structure appears to fall apart.[15] Philosophical anthropology will pose the questions as to where the conflicts between nature and culture arise, what form they take and how they are represented and how certain cultures and individuals take this conflict into account. It also poses the question, in keeping with Durkheim, as to whether the fact that every individual is basically an anarchist who tries to avoid the collective rules and norms perhaps indicates that this anarchism may actually be rooted in the individual's biological structure.

According to Bataille's anthropology, however, what is paradoxical, or the "rupture" lies in the fact the in the *two natures* (or the double determination through biology and society) the opposition between being separated and being required to belong together and wanting to belong together among individual units is practically predetermined as if it were programmed. The first nature provides the precondition of the continuity of the life of the species through the sex drive that unites separated individuals intermittently, whereby the ultimate, decisive rupture or what Bataille calls the discontinuity of life, namely death, while not stoppable, can be overcome and it is not until one becomes conscious of this that life itself receives its significance. The first nature, however, also implants the possibility of a second nature in the human being, which brings about permanent communication among the ephemeral individuals, who otherwise have developed as lonely and isolated individuals and in so doing creates society. At the same time, however, society most strictly regulates those impulses that make continuity possible by constraining sexuality with norms and taboos.

The quotes that have already been presented above point to one pole of Bataille's objectives in developing an anthropology that identifies the objective prerequisites for human existence that is also valid for reflective thinking. The other pole is the evidence that the human being can only be a human as a cultural being, who, through a subjective awareness of death clearly comprehends the objective limits of his or her being (this brings Vico's explanation of "culture" to mind) and attempts to overcome them. Bataille attaches these subjective and objective sides of the being to that *fracture* point of subjectiv-

---

[15] Here the postulate of a universal biological foundation remains problematic because it only appears in the culturally broken representations, notions and attitudes. Even if the sex drive is assumed to be a biological constant, its emotional form in eroticism remains. Thus, transgression can only occur in the domain of culture.

ity that owes its existence to the paradox of the *necessity* of norms and the *desire to overstep their boundaries.* This desire to overcome the world of self-created order is in turn postulated as an objective fact and is seen as possessed by all human beings as cultural beings and is rooted in the physiological fact of sexual reproduction (as individual delimitation) and thus in an objectively determined instinct. However, desire is a collectively and subjectively determined experience that can lead the individual's potentially creative perception of death to a new awareness of joy of life, since the world of work and order has the tendency to cover up death (or to repress awareness of death as well as sexuality).

The wish for continuity of the discontinuous existence by transgressing the limits of experience is at the foundation of religion and sacredness. The fundamental paradox appears as a problem of the victim who, through the act of transgression, i.e. murder, is supposed to lead to an extension of life but in one's consciousness this very transgression connotes fear, disgust and horror.

For Bataille the key position is taken by the contradiction of preservation and destruction of that continuity that can only be maintained and experienced through discontinuous action. An essential part of this is the terrifying insight that it is the desire for continuity that, even if it grew out of physiology, leads to *the negation of the desired object* through reflected action, this negation being the elimination of the individuality of another individual. Bataille describes this in the formulation below that brings Hegel to mind, although it goes beyond Hegel's approach in its emphasis on the primacy of the senses and of the body as well as of the immediacy of experience:

> "... It is the human world, shaped by a denial of animality or nature, denying itself, and reaching beyond itself in this second denial, though not returning to what it had rejected in the first place" (1986: 83).

This is, where mankind's sovereignty lies for Bataille in truth, a point he is stressing throughout his "systemic" writings, ranging from the discussion of palaeolithic cave paintings to the rise of totalitarian state-control. The impact of Kojève's philosophy is immediately apparent. Bataille uses Kojève's main thesis as a motto for his treatise on *Theory of Religion*, in which desire is also seen as the driving force for self-awareness but it does not suffice as an explanation for human culture, which only comes about because desire provides the impetus to carry out action that is intended to satisfy desire. Yet this can only come about through negation, the destruction, or at the least the transformation of the desired object:

> "In order to appease one's hunger food must be destroyed or at least be

transformed. This is why action is always 'negation' (Based on a quotation from Kojève's *Introduction to the Reading of Hegel* in Bataille 1994a[1973]).

Bataille also sees desire as the driving force, as Kojeve did when the latter identified knowledge with passive quietude and desire as dis-quieting element that moves man to action. However, his main focus in this context is on the area of the erotic and sacred, in which the erotic conscious play of the lovers becomes a paradigm of the transgression of the normal social world that leads to especially great suffering for the very reason that it strives for the impossible. This is the kind of rupture of consciousness that also became a leading topic of eroticism for Michel Leiris in his theory of the bullfight.[16]

Thus the one basic figure or disposition of the emotions and of the consciousness, desire, is elaborated in the three surrealistic anthropologists in order to establish three domains of human existence: Leiris develops a theory of aesthetics, Caillois a theory of play, and Bataille, who incorporates both theories, a theory of society of norm (or taboo) and transgression.[17] The reverse side of the suppression or the elimination of transgression even in the ritual sphere in most of the "modern" societies was expanded on by Leiris insofar as he assumes that the greatest atrocities take place in these very societies, since eliminating the temporary emotional forms of transgression (in a celebration, rite or game) leaves only a "mutilated life" of boredom (Leiris, 1982: 38).

Bataille describes his reaction to a dream, which consists of him actually accepting himself as the philosopher of laughter, without having written even one book about it. He arrives at the spontaneous insight that the experiences of laughter, eroticism, ecstasy and death inscribed themselves into one single perspective. But to achieve the fractureless transition from the dream to the reflection on his work, he considers an unfinished task.

For Bataille, the ultimate transgression consists therefore in writing about eroticism and sacredness: writing as form of excess therefore requires a short reference to this key for the social formation that again is based on a natural principle.

A special form of transgression is its expression in the excess, in wasteful consumption, also in the free expenditure of energies, material and emotional. For this reason the significance of excess and waste for the development of

[16] See the chapter on the *Tauromachie* of Leiris in this volume.

[17] Equivalent, if not as comprehensive approaches are not found until the late 60s and 70s in the empirically oriented English social anthropology, with the work of Victor Turner (1967) and Mary Douglas (1969) the latter being dedicated to the problem of paradox of those widespread classification forms that lead to ambivalences and ambiguities that cannot be broken up in binary structures and question the classic oppositions of sacred and profane.

society, especially in the economic and political domains cannot be excluded in the turn from eroticism to economy or in looking at the economic aspects of eroticism.

For Bataille, there are two purposes to which the production of goods for the elimination of excess can be ascribed: One of them belongs to the world of work and order and is the stockpiling of items of worth for a later point in time, saving, budgeting and calculating.

On the other hand, life by its very nature is designed for waste and produces goods in excess, be it solar energy or sexual reproduction. In the human sphere, not everything is oriented toward conserving what currently exists. There is another purpose of production in the cultural sphere to which eroticism and sacrifice belong or so-called "unproductive expenditures" such as the exchange of sacrifices (for this reason, in his work on economy, Bataille frequently refers to the *potlatch*, the extreme or "pure form" of waste that was dealt with by Marcel Mauss). For Bataille these include each and every luxury, all cults and rites, especially sacrifice, wars, or perverse sexual practices, all of which have their end in themselves and, as in the case of sacrifice, produce the order of the intimacy of the sacred by increasing the experience of the moment.[18]

This may sound like a teleological reading of nature, but what was ultimately of greatest significance to Bataille is the ethical call for the *sovereignty* of the human being. Through various forms of excess, non-calculating and non-productivity, human beings liberate themselves from oppression through biological urges *via* second nature, namely the rules of society. Yet from these rules humans can liberate themselves through a *second negation*, and that is the sign of their true sovereignty, the activities of excess being the enactment of transgression, only possible due to the reflexion about mortality.

It is true that in a review of Caillois' work Bataille issues a warning not to overestimate the sacred as a "pure" category because the background of the profane world continues to be maintained in orgies, celebrations and sacrifices as calculations for instrumental objectives such as maintaining the fertility of the fields. However, as they run their course, celebrations develop the kind of dynamics that lead to the fact that the celebration itself takes on a higher value or a value as such, when he says, that "in the course of festivals, the goals have less meaning than the festival itself" (Bataille 1994a: 118, from his Caillois review of 1951).[19] Yet since the pleasure leads to just as intensive a "con-

[18] Here the above-mentioned loss of individuality of abnormal sexual practices in fantasy products takes on significance from the point of view that they are extracted from the domain of the sacred.

[19] For a paradigmatic example see my chapter on the Japanese Matsuri in this volume; Bataille refers here to the now eminent view – after the performative turn in anthropology – that the ritual activity has its own *raison d'être* and is therefore effective, as the performance carries away actors and participant in unexpected ways, revamping their perception of reality, often radically, and that applies even when and if, maybe because of its redundant features.

summation" as the sacrificial rite and thus can flare up to an intensity that destroys ("eats up") everything, excess (both waste and plethora), whose end point is death, remains so terrifying and we normally recoil from it.

Thus, despite all the wasteful consumption, every celebration remains subject to the "agony of consciousness" of not being able to let go. This is why ultimately the celebration is framed by the limits of reality, the negation of which is actually supposed to be the major point (Bataille 1989: 54).

In the end, however, it is the awareness of death that is finally able to shed light on the values of life and which also connects sacredness with eroticism in that with this celebratory waste the human being becomes sovereign and at the same time becomes capable of making the sacred immanent. The potential of both domains and the violent act of the excessive exhaustion is caused by the *desire for the impossible*, which is the *transcendence beyond transgression*.

What then remains beyond the recognition of the limit, of the transgression of speaking and writing, is the revelation of the "presence of *sensuality*" (Bataille 1979: 207; his emphasis), which puts it beyond speech. Sensuality may be conceived as the rupture of consciousness, of reality and perception, and the very attempt of transgressing the experiential level through reflection brings the rupture to our awareness, increasing its power of desolation and discontinuity, so that the continuity which we want to achieve in writing, in keeping in the memory, of transmission and tradition, of authentically speaking and writing are nothing but forms of the imaginary, of the figments of a mind which tries to preserve something beyond the moment of the experience itself. There lies the final rupture.

Thus Bataille reaches the same conclusion on which Leiris appears to base his concepts of *Tauromachie*: perfection cannot be perceived until the element of the *flaw* comes into play that is found in the potentiality of the perception of death. For Leiris this "sinister" is the original source of *aesthetics*, while for Bataille it is the original source of *eroticism* and thus for both it is founded in *sacred play* for which Caillois was the Muse to both.

There seems to me no better summary of these positions reached by the French *avant-garde* of ethnographer-artists of the surrealist persuasion than the insight by Foucault that the true nature of transgression as well as of limit and their complex intertwining have come to the fore in modern philosophy for the first time that clearly and uncompromisingly:

"Transgression contains nothing negative, but affirms limited being – affirms the limitlessness into which it leaps as it opens this zone to existence for the first time. But correspondingly, this affirmation contains nothing positive: no content can bind it, since, by definition, no limit can possibly restrict it. Perhaps it is simply an affirmation of division; but only insofar as division is not understood to mean a cutting gesture, or the establishment of a separation or the measuring of a distance, only retaining that in it which may designate the existence of difference" (Foucault 1977: 35-6).

# HERMES

# Seduced Seducers

*Experiencing*

*In England people make much of becoming totally dispassionate and freethinkers in moral matters: Spencer, Stuart Mill. But they do nothing but formulate moral sentiments. Something altogether different is required: for once, to feel something different (something other) and to be able thoughtfully to analyse this afterwards. That means, dear moralist, new inner experiences (Nietzsche).[1]*

One could not easily imagine a more pithy statement, or passionate plea in response to the dilemma besetting the anthropological profession since its inception as empirical study with the – until recently – unspoken agreement of the majority of its practitioners about the canon of methodology as introduced by Malinowski through the oxymoron "participant observation". Nietzsche's "revaluation" is indeed a turning upside-down of the agreed modern practice of doing science by putting ethics as experience before epistemology.

What field is better equipped than anthropology to put these precepts into practice, where, as Malinowski formulated it, fieldworkers aim "to grasp the native's point of view, *his* relation to life, to realise *his* vision of *his* world" (Malinowski 1961: 25, his emphasis) through what he labelled "plunging into the life of natives" (1961:7 and 22). In the first quarter of this century, the new "science of mankind" was based on the methodological primacy of experience of Otherness *via* the Self, which could be called an "immersion therapy". In the last quarter of the century the discussion about ethnography seems to revolve around the problem of analysis not of data but of writing about others, not of the method of being with others, but merely of the product, the process of knowledge acquisition becoming expendable.

While the instigator of "thick description", Clifford Geertz, has doubtlessly done the long-overdue job of deconstructing the process of writing ethnography, his critique to bring the author into the text seems to have gone to the extreme sarcastic position, possibly born from despair about the impossibility of the task, of declaring all such attempts as basically futile. On the other hand, he does understate the importance of the self-reflexive stance, which only the encounter in the field can generate.

The ethnographic enterprise is supposed to range from participation through mediation to communication, or from understanding to interpretation,

[1] 1969: 203; my translation; emphasis in the original.

as I once put it[2]. Knowledge is authenticated by participation while the communication could potentially lead to emancipation of self and others, whereby the latter do not need us to authenticate them. To establish the status of that kind of knowledge which participatory research obtains must remain an urgent task, coming before consideration of the form, which the transmission of this knowledge takes. The anthropologist may often feel like the mythical blind seer Teiresias who after having been granted the boon of changing his sex, when rechanged into a man and asked how it felt to be female could not recall the experience. But then the anthropologist knows that "the other establishes me in truth: it is only with the other that I feel I am 'myself'" (Barthes 1990: 229); without pretending to "be the Other" in the Diltheyan mode of "empathetic re-experiencing" (*Nachempfindung*). The anthropologist is more beholden to the insight that the "me" that he writes about is a self established as a composite after having encountered the Other, as Self transformed. It is this transformation process which I shall pursue in the following through a diversity of perspectives.

### The Metaphor of Hermes

Over the years, a variety of different metaphoric comparisons has been applied by practitioners to the anthropologist's fieldwork activities in order to convey the importance as well as the existential, epistemological and moral dialectic inherent in the figure of the stranger who as participant observer has to shuttle between contrasting attitudes to the Other, between nearness and distance, engagement and detachment, involvement and critique, experience and analysis. Following previous suggestions[3]. I shall therefore refer to Hermes in his function as "messenger" who straddles the worlds of gods, humans and the dead. I thereby take cognisance of two aspects of Hermes' nature, on the one hand of the bridge from being with others to writing about others, while on the other through the intimation of Hermes as seducer I refer again to the double bind, between self and other in the field as well as the researcher's self in relation to readers.

I shall engage in a polemic deconstruction of some of what I consider excessive statements by post-modern deconstructionism, but I shall not main-

---

[2] "Von der Teilnahme über die Mitteilung zur Vermittlung" (1980, *Paideuma* 26).

[3] See chapter on Satire in this volume; the metaphor of Hermes has of course been usefully applied by Crapanzano 1987 and 1992. I do however differ from his approach by underplaying the psychoanalytic connotation in Crapanzano's "Hamlet's Desire", while stressing more the seductive qualities of Hermes as against his vacillations as mediator as implied in Crapanzano's "Hermes' Dilemma".

tain this mode of the trickster's puckish delight in subversion consistently throughout, as I want to carry on what Geertz has called the "hackneyed" discussion of the epistemological status of fieldwork.

By circling the problem from historical as well as epistemological angles, the overriding metaphor remains the one of the anthropologist as trickster, which however may end in the logical absurdity of the deceived deceiver of Radin and Kerényi (see Koepping 1985), which nevertheless may be an existentially perceived truth. I intentionally make use of the ambiguity of Hermes who not only subverts through clumsiness and pretended naivety, but as one who through applying charm, stealth and cunning becomes the creative genius of the boons of mankind. I therefore take Hermes as icon for the herald and messenger who through dialogic encounter, through speaking and other forms of *seductive communication*, engages in a process of gaining knowledge, while as translator *revealing and hiding truth* and "half-truth" in this very process of communication.

As Hermes was also the inventor of the lyre, the comparison to the seduction through music to which the listener succumbs is implied in my pleading for a rethinking of the modes – and metaphors used for that mode – of fieldwork as more than "data-gathering" activity. I suggest that the often aggressive epithet used for the gaining of "information" (like the cracking of codes, investigations or surveying) be recast in the mode of "surrender", a word which most critics of Malinowski's assumedly "imperialist" posture conveniently overlook in his oeuvre where he uses it – without epistemological implications – in his "*Diary*" as follows: "I went to the village and I surrendered artistically to the impression of a new *Kulturkreis*".

The epistemological elaboration of "surrender" as a key concept for doing research, relating it to a "catch" (the conceptualisations in written work) has been introduced by Kurt Wolff in several publications since 1976.[4] I shall refer more extensively to them, further on: suffice it here, in order to avoid immediate misunderstandings, to state that the term "surrender" (*Hingebung*) does not entail a "giving up" (which would be *Aufgeben*) of self or a "merging" of self and other. Surrender rather implies the attentiveness with which we listen to musical performances, or that characteristic of lovers' relationships, these relationships which lead not to a losing of self but to a finding of it, as expressed in the medieval concept of *amor ut intelligam* ("to love in order to understand" by St. Augustine) which should, in Wolff's understanding of social science research, accompany, or be the foundation of our "intellectual curiosity" (see Wolff 1976).

Yet I do not think that any one metaphor or one single trickster icon however versatile and multifaceted will suffice to figuratively encompass the

---

[4] The root-words of these metaphors contain a strong element of the haptic sense, which may or may not be a typical feature of Indo-European languages.

ambiguities of the ethnographic enterprise as *practice of living* as well as *practice of writing*. We may have to resort to a variety of such figures. George Steiner has recently made a bold and convincing suggestion to conflate and focus the European intellectual attitudes to the world in the fourfold iconicity of Prometheus/Faust, Hamlet, Don Quixote and Don Juan which Arnold Hauser has previously shown to be emanations of a narcissistic consciousness (Hauser 1964), which I in turn like to conceive of as typical European forms of tricksterhood[5]. I will therefore here try to extend the fourfold division by the figure of Hermes who shares a number of traits with the other four, while lacking some of theirs. While Hermes as critic and interpreter goes beyond the self-referentiality of the other four tricksters, he shares the inventiveness and cunning of Prometheus (who lacks charm while Hermes lacks the other's *libido sciendi* as well as the rebellious attitude, being more diplomat than revolutionary); the charm of Don Juan (lacking his desperation, but charming his way out of desperate situations); the played naivety of Don Quixote (lacking his delusions and showing not much of the holy fool trait). Similarities with the vacillations of Hamlet seem to spring from his ability at dissimulation or performative skills of pretence, while in his beguiling musicality he resembles the singer Orpheus. However, Hermes' main trait is his multilingualism, his ability to carry messages between different realms of the universe, being able to cross boundaries, protecting travellers, and to be "persuasive" in his function as diplomat, psychopomp and adjudicator. As master of dissimulation, he could take on strange disguises and play the part of the perfect thief.[6] He is also the master and guardian of "secret knowledge" adduced later to him (as a double of the Egyptian god Thot who invented sciences, writing, numbers and books), and his charm was apparently strong enough to attract Aphrodite out of which union the hermaphrodite was born (see also Brown 1969), so that the metaphorical use of the *psychopomp* may conceivably be interpreted as a marriage between science and sensuality, linking us back to the Platonic image of the connection between Eros and truth.

## *Seduction and Annihilation: Europe's Quest*

I here put my options on Hermes as metaphoric image for the fieldwork encounter – other trickster icons would certainly throw a different light on our understanding of the nature of ethnographic work – because of the seductive

---

[5] See chapter on the Trickster in this volume.

[6] In this essay I intentionally abstain from comparing Hermes as thief with anthropologists as appropriators of indigenous knowledge. Such equation would be an oversimplification whichoversimplification, which however has been repeatedly implied, in particular in the post-colonial climate of intellectual rectitude. My contentions about re-appropriation will become clear in a later section through recourse to the musical mode of "recital".

qualities of his dialogic disposition and because European history starts with the metaphor of a seduction through the myth of Europa and Zeus, a seduction which – according to Steiner's pessimistic assessment of the modern European consciousness – ends in a boundless striving for destructiveness which can only find its fulfilment in utter annihilation. Whether anthropology's search for this Other is an attempt to overcome the destructive impulses which permeate reality – where reality overtakes anthropology by throwing its essentialist theoretical concept of cultural difference back at it through using it to legitimate genocide and other atrocities –, whether its endeavour can be perceived as an answer to the only vision which could – in Steiner's thinking – save the occidental consciousness from annihilation by merging the Judaeo-Christian and the Greco-Roman worlds, the unfinished project of the Renaissance to weld Athens and Jerusalem together, remains an open challenge. It is the challenge which philosophy has begun to accept through the writings of Levinas who develops what he himself calls an anti-totalitarian, anti-Platonic and anti-Heideggerian philosophy which rests not on the claim for Being and Subject as self-fashioned, but in which the Other becomes as much of a focus as does desire and the messianic impulse of Judaism (Levinas 1961).

### Anthropology as Redemptive Process?

The question remains whether anthropology can contribute to this kind of Salvationist enterprise of welding culturally divergent ontologies together through the moral stance of exposing the Self to them. Forms of perceiving anthropology as a redemptive process were entertained by some of its practitioners. Lévi-Strauss gave a negative answer with his notion of cultural entropy. By contrast we may infer a more positive image from Malinowski's vision of the aims of anthropological fieldwork, the metaphorical suggestiveness of which has to my knowledge not been perceived (least of all, by any of the busy deconstructionists who still seem to revel in anti-imperial pounding of other chests).

There exists however an original metaphorical relation to redemptive processes. In his introduction of 1922 to *Argonauts of the Western Pacific*, Malinowski refers to the collecting of demographic and census information of kinship terms and genealogies as "dead material" (1961: 5), which become, nevertheless, the "firm skeleton of the tribal life" (1961: 11). This, as may be recalled, he later designates as the firm foundation for the "constructive drafting ... of the charters of native institutions", whereby those whose life is largely determined by them are not aware of the values governing the institutions or are unable to formulate these coherently (Malinowski 1935: 137). The *second* feature to be aimed for is the "intimate touches of native life" (Malinowski 1961: 17), to acquire "the feeling" and "being in touch with the natives" (1961: 8). He summarises this double requirement by contrasting his own approach with previous scientific work: "... we are given an excellent skeleton, so to speak, of the tribal constitution, but it lacks flesh and blood" (1961: 17), and repeating emphatically: "... the full body and blood of actual native life fills out soon the skeleton of abstract constructions" (1961: 18). These are obtained through attention to the ethnographer's breaches of etiquette (1961: 8) or those *"imponderabilia* of actual life" (1961: 18; his emphasis) such as the routine activities of body care, food preparation and eating, as well as through a knowledge of the meaning of the "intimacy" of family life – as opposed to the ideal concept – as expressed in "the affection, the mutual interest, the little preferences, and the little antipathies" (1961: 19).

The *third* aim of scientific fieldwork, as he calls it, is recording "the native's views and opinions and utterances" which make up the "spirit" of native life as well as ethnographic work (1961: 22), and, seeking to "convince those Here that one has been There", claimed as an important novelty by some deconstructionists and textualists like Geertz, Malinowski adds a "third commandment": to "formulate the results in the most convincing manner" (1961: 23). What then did Malinowski end up with: anthropomorphisation of data or redemption of the researcher?

## *A Personal Encounter*

It has become customary for anthropologists to authenticate their data or deliberations through reference to a field-incident, as exemplified by the indignant reply of Lévi-Strauss to his critic Gurvitch: "They are my witnesses". I shall therefore follow suit and relate one such incident from fieldwork in Japan in 1966, because the incident is one, which first made me aware of the precariousness of the ethnographic method and thus ultimately led to the present meta-discourse on participation[7].

When I approached the foundress of one of the many post-war so-called "New Religions" *(Shinko Shukyo)* in Japan, the late Mrs. Sayo Kitamura of *Odoru Shukyo* ("Dancing Religion") or *Tensho Kotai Jingu Kyo* ("Religion of the Heavenly Shining Goddess and the Sacred Shrine"), she got rather tired of my insistent questioning about her relation to the deity, which was assumed to speak through her mouth and reside in her belly, and of my inquiring about the state of "non-ego" *(muga)* which followers were believed to achieve through participation in the ritual "dance of loosing one's ego" *(muga-no-odori)*. She curtly advised me: *"Bakayaro"* ("you simpleton" or "stupido")! – "You try to

---

[7] See chapter on Shamanism in this volume.

grasp with your head what you can only achieve through your heart (*kokoro*). You should participate in the dance of non-ego!" (See Koepping 1968, 1980b; 1994a, 1999)!

The meaning of Mrs. Kitamura's advice seems clear: she meant me to abandon my questioning, observing, interviewing and all forms of ratiocination in order to gain "understanding" or insight by joining in the dance of her followers, which would help me to reach the state of emptiness which would reveal the divinity and thereby answer all my questions through experience. To put it differently, the message seemed to be – and it was startling for me at that time and has remained startling until today – that I surrender to the occasion, leaving my scholarly interests and orientations and my rationality aside. For the sake of the participatory requirement, I realised that she was right, but I also realised that I could not give in to the occasion – for, as Gouldner put it once, I had to satisfy both requirements of my professional life, those of passion as well as of reason. Because without passion "man would be a computer, but without reason he would be a naked ape".

Mrs. Kitamura was right insofar as my professed belief in gaining knowledge through participation should entail immersion in the activities, but besides observing my own self in this process of participation, and the activities of others, I was also committed to conveying my insights to the outside world. The latter required me to attain distance instead of involvement, detachment instead of engagement, or at least always the application of rational analysis in order to gain a horizon of reflexivity, and reflection on what the group was trying to do in the light of a wider context, be it that of modern Japan or that of the correlation of messianic movements to social, political or economic circumstances in other times and other places.

My initial self-set task was for a comparative analysis, informed by theories as well as descriptions already available on similar phenomena outside Japan. Little was I prepared to encounter a wall of non-comprehension for my task of "writing about" by inquiring from "outside" among the practitioners of the group who, like the foundress, wanted me to become a member, a part of their community of believers.

### Selected Contexts of the Field-Encounter

The foundress and the group members (largely the several dozen key administrators and missionaries at headquarters in the town of Tabuse, as well as several hundred members coming on pilgrimages or work-duties for several days, sometimes two weeks, to the headquarters, and later many individual members all over Japan and overseas) were prepared to let me as "foreigner" share in their experiences. This was a relief and surprise for me at the same time – as it would be for anyone else who has tried to do participant research in Japan – since foreigners are usually a category of persons who are considered "crazy" or "odd" (*henna gaijin*): if they try to emulate Japanese ways too closely, they easily become a laughing stock as well as a source of embarrassment.

The group I encountered had no qualms about my notion of participation which often creates the greatest difficulties in other research areas: Anthropologists who are neither doctors or nurses, nor development agents with specialised knowledge, cannot easily justify or legitimate their presence, not to speak of their wish to participate like "one of them". However, the members of this religious group could not understand the reason for writing about them through the tool of rational inquiry: The only way any writing was to be done was as "testimony" to conversion and to the experience of divine blessing in order to spread the truth of their gospel. I, on the other hand, was willing to participate and share in their experiences, happy to get away from the often only vicarious way of "gazing at Otherness" so common in most fieldwork, but I was not prepared to surrender to the degree of "becoming one of them", to fake conversion or even to give up my analytic task.

The compromise reached in the end was for the group to accept the idea of my writing about them as approximating their notion of conversion literature while granting the foreigner the freedom or spleen of a "learned man" (*erai hito*), as those who write books for a living in Japanese society are known by people in the countryside. However, being in close contact with many adherents at the headquarter of a foundress of teachings which were literally taken as "God's truth" for world salvation, at a place which was to be the "future paradise" (*tengoku*) on earth, I was also often challenged in my private self when involved in questions of truth or of "my beliefs". I soon realised that I could not bring off a "neutral" stand, nor could I fake belief in their specific truth: the encounter led me to rethink my own beliefs of which my professional anthropological pursuits are an inseparable part.

### Authentication

My example touches directly on the issue of the authenticity of the researcher. While it has become customary to claim that a written ethnography gains its authenticity through reference to fieldwork, in the recent deconstructionist literature the concept seems to be devalued to mean the "persuasiveness of fiction" and not the existentially and morally more challenging question of what authenticity truly entails, the "being true to oneself". The question which we ought to be able to answer is not whether we are convincing to a readership but whether our findings rely on an authentic human being's involvement with other human beings, and that question can only be assessed through attention to the primary praxis of fieldwork, not by reference to good or bad writing or to rhetorical adumbrations. What does "being true to oneself" entail, in general terms, for the anthropological profession? Surely, the reader will say, no answer can be expected or given in detail as only the researchers could answer this for themselves. I recently wrote confidently on this as follows: "The only authenticity we may claim in this enterprise we derive from our participation in other ways of perceiving reality, and not from the casual voyeurism of the tourist or the persuasiveness of our 'fictions' in our world" (Koepping 1994b: 25). I still maintain this position, but with an extension or rather addition resulting from a variety of influences which forced me to re-think my position, influences ranging from "re-creating" the field-encounter in my memory to the literature of the Writing Culture adherents, from teaching fieldwork methods to undergraduates through rereading carefully Malinowski's introduction to *Argonauts* to encountering colleagues thinking about similar problems during conferences. As the reaction to my participatory attempts in the field showed to me then, and more pronouncedly shows now, my informants did share to a degree my own idea of true knowledge to be gained through action and experience, but we parted at the point where I insisted on holding to my own beliefs which included the aim of writing about them in an analytic way. Nevertheless, in spite of disagreements true dialogic interactions did develop, because of the differences being maintained, I would think, because we – informants and myself – were indeed mutually curious and willing not only to suspend pre-judgements, but also to suspend disbelief in the possibility of a meeting of thought and feeling[8].

## Two Forms of Access to Reality: Knowledge of the Head and the Heart

Little was I prepared to encounter a cultural setting where a split of two kinds of knowledge was taken for granted, where knowledge through giving in and surrendering to experience was considered the highest form of realising full humanity while all ratiocination was considered an inferior form of living, a form which the foundress Mrs. Kitamura made responsible for the "decline of the world" (using the Buddhist term *mappo*, the third of three ages after the death of Shakyamuni, being the age of decline before the Apocalypse).

While I was not prepared to relinquish my own pursuit of rational analysis, the encounter with this different concept of knowledge made me aware not only that anthropology was caught in the same bind which Mrs. Kitamura was

---

[8] Crapanzano in his ethnography *Tuhami* quite rightly pointed to the necessity of "mutual recognition", and I would even go further by insisting on mutual constitution between researcher and interlocutor, and by implication, their respective cultural embeddedness.

describing, but that the close encounter of participation was indispensable as a praxis in order to be able to detect the similarity or difference on a more than intellectual level of game-playing. I was challenged in my belief that I could possibly keep my personal self-separate from my professional self. And I now became aware that the professional orientation to write and be involved with analysis does belong to my authenticity.

Authenticity thus encompasses the combination of what Gouldner called the two forms of knowledge, knowledge as information as well as knowledge as awareness (1972: 493)[9], whereby the latter as self-reflective mode cannot come about without participation and engagement with concrete others. This engagement and participation does involve the full Self, not a compartmental-ised section of it, since, as Diamond once expressed it, when we talk about generalised others we are most inauthentic. Roland Barthes put it very aptly by quoting Nietzsche:

> "Supposing that we experienced the other as he experiences himself – which Schopenhauer calls compassion and which might more accu-rately be called a union within suffering, a unity of suffering – we should hate the other when he himself, like Pascal, finds himself hate-ful" (Barthes 1990: 174).

In his own comment Barthes continues this line of thought: "Now, whatever the power of love, this does not occur: I am moved, anguished, for it is horri-ble to see those one loves suffering, but at the same time I remain dry, water-tight. My identification is imperfect" (1990: 57).

There is no guarantee that we can ever bridge successfully the gap between experience and analysis or between the two forms of existence which Levinas labelled the different attitudes to the world: either we are giving in to it and are taken over by it (then we are existing in the mode of ecstasy), or we appro-priate and assimilate it to us (then we are in the mode of knowledge), but prior to both are forms of enjoyment (*jouissance*) and all enjoyment is a way of being (Levinas 1987: 63). But, we might add, our way of being is in different worlds. While we may reach an understanding through reaching out to the other, by imagination, or by negotiation of meaning, we will not be able to change places. Rosaldo's example of understanding the head-hunter's rage refers to the flash of recognition of meaning through our own hurt and the accompanying 'natural' reaction of rage, but it is "his" hurt and rage, or in Laura Bohannan's words: "The greater the extent to which one has lived and participated in a genuinely foreign culture and understood it, the greater the extent to which one realises that one could not, without violence to ones per-sonal integrity, be of it" (Bowen 1964: 291).

---

[9] For a similar position emerging see also Lane Kauffmann 1990.

*Appropriations of Self and Other*

Rethinking the field-encounter with a religious foundress, I would now state that only through this encounter could I become aware of the second pole of my authenticity as anthropologist and person: the aim to analyse and write or what Roland Barthes would have called "the pleasure of the text". Yet, I could only give in to that by having first given in to the encounter. Thus both forms of praxis belong certainly to the anthropologist's authenticity, and no matter how many texts I read previously or subsequently, the encounter remains the primary source for the reflexivity to take place. The example of the encounter also makes it clear that no form of "text-positivism", no laying open all possible memories of influences, whether before, during or after the field encounter, can help to elucidate the sources of my interpretations of Japanese attitudes to knowledge, which – while partial in spite of all the above given contextual analysis – are my own "map" to make sense of a plethora of single incidences; whether it provides a reader with the same map is open to debate.

The encounter clarified many questions I had about Japanese religiosity and many previously incomprehensible behavioural incidences fell into place. However, the meaning of what Mrs. Kitamura said also was informed by previous experiences in Japan, including misunderstandings. Moreover, the epistemological and existential impossibility of the task of anthropology became clear to my startled re-cognition: how could I have or pretend to have similar participatory access to half a dozen messianic groups?

My above given translations and interpretations of Japanese concepts of knowledge are certainly re-appropriations of my own experiences for other purposes, like the one at hand of presenting an essayistic approach, re-appropriations in the light of information and purposes which were not at issue at the time of the encounter in the field or of its first analysis.

The encounter ultimately also made sense of my anthropological vocation (for the time being), but foremost made me realise my difference through the alterity of the Other, throwing me back upon my own alterity and forcing me to explain myself to myself, authenticating myself not only to the Other, but also to the Self (and in this sense of course also legitimating my continuation of research as well as writing). The encounter itself is possibly responsible for my quoting of Levinas in this context, but certainly is decisive – here and now – for my agreement with or critique of Malinowski or other colleagues who have addressed the problem of Otherness in fieldwork and writing, or for my quoting certain authors and not others in the essay: put simply, I read my own culture history and my intellectual heritage in the light of the field-encounter. And that is, after all, what comparative anthropology is really about, namely to re-read and re-interpret the Self as individual life-history as well as from the point of a collective memory, thus critically re-appropriating it for personal (and professional) purposes.[10]

Jean Pouillon put the dilemma very aptly as follows: "The notion we have of others is a function of what we are ourselves", and, so he continues, a proper anthropology comes about through the integration of our "prejudiced" ideas and what we know about others. But how, he asks, can our "prejudiced" ideas become true knowledge: "This means admitting that he (the anthropologist) can become conscious of the traditions which orient his thought, that he can judge them and need no longer submit to them even if he still accepts them" (Pouillon 1980: 37-39).

This does sound like the advice of Gadamer that while we may not be able to overcome our prejudices the chance at least exists "to free ourselves through reflection from that which otherwise oppresses us unbeknown to us".[11] This still leaves open the question: how do reflection and self-reflection (reflexivity) get set into motion? Before trying to prove that self-referentiality does not open the way to this, I take a detour through a discussion of another familiar form of re-appropriation in the field of artistic re-creation in the musical modality.


*Original and Copy: Citation and Re-Cital*

While the research subjects (partners of a dialogue) provide the original information (possibly maieutically induced), they end up disembodied in the literal sense of the word, made over into new bodies in the "body of the text" providing the "pleasure of the text" to distanced readerships, thus loosing control and power in a similar way as do researchers when writing, although the latter's disempowerment is at least mitigated by the control over the authorial shaping of texts as "woven things" (I shall later discuss the power of seduction the informant retains). This problem relates to the "appropriation" of knowledge in the written text to which I shall turn now.

An issue that relates directly to the notion of appropriation is that of the translation from experience to expression (Dilthey's *von der Erfahrung zum Ausdruck*), the problem of "citation". Some textualists convey the impression that we would be closer to the truth or would gain a more accurate picture of the Other (or the Other and the Self of the researcher in their interactions) if we only had all the field notes and diaries of fieldworkers and thus could re-

---

[10] For an extension of this idea by a researcher who reads his fieldwork through Forster's works and *vice versa*, see Rapport 1994.

[11] "Die Reflexion befreit, indem sie durchschaubar macht, von dem, was einen undurchschaut beherrscht"( see Gadamer 1975: 283-316).

construct their "path" (a typical example with these aims is the collection of field notes or rather of meta-discussions on field notes in Sanjek 1990). It should be abundantly clear that a return to a new text-positivism is futile as every text is the absorption and transformation of other texts[12]. Since Schleiermacher, interpretation always entails the appropriation of a "text", the past, while addressing the present and the future. The original is thus appropriated for the present audience's (and interpreter's) relevance. Pouillon put it cogently by positing as minimum requirement to translate "faithfully from the 'language of departure'" and "intelligibly to the 'language of arrival'" (Pouillon 1980: 38).

It is for this reason that conductors of Beethoven's symphonies and performers of Schubert's *Lieder* are hailed as "creative" persons, as they "re-create" and are insofar original and creative because while taking both sides into account they are appraised by the "taste" of the present as to how a symphony or a *Lied* should sound, while the – audience rarely cares whether Beethoven or Schubert would have played or sung it in the same way. It is not the identity of the copy, the exact replica, which is desired but a "convincing" rendering of an original in what is appropriately called a "re-cital". The very problem of the age of exact mechanical or electronic reproduction (Disneyland or Hearst's collection mania are the serious examples, the ironic breaking of this fad in the works of Roy Lichtenstein or Andy Warhol the playful comments on it) is that it leaves the audience rather listless, as a million Raphael Madonnas or the rebuilding of Medieval townships are known to be exactly what they try to hide: fake imitations, without life or "spirit".[13]

By contrast, each "re-creation" of a piece of music or a dramatic role by a gifted artist is considered unique, riveting, soul-stirring and possibly "cathartic" in Schiller's sense, because the interpreter "got it right" in accordance with the taste and the imagination as well as the desire (the fantasy) of the audience. This experience is replicated and re-experienced by anybody who reads a poem the first or the hundredth time for private pleasure (or edification), when the pleasure is not derived from the author's intentions but from the relevance the reader, listener or viewer attaches to the occasion, Clifford's statement that "ethnographers can no longer claim this sort of originary or creative role, for they must always reckon with predecessors", because "one writes among, against, through, and in spite of them", is misleading in the light of a classical hermeneutic framework (it would barely hold in a positivistic environment; see Clifford 1990: 55)[14]. Australian Aboriginal religious practitioners and artists could have taught Clifford a different perspective.

---

[12] For an incisive critique along these lines, see Kauffmann 1990.

[13] For a critique of this search for authenticity in the replication see also Hillel Schwartz, *The Culture of the Copy*, Cambridge, MA., 1996.

[14] See my comments on intertextuality in chapter one of this volume.

Aborigines of the Northwest of Western Australia "touch up" the paintings on rocks where the *Dreamtime* creator beings left their "imprint": this re-painting activity is enacted in periods of sacred time, during seasonal "increase" ceremonies, in truly "re-creational" time, in order not only to "remember" (or anamnetically re-collect the ancestor creators), but specifically to effect the increase of all species, thus perceiving "re-creation" as a creative act (repeating the *Dreaming* as the Creation[15]).

By re-creation the present performers appropriate indeed the powers of the original creators, and in this sense each appropriation has to encompass an apprehension or rather comprehension, an understanding of the creative original process. Each reading (or writing or playing of music or conversation) is an original experience: that is the true message of the art of interpretation. This also empowers each reader as last interpreter while the author loses control over the production, as does the mediator. In my present frame of reference, the informant as well as the translator/mediator-anthropologist must empower the reader to make sense of the product. As I tried to show through the explication of a personal field-encounter, another feature gets short shrift if "originality" in appropriation and re-casting in interpretation is denied: the transformation of the researcher involved in an encounter has to be taken into account, in particular the changing of his theoretical perspective or personal frame of interpreting his and other cultural arrangements in critical "re-appraisal" or what I have called previously the "emancipatory" effect of research (which may work also for the research partner).

### A Breakdown of Occidental Confidence?

In regard to the Malinowskian "spirit" of gained information, Geertz speaks of an "ethnographic ventriloquism: the claim to speak not *just about* another form of life but to speak from within it" (Geertz 1988: 14), making Malinowski's ethnography (meaning his fieldwork) an "oddly inward matter, a question of self-testing and self-transformation, and making of its writing a form of self-revelation", which, so concludes Geertz, dramatised for Malinowski "his hopes of self-transcendence", while for most descendants, "it dramatises their fears of self-deception" (Geertz 1988: 22-23). It is difficult to imagine that Geertz as advocate of "thick description" here resorts to such pessimistic views about anthropology's search for what is human in us all. An uncharitable explanation would be to see this remark not as rhetorical hyperbole but as based on the world-view of a hermeneutics of suspicion, which may be the logical outcome of an attitude of misanthropy (see Koepping 1995). As originally defined by Kant and further developed by Helmuth Pless-

---

[15] See chapter on the Dreaming in this volume.

ner, the misanthrope is convinced that human nature is governed by egoism and deceit, resulting often from a feeling of failure (see Plessner 1974: 213). This is a trait discernible very early on in the written works of Geertz. Thus in 1968 he claimed that "the relationship between an anthropologist and his informants rests on a set of partial fictions half seen through", having first asserted that the tears which many anthropologists see in the eyes of informants "are not really there" (Geertz 1968), for which the unacknowledged original is Evans-Pritchard's note: "... an anthropologist has failed unless, when he says goodbye to the natives, there is on both sides the sorrow of parting" (Evans-Pritchard 1951: 79).

We may quibble with Evans-Pritchard whether all field encounters are amiable, as in many field situations there may have been a mixture of hate and love, of greed and anger, there may have been moments of suspicion and disgust, and there may also be relief at the parting of the stranger who knows so much, who was such a pestering nuisance, and on the ethnographer's side the expectation of reward, fame and re-union with "civilised" life. But there will always be sorrow on both sides if engagement and negotiation over a long period have occurred (other forms of anthropological fieldwork are not under discussion here). Otherwise, we find that which Evans-Pritchard labelled "competent" ethnographic work, but if it was only won through physical proximity and if fieldwork did not affect "the entire personality, the total human being", no "deeper level of understanding" will have been reached (Evans-Pritchard 1951: 82).

Twenty years later, Geertz states categorically that modern anthropology – in contrast to the founding fathers and mothers to whom he grants superior rhetorical skills – has become the business of "half-convinced writers trying to half-convince readers of their half convictions" (Geertz 1988: 139). As clue to the conviction about the "prevalence of deceit" (to use one of Bailey's recent titles) the incident, which Geertz reports about his fieldwork, offers itself, when he refused to lend his typewriter to an indigenous aspiring author, which led to a break-up of the relationship. Geertz puts this into the following framework of polite deceit:

> "Borrowing ... my informant was, tacitly, asserting his demand to be taken seriously as an intellectual ..., i.e. a peer; lending it, I was, tacitly, granting that demand ... We both knew that these agreements could be only partial: we are not really colleagues ..." (Geertz 1968).

As Simmel pointed out at the beginning of this century about the emptiness of social courtesy, we should not infer from their observance any esteem or devotion (1950: 400).

Early insight to this effect comes from Pascal's treatise *"Trois discourses sur la condition des grands*" of 1560 where he advised that one could require that one greets a duke but one cannot require that one hold him in esteem. One could argue with Geertz against himself: he did not see the "winks", but mistook courtesy on his side for showing of esteem (the base reason may have been plain inconvenience) and inferred that the informant's request for courtesy implied an equality he, Geertz, did not believe to be there in the first place, a result – if I may speculate – possibly of the lack of the very same confidence which he requires of present writers of ethnography.

While chiding Geertz for trying to wheedle his way out of this conundrum through recourse to a theory of "cross-cultural communion" for a case which is a straightforward personal miscommunication or a clash of personalities, Robert Jay admits in the same breath that he too mismanaged personal relations, as he could not remember a single personal informant, and that "any awareness I had of particular individuals as they related personally to me, to others, and to their own lives, except as it bore on my perception of such patterning" – of systems of rice agriculture as dynamic of social and economic power – "slipped by me, or, if registered because of some intimacy in my relation with them, got set apart into the separate realm of my private life" (Jay 1969: 376). Jay admits in retrospect that the facile distinction which he made in his earlier fieldwork between relevance and responsibility, the former being related to the scientific project, the latter being relegated to the "private" or "personal" level, cannot be maintained, because relevance as knowledge and responsibility as action are inextricably intertwined in the relationship between researcher and informant (1969: 377-378).

### Humour, Self-Irony and Surrender to Seduction

Jay's "confessions" are an example of insight about the limitations of the Self won after fieldwork; but it is the very attention to "scientific" anthropology which brings about this realisation of the lack, dimly felt in the field, leading now to a new "self-realisation", rejecting the old "me" and creating a future "me" with different orientations, thus leading to a transformed condition of being in the world.

This is also the conclusion to which Lévi-Strauss comes in his reading of Rousseau's *Confessions*: The long reliance of European thought on the self-fashioning Cartesian *"cogito"* cannot establish the Self as a reflexive object of the reflecting subject. For Lévi-Strauss, Rousseau's importance lies in his realisation that – against the attempt of Montaigne – the Self has to be established as a third person through the dialogic interrogation only possible through the presence of others, in order to arrive at the insight of Rimbaud's "je est un autre". Lévi-Strauss therefore agrees with Rousseau in the pronouncement that "when I hear music, I am hearing myself through it".[16]

It is from this perspective surprising that Lévi-Strauss, who had previously indicated that no particular view of the world should be considered as superior and that anthropologists have to follow Rousseau's adage that one has "to refuse oneself in oneself in order to accept oneself in others" (Lévi-Strauss 1973: 242), does not get to the point of criticising his own society but rather feels himself as a "amputated being" (Sontag 1966: 69-81). At the same time chiding those anthropologists who criticise their own society while becoming most conservative in supporting even the abstruse customs as soon as they enter the field. But if no society has the prerogative of the "good life", then criticism at both ends should be possible. Standing aloof from engagement is that very attitude which came into prominence with the notion of Scheler and later of Mannheim about the "free-floating class of the intelligentsia", and it is an attitude the anthropologist cannot afford. If anthropology chooses to deny its own precepts of the suspension of disbelief in the impossibility of the "psychic unity of mankind" underlying the fieldwork endeavour, it should indeed not be surprised to be taken (by informants and readers) as untrustworthy as that cosmopolitanism which Rousseau regarded with great suspicion. We cannot retain the attitude of the limping Oedipus if we want to do fieldwork. The adherents of the *Writing Culture* form of deconstruction – a major pursuit of Cultural Studies – are feeding into and relying on the very notion of the untrustworthiness of all re-creative productions, maybe because, as Barnes suggested, they are "discouraged with the partial and philosophical difficulties of discovering what goes on in the real world" and therefore diverting "their energies to exegesis to the industry and other self-contemplating pursuits" (Barnes 1979: 188).

In contrast to Robert Jay's attitude stands that of Laura Bohannan who during fieldwork realised her own "tricksterhood" as follows: "I was one who seems to be what he is not and who profess [*sic*!] faith in what he does not believe" (Bowen 1964: 290). She achieved the supreme feat of self-irony when she joined in the laughter of her informants performing a pantomime in her face about the anthropologist as a writer, but also, perceived the unacceptable side of the Other when they laughed about a blind man stumbling about, stating: "In an environment in which tragedy is genuine an [*sic*!] frequent, laughter is essential to sanity" (Bowen 1964: 295), and further:

"These people know the reality and laugh at it. Such laughter has little

---

[16] See Lévi-Strauss' address in Geneva for the 250th anniversary of Rousseau's birth (Lévi-Strauss 1973).

concern with what is funny. It is often bitter and sometimes a little
mad, for it is the laugh under the mask of tragedy, and also the laughter
that masks tears. They are the same" (Bowen 1964: 297).

But she could not share in that laughter, or as she put it: "It is an error to
assume that to know is to understand and to understand is to like" (Bowen
1964: 291). Here we are on different ground, argued from the level of experience with Otherness, of being-for (to use Heidegger's and Zygmunt Bauman's
terminology) in togetherness, not the distancing reflection of one's own writing. Bohannan thus avoided the pitfall of moral indifference or condescension,
which Bauman characterised once as the attitude "you are wrong, I am right,
... the fact that I bear with your Otherness does not exonerate your error, it
only proves my generosity" (Bauman 1992: XXI). Bauman therefore calls for
a dialogic acknowledgement of the equivalence of knowledge-producing discourses, when we take this legitimacy of the interests of others seriously. That
would be true tolerance as well as a sign of solidarity (the only value Bauman
wants to save from modernity's project).

    Bohannan achieves this kind of insight through a sense of the anarchic
power of humour which, as the art of balancing between self-enjoyment and
sympathy for the suffering, has been perceived as a sign of true humanity
since Roman times; or as Friedrich Schlegel, the great theoretical mind of the
German Romantic Movement of the 1820s put it: "Irony contains something
of and creates a feeling for the insoluble struggle between the impossibility
and at the same time the necessity of compete dialogue. With irony one surpasses one's self"[17].

    Any other attitude, such as the indignation ("but I was a fieldworker" or
"that is beyond the bounds of scholarly civility") of some members of the
anthropological profession, who reacted violently against the charge by Sangren and Jarvie that deconstruction was the best excuse for armchair-ethnol-
ogy since Frazer, would have been regarded by the Romans as the vice of
*gravitas,* that "heaviness" which is the very opposite of the levity of the poetic
imagination of which Schlegel again said in unsurpassed clarity the following:
"Behind the creative impulse stands the buffoon, and the inspirational force of
poetry is the divine breath of irony, permeated by truly transcendental buffoonery".

    It is this buffoonery of the trickster who delights in his own pranks and the
faults or folly of others, or as La Rochefoucauld said: "If we had no faults we
would not derive so much pleasure discovering them in others"[18] (1959: 72),

---

[17] From *Friedrich Schlegel, 1794-1806, seine prosaischen Jugendschriften* (ed. J. Minor) Vienna
1882. The fragment is from 1797. For translation see Szondi 1988: 66.

[18] "Si nous n'avions point de défauts, nous ne prendrions pas tant de plaisir a en remarquer dans les
autres."

which makes the encounter with the other a salutary experience. The limitations as well as the surpassing of boundaries only become clear to us when we see ourselves as third parties through encountering the other. But fieldwork is beset with the very *illiberality* in which we are caught, following Schlegel, when we are creative. Therefore, to be able to analyse we have to embrace distance, for only then do we gain freedom from our undivided attention to a task. We have then, after all, to revert to writing, and writing leads to the irreverent freedom of the buffoon, the trickster, the sender of messages, to Hermes as herald.

There is a very fine example of reflection by an ethnographer about the attempt to escape the self-referentiality of the monologic disposition and the temptation to write. Michel Leiris commented on the Djibouti-Dakar expedition as follows:

> "Intense work, to which I give myself with a certain assiduousness, but without an ounce of passion. I'd rather be possessed than study possessed people, have carnal knowledge of Zarina, rather than scientifically know all about her. For me, abstract knowledge will never be anything but the second best" (1934: 324).

Leiris was one of the few who saw that dangerous poison which lies behind the demand and the aim to publish an ethnography of lived experience, that which Susan Sontag has called the revenge of the intellect upon art, as each interpretation implies that the original is not good enough. Such a hermeneutic is not only aggressive but also impious:

> "From the start, writing this journal, I have struggled against a poison: the idea of publication" (Leiris 1934: 215).

He adds also a melancholic note:

> "In the year 1933 I returned and had at least destroyed one legend: that of travelling as the possibility or escaping oneself ..." (1939: 202-203).

When he produced finally a text, Leiris says about it:

> "I like very much what Genet told me when we met first: 'I write in order to be loved' – that seems to me of unconditional sincerity" (1934: 209).

Thus, while wishing in vain to embrace the research subject, he ends up yearning to embrace the reader: from the impossible to the potential. This is possibly the same attitude, which Devereux suspected behind all writing: the surpassing of anxiety (of Otherness in the Self?) through method (i.e. writing).

## Letting Go

Behind Leiris stands another problem, that of the constant seduction of the Other and by the Other. As Burridge once formulated it, anthropology stands at the cross-roads of European philosophies, between Platonic Eros and Christian love, between the "faith in the rationally objective" as antidote to what he calls: "... the inertial human drift toward a viewpoint based wholly on the participation and inter-relatedness" (Burridge 1973: 12). Michael Jackson referred to it recently in similar terms:

> "My own fieldwork among the Kuranko had reflected a profound dilemma. On one hand I found myself striving for a wealth of data, which I could convert into a book, a durable object that might make my name. But on the other hand I felt my ego threatened by a world of opaque languages, bizarre customs, and oppressive living conditions. Running counter to this will to amass knowledge was a profound desire to give up and let go, to allow my consciousness to be flooded by the African ambience" (Jackson 1989: 163).

Jackson's conclusions *for* anthropology are worth quoting as well. Relying on Gadamer's notion of the ongoing tradition and its reflective appropriation, he states:

> "An anthropology which so forthrightly reflects upon the interplay of biography and tradition and makes the personality of the anthropologist a primary datum entails a different notion of truth than that to which a scientific anthropology aspires. It is a notion of truth based less upon epistemological certainties than upon moral, aesthetic, and political values" (1989: 167).

For Jackson meanings are created inter-subjectively as well as inter-textually, embodied in gestures as well as in words: "... quite simply", he says, "people cannot be reduced to texts any more than they can be reduced to objects" (1989: 184).

The dilemma appearing here, that between "giving in" to the Other and "giving in" to the text, was clearly perceived by Kurt Wolff who offered the prospect of surrender as a methodical answer, derived from phenomenology and existentialism, as a synonym for "total experience" (1976: 22) as follows under the requirement of "identification":

> "... In surrender the individual identifies (the main point of the attitude, besides suspension of received notions, the pertinence of everything, the total involvement and the risk of being hurt): in surrender the individual identifies with it, its occasion, moment, object, self. But identification [sic!] is the aim of surrender, not the aim of the catch. For if it were the aim of the catch, surrender would not be cognitive love, the surrenderer would not want to know, but, by definition, would want to identify, assimilate, go native, or change in some other fashion; the experience of surrender would be consummated as a state and remembered as an episode – perhaps even as a turning point. But since the surrenderer wants to know, there is the love of the catch, of understanding, conceiving, considering so that others can be told what has occurred, must lose himself to find himself, not to lose himself, otherwise he would be self-destructive" (1976: 23).

If it were not so, if surrender would mean identifying assimilation or kow-towing to every whim of others, always being polite, one might also end up disgusted with oneself when leaving the field. Dialogic appropriation and casting in a new context or confrontation, implies the coming to the fore of conflicts. As an Aborigine said to Stanner:

> "White man, him go different. Him got road belong himself" (Stanner 1979: 24).

Acknowledging the autonomy of difference is the precondition for the attaining of self-respect, by not making the Other over into the Self or the Self becoming Other. Dialogue also has to show the Otherness of the Other to that other, giving him or her autonomy of Self. Only if this is realised in engagement, the statement that the anthropological enterprise is "the comprehension of the self by the detour of the comprehension of the other" (with which Rabinow modernises Malinowski's adage of 1922; see Rabinow 1977: IX) can be agreed upon without making the Other only a tool. With this we must finally agree with Nietzsche's insight with which I started the essay: It may be time to put ethics before epistemology (as also pursued by Levinas). A secondary epistemological result entails the insight that translation of messages means, "it is finally not some mysterious primitive philosophy we are studying, but the extreme potentialities of our own thought and our own language" (Lienhardt 1954: 97).

### Which Catch?

The catch of surrender seems to me to lie in several results. One is the *risk* we run by embracing a method of gaining knowledge which involves the Self as subject and object at the same time, and a subject as third person which can only come to the fore through encounter with concrete others. It entails the risk, as Zygmunt Bauman pointed out, not to be taken as a kind of knowledge compatible with the "scientific community":

> "The price a theory which subjects itself to the text of authentication pays for pulling down the barrier dividing the experimenter and his objects ... is likely to be considered exorbitant by a science concerned more with certainty than with the significance of its results" (1976: 109).

Participation rests on the desire to reach out personally without the guarantee of reciprocity and for this reason the method is endemically ridden with irregularity and cannot be taught or learned: It certainly cannot be required of all, for it has to remain a personal decision. Surrender however can only be achieved if *alterity* retains its seduction, and this it can only retain if it is permitted autonomy as difference. Seduction is therefore the life-blood of the field-encounter: to want to know the Other, but never be able to achieve complete union, being aware of this divisiveness without despondency or self-disgust (about which Nietzsche warned as much as about the adulating attitude as detrimental to historical studies), to retain as well as regain the utopian desire with the knowledge that fulfilment would end the seductiveness of alterity which would then become, as Levinas put it, "banalised and dimmed in a simple exchange of courtesies which are signs of the interpersonal", and I would add, of impersonal "commerce". That remains the challenge of fieldwork (for this view of Levinas see also Bauman 1995: 60).

Only this way can seduction itself retain its ironic form which provides "a space, not of desire, but of play and defiance", because, as Baudrillard extends his explanation of the concept, "the law of seduction takes the form of an uninterrupted ritual exchange where seducer and seduced constantly raise the stakes in a game that never ends" (1990: 21-22). The anthropologist must surrender to seduction which in this case has several faces: the seduction of the field (and the *imagination* about it), of the Other, and by the imagined Other, and of text as well as reader. But this is also the only way by which the ethnographer can maintain hope: "The togetherness of being-for is cut of the same block as hope, ... but what keeps the hope alive is precisely the un-fulfilment" (Bauman 1995: 69).

The ethnographer is a Hermes who has not been called to receive a mes-

sage, but becomes possibly seductive through being and remaining an enigma
to the host community, seducing the Other to engage. While the power differ-
ential, on moral as well as epistemological levels, has often been described as
insurmountable, the argument forgets the power of seduction of the Other
over the ethnographer's imagination. It must be added that the seduction of
Otherness in the field-encounter is ultimately also one of the ethnographer's
own making: his imagination projects the desire to reach this imagined Other
in reality.

Two forces of seduction, therefore, move the ethnographer, his desire to
engage on both levels, the field-level as well as the level of writing. But both
are to a large degree projections of his own desires, his system of imaginings:
he is therefore ultimately seduced by his own desire, which does not emerge
through solipsistic existence. Indeed, a strange messenger: Hermes as seduced
seducer!

A final catch emerges for me from the essay of writing about the field
engagement in relation to the praxis of writing: it is the insight into what
Roland Barthes called under the word *potin* (gossip) in his *A Lover's Discourse* the "wickedness" of the third-person pronoun:

"... it is the pronoun of the non-person, it's absent, it annuls ... For me,
the other [*sic!*] cannot be a referent: you are never anything but you. I
do not want the Other to speak of you" (Barthes 1990: 185).

While I should have liked to address the readership as "you" (even if
unknown, imagined), I have referred to the generalised Other, the colleague
anthropologist. Worse, the Other of my field encounter becomes the generalised "they" (see also Favret-Saada's critical re-assessment of this issue;
Favret-Saada 1979), but that is the inauthenticity of all discourse as opposed
to lived dialogicity, a discourse that, as Barthes also intimated, leaves me
caught in a cage:

"I do not get out of the system" of the *"image-repertoire"*.[19]

Yet in dialogical engagement, it is the Other who makes an appearance when
we surpass the Self. We may have to suspend disbelief in the unity of humankind as a moral community, even if we have to surrender to the epistemological diversity of ontologies. Nothing prevents us from the moral "but". Only
one catch is clear: It is not through inter-textuality that we become authentic,
but in the realm of *Zwischenmenschlichkeit*, the "interhuman" interphase.

---

[19] From Barthes 1990: 233 about the words vouloir/saisir.

# Selected Bibliographic References

André, J.-M. 1994: *Griechische Feste. Römische Spiele*. Stuttgart.
Antoni, Klaus 1993: Yasukuni-Jinja and Folk-Religion. In: Richard Mullins, Susumu Shimazono and Paul Swanson (eds.), *Religion and Society in Modern Japan*. Berkeley.
Apte, M. 1985: *Humor and Laughter. An Anthropological Approach*. Ithaca.
Arai, Ken 1996: New Religions. In: Noriyoshi Tamaru and David Reid (eds.), *Religion in Japanese Culture*. Tokyo.
Araki, Michio 1986: Sezokuka ippanka tanni seiyo no sezokuka ka soretomo atarashii sozo e no katei ka? In: *Toyo Gakujutsu Kenkyu* 25(1).
Artaud, Antonin 1970: Heliogabale ou l'anarchiste couronné. In: A. Artaud, *Oeuvres complètes* vol.7. Paris.
Asad, Talal 1993: *Genealogies of Religion*. Baltimore.
Ashkenazi, Michael 1993: *Matsuri. Festivals of a Japanese Town*. Honolulu.
Assmann, Aleida 1989: Feste und Fasten. In: W. Haug & R. Warning (eds.), *Das Fest*. München.
Augé, Marc 1998: *A Sense for the Other*. Stanford.
Averbuch, Irit 1995: *The Gods Come Dancing*. Ithaca.
Babcock-Abrahams, Barbara 1975: A Tolerated Margin of Mess. In: *Journal of the Folklore Institute* 11: 147-86.
Babcock, Barbara (ed.) 1978: *The Reversible World*. Ithaca.
---1978: Liberty's a Whore. In: B. Babcock (ed.), *The Reversible World*. New York.
Bailey, F.G. 1991: *The Prevalence of Deceit*. Berkeley.
---1996: Cultural Performance, Authenticity and Second Nature. In: David Parkin, Lionel Caplan and Humphrey Fisher (eds.), *The Politics of Cultural Performance*. Oxford.
Bakhtin, Mikhail 1968: *Rabelais and His World*. Cambridge, Mass.
----1979: *Die Aesthetik des Wortes*. Frankfurt.
Barnard, F.M. 1969: *Herder on Social and Political Culture*. Cambridge, MA.
Barnes, J.A. 1979: *Who should know what?* Harmondsworth.
Barthes, Roland 1990: *A Lover's Discourse*. Harmondsworth.
Bataille 1949: Rezension von Malcolm de Chazal, 'Sens-plastique', 1948 (transl. in Bataille 1994b).
Bataille 1951: Rezension von Roger Caillois, 'L'homme et le Sacré'. (transl. in Bataille 1994b).
Bataille, Georges 1957: *L'Erotisme*. Paris. (English transl. as "Erotism" by Mary Dalwood, San Francisco, 1986).
---1981: *Die Tränen des Eros*. (French orig., 1961). München.
---1988: *The Accursed Share*, vol.1. (French orig., 1967).
---1994a[1973]: *Theory of Religion*. New York.
---1994b: *The Absence of Myth*. (ed. Michael Richardson). London.
---1998: *Essential Writings*. (ed. Michael Richardson). London.
Bateson, Gregory 1936: *Naven*. Cambridge.
---1956: The Message 'This is Play'. In: B. Schaffner (ed.), *Group Processes*. New York.
Baudrillard, Jean 1968: *Le System des Objets*. Paris.
---1990: *Seduction*. Montreal.
Bauman, Richard 1986: *Story, Performance and Event. Contextual Studies of Oral Narrative*. Cambridge.
Bauman, Zygmunt 1973: *Culture as Praxis*. London and Boston.
---1976: *Toward a Critical Sociology*. London.
---1994: *Intimations of Postmodernity*. London.
---1995: *Life in Fragments*. Oxford.
Behler, Ernst 1966: *Schlegel*. Hamburg.
Bell, Catherine 1992: *Ritual Theory, Ritual Practice*. New York.

282 Shattering Frames

---1997: *Ritual. Perspectives and Dimensions*. Oxford.
Bell, Daniel 1977: The return of the sacred? In: *British Journal of Sociology* 28(4).
Berger, Peter 1969: Christian Faith and the Social Comedy. In: C. Heyers (ed.), *Holy Laughter*. New York.
Berlin, Isaiah 1980: *Vico and Herder*. (Orig. 1976). London.
Berndt, Ronald M. 1951: *Kunapipi*. Melbourne.
---1951: Influence of European Culture on Australian Aborigines. In: *Oceania* 23: 229-235.
---1952: *Djanggawul*. Melbourne.
---1976: *Love Songs of Arnhemland*. Melbourne.
Berndt, Catherine & Ronald Berndt 1951: Sexual Behavior in Western Arnhem Land. In: *Viking Fund Publications in Anthropology* 16. Washington.
Bhabha, Homi 1994: *The Location of Culture*. London.
Bjornson, Richard 1977: *The Picaresque Hero in European Fiction*. Madison.
Blackburn, Alexander 1979: *The Myth of the Picaro*. Chapel Hill.
Blacker, Carmen 1975: *The Catalpa Bow. A Study of Shamanistic Practices in Japan*. London.
Bloch, Maurice 1974: Symbols, Song, Dance and Features of Articulation. In: *Archives Européennes de Sociologie* 15: 55-81.
---1989: *Ritual, History and Power*. London.
Bloch, Ernst 1977: Das Prinzip Hoffnung. In: E. Bloch, *Gesamtausgabe* Bd. 5. Frankfurt/M.
Boas, Franz 1911: *The Mind of Primitive Man*. New York.
---1968[1940]: *Race, Language and Culture*. New York.
Böll, Heinrich 1973: *Group Protrait with Lady*. New York.
Bohman, James 1999: Practical Reason and Cultural Constraint. Agency in Bourdieu's Theory of Practice. In: Richard Schusterman (ed.), *Bourdieu. A Critical Reader*. Oxford.
Bourdieu, Pierre 1977: *Outline of a Theory of Practice*. Cambridge.
Bowen, Elenore Smith 1964: *Return to Laughter*. New York (orig. 1954; alias Laura Bohannan).
Bowman, Glenn 1997: Identifying versus identifying with 'the Other': Reflections on the Siting of the Subject in Anthropological Discourse. In: Allison James, Jenny Hockey and Andrew Dawson (eds.), *After Writing Culture*. London.
Breysig, Kurt 1906: Götter und Heilbringer. In: *Zeitschrift für Ethnologie* 38: 536-610.
Buchler, Ira 1978: The Fecal Crone. In: Ira Buchler and Kenneth Maddock (eds.), *The Rainbow Serpent*. The Hague.
Burckhardt, Jacob 1939: *Kultur und Kunst der Renaissance in Italien*. Wien-Leipzig.
Burkert, Walter 1985: *Greek Religion*. (German orig. 1977). Cambridge, Mass.
Burridge, K.O.L. 1973: *Encountering Aborigines*. New York.
Burton, G. 1993[1651]: *Anatomy of Melancholy*. Oxford.
Butler, Judith 1997: *Excitable Speech. A Politics of the Performative*. New York.
---1999: Performativity's Social Magic. In: Richard Schusterman (ed.), *Bourdieu. A Critical Reader*. Oxford.
Caillois, Roger 1950: *L'homme et le sacré*. (German ed., 1982). Paris.
---1958: *Les jeux et les hommes*. Paris.
Casagrande, Joseph 1960: *In the Company of Man*. New York.
Cassirer, Ernst 1969: *The Problem of Knowledge*. New Haven.
Castaneda, Carlos 1971: *A Seperate Reality*. New York.
Chandler, Frank W. 1898: *Romances of Roguery*. London.
Clarke, Peter, and J. Somers (eds.) 1994: *Japanese New Religions in the West*. Folkstone.
Clifford, James 1988: *The Predicament of Culture*. Cambridge, MA.
---1990: Notes on Fieldnotes. In: R. Sanjek (ed.), *Fieldnotes*. Ithaca.
Cohen, Anthony P. 1992: Self-conscious Anthropology. In: Judith Okely and Helen Callaway (eds.), *Anthropology and Autobiography*. London.
Comaroff, Jean and John Comaroff 1985: *Body of Power, Spirit of Resistance*. Chicago.
Conklin, H.C. 1955: Hanunoo Color Categories. In: *Southwestern Journal of Anthropology* 11: 339-344.

Connerton, Paul 1989: *How Societies Remember*. Cambridge.

Cox, H. 1969: *The Feast of Fools: A Theological Essay on Festivity*. New York.

Crapanzano, Vincent 1987: Editorial. In: *Cultural Anthropology* 2(2).

---1992: *Hermes' Dilemma and Hamlet's Desire*. Cambridge, Mass.

Csordas, Thomas J. (ed.) 1994: *Embodiment and Experience*. Cambridge.

Curtius, Ernst Robert 1953: *European Literature and the Latin Middle Ages*. (German orig. Bern, 1948). London.

Czaplicka, M.A. 1969[1914]: *Aboriginal Siberia*. Oxford.

Davis, Nathalie Zemon. 1965: *Society and Culture in Early Modern France*. Stanford.

Davis, Winston 1980: *Dojo: Magic and Exorcism in Modern Japan*. Stanford.

De Mille, Richard (ed.) 1976: *Castaneda's Journey. the Power and the Allegory*. Sta. Barbara.

De Vries, Jan 1933: The Problem of Loki. In: *Folklore Fellows Communications*, vol.110. (Helsinki).

Derrida, Jacques 1974: *Glas*. Paris.

Détienne, Marcel 1977: *The Gardens of Adonis*. Hassocks.

Détienne, Marcel & Vernant, Jean-Pierre 1978: *Cunning Intelligence in Greek Culture and Society*. Sussex.

Devereux, Georges 1967: *From Anxiety to Method in the Behavioral Sciences*. Paris.

---1981: *Baubo*. Frankfurt/M.

Devisch, R. 1985: Approaches to Symbol and Symptom in Bodily Space-Time. In: *International Journal of Psychology* 20: 389-415.

Diamond, Stanley 1974: *In Search of the Primitive*. New Brunswick.

Doi, Takeo 1973: *The Anatomy of Dependence*. Tokyo.

Doniger O'Flaherty, Wendy 1980: Dionysos and Siva. In: *History of Religions* 20: 81-111.

Douglas, Mary (ed.) 1970: *Witchcraft, Confessions and Accusations*. London.

---1975: *Implicit Meanings*. London.

---1984[1966]: *Purity and Danger*. London.

Dumézil, Georges 1924: *Le Festin d'immortalité*. Paris.

---1959: *Loki*. (extended German ed.). Darmstadt.

---1970: *Du Mythe au Roman*. Paris.

Eco, Umberto 1973: Is There a Way of Generating Aesthetic Messages in an Edenic Language?. In: S. Bann & J.E. Bowlt (eds.), *Russian Formalism*. Edinburgh.

Eliade, Mircea 1951: *Le Chamanisme et les Techniques Archaïques de l'extase*. Paris.

---1973: *Australian Religions*. Ithaca.

Elias, Norbert 1969: *The Civilizing Process*. New York and Cologne.

Elkin, A.P. 1930: Rock-Paintings of North-West Australia. In: *Oceania* 1: 257-279.

---1977[1945]: *Aboriginal Men of High Degree*. 2nd ed. New York.

Erasmus of Rotterdam, D. 1515: *Encomium Moriae*. (In Praise of Folly).

Evans-Pritchard, Edward Evans 1951: *Social Anthropology*. London.

---1965a[1929]: Some Collective Expressions of Obscenity in Africa. In: E. Evans Pritchard, *The Position of Women in Primitive Societies and Other Essays*. London.

---1965b: Some Zande Animal Tales from the Gore Collection. In: *Man* 65: 70-79.

Fanon, Frantz 1967: Toward the African Revolution. New York.

Favret-Saada, Jeanne 1979: *Die Wörter, der Zauber, der Tod: der Hexenglaube im Heimatland von Westfrankreich*. Frankfurt.

Firth, Raymond 1957: Malinowski as Scientist and as Man. In: R. Firth (ed.), *Man and Culture. An Evaluation of the Work of Bronislaw Malinowski*. New York.

---1967: Ritual and Drama in Malay Spirit Mediumship. In: *Comparative Studies in Society and History* 9.

Foster, Hal 1985: *Recordings: Art, Spectacle, Cultural Politics*. Port Townsend.

Foucault, Michel 1966: *Les Mots et les choses*. Paris.

Frazer, Sir James 1913: *The Golden Bough. Part VI: The Scapegoat*. 3rd ed. London.

Frenzel, Elisabeth 1976: *Motive der Weltliteratur*. Stuttgart.

Freud, Sigmund 1913: *Totem und Tabu*. (English ed. Totem and Taboo. New York: Moffat, 1918). Vienna.
---1950: Negation. In: J. Strachey (ed.), *Collected Papers*. New York.
Frobenius, Leo 1932: *Schicksalskunde im Sinne des Kulturwerdens*. Leipzig.
---1933: *Kulturgeschichte Afrikas*. Frankfurt/M.
Gadamer, Hans Georg 1965: *Wahrheit und Methode*. Tuebingen.
---1975: Replik. In: J. Habermas, D. Henrich, and J. Taubes (eds.), *Hermeneutik und Ideologiekritik*. Frankfurt.
Gaster, Th. 1987: Seasonal Ceremonies. In: M. Eliade (ed.), *The Encyclopedia of Religion*. Vol.13. New York.
Geertz, Clifford 1967: Under the Mosquito Net. In: *New York Review of Books* 14(9).
---1968: Thinking as a Moral Act. In: *Antioch Review* 28.
---1973: *The Interpretations of Cultures*. New York.
---1975: *Islam Observed*. Chicago.
---1988: *Works and Lives. The Anthropologist as Author*. Stanford.
Gell, Anthony 1998: *Art and Agency*. Oxford.
Giddens, Anthony 1984: *The Constitution of Society: Outline of a Theory of Structuration*. Cambridge.
---1997: *The Transformation of Intimacy*. Cambridge.
Gill, Carolyn B. 1995: *Bataille. Writing the Sacred*. London.
Girard, René 1972: *La violence et le sacré*. (English ed. 1977. Baltimore). Paris.
Gluckman, Max 1952: Rituals and Rebellion in South-East Africa. In: M. Gluckman, *Order and Rebellion in Tribal Africa*. New York.
---1955: *Custom and Conflict in Africa*. Oxford.
Goffman, Erving 1974: *Frame Analysis*. London.
Goldwater, Robert 1967[1938]: *Primitivism in Modern Art*. New York.
Gomperz, Theodor 1964[1901]: *Greek Thinkers*. London.
Gouldner, Alvin 1971: *The Coming Crisis of Western Sociology*. London.
---1973: *For Sociology*. Penguin.
Greenblatt, Stephen 1991: *Marvelous Possessions*. Oxford.
Grimm, Jacob 1981: *Deutsche Mythologie*. 3 Bde. (orig. 2$^{nd}$ ed. 1844). München.
Grotowski, Jerzy 1969: *Towards a Poor Theatre*. London.
Handelman, Don 1979: Is Naven Ludic? In: B. Kapferer (ed.), The Power of Ritual, *Social Analysis* 1 : 177-192. (Adelaide).
---1981: The Ritual Clown. In: *Anthropos* 76: 321-70.
---1993: The Absence of the Others, the Presence of Texts. In: Smadar Lavie, Kirin Narayan, and Renato Rosaldo (eds.), *Creativity/Anthropology*. Ithaca.
Hardacre, Helen 1986: *Kurozumi-Kyo and the New Religions of Japan*. Princeton.
Harner, Michael (ed.) 1971: *Hallucinogens and Shamanism*. London.
Harootunian, H.D. 1988: *Things Seen and Unseen: Discourse and Ideology in Tokugawa Nativism*. Chicago.
Harris, Marvin 1964: *The Nature of Cultural Things*. New York.
---1968: *The Rise of Anthropological Theory*. New York.
Harrison, J. 1921: *Epilegomena to the Study of Greek Religion*. Cambridge.
Hastrup, Kirsten 1995: *A Passage to Anthropology*. London.
Hauser, Arnold. 1964: *Der Ursprung der modernen Kunst und Literatur*. München.
Haustein, Lydia 1997: *Primitivismus. Vom Aufbruch der Moderne zur Internationalisierung Zeitgenössischer Kunst*. Unpubl. ms., 49 pp.
Hazard, Paul 1965: *European Thought in the Eighteenth Century*. Harmondsworth.
Heidegger, Martin 1927: Sein und Zeit. Tuebingen.
---1969: *Zur Sache des Denkens*. Tuebingen.
Herder, Johann Gottfried 1967: *Auch eine Philosophie der Geschichte. Zur Bildung der Menschheit 1774*. Frankfurt.

---1976: *Journal meiner Reise im Jahre 1769*. Stuttgart.

---1982: *Werke*. Berlin und Weimar.

Hertz, Robert 1909: La Prééminence de la Main Droite: Étude sur la Polarité Religieuse. In: *Revue Philosophique* LXVIII: 553-80. (English transl. by Rodney Needham, *Death and the Right Hand*, Oxford 1960).

Hill, Christopher 1972: *The World Turned Upside Down*. London.

Hillman, Richard 1992: *Shakespearean Subversions*. London.

Holtom, D.C. 1943: *Modern Japan and Shinto Nationalism*. Chicago.

Hori, Ichiro 1951: *Waga kuni Minkan Shinko-shi no Kenkyu*, 2 vols. Tokyo.

---1968: *Folk Religion in Japan*. Chicago.

Horkheimer, Max 1971: *Montaigne und die Funktion der Skepsis*. Frankfurt.

Horkheimer, Max and Theodore W. Adorno 1969: *Dialektik der Aufklärung*. Frankfurt/M.

Howell, Signe 1995: Whose Knowledge and Whose Power? A New Perspective on Cultural Diffusion. In: Richard Fardon (ed.), *Counterworks - Managing the Diversity of Knowledge*. London.

Huizinga, J. 1956: *Homo Ludens*. Hamburg.

Humboldt, Alexander von 1844: *Cosmos*. New York and London.

---1967: *Über die Kawi-Sprache auf der Insel Java* (facsimile reprint of orig. work of 1836). Berlin.

Humphrey, Caroline and James Laidlaw 1994: *The Archetypical Actions of Ritual. A Theory of Ritual Illustrated by the Jain Rite of Worship*. Oxford.

Husserl, Edmund 1913: *Ideen zu einer reinen Phaenomenologie und phaenomenologischen Philosophie*. (Transl. Boyce Gibson, *Ideas*. London 1969).

---1960: *Cartesian Meditations*. (Transl. by Dorion Cairns). The Hague.

---1965a: Philosophy as Rigorous Science. In: E. Husserl, *Phenomenology and the Crisis of Philosophy*. (Transl. by Quentin Lauer). New York.

---1965b: Philosophy and the Crisis of European Man. In: E. Husserl, *Phenomenology and the Crisis of Philosophy*. (Transl. by Quentin Lauer). New York.

Hyers, C. (ed.) 1969: *Holy Laughter*. New York.

Hymes, Dell (ed.) 1969: *Reinventing Anthropology*. New York.

Ivy, Marilyn 1995: *Discourses of the Vanishing*. Chicago.

Jackson, Michael 1989: *Paths toward a Clearing*. Bloomington.

Jacobson, R. 1960: Closing Statement: Linguistics and Poetics. In: T.A. Sebeok (ed.), *Style in Language*. Cambridge, Mass.

James, Wendy 1995: Whatever Happened to the Enlightenment? Introduction. In: W. James (ed.), *The Pursuit of Certainty - Religious and Cultural Formulations*. London.

Jamin, Jean 1980: Un Sacré Collège pour les Apprentis Sorciers de la Sociologie. In: *Cahiers Internationaux de Sociologie* 68: 5-30.

Jansen, Marius B. (ed.) 1989: *Changing Japaneses Attitudes toward Modernisation*. Princeton.

Jay, Robert 1969: Personal and Extrapersonal Vision in Anthropology. In: Dell Hymes (ed.), *Reinventing Anthropology*. New York.

Jennings, Sue 1995: *Theatre, Ritual and Transformation. The Senoi Temiars*. London.

Jensen, A.E. 1960: *Mythos und Kult bei Naturvölkern*. Wiesbaden.

Josephides, Lisette 1997: Representing the Anthropologist's Predicament. In: Allison James, Jenny Hockey, and Andres Dawson (eds.), *After Writing Culture*. London.

Kandinsky, Wassily 1952: *Über das Geistige in der Kunst*. Bern.

Kant, Immanuel 1764: Untersuchung ueber die Deutlichkeit der Grundsaetze der natuerlichen Theologie und der Moral. In: F. Kaulbach (ed.), *Immanuel Kant*. (1969) Berlin.

---1792: *Vorlesungen über Logik*. (ed. Kowalewski, 1924). Königsberg.

Kapferer, Bruce 1979a: Ritual Process and the Transformation of Context. In: *Social Analysis* 1: 3-20. (Adelaide).

---1979b: Postscript. In: Bruce Kapferer (ed.), The Power of Ritual. *Social Analysis* 1: 192ff. (Adelaide).

---1997: *The Feast of the Sorcerer. Practices of Consciousness and Power*. Chicago.

Kaufmann, Walter 1950: *Nietzsche*. New York.

Kauffmann, Lane 1990: The Other in Question. In: T. Maranhäo (ed.), *The Interpretation of Dialogue*. Chicago.

Kendall, Laurel 1996: Initiating Performance. The Story of Chini, A Korean Shaman. In: Carol Laderman and Marina Roseman (eds.), *The Performance of Healing*. London.

Kerényi, Carl 1938/40: Vom Wesen des Festes. Antike Religion und Ethnologische Religionsforschung. In: *Paideuma* 1: 59-74.

---1944: *Hermes der Seelenführer*. Zürich.

---1956: The Trickster in Relation to Greek Mythology. In: Paul Radin (ed.), *The Trickster: A Study in American Indian Mythology*. London.

---1959: *Prometheus*. Hamburg.

Kitagawa, Joseph M. 1966: *Religion in Japanese History*. New York.

Kluckhohn, Clyde 1967: *Mirror for Man*. Greenwich, Conn.

Kluckhohn, Clyde & O. Pufer 1959: Influences during the Formative Years. The Anthropology of Franz Boas. In: *American Anthropological Association Memoir* 89: 4-281.

Koch, K. 1995: Liturgie und Theater. In: *Stimmen der Zeit* 1: 3-16.

Kohl, Karl-Heinz 1987: *Abwehr und Verlangen*. Frankfurt.

Kolakowski, Leszek 1975: *Husserl and the Search for Certitude*. New Haven and London.

---1976: *Der Mensch ohne Alternative*. München.

Konnecker, Barbara 1966: *Wesen und Wandlung der Narrenidee im Zeitalter des Humanismus*. Wiesbaden.

Koepping, Klaus-Peter 1967: Sekai Mahikari Bunmei Kyodan. In: *Contemporary Religions in Japan* Viii(2): 101-134.

---1968: Pattern and Function in Cultural Processes. In: *Proceedings of the VIIIth International Congress of Anthropological and Ethnological Sciences, Tokyo* 3: 116-117.

---1973: Participant Observation, problem and promise of a research method. In: *Occasional Papers in Anthropology* 1: 31-68. Brisbane: Univ. of Queensland Anthropology Museum.

---1974: *Religiöse Bewegungen im modernen Japan*. Köln

---1975: From the Dilemma of the Ethnographer to the Idea of Humanitas. In: *Occasional Papers in Anthropology* 4: 124-136. Brisbane: Univ. of Queensland Anthropology Museum.

---1977a: The Ethics of Planning. In: J. Western and P. Wilson (eds.), *Planning Turbulent Environments*. Brisbane.

---1977b: Ideologies and New Religious Movements, the Case of Shinreikyo. In: *Japanese Journal of Religious Studies* 4(2-3): 103-150.

---1977c: Castaneda and Methodology in the Social Sciences – Sorcery of Genuine Hermeneutics? In: *Social Alternatives* 1: 1. Brisbane.

---1980a: lst die Ethnologie auf dem Wege zur Mündigkeit. In: *Paideuma* 26: 21-40.

---1980b: Japanese Religious Movements: The Semiology of Revolutionary Movements. In: *Anthropological Forum* IV(3-4): 375-384. Perth.

---1981a: Religion in Aboriginal Australia. In: *Religion* 11: 367-91.Lancaster.

---1981b: Lachen und Leib, Scham und Schweigen, Sprache und Spiel. In: H.-P. Duerr (ed.), *Der Wissenschaftler und das Irrationale*, Bd.1. Frankfurt.

---1983: *Adolf Bastian and the Psychic Unity of Mankind*. Brisbane.

---1984 Trickster, Schelm, Pikaro. In: *Kölner Zeitschrift für Soziologie und Sozialpsychologie*, Special Issue No. 26: "Ethnologie als Sozialwissenschaft". (eds. By Rene Koenig, W.E. Müller, K.-P. Koepping and P. Drechsel.)

---1985: Baubo und Priapos. Ethnographische Materialien zur mythischen und rituellen Symbolik der Geschlechterbeziehungen. In: Siegfried Müller (ed.), *Graffiti*. Bielefeld.

---1987a: Unzüchtige und enthaltsame Frauen im Demeterkult. In: H.P. Duerr (ed.), *Die Wilde Seele*. Frankfurt/M.

---1987b: Anamnesis. In: M. Eliade (ed.), *The Encyclopedia of Religion*. Vol.1. New York.

---1988: Nativistic Movements in Aboriginal Australia. In T. Swain & D.B. Rose (eds.), *Aboriginal Australians and Christian Missions*. Bedford Park, South Australia.

---1989: The Voice of Masks and the Face of Deities. In: K.-P. Koepping (ed.), *The No Masks of Soei Ogura*. Melbourne.

---1994a: Manipulated Identities: Syncretism and Uniqueness of Tradition in Modern Japanese Discourse. In: Charles Stewart and Rosalind Shaw (eds.), *Syncretism/Antisyncretism*. London.

---1994b: Ethics in Ethnographic Practice: Contextual Pluralism and Solidarity of Research Partners. In: K.-P. Koepping (ed.), *Anthropology and Ethics. Special volume of Anthropological Journal on European Cultures*, 3(2): 21-38.

---1997a: Obszönität. In: C. Wulf (ed.), *Vom Menschen. Handbuch Historische Anthropologie*. Weinheim.

---1997b Ekstase. In: C. Wulf (ed.), *Vom Menschen. Handbuch Historische Anthropologie*. Weinheim.

---1997c (ed): *Games of Gods and Man. Essays in Play and Performance*. Muenster.

---1998: Inszenierung und Transgression in Ritual und Theater – Grenzprobleme der performativen Ethnologie. In: Bettina Schmidt und Mark Münzel (ed.), *Ethnologie und Inszenierung*. Marburg.

---1999: Collective Identity and the Discourse on Cultural Hegemony in Japanese Syncretism. In: *Bulletin of the Royal Institute for Inter-Faith Studies* 1: 105-136. Amman, Jordania.

---2000: Bauch haben. Die Inszenierung von Gemeinschaftsgefühl in Japan. In: Claudia Benthien, Anne Fleig und Igrid Kasten (eds.), *Emotionlität*. Köln.

Koepping, Klaus-Peter (with B. Schnepel) 1997: Die Umkehrung des Blicks: Akkommodierung von 'Inauthentischem' in festlichen Inszenierungen in Japan und Indien. In: E. Fischer-Lichte (ed): *Theatralität und Authentizität*. Berlin.

Koepping, Klaus-Peter and Ursula Rao (eds.) 2000: *Im Rausch des Rituals*. Münster.

Koepping, Klaus-Peter and Klaus Buchheit 2001: Bastian. In: Christian Feest and Karl-Heinz Kohl (eds.), Wörterbuch der Ethnologen. Stuttgart.

Kranz, Walter 1971: *Die Griechische Philosophie*. Muenchen.

Kulick, Don and Margaret Wilson (eds.) 1995: *Taboo: Sex, Identity and Erotic Subjectivity in Anthropological Fieldwork*. London.

Kuper, Adam 1983: *Anthropology and Anthropologists*. London.

---1988: *The Invention of Primitive Society*. London.

La Rochefoucauld 1868: *Oeuvres*. Paris.

---1959: *Maxims*. Harmondsworth.

Langer, Susanne K. 1951: *Philosophy in a New Key*. New York.

Laube, Johannes (ed.) 1995: *Neureligionen: Stand ihrer Erforschung in Japan. Ein Handbuch*. (Zusammengestellt von Inoue Nobutaka, Komoto Mitsugi, Shioya Masanori, Shimazono Susumu, Tsushima Michihito, Nishiyama Shigeru, Yoshihara Kazuo, Watanabe Masako).

Lawrence, Peter 1964: *Road Belong Cargo*. Manchester.

Layard, John 1957: Critical Notes on the Trickster. In: *Journal of Analytical Psychology* 2: 106-11.

Le Goff, Jacques 1980: *Time, Work, and Culture in the Middle Ages*. Chicago.

---1988: *The Medieval Imagination*. Chicago.

Leach, Edmund 1957: The Epistemological Background to Malinowski's Empiricism. In: R. Firth (ed.), *Man and Culture*. New York.

Leiris, Michel 1934: *L'Afrique fantôme*. Paris.

---1934: Le Culte des Zars á Gondar. In: *Aethiopica* II, 3(July): 96-103.

---1939: *L'Age d'homme*. Paris.

---1948: *La Règle du Jeu*. Paris.

---1963: De Bataille l'impossible à l'impossible 'Documents'. In: *Critique* 15: 195-96.

---1982: *Spiegel der Tauromachie, eingeleitet durch Tauromachien*. (French orig., 1980). München

Lepenies, Wolfgang 1976: *Das Ende der Naturgeschichte*. München.

---1988: *Autoren und Wissenschaftler im 18. Jahrhundert*. München.

Levin, David Michael 1970: *Reason and Evidence in Husserl's Phenomenology*. Evanston.

Levinas, Emmanuel 1961: *Totalite et Infini*. Den Haag.

---1987[1947]: *Time and the Other*. Pittsburgh.

Lévi-Strauss, Claude 1971[1955]: *Tristes Tropiques*. New York.
---1973a: *Anthropologie Structurale*. Paris.
---1973b: *Anthropologie Structurale II*. Paris.
---1976: *Structural Anthropology*. New York.
---1988: *The Jealous Potter*. Chicago.
Lewis, Ioan M.1968: Book Review of Malinowski's Diary. In: *Man* 3: 348-9.
Lewis, Ioan.M. 1971: *Ecstatic Religion*. Harmondsworth.
Lichtenberg, Georg Christoph 1968: *Schriften*. München.
Lienhardt, Godfrey. 1954: *Social Anthropology*. London.
---1961: *Divinity and Experience*. Oxford.
Lindsay, Jack 1965: *The Clashing Rocks*. London.
Lock, Margaret 1993: Cultivating the Body: Anthropology and Epistemologies of Bodily Practice and Knowledge. In: *Annual Reviews of Anthropology* 22: 133-155.
Lommel, Andreas 1952: *Die Unambal*. Hamburg.
Luther, Martin 1982: An den christlichen Adel deutscher Nation. In: K. Bornkamm and G. Ebeling (eds.), *Ausgewählte Schriften*. Bd.1. Frankfurt/M.
Lynch, W. 1969: The Humanity of Comedy. In: C. Hyers (ed.), *Holy Laughter*. New York.
Lyon, M.L. & J.M. Barbalet 1994: Society's Body: Emotion and the 'Somatisation' of Social Theory. In: Thomas J. Csordas (ed.), *Emotion and Experience*. Cambridge.
Malinowski, Bronislaw 1926: *Crime and Custom in Savage Society*. London.
---1929: *The Sexual Life of savages in North-Western Melanesia*. London.
---1935: *Coral Gardens and Their Magic*. Bloomington.
---1944: *Freedom and Civilisation*. New York.
---1961[1922]: *Argonauts of the Western Pacific*. New York.
---1967: *A Diary in the Strict Sense of the Term*. New York.
Mannheim, Karl 1960; 1971[1932]: *Ideology and Utopia*. London.
Marett, R.R. 1912: *The Threshold of Religion*. London.
Marglin, Frédérique Apffel 1990: Refining the Body. Transformative Emotion in Ritual Dance. In: M.O. Lynch (ed.), *Divine Passions. The Social Construction of Emotions in India*. Berkeley.
Markarius, Laura 1969: Le Mythe du trickster. In: *Revue de l'histoire des religions* 175: 17-46.
---1974: The Magic of Transgression. In: *Anthropos* 69: 537-52.
Maturana, Humberto and Francisco Varela 1987: *Der Baum der Erkenntnis*. Bern.
Miller, Roy Anthony 1982: *Japan's Modern Myth*.Tokyo.
Mishima, Yukio 1958: *Confessions of A Mask*. New York.
Miyake, Hitoshi 1993: Religious Rituals in Shugendo. In: Mark Mullins, Susumu Shimazono and Richard Swanson (eds.), *Religion and Society in Modern Japan*. Berkeley.
---1996: Folk Religion. In: Noriyoshi Tamaru and David Reid (eds.), *Religion in Japanese Culture*. Kodansha International.
Moeran, Brian 1985: *Okubo Diary*. Stanford.
Morgenstern, Christian 1979: *Werke*. München.
Morphy, Howard 1995: Aboriginal Art in a Global Context. In: Daniel Miller (ed.), *Worlds Apart - Modernity Through the Prism of the Local*. London.
Morris, Ivan 1975: *The Nobility of Failure*. Tokyo.
Mulvaney, D.J. and J.H. Calaby 1985: *So Much That is New: Baldwin Spencer 1860-1929. A Biography*. Melbourne.
Munn, Nancy 1970: The Transformations of Subjects into Objects in Walbiri and Pitjantjatjara myth. In: Ronald Berndt (ed.), *Australian Aboriginal Anthropology*. Nedlands.
Needham, Rodney 1975: Polythethic Classification. In: *Man N.S.* 10: 349-69.
Niehaus-Pröbsting, H. 1988: *Der Kynismus des Diogenes und der Begriff des Zynismus*. Frankfurt/M.
Nietzsche, Friedrich 1966: *Beyond Good and Evil*. (transl. Walter Kaufman) New York.
---1969[1888]: *Umwertung aller Werte*. Vol.I. München.
---1980: *Werke*. München.

Norbeck, Edward 1970: *Religion and society in modern Japan*. Houston.

Brown, Norman 1969: *Hermes the Thief*. New York.

Ohashi, Ryosuke 1998: Zum japanischen Kunstweg – Die ästhetische Auffassung der Welt. In: Hans Belting und Lydia Haustein (eds.), *Das Erbe der Bilder*. München.

Ortiz, Alfonso 1972: Ritual Drama and the Pueblo World View. In: A. Ortiz (ed.), *New Perspectives on the Pueblos*. Albuquerque.

Otto, Rudolph 1963: *Das Heilige* (1917). München.

Parker, Alexander A. 1967: *Literature and the Delinquent*. Edinburgh.

Paulme, Denise 1977: The Impossible Imitation in African Trickster Tales. In: R. Lindfors (ed.), *Forms of Folklore in Africa*. Austin (Tex.).

Pelton, Robert D. 1980: *The Trickster in West Africa*. Berkeley and Los Angeles.

Perloff, Marjorie 1995: Tolerance and Taboo: Modernist Primitivism and Postmodernist Pieties. In: Elazar Barkan and Ronald Bush (eds.), *Prehistories of the Future*. Stanford.

Petri, Helmut 1950: Kurangara. In: *Zeitschrift für Ethnologie* 75: 43-51.

---1952: Der Australische Medizinmann. In: *Annali Lateranensi* 16: 159-317.

---1954: *Sterbende Welt in Nordwest-Australien*. Braunschweig.

Pieper, J. 1963: *Zustimmung zur Welt. Eine Theorie des Festes*. München.

Plessner, H. 1974[1953]: Über Menschenverachtung. In: H. Plessner (ed.), *Diesseits der Utopie*. Frankfurt.

---1974: Anthropologie der Sinne. In: Hans-Georg Gadamer und Paul Vogler (eds.), *Neue Anthropologie*, Band 7: *Philosophische Anthropologie*, Zweiter Teil. Stuttgart.

Plutschow, Herbert 1996: *Matsuri. The Festivals of Japan*. Richmond.

Pohlenz, Max 1948: *Die Stoa*. Goettingen.

Pouillon, J. 1980: Anthropological Traditions. Their Uses and Misuses. In: Stanley Diamond (ed.), *Anthropology. Ancestors and Heirs*. The Hague.

Powdermaker, Hortense 1966: *Stranger and Friend. The Way of an Anthropologist*. New York.

Pratt, Mary Louise 1992: *Imperial Eyes*. London.

Preuss, Karl Theodor 1912: *Die Nayarit-Expedition*. Leipzig.

---1933: *Der religiöse Gehalt der Mythen*. Tuebingen.

Rabinow, Paul 1977: *Reflections on Fieldwork in Morocco*. Berkeley.

---1988: Reply to Sangren "Rhetoric and the Authority of Ethnography". In: *Current Anthropology* 29(3).

Radin, Paul 1914: Religion of North American Indians. In: *Journal of the American Folklore Society* 27: 335-731.

---1933: *The Method and Theory of Ethnology* (1987, ed. by Arthur Vidich). Cambridge, Mass.

---1956: *The Trickster: A Study in American Indian Mythology*. London.

---1957[1937]: *Primitive Religion*. London.

---1953: *The World of Primitive Man*. New York. (Re-edited 1971 by Stanley Diamond) Westport, Conn.

Rapport, Nigel 1990: Surely everything has already been said about Malinowski's Diary! In: *Anthropology Today* 6(1): 6-9.

---1994: *The Prose and the Passion*. Manchester.

Ratzel, Friedrich 1887: Die Afrikanischen Bogen. In: *Abhandlungen der Kaiserlich-Sächsischen Gesellschaft der Wissenschaften, Phil. Hist. Klasse* 13(3).

Reinach, Adolf 1953: *Die apriorischen Grundlagen des buergerlichen Rechts*. München.

Richie, Donald 1991: *Geisha, Gangster, Neighbour, Nun*. Tokyo.

Ricketts, Mac Linscott 1965: The North American Trickster. In: *History of Religion* 5: 327-50.

Rohner, Ronal P. 1966: Franz Boas, Ethnographer of the Northwest Coast. In: J. Helm (ed.), *Pioneers of American Anthropology*. Seattle.

Rorty, R. 1980: *Philosophy and the Mirror of Nature*. Princeton.

Rousseau, Jean Jaques 1981: Träumereien eines einsamen Spaziergängers. In: H. Ritter (ed.), *Rousseau. Schriften*, Bd. 2. München.

Sahlins, Marshall 1985: *Islands of History*. London.

Sangren, Steven P. 1988: Rhetoric and the Authority of Ethnography. In: *Current Anthropology* 29(3): 405-424.
Sanjek, Roger (ed.) 1990: *Fieldnotes*. Ithaca.
Sansom, G.B. 1958-1969: *A History of Japan*. 3 vols. Stanford.
Satow, Sir Ernest 1983: *A Diplomat in Japan*. Tokyo.
Schieffelin, Edward 1993: Performance and the Cultural Construction of Reality. In: Smadar Lavie, Kirim Narayan, and Renato Rosaldo (eds.), *Creativity/Anthropology*. Ithaca.
---1996: On Failure and Performance. Throwing the Medium out of the Séance. In: Carol Laderman and Marina Roseman (eds.), *The Performance of Healing*. London.
Schiffer, Wilhelm 1967: Necromancers in the Tohoku. In: *Contemporary Religions in Japan* 8(2).
Schlegel, Friedrich 1972: *Schriften zur Literatur*. München.
Schmid, Wilhelm 1987: *Die Geburt der Philosophie im Garten der Lüste*. Frankfurt.
Schoene, Albrecht 1982: *Aufklaerung aus dem Geiste der Experimentalphysik*. München.
Schutz, Alfred 1970: *On Phenomenology and Social Relations*. (H.R. Wagner ed.) Chicago.
Schuetz, Alfred 1932: *Der sinnhafte Aufbau der Sozialen Welt* (2nd ed. 1967). Wien.
---1971: *Gesammelte Aufsätze*. Konstanz.
Scott, David 1992: Anthropology and Colonial Discourse: Aspects of the Demonological Construction of Sinhala Practice. In: *Cultural Anthropology* 7: 301-326.
Screech, M.A. 1979: *Rabelais*. London.
---1980: *Erasmus, Ecstasy and The Praise of Folly*. London.
Seaford, Richard 1994: *Reciprocity and Ritual*. Oxford.
Segalen, Victor 1987: Exoticism. In: *Normal* 3.
Seidel, Michael 1979: *Satiric Inheritance*. Princeton.
Shimazono, Susumu 1982: Charisma and the Evolution of Religious Consciousness: The Rise of the Early New Religions of Japan. In: *The Annual Review of the Social Sciences of Religion* 6.
---1993: The Expansion of Japan's New Religions into Foreign Cultures. In: M.R. Mullins, S. Shimazono, and P. L. Swanson (eds), *Religion and Society in Modern Japan*. Berkeley.
---1995: In the Wake of Aum. In: *Japanese Journal of Religious Studies* 22(3-4).
---1996: Aspects of the Rebirth of Religion. In: Noriyoshi Tamaru and David Reid (eds.), *Religion in Japanese Culture*. Tokyo.
Simmel, Georg 1950: *The Sociology of Georg Simmel*. (ed. by K. Wolff.) New York.
---1968: *Das individuelle Gesetz*. Frankfurt.
---1983/1992[1901]: *Schriften zur Soziologie*. Frankfurt.
Sloterdijk, Peter 1983: *Kritik der Zynischen Vernunft*. Frankfurt.
Slotkin, J.S. (ed.) 1964: *Readings in Early Anthropology*. Chicago.
Sokolowski, Robert 1964: *The Formation of Husserl's Concept of Constitution*. The Hague.
Sontag, Susan 1966: The Anthropologist as Hero. In: E. Nelson Hayes and Tanya Hayes (eds.), *Claude Lévi-Strauss – The Anthropologist as Hero*. Cambridge.
---1982: Against Interpretation. In: *A Susan Sontag Reader*. New York.
Sperber, Dan 1985: *On Anthropological Knowledge*. Cambridge.
Spies, Werner 1988: *Kontinent Picasso*. München.
Spitz, L.W. 1955: Natural Law and the Theory of History in Herder. In: *Journal of the History of Ideas* 16: 453-75.
Stanner, W.E.H. 1966: On Aboriginal Religion. In: *Oceania Monograph* 11. Sydney.
---1979: *White Man Got No Dreaming*. Essays. Canberra.
Starobinski, J. 1994: *Gute Gaben, Schlimme Gaben. Die Ambivalenz sozialer Gesten*. Frankfurt/M.
Stocking, George W. 1968: Empathy and Antipathy in the Heart of Darkness. In: *Journal of the History of Behavioural Sciences*. pp.189-194.
---1987: *Victorian Anthropology*. New York.
Strathern, Andrew 1996: *Body Thoughts*. Ann Arbor.
Strehlow, T.G.H. 1947: *Aranda Traditions*. Melbourne.
---1964: Personal Monototemism in a Polytotemic Community. In: *Festschrift für A.E. Jensen*. München.

Syrkin, Alexander Y. 1982: On the Behavior of the 'Fool for Christ's Sake'. In: *History of Religions* 22: 150-71.

Szondi, Peter 1986: *On Textual Understanding*. Manchester .

Tamaru, Noriyoshi 1987: The Concept of Secularization and its Relevance for the East. In: *The Journal of Oriental Studies* 26(1).

Tambiah, Stanley J. 1979: A Performative Approach to Ritual. In: *Proceedings of the British Academy* 65: 113-169.

---1985: *Culture, Thought and Social Action*. Cambridge, MA.

Tensho Kotai Jingu Kyo (no date): *Mioshie*. Tabuse.

---1954: *The Prophet of Tabuse*. (orig.: *Tabuse no Yogensha*) Tabuse.

Todorov, Tsvetan 1984: *The Conquest of America. The Question of the Other*. New York.

Torgovnick, Marianna 1990: *Gone Primitive*. Chicago.

Turner, Terence 1977: Transformations, Hierarchy and Transcendence. In: Sally F. Moore and Barbara G. Myerhoff (eds.), *Secular Ritual*. Assen.

---1994: Bodies and Anti-Bodies: Flesh and Fetish in Contemporary Social Theory. In: Thomas J. Csordas (ed.), *Embodiment and Experience*. Cambridge.

Turner, Victor 1957: *Schism and Continuity in an African Society*. Manchester.

---1969: *The Ritual Process*. Chicago.

---1977: Variations on a Theme of Liminality. In: Sally F. Moore and Barbara G. Myerhoff (eds.), *Secular Ritual*. Assen.

---1986: *From Ritual to Theatre*. New York.

Tylor, Ernest Burnett 1865: *Researches into the Early History of Mankind and its Development of Civilization*. London.

---1871: *Primitive Culture*. London.

Van Bremen, Jan and D.P. Martinez (eds.) 1995: *Ceremony and Ritual in Japan*. London.

Van Gennep, Arnold 1909: *Les rites de passage*. Paris.

---1960: *The Rites of Passage*. London.

Van Ström, Ake 1975: *Germanische Religion*. Stuttgart.

Vernant, Jean-Pierre 1980: *Myth and Society in Ancient Greece*. Brighton.

Veyne, Paul 1994: *Brot und Spiele*. München.

Vico, Giambattista 1966[1744]: *Scienza Nuova*. (German ed. by E. Auerbach). Hamburg.

Waldenfels, Bernhard 1990: *Der Stachel des Fremden*. Frankfurt.

Weber, Max 1918/19: Wissenschaft als Beruf. In: F. Jonas, *Geschichte der Soziologie* 4.

Welsford, Enid 1961[1935]: *The Fool*. New York.

Willis, Roy 1975: *Man and Beast*. Paladin.

Wilson, Monica 1957: *Rituals and Kinship among the Nyakyusa*. London.

Wolf, Eric 1974: Forword. In: S. Diamond, *In Search of the Primitive*. New Brunswick, N.Y.

Wolfe, Patrick 1999: *Settler Colonialism and the Transformation of Anthropology*. London.

Wolff, Kurt 1976: *Surrender and Catch*. Dordrecht.

---1994: Surrender and the Other. In: Koepping, K.-P. (ed.), Anthropology and Ethics. *Anthropological Journal on European Cultures* 3(2).

Worsley, Peter 1957: *The Trumpet Shall Sound*. London.

Wright, Mills C. 1970: *The Sociological Imagination*. Pelican.

Young, Michael (ed.) 1979: *The Ethnography of Malinowski*. London.

Yourcenar, Marguerite 1985: *Mishima oder die Vision der Leere*. München.

# Picture Credits

*Figures 1* and *2* are taken from a Catalogue, accompanying the exhibition of the group COBRA at the Hypo-Kunsthalle München in 1998. The panels are two of six of *Les Transformes* of 1951 by Jean-Michel Atlan and Christian Dotremont. Published on p.110 and 111 of the Catalogue. München: Hirmer, 1997.

*Figure 3* is a portrait of Lévi-Strauss, reproduced as cover-illustration of David Pace, *Claude Lévi-Strauss, the Bearer of Ashes*, London: Routledge, 1983. Source Jacques Haillot Camera Press, London.

*Figure 4* is a photo of Adolf Bastian around 1900, published in *Baessler-Archiv*, Band X at the occasion of the commemoration of Bastian's 100th birthday. The Directors of the Ethnological Section of the National Museum of Anthropology, Berlin, edited by Alfred Maas. Berlin 1906: Dietrich Reimer. Frontiscpiece.

*Figure 5* is a photo of Malinowski, taken by *Life-Magazine* of the scholar at Yale University in 1942, published in Raymond Firth (ed.), *Man and Culture*. New York: Harper, 1957.

*Figures 6* to *13* are photos taken by the author.

*Figure 14* is a portrait of Michel Leiris around 1966, used as copy by the painter Francis Bacon.

*Figure 15* is a drawing by André Masson, published in Michel Leiris's, *Tauromachie* of 1982 (a bilingual, French and German edition) on p.74. München: Matthes und Seitz.

*Figure 16* is a photo of Georges Bataille around 1933, published in the re-edition of the *Encyclopaedia Acephalica*, edited by Georges Bataille, originally published in the *Documents* of 1929 and 1930. London: Atlas Press, 1995, p.8.

# About the Author

Klaus-Peter Koepping, born 1940, is at present professor of anthropology at the University of Heidelberg. His interests extend to the history of anthropological theory, the existential and epistemological foundations of fieldwork methodology, theories on myth and ritual and the anthropology of embodiment and performance. After reading in Bonn and Hamburg for a law degree, he started his interests in anthropology at the University of Cologne under Helmut Petri and in comparative sociology under Rene Koenig. Adding Japanology and, for a short time linguistics, he finally decided to do his research in Japan on the newly founded religions of messianic and millenarian persuasion. From the mid-60s until now he extended his research interests from new religions to traditional village festivals, folk-religious practices as well as traditional Shinto rituals.

Outside of his main research focus of Japan, he did fieldwork in the United States among the Hopi, in Australia in Queensland settlements of Aborigines,in New Guinea on the Huon Peninsula in villages strongly influenced by German missions, finally in the late 70s in Afghanistan among nomadic groups in the province of Baghlan, in Taiwan among old Malay populations, and in South Australia on the descendants of the Old Lutheran emigrant communities. After his first fieldwork period he took up an appointment at the University of California at Berkeley, then at Fullerton State University, moving in 1972 to Brisbane, Australia, where he was member of the Department of Anthropology and Sociology until 1984. Having had overseas visiting appointments in Japan (Sophia University), in Canberra (as fellow of the Research School of the ANU), in the Philippines (Ateneo de Manila and Silliman University in Dumaguete City on Negros), at Bielefeld and Mainz Universities, he was offered the Baldwin Spencer Chair of Anthropology at Melbourne University in the capacity of a foundation professorship in 1985. After establishing a successful Department there, having also taken on the responsibilities for founding a School of Asian Studies, he moved to his present position at Heidelberg University in 1991. Since his move to Germany he has been guest professor in Japan at Nagoya City University and other Japanese institutions. Being a member of the research group on theatricality funded by the German Science Foundation (chaired by Erika Fischer-Lichte) since 1997, his interests at present combine the comparative study of rituals and theatrical performances as well as research on phenomena of culture change and hybridity, while at the same time keeping his historical curiosity as serious hobby alive about the influence of an anthropological attitude on modern thought, in particular in the period of the early 20th century with its emanations in primitivism and surrealism as well as through the re-evaluation of the myths and rituals of Greek antiquity, in particular as they pertain to notions of sensuality, embodiment and the coping with ambiguity and contingency.